How is the Weather?

by Jim Collins

PEARSON
Scott Foresman

Editorial Offices: Glenview, Illinois • Parsippany, New Jersey • New York, New York
Sales Offices: Needham, Massachusetts • Duluth, Georgia • Glenview, Illinois
Coppell, Texas • Sacramento, California • Mesa, Arizona

umbrella

You plan a special day. Will the weather be perfect for your plans? Could bad weather spoil your plans?

How can you find out about the weather? This book is about changes in the weather.

---
spoil: ruin

thermometer

beach ball

This family is ready for the beach. They want to picnic and swim. How do they know that it will be a good day for the beach? They looked at the thermometer outside their house.

The thermometer shows the temperature. It shows how hot or how cold the air is.

This man is fishing at the beach. He likes this cool, cloudy day.

How did he know that today would be a good day for fishing at the beach? Before he went fishing, he listened to the weather reporter on television.

---

weather reporter: person who reports the weather news

Will the team be able to play?

The team is ready to play. But it is raining. When will the rain stop? What can they do to find out? They can listen to a weather report on the radio.

Sometimes the weather can spoil the plans that people make.

hot air balloon

Will they ride on this windy day?

This family is going to ride in a hot air balloon. They can't wait to be up in the sky. It is very windy. They can't go up in the air today. The weather has spoiled their plans!

snow

How much snow fell?

These girls are measuring how much snow fell during the night. They plan to go sledding. They want to build a snowman.

The weather did not spoil their plans.

Everyone likes to stay comfortable in all kinds of weather. We use warm clothes, and we heat our homes to stay warm. We use cool clothes, fans, and swimming pools to stay cool. What do you need most for today's weather?

Y0-DRY-697

ADAMEC

Statistical Analysis in Biology

By the same Author

*The Measurement of Linkage
in Heredity*

Statistical Analysis in Biology

by

K. MATHER

D.Sc., Ph.D.
Professor of Genetics in the University of Birmingham

With a foreword by

R. A. FISHER

Sc.D., F.R.S.
Arthur Balfour Professor, University of Cambridge

METHUEN & CO. LTD. LONDON
11 NEW FETTER LANE, E.C.4

First published January 14, 1943
Second Edition, Revised, December 1946
Third Edition August 1949
Fourth Edition 1951
Reprinted 1960
Fifth edition 1964
Reprinted 1966
Printed and bound in Great Britain by
Butler & Tanner Ltd, Frome and London
Catalogue No. 12/3832/62
5.2

FOREWORD

ONE of the most encouraging features about the modern statistical methods, which have developed in this country during the last fifteen years, is the readiness with which they are applied in aid of practical research. The enterprise and facility with which the younger biologists in particular have exploited these methods, and the stimulus they have found in them for the advancement of their own studies, constitute the real proof of their value. In a well-designed experiment every feature of the analysis has a meaning relevant to the understanding of the situation which the experiment was intended to explore. The earlier statistical literature, on the other hand, abounds in mathematical artefacts the interpretation of which is as ambiguous as their calculation is tortuous and indirect. At the present time it is the elementary expositions which suffer most from this academic tradition, for these are naturally more timid and imitative than more advanced works.

Dr. Mather has already illustrated the power of these methods in genetic analysis, in his work on *The Measurement of Linkage in Heredity*, a book which every geneticist would be wise to have by him. The present work, designed as a more general introduction to statistical methods for biological investigators, shows the same practical grasp of the essentials of good experimentation, and the same deliberate avoidance of what is extraneous. It is very simply written, and by well-chosen examples exhibits every step of the processes needed. The careful reader should rapidly acquire a repertoire of techniques appropriate to very varied circumstances.

R. A. FISHER

This impatience was very foolish, and in after-years I have deeply regretted that I did not proceed far enough at least to understand something of the great leading principles of mathematics, for men thus endowed seem to have an extra sense.

CHARLES DARWIN

General impressions are never to be trusted.

FRANCIS GALTON

PREFACE

STATISTICS is the concern of two different groups of scientist. The first group, of mathematical statisticians, is interested in developing the theory and extending the applicability of their subject, while the second group, which consists of non-mathematicians, is concerned largely with using the methods already available as tools in their own researches. Among this latter group biologists are forced by the peculiarities of their experimental material to occupy a leading position; for it is very rarely that the full value of a biological experiment can be realized before the observations have been subjected to a suitable statistical analysis.

This separation into two groups, which might be termed respectively the makers of statistics and the users of statistics, is not, of course, complete. The mathematician must be able to appreciate the problems met by the users of his product, or his work will be sterile. Similarly, the biologist must have a sufficient knowledge of statistical theory to know how far present-day methods will take him and at what point he must turn to the statistician for further help and advice. That the full development of the subject is dependent on such co-operation is amply shown by the great advances which have resulted from the association of R. A. Fisher and his school with the agronomical and other biological research carried out at the Rothamsted Experimental Station and elsewhere.

As a non-mathematician I cannot pretend to more than a passing acquaintance with those branches of statistics which are peculiarly the province of the mathematician. But as a biologist I can appreciate both the necessity for a better understanding of the potentialities of statistics amongst experimentalists, and the difficulties they feel in approaching a science which has a theory and language so unlike their own. Much has been done by R. A. Fisher's two books, *Statistical Methods for Research Workers* and *The Design of Experiments*, to assist biologists in this direction, and I hope the present work will also be of material help in a somewhat different way. I have concentrated on trying to show the scope of the various methods, how they are interrelated and how they fulfil the conditions necessary for satisfactory analysis.

This treatment will, no doubt, be subjected to two types of criticism. First of all, the mathematician may object that it is unsound, as, while resting on a mathematical basis, it avoids proof of the various propositions and distributions used. To him I would reply that such proofs are not difficult to find elsewhere and that, in any case, the need of the biologist is not so much to understand the construction of these distributions as to obtain a knowledge of the extent to which they help him and of how he should set about using them. His needs are not those of the mathematician. The second criticism may be made by the biologist who maintains that the book is of too advanced a mathematical standard. To defend myself against this attack I must point out two things, viz. that simple algebraic manipulation and elementary differential calculus are taught as routine to many school-children, and that as a matter of experience I have found this very treatment helpful in teaching statistics both to myself and to others during the last seven years or so. The main work involved is that of learning the vocabulary and grammar of the symbol language with which ideas are expressed and developed mathematically. This is, after all, no more difficult than acquiring a working knowledge of some spoken language. Indeed, to many of us it is easier, as there are no exceptions to be memorized. I have tried to lessen some of the labour by gradually working up to the more mathematical parts, which are mainly in the later chapters.

Statistics and microscopy occupy a very similar position in biology. Both have been, and are, the subject of study by non-biological specialists, yet the use of existing facilities in both is necessary for the full development of the biological sciences. Their difference lies in the fact that biologists are early introduced to the use of the microscope, but are, at present, forced to pick up a knowledge of statistics for themselves when they have, perhaps somewhat reluctantly, found it to be necessary. A modification of biological teaching to include the elements of statistical analysis would have a profound and very beneficial effect.

Many sample analyses are given as examples in the text. The questions at issue are often somewhat trivial; they have been chosen solely with the object of illustrating the argument. The data treated have been taken from many fields of research but inevitably will show a preponderance from those branches, especially my own subject of genetics, with which I am familiar.

Whatever the nature of the data, the examples should be worked through carefully by anyone wishing to derive full benefit from the book, as it is the treatment, not the subject matter, which is of importance.

I have to thank Dr. C. H. Cadman and Mr. L. G. Wigan for reading and criticizing the text. Miss B. Schafer has been of great assistance in preparing the manuscript and the late Mr. H. C. Osterstock is responsible for drawing most of the diagrams. I am especially indebted to Professor R. A. Fisher for his advice, not only in the preparation of this book, but also on the many occasions when he has helped me over troublesome difficulties.

Tables I–IV are abridged from *Statistical Tables for Biological, Agricultural and Medical Research*, by R. A. Fisher and F. Yates, with the kind permission of the authors and of the publishers, Messrs. Oliver and Boyd. When fuller versions of these tables are necessary, reference should be made to the originals.

October 1942 K. M.

PREFACE TO THE SECOND EDITION

DURING the period which has elapsed since the appearance of the first edition, my attention has been drawn to a number of misprints, ambiguities and inaccuracies which it contained. I wish to thank all those correspondents, especially Mr. K. Williams, who have helped me in this way. I trust that, as a consequence, this edition will be less open to misunderstanding.

A number of suggestions have also been made to me in regard to problems and techniques which received no mention in the first edition, and yet which might increase the usefulness of the book and render it of value to a wider public. While sympathizing with many of them, I have found it impossible to include them all if an unjustifiable expansion of the book was to be avoided. A thirteenth chapter has, however, been added. It includes accounts of the angular and probit transformations. These were chosen not merely as illustrating the widely used and special techniques of toxicology and biological assay, but also to show the general value of transformations in rendering data more manageable.

July 1945 K. M.

CONTENTS

CHAPTER		PAGE
I	INTRODUCTORY	9

    1. THE NATURE OF STATISTICS. 2. POPULATIONS AND SAMPLES. 3. DIAGRAMS AND GRAPHS

II	PROBABILITY AND SIGNIFICANCE	14

    4. SIMPLE PROBABILITY. 5. COMPOUND PROBABILITY. 6. AGREEMENT WITH HYPOTHESIS. 7. SIGNIFICANCE

III	DISTRIBUTIONS	25

    8. THE NORMAL DISTRIBUTION. 9. THE MEAN AND STANDARD DEVIATION. 10. FITTING THE NORMAL CURVE. 11. SKEWNESS AND KURTOSIS. 12. THE POISSON SERIES. 13. THE MEAN AND VARIANCE OF THE BINOMIAL DISTRIBUTION

IV	TESTS OF SIGNIFICANCE	41

    14. THE NORMAL DEVIATE. 15. THE t DISTRIBUTION. 16. THE z DISTRIBUTION. 17. THE χ^2 DISTRIBUTION. 18. THE INTERRELATIONS OF c, t, χ^2 AND z, AND THEIR USE IN ANALYSIS

V	THE SIGNIFICANCE OF SINGLE OBSERVATIONS, SUMS, DIFFERENCES AND MEANS	50

    19. SINGLE OBSERVATIONS. 20. THE VARIANCE OF SUMS, DIFFERENCES AND MEANS. 21. THE SIGNIFICANCE OF MEANS AND DIFFERENCES OF MEANS

VI	DEGREES OF FREEDOM AND THE ANALYSIS OF VARIANCE	61

    22. THE INDIVIDUALITY OF DEGREES OF FREEDOM. 23. THE PRINCIPLES OF PARTITION. 24. THE ANALYSIS OF VARIANCE. 25. INTERACTIONS BETWEEN MAIN EFFECTS. 26. INCOMPLETE ANALYSIS

VII	PLANNING EXPERIMENTS	86

    27. THE FACTORIAL EXPERIMENT. 28. AN EXPERIMENT WITH THREE FACTORS. 29. THE CONTROL OF ERROR. 30. CONFOUNDING

VIII	THE INTERRELATIONS OF TWO VARIABLES	109

    31. LINEAR REGRESSION. 32. THE SAMPLING ERROR OF REGRESSION CONSTANTS. 33. THE DIFFERENCE BETWEEN TWO REGRESSION COEFFICIENTS. 34. THE USE OF CONCOMITANT OBSERVATIONS

IX	POLYNOMIAL AND MULTIPLE REGRESSIONS	129

    35. TESTING LINEARITY OF REGRESSIONS. 36. THE CHOICE OF ORDER OF A POLYNOMIAL. 37. THE CALCULATION OF A POLYNOMIAL REGRESSION. 38. REGRESSION ON TWO OR MORE VARIATES. 39. DISCRIMINANT FUNCTIONS

X	CORRELATION	160

    40. INTER-CLASS CORRELATION. 41. THE COMBINATION OF INTER-CLASS CORRELATION COEFFICIENTS. 42. PARTIAL CORRELATION. 43. INTRA-CLASS CORRELATION

CONTENTS

CHAPTER		PAGE
XI	THE ANALYSIS OF FREQUENCY DATA	174

44. χ^2 AND THE NORMAL DEVIATE. 45. THE VARIOUS FORMS OF χ^2. 46. PARTITIONING χ^2. 47. THE EFFECT OF FITTING A PARAMETER. 48. HETEROGENEITY OF DATA. 49. THE 2×2 CONTINGENCY TABLE. 50. THE $2 \times j$ TABLE. 51. THE GENERAL CONTINGENCY TABLE

XII	ESTIMATION AND INFORMATION	203

52. PROBABILITY AND LIKELIHOOD. 53. THE METHOD OF MAXIMUM LIKELIHOOD. 54. INEFFICIENT STATISTICS. 55. SIMULTANEOUS ESTIMATION. 56. COMBINED ESTIMATION AND HETEROGENEITY TESTS. 57. PLANNING EXPERIMENTS. 58. FIDUCIAL PROBABILITY

XIII	SOME TRANSFORMATIONS	234

59. THE ANGULAR TRANSFORMATION. 60. THE PROBIT TRANSFORMATION

	GLOSSARY OF TERMS	253
	TABLES	258
	INDEX	265

CHAPTER I

INTRODUCTORY

1. THE NATURE OF STATISTICS

STATISTICS is the mathematics of experiment. Experiments are conducted with the object of answering some question or questions in which the experimenter is interested; but it is seldom that the answer can be seen before the results have been subjected to some form of analysis. For the results of an experiment, especially a biological experiment, commonly show the influence of many factors other than those whose investigation forms the reason of the research. Some of these disturbances may be traced to known or partially known causes, but the majority are unaccountable and constitute sources of potential error in the interpretation of the results. The objects of statistical analysis are (i) to reduce the data, which because of their very bulk and complexity are incapable of being fully comprehended by the mind of the experimenter, to a few easily understood quantities containing most, if not all, of the information relevant to the subject under investigation; and (ii) to assess the meaning and importance of these quantities while making due allowance for the errors caused by disturbing influences.

Every experiment is of necessity limited in scope. Its results afford a sample of what would be observed if all the material of the particular kind under investigation was subjected to the special circumstances of the experimental procedure. Yet the hypothesis which seeks to explain the resulting observations must account equally well for the outcome of any of the many other possible experiments of the particular kind under consideration. Thus, if experimental science is not to be dismissed as meaningless, it must be held possible to draw conclusions of general validity from the results of necessarily restricted experiments, i.e. it must be held possible to argue from the particular to the general. To the extent that statistics is developed to facilitate such arguments it is the mathematics of inductive reasoning, in contradistinction to other branches of mathematical science which are concerned with deducing the logical consequences of a given set of postulates. This is not to say that statistical analyses never involve deduction. Not infrequently they do, as when testing the adequacy of a given hypothesis to account for or explain particular observations. But hypotheses are seldom so precisely formulated as to be capable of being tested before the data have been made to supply, by inductive reasoning, some quantity necessary to their full specification. Statistical operations reflect that alternation of induction and deduction which is so characteristic of experimental science.

2. POPULATIONS AND SAMPLES

The primary concept of statistics is that of the infinitely large hypothetical population of which the observed data form a sample. It is to the population, which is characterized and described by certain quantities, termed parameters, that the hypothesis with which the experimental results are being compared, or to whose specification they are contributing, applies. The population is the statistical way of representing the hypothesis, or rather its consequences, and the sample is the way of representing the observations. Thus suppose we consider the time-honoured example of tossing a coin. The hypothesis is that the coin is true or unbiased, i.e. that the chances of its showing a head or tail after tossing are equal. The population comprises an infinitely large number of tosses of the coin and, of course, exactly half the population shows heads and exactly half shows tails. The population is in fact characterized by the parameter $\xi=\frac{1}{2}$, where ξ is the proportion of heads, or tails.

We sample the population by tossing the coin and observe either a head or a tail. This observation may be tested for agreement with hypothesis, i.e. we may undertake an analysis designed to determine whether it could reasonably be considered as a sample of the population which the hypothesis generates. Clearly in this case it can, as one or other result of tossing must be obtained. But we may toss the coin a large number of times, and then more possibilities would exist. If a_1 heads and a_2 tails are observed, we know that a_1 roughly should be equal to a_2 if the observations are really a random sample of this population. The degree to which a_1 and a_2 depart from this expected equality affords a means of reaching a decision as to whether observation agrees with hypothesis or not. This operation is what we shall come to know as a test of significance.

The data could, however, be used in another way. Just as the population is characterized by the parameter $\xi=\frac{1}{2}$ when ξ is the theoretical proportion of heads, the sample is characterized by the statistic $x=\dfrac{a_1}{a_1+a_2}$, x being the observed proportion of heads. Now ξ and x are clearly related since, as a_1 and a_2 increase, x must approach closer and closer towards ξ in value. But equally clearly x will not in general equal ξ as its value is subject to chance errors of sampling from the population. We must then regard x not as telling us the exact value of ξ but as affording an estimate of this value. This distinction between the parameter specifying the population and the statistic which represents all that a sample can tell us about the parameter is very important in statistical theory and will be encountered again on many occasions. The statistic, or estimate of a parameter, is subject to sampling errors whose magnitude may, however, be calculated exactly, and so although it is impossible to find ξ from x it is possible to say rigorously, solely from what is known about x, that ξ lies within a given range of values with a given probability.

The question of rigour in such cases is interesting. The conclusions drawn concerning ξ are not certain, but they are none the less rigorous as the nature and degree of the uncertainty can be stated exactly. This is equally true of conclusions drawn from a test of significance. Even though it may not be possible to say with certainty that an observation is or is not a sample from the population, it is possible to state exactly the degree of probability of either alternative being true. Uncertainty does not preclude rigour, provided that the degree of uncertainty is itself exactly known.

Rigorous statements, even though they are uncertain statements, must be based solely on known facts, since it is only on this basis that the degree of uncertainty can be stated. In our example of estimating ξ, the statement of its value, or rather of the limits to its value, must be based only on the data contained in the observed sample, since these data represent the sum total of our accurate knowledge about the coin. It would be fatal to the rigour of the conclusions to attempt the introduction into the analysis of speculative controlling agents whose existence was unproven or whose effect was unmeasured. The idea, for example, that greater weight must be accorded to the possibility of $\xi=\frac{1}{2}$, as compared with any other single value, because the mint responsible for the coin is unlikely to send out a biased product, is useless. It contributes nothing accurate to our data. If, however, it is possible to give the range and frequency of the values of ξ shown by the coins emerging from the mint in question, the additional data are precise and they can be incorporated in the calculation with profit. In doing this we are clearly not transgressing the rule that any statement about the parameter must be based solely on the data of observation, for the detailed knowledge of the distribution of bias in the mint's coins must have originated from a series of precise observations.

The method of incorporating extra information of this particular type in the analysis is worth noting. It would be used to describe a super-population of coins each of which gives a population of throws like the one whose sample is discussed above. Clearly this super-population can only be adequately specified if the range and frequency of bias in coins are accurately known. In the absence of such knowledge the super-population cannot be used, though, as will be seen in Chapter XII, attempts have been made to employ it as a means of analysis by giving it characteristics based on *a priori* arguments. Such arguments introduce a subjective element into an analysis otherwise solely concerned with objective experimental data. In consequence they cannot be considered as anything but misleading.

Thus statistical analysis must aim at making the data tell their own story in such a way that their true value and degree of trustworthiness may be accurately assessed. Under-assessment of value is wasteful and over-assessment is misleading. Both must be avoided. Fisher's co-ordination of his own analysis of the problem of estimation with the use of the exact tests of significance derived by Pearson, 'Student' and himself make this aim capable of achievement by means that are illustrated in the succeeding chapters.

3. DIAGRAMS AND GRAPHS

Before turning to the discussion of the methods by which satisfactory statistical analyses are made, a word about diagrams and graphs is necessary.

Diagrams and graphs share with statistical analyses the purpose of separating the relevant from the irrelevant in the data and presenting the results in such a way that this distinction is reasonably obvious. The methods of achieving this end are, however, very different in the two cases. In an analysis the procedure is that of reducing the data to a few numbers which have certain definite and known properties and which can hence be used as the basis of rigorous statements. A diagram is, on the other hand, merely a geometrical representation of the data, carried out in such a way that any marked trends are obvious on inspection. It can never replace statistical analysis because the interpretation of a diagram is essentially subjective. This is not, however, to say that diagrams are useless; on the contrary, they are invaluable as adjuncts to statistical analysis, in two ways. In the first place, when used as a preliminary to the analysis, they serve to draw the attention of the experimenter to the salient features of his data and frequently ensure that he does not overlook some unexpected relationship. In doing this a diagram will generally suggest the form of analysis most appropriate to the data. Secondly, diagrams are of value when used subsequently to the analysis in order to display the results. Other persons interested in the work can then understand the findings quickly and easily, in a way that non-geometrical representation seldom permits.

The forms which diagrams and graphs can take are too numerous to be detailed here, though certain types will be illustrated later. No matter, however, what form a diagram assumes, it should always be made as simple as is compatible with the purpose in mind. Excessive elaboration defeats its own end, because it obscures the important features of the data both from the experimenter and from his subsequent readers.

CHAPTER II

PROBABILITY AND SIGNIFICANCE

4. SIMPLE PROBABILITY

ONE of the fundamental concepts of statistics is that of probability. It is an idea with which most of us are familiar in a general way, but a precise definition of the term is necessary before it can be applied to the analysis of experimental data.

When we speak of the probability of an event we imply that circumstances do not allow us to determine its regular occurrence, so that at a given opportunity the event may or may not happen; but over an extensive series of opportunities it will take place in a characteristic proportion of cases. This proportion may be expressed numerically. Thus we can toss a penny and it may come down 'heads', though on the other hand it may equally show 'tails'. Under the ordinary conditions of tossing it is not known which of these two possibilities will be realized by any spin. If, however, the penny is tossed a large number of times, assuming the absence of bias, we expect that the coin will show heads and tails in equal proportions of the trials. The probability of each result is then $\frac{1}{2}$. In general the probability of occurrence of an event may be defined in the following way: If, out of a very large number, n, of similar occasions on each of which a given event may occur, that event actually happens in a cases, the probability of the occurrence of the event is $\frac{a}{n}$. With a limited number of trials, such as must always content us in practice, the proportion of successes may not exactly equal $\frac{a}{n}$, but the larger n, and hence a, become, the more closely will the ratio of number of successes to number of trials tend to approach the true probability.

The probability of an event is sometimes predictable from the data given. Thus in the case of the character 'fern' leaf in *Primula sinensis* our previous experience is compatible with the belief that fern differs from the normal palm type by a single recessive gene. Fern is always homozygous ff, while palm may be Ff or FF. If a heterozygous palm is crossed with a fern (Ff×ff), it is expected according to simple mendelian theory that half the progeny will have palm and half fern leaves. So the probability of any individual being fern is predictable from previous knowledge of gene transmission. Such a forecast is, however, not always possible. Suppose that seed had been collected from a fern plant exposed to open pollination by both fern and palm individuals. In the absence of any knowledge as to the frequency of the various kinds of pollination and as to the constitution of the palm plants, i.e. whether homozygous or heterozygous, it would be impossible to predict the probability of any individual in the progeny being fern, because there are three possible types of cross, each giving different expectations. In such cases it is necessary to resort to estimation from experimental data in order to determine the probability. But the probability of any plant being fern is always a characteristic property of the particular sample of seed and may be found by suitable methods.

5. COMPOUND PROBABILITY

Just as the probability of one individual being of a given type may be determined, it is also possible to ascertain that of finding pairs or higher groups containing given numbers of individuals of each type. Consider the case of a family of five plants raised by back-crossing a heterozygous palm by fern (Ff×ff). The probability of each plant being palm is $\frac{1}{2}$ and of its being fern is also $\frac{1}{2}$. What is the probability that the family will consist of four palms and one fern?

Let us label the five plants, A, B, C, D and E. Two equally likely types of family may be distinguished according to whether A is palm or fern. Similarly the leaf form of B may be used to separate two types of family. Then since B's leaves cannot be considered as determined by those of A, 2×2 types of family, all equally likely, can be recognized by the simultaneous leaf forms of these two plants. On extending this argument it is seen that there are 2×2×2×2×2 or 2^5 kinds of family all of equal probability, distinguishable when the leaf forms of all five plants are taken into account. The probability of any one of these families is clearly $\frac{1}{2^5}$ or 2^{-5}. So the problem reduces to that of finding what proportion of these 2^5 families consists of 4 palms and 1 fern. The fern plant may be A, B, C, D or E, but once it has been decided which of the five is of this kind, the family is completely specified, since all the rest must be palm. Hence there are only five different families which will fulfil the stated condition, viz. $A^f\ B^F\ C^F\ D^F\ E^F$, $A^F\ B^f\ C^F\ D^F\ E^F$, $A^F\ B^F\ C^f\ D^F\ E^F$, $A^F\ B^F\ C^F\ D^f\ E^F$ and $A^F\ B^F\ C^F\ D^F\ E^f$, where F is palm and f is fern. So the required probability is 5 out of 32, i.e., $\frac{5}{32}$ or 0·15625.

In the above example the chance of finding a family of four ferns and one palm would also be 0·15625, as five of the 32 equally likely families would fulfil this requirement. These five would be specified by A, B, C, D or E being palm, the others being fern. If, however, the probabilities of any individual being palm and fern were not equal, the situation would be rather different, because the 32 types of family would not be expected equally often. Where, for example, the plants were from F_2 seed obtained by selfing a heterozygous palm (Ff×Ff) palm and fern would be expected with probabilities of $\frac{3}{4}$ and $\frac{1}{4}$ respectively. A would then be palm in $\frac{3}{4}$ and fern in $\frac{1}{4}$ of the cases, and similarly for B. The probability of both A and B being palm would be $\frac{3}{4}\times\frac{3}{4}$, of A being palm and B fern $\frac{3}{4}\times\frac{1}{4}$, of A fern and B palm $\frac{1}{4}\times\frac{3}{4}$ and of both being fern $\frac{1}{4}\times\frac{1}{4}$. By extending this argument it will be seen that the probability of obtaining any one of the different families which contain four palms and one fern would be $(\frac{3}{4})^4(\frac{1}{4})^1$. There would again be five equally likely families answering to the requirement of four palms and one fern, so the total would be $5(\frac{3}{4})^4(\frac{1}{4})$ or 0·39551. It will also be seen that the chance of getting a family with four ferns and one palm is $5(\frac{3}{4})(\frac{1}{4})^4$, and so differs from its reciprocal.

We may recognize two steps in the calculation of a compound probability. The first is the determination of the number of types of family that fulfil the given requirements. The second is that of finding the probabilities of each of these types. In the above examples there were five types of family, distinguishable only by the order in which the leaf forms occurred and so all equally suitable. In the F_2 plants these five were all equally probable with an expectation of $(\frac{3}{4})^4(\frac{1}{4})$. The final probability was the product of these two figures.

The further application of these rules may be illustrated by a somewhat more complicated example. What is the probability of a family of two palms and three ferns in the case of F_2 plants?

To find the number of suitable families we first note that the family is specified when it is known which two of the five plants are palm. Let these two palms be distinguished as first and second. The first may be any one of five plants, but when this is fixed the possibilities for the second are more limited. It must be one of the remaining four plants. So the first palm may be assigned in five ways and the second in four. Furthermore, there is no reason to believe that the first one determines the second, other than in limiting the number of plants which may fill this role. Hence the total number of ways of jointly assigning the two is 5×4, or 20. This is called the number of permutations of five taken two at a time and is written $_5P_2$. It may also be expressed in factorial notation as $\frac{5!}{(5-2)!}$, where $5!=5\times4\times3\times2\times1$ and $(5-2)!=3!=3\times2\times1$. But of these 20 ways some are identical, for we have formally distinguished the palms as first and second and so drawn a distinction between the cases, say, when A is the first palm and B the second and when B is the first palm and A the second. This distinction arises solely from the method of approach and has no real meaning. A little consideration will show that the 20 ways consist of 10 such pairs. So the number of types of family with two palms and three ferns is $\frac{5 \times 4}{2}$. This is the number of combinations of five taken two at a time and is written as $_5C_2$. In the factorial notation it is $\frac{5!}{(5-2)!\, 2!}$. It should be noticed that $_5C_2$ is the same as $_5C_3$, since

$$\frac{5!}{(5-2)!\, 2!} = \frac{5!}{3!\, 2!} = \frac{5!}{3!\, (5-3)!}$$

The essential difference between permutations and combinations is that the former takes into account order, which the latter neglects.

Having decided that there are 10 types of family, it is next necessary to find the probability of each. The probability that an individual will be palm is $\frac{3}{4}$, and so the chance of two being palm simultaneously is $(\frac{3}{4})^2$. Similarly the chance of finding three ferns is $(\frac{1}{4})^3$ and so a family of two palms and three ferns has a probability of $(\frac{3}{4})^2(\frac{1}{4})^3$. Multiplying this by the number of suitable types of family, which are clearly all equally likely, we get as the probability of a family of two palms and three ferns $10(\frac{3}{4})^2(\frac{1}{4})^3$ or $10 \times \frac{9}{1024}$, i.e. 0·08789. There are also 10 families containing 3 palms and 2 ferns, as $_5C_2 = {_5C_3}$. But these each have a probability of $(\frac{3}{4})^3(\frac{1}{4})^2$ and so the total probability of a family of this type is $10(\frac{3}{4})^3(\frac{1}{4})^2$.

The expectations of obtaining five plants of which four, three, two and one are palm have now been found. Only two further possibilities remain, viz. families with five palm or five fern plants. Following the same methods of calculation it can easily be shown that these two types of family are expected in $(\frac{3}{4})^5$ and $(\frac{1}{4})^5$ of cases respectively. So the probabilities of the six types of family are:

5F	4F 1f	3F 2f	2F 3f	1F 4f	5f	Total
$(\frac{3}{4})^5$	$\frac{5!}{4!\, 1!}(\frac{3}{4})^4(\frac{1}{4})$	$\frac{5!}{3!\, 2!}(\frac{3}{4})^3(\frac{1}{4})^2$	$\frac{5!}{2!\, 3!}(\frac{3}{4})^2(\frac{1}{4})^3$	$\frac{5!}{1!\, 4!}(\frac{3}{4})(\frac{1}{4})^4$	$(\frac{1}{4})^5$	1·0
0·23730	0·39551	0·26367	0·08789	0·01465	0·00098	1·0

The second line of the table gives the probabilities in factorial notation, and the third line in decimals.

These results can be arrived at by the simple expansion of the expression $(\frac{3}{4} + \frac{1}{4})^5$. Such a binomial series can be used to find the expectation of the various possible types of family for any case involving two alternative types. Where p is the probability that an individual will be of one type and q $(=1-p)$ that it will be of the other type, there being k individuals in the family, the appropriate binomial is $(p+q)^k$. The chance of getting a family containing r individuals of the first type, the remaining $k-r$ being of the second, is then

$$\frac{k!}{(k-r)!\,r!}(p)^r(q)^{k-r}$$

As an example of the use of the binomial expansion consider the case of families of six obtained by backcrossing heterozygous palm to fern (Ff×ff). The two types, palm and fern, are expected with equal frequency in the next generation. So $p=q=\frac{1}{2}$ and $k=6$. The series of expectations will be given by the expansion of $(\frac{1}{2}+\frac{1}{2})^6$. These are:

6F	5F 1f	4F 2f	3F 3f	2F 4f	1F 5f	6f
$(\frac{1}{2})^6$	$\frac{6!}{5!\,1!}(\frac{1}{2})^5(\frac{1}{2})$	$\frac{6!}{4!\,2!}(\frac{1}{2})^4(\frac{1}{2})^2$	$\frac{6!}{3!\,3!}(\frac{1}{2})^3(\frac{1}{2})^3$	$\frac{6!}{2!\,4!}(\frac{1}{2})^2(\frac{1}{2})^4$	$\frac{6!}{1!\,5!}(\frac{1}{2})(\frac{1}{2})^5$	$(\frac{1}{2})^6$
0·015625	0·093750	0·234375	0·312500	0·234375	0·093750	0·015625

where the third line of figures is the evaluation of the second line.

Where an individual may fall into one of more than two classes the expression whose expansion gives the series of probabilities is known as a multinomial. The general form is

$$(p_1+p_2+p_3+\ldots+p_j)^k$$

The expectation of a family containing r_1 of the first kind, r_2 of the second, ... r_j of the jth kind is given by

$$\frac{k!}{r_1!\,r_2!\,r_3!\,\ldots\,r_j!}(p_1)^{r_1}(p_2)^{r_2}(p_3)^{r_3}\ldots(p_j)^{r_j}$$

6. AGREEMENT WITH HYPOTHESIS

Given the probabilities of obtaining various kinds of family on any hypothesis, it is possible to determine how well or ill any observed family accords with that hypothesis. The series of calculated probabilities tells us the frequency with which to expect a result like the one observed. It is then necessary to decide whether this frequency is sufficiently high to justify the belief that the data accord reasonably well with the primary hypothesis, or whether such a result would be expected so rarely that its occurrence must be taken to indicate that the hypothesis is invalid and incapable of explaining the observed data. This is the principle of all tests of significance.

Example 1. Two plants of *Primula sinensis*, one pin and the other thrum, were crossed together and a family of eleven plants grown from the seed so obtained. Of these eleven two were thrum and nine were pin. Does this agree with the hypothesis that pin differs from thrum by a single gene ?

Now if the difference is due to a single gene the cross would be of the type Ss×ss and each plant in the progeny would have a half chance of being thrum and a half of being pin. Then with a family of eleven plants the various types of segregation would be expected with frequencies given by the expansion of $(\frac{1}{2}+\frac{1}{2})^{11}$. These are set out in Table 1. The chance of getting nine pins and two thrums is thus $\frac{55}{2048}$, or about 1 in 37. This type of family appears to be but rarely expected on the basis of a single gene difference and the hypothesis might be considered to be suspect.

There is, however, one important drawback to the use of the expectation of the observed type of family for a direct test of this kind, viz. that as the number of plants increases, the chance of getting any type of family, even though it be a very good fit with expectation, decreases rapidly. In a backcross, for example, we expect half the plants to be of each kind and so families with an exact 1 : 1 ratio are showing a perfect fit. Yet the chance of getting such a family diminishes as the size of the family grows larger (see Table 2).

Thus the isolated probability of an observed type can be very misleading and cannot be employed in a test of significance. We use instead the probability of getting as bad or worse a fit on the hypothesis in question. In the case of the perfect 1 : 1 ratios of Table 2 this is clearly constant at 1, no matter what the family size may be.

In the segregation for pin and thrum any family containing nine, ten or eleven pins agrees with the hypothesis as badly as or worse than the progeny in question. But we have no reason to expect that the deviation from the perfect 1 : 1 shall occur in either the direction of more thrums or of more pins. So families with nine, ten or eleven thrums also agree as badly or worse with hypothesis than our observed progeny. Hence it is necessary to sum the probabilities of all six kinds of families containing nine or more plants of either kind. These are shown in heavy type in Table 1 and summation gives $\frac{(1+11+55+55+11+1)}{2,048}$ as the required probability. This is 0·065, or about 1 in 15. When considered in this way agreement with hypothesis is not nearly so bad as it first appeared, and indeed would not generally be considered to be unduly poor. It is true that the probability is rather low, but if we were to take such data as contradicting hypothesis we should be deluding ourselves once in every fifteen trials. This is rather too often for most purposes, and so such

TABLE 1
The Expansion of $(\tfrac{1}{2}+\tfrac{1}{2})^{11}$

No. of thrums	0	1	2	3	4	5	6	7	8	9	10	11	Total
Expectation	$\tfrac{1}{2048}$	$\tfrac{11}{2048}$	$\tfrac{55}{2048}$	$\tfrac{165}{2048}$	$\tfrac{330}{2048}$	$\tfrac{462}{2048}$	$\tfrac{462}{2048}$	$\tfrac{330}{2048}$	$\tfrac{165}{2048}$	$\tfrac{55}{2048}$	$\tfrac{11}{2048}$	$\tfrac{1}{2048}$	1

TABLE 2
The Probability of a Perfect 1 : 1 Ratio with Various Sizes of Family

Size of family	2	4	6	8	10	40	80
Probability of getting a perfect 1 : 1 ratio	0·500	0·3750	0·3125	0·2709	0·2461	0·1254	0·0889

a result would not be described as differing significantly from expectation.

7. SIGNIFICANCE

This question of the significance of results is one which frequently causes confusion. The probability of obtaining a fit as bad or worse may be calculated exactly; but a subjective decision is always involved when the meaning of the probability is considered. The level of probability which is considered to indicate a significant departure is really the level of admissible error, since the rejection of an hypothesis when it shows the data to have a probability of one in n means that it will be wrongly rejected once in n times. It seems to be generally agreed that a probability of 0·05, i.e. 1 in 20, indicates a suspiciously large departure from expectation, while 0·01 or 1 in 100 should be taken as showing a real discrepancy between the data and expectation. These are, however, not rules and the decision must always be dependent to some extent on the circumstances of the case. Where much hangs on the outcome of the test it might be desirable to adopt a more exacting standard, while if the decision has only trivial consequences a higher probability might be taken as significant. One rule can, however, be laid down. In presenting the results of any test of significance the probability itself should be given. The reader is then in a position to form his own opinion as to the justification of the acceptance or rejection of the hypothesis in question.

In judging the significance of results all relevant information must be taken into account. Where an isolated set of data has a probability as low as 1 in 100 the departure from expectation would be considered to be real. But if 100 such sets of data are analysed and one of them shows a probability of 0·01 it clearly should not be taken as indicating a departure from hypothesis, because a fit as poor as this is expected once in 100 sets of data. Table 3 gives the results of analysing 100 back-crosses for the gene determining yellow body colour in *Drosophila melanogaster* (Mather's data). The probability of obtaining as bad or worse a fit has been calculated for each family separately and the families then classified according to these probabilities.

Now the grand totals of yellow and not-yellow flies were 5,273 and 5,329 respectively. These are in good agreement with the expected 1 : 1 ratio. But one family has a probability of less than 0·02. This would, if occurring individually, indicate a significant, or at least a suspiciously large, departure from expectation. In the present case we attach no significance to it, as not one but two families showing such poor agreement are expected. In other words, the evidence for agreement with

TABLE 3

Distribution of Probabilities of finding a Fit with Hypothesis as bad as or worse than that observed in 100 Backcrosses for Yellow Body Colour in Drosophila melanogaster

Probability of a fit as bad as or worse than that observed	1·0–0·95	0·95–0·90	0·90–0·80	0·80–0·70	0·70–0·50	0·50–0·30	0·30–0·20	0·20–0·10	0·10–0·05	0·05–0·02	0·02–0·01	0·01–0·00
Number of families expected	5	5	10	10	20	20	10	10	5	3	1	1
Number of families observed	4	4	10	9	18	24	12	13	2	3	1	0

TABLE 4

Distribution of Probabilities of finding a Fit with Hypothesis as bad as or worse than that observed in 20 Pairing Tests of Random Numbers

Probability of a fit as bad as or worse than that observed	1·0–0·95	0·95–0·90	0·90–0·80	0·80–0·70	0·70–0·50	0·50–0·30	0·30–0·20	0·20–0·10	0·10–0·05	0·05–0·02	0·02–0·01	0·01–0·00
Number expected	1	1	2	2	4	4	2	2	1	0·6	0·2	0·2
Number observed	2	0	0	7	4	3	0	2	1	0	1	0

hypothesis is actually rather better than random sampling would lead us to expect. It will be observed that, in general, the agreement between the number of families expected and the number observed to have probabilities between given levels is quite good in these data.

The table might also be read in the reverse direction. For example, 18 families have a probability of 0·8 or higher. On the basis of random sampling we should expect 20 out of the 100 to fall in this class. Agreement of observation and expectation is again good. If too many families, say 50 out of 100, had shown a probability as high as or higher than 0·8, the hypothesis would have been just as suspect as if too many families had shown a very low probability. A ratio of 1 : 1 is indeed expected, but the theory of random sampling leads us also to expect a certain measure of departure from this perfect ratio in finite samples, such as we must always use in practice. If this departure is not realized, something is wrong. Excessively good agreement might be due to selection of data, a very dubious and misleading practice, or to interdependence of the genotypes of the individuals in a family, in a way that would lead to reduced variability. Agreement with hypothesis demands that no exceptionally wide departures from expectation should be observed, but it also demands that a certain range of departure should be found, according to the sampling technique used. Excessively good agreement is as much a disproof of hypothesis as is excessively bad agreement.

There is a second way in which apparently significant departure from expectation may be spuriously obtained, viz. by the application of a number of different tests of significance to the same data. If 100 such tests are applied, one is expected to show a probability of as low as 0·01, and such a result must not be taken to indicate that the data really depart from expectation. This may be illustrated by the following case. One hundred numbers, ranging from 0 to 9 inclusive, were taken from Fisher and Yates's table of random numbers. Now if these numbers are really random, any pair of them should have a probability of 0·1 of being identical. Hence if each number is compared with its successor, the first being taken as the successor of the hundredth, one hundred comparisons will be made and ten identities are expected. Actually in the set of numbers used 8 such identities were found. Similarly each number can be compared with the next but one, the next but two, and so on. In every case 10 identities are expected out of the hundred comparisons made. Twenty such tests were applied, and the probability of each result was calculated. The twenty probabilities are grouped, as in the case of the *Drosophila* data, and given in this form in Table 4. One of the twenty tests of randomness gave a result with the probability as low as 2%. This cannot, however, be judged significant, as we expect to get a single test showing a fit as bad as this in two out of every five trials, each of which includes twenty such tests. A perusal of the distribution of probabilities shows that they accord reasonably well with that expected on the basis of random sampling. There is a tendency to bunch in the 0·8–0·7 region, but this may be due in part to the use of only 100 numbers. There is no reason to doubt that these numbers were indeed random.

So unless all the available information is taken into account, the result of a test of significance may be misleading. Several bodies of data can very often be combined into one test of significance, the decision as to the significance of departure then being more easily taken. Methods of doing this will be illustrated later.

Finally, it must always be borne in mind that a hypothesis can never be completely disproved, still less proved, by the calculation of such a probability. It can only be rendered more or less likely, since however small the probability may be, such a result as the one observed is expected if sufficient trials are made, in spite of our surprise that it should occur in the very trial we ourselves conduct.

REFERENCES

FISHER, R. A., and YATES, F. 1943. *Statistical Tables for Biological, Agricultural and Medical Research.* Oliver and Boyd. Edinburgh. 2nd ed.

CHAPTER III

DISTRIBUTIONS

8. THE NORMAL DISTRIBUTION

THE binomial distribution $(p+q)^k$, where $p+q=1$, can only be used as a basis for the analysis of data where the quantities p and k are known. In the genetical examples treated in the foregoing chapter these parameters are fixed by mendelian theory and the magnitude of the experiment respectively.

Many kinds of data are, however, incapable of being treated in this way because they provide no basis for the fitting of numerical values to p and k. Thus the height of a maize plant is variable just as is the number of fern plants in a family of Primulas, but it is impossible to say how many factors are influencing the height. In other words, we do not know the value of k. Furthermore, we do not know how often or how far each factor affects the height of the plant, i.e. we do not know p. So it is impossible to find the curve of variation of such heights from a consideration of the binomial series.

There is, however, a way of avoiding this difficulty. The number of factors influencing the height of a maize plant cannot be determined, but it is certainly large, for in addition to the many genes there will be innumerable environmental conditions, climatic, edaphic and biological, all playing their part in determining this one character. Now, provided that neither p nor q is of the magnitude of $\dfrac{1}{k}$ or less, as k becomes larger and larger the frequency distribution obtained by expanding $(p+q)^k$ approaches more and more closely to a curve which has the formula

$$m = \frac{1}{\sigma\sqrt{2\pi}} e^{-\frac{(x-\mu)^2}{2\sigma^2}}$$

where m is the frequency of the class x. This limit to the binomial is called the Normal Curve of Errors, or for short, the Normal Curve. It will be observed that its formula contains neither p nor k, but is characterized by two new parameters, μ and σ. These two quantities are seldom fixed by hypothesis, but, unlike p and k, can easily be estimated from experimental data such as those concerning the height of maize plants.

Before considering the estimation of μ and σ, it should be pointed out that the normal curve is also the limit towards which the distribution

$$(p_1+q_1)(p_2+q_2)(p_3+q_3) \ldots (p_k+q_k)$$

tends. This means that it has a very wide application in covering the case where the k factors are exerting unequal influences on the character in question. Nor does this close the account of the usefulness of the normal curve, for it is the limit of the multinomial distribution too. As might then be expected, many sets of observed data have been found to conform to the normal curve.

9. THE MEAN AND STANDARD DEVIATION

The nature of the two quantities characteristic of the normal curve, viz. μ and σ, can perhaps be understood most easily from a geometrical representation. Fig. 1 shows a sample normal curve which, as will be observed, is continuous and symmetrical, unlike the binomial which is neither continuous nor in general symmetrical. The shape is such that there is a point of maximum slope on either side of the centre line, or axis of symmetry. The distance, along the abscissa, of this centre line from the origin of the axes is μ, and the distance of each point of maximum slope from the centre line, also as measured along the abscissa, is σ. Thus μ fixes the position of the curve and σ determines its width.

It has already been stated that these two quantities are seldom fixed by hypothesis, and that in consequence they must always be estimated from the experimental data themselves. Three main ways of finding μ suggest themselves. Two of them depend on this parameter's property of marking the centre of the curve. The first consists of taking the simple average of all the observations. This estimate of μ is termed the mean of the distribution. The second way is to use as the estimate of μ the magnitude of that observation which has an equal number of others smaller and larger than itself. This is termed the median of the distribution. The third way of finding μ depends on the fact that it is this class which is most frequent, i.e. that the value of m is greatest at this value of x in the graph. μ as found in this way is the mode of the curve. These three characteristics can all be used as estimates of μ in the case of the normal curve, as they coincide, but in other curves, notably asymmetrical ones, they have different values.

Two ways of estimating σ have been proposed, and as might be expected both depend on finding the average magnitude of the deviations of the various observations from the centre of the curve. The simplest way is to take the average of these deviations, ignoring any question of sign, i.e. taking no account of which side of the centre the particular observation lies. This gives the mean deviation from which σ is estimated. The more complex way consists of squaring all the deviations, so removing any difficulty introduced by sign, finding the mean of these squares and taking its square root. This is termed the standard deviation, and is a direct estimate of σ.

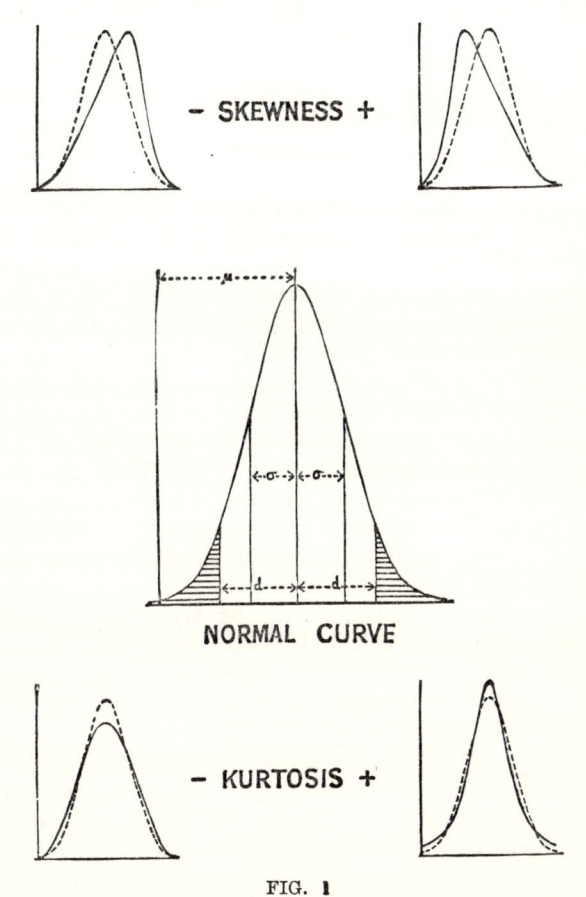

FIG. 1

In the centre, a normal distribution showing how the mean, μ, fixes the position of the curve, and the standard deviation, σ, measures its spread. The shaded portions are the tails cut off by the ordinates marking the deviation, d. The four corners illustrate how curves showing Skewness and Kurtosis (solid line) deviate from the normal distribution (broken line)

Now these various ways of estimating μ and σ would all lead to the same value, viz. the true value, of each parameter if an infinitely large number of observations were available; but it is clear that with the limited samples obtainable in practice they will differ among themselves. It is thus necessary to decide the questions of which is the best estimate of μ, mean, median or mode, and which gives a better estimate of σ, mean deviation or standard deviation. Discussion of the considerations involved in answering these questions must be deferred to a later chapter, and it must suffice for the present to say that μ is most efficiently estimated by the mean, and σ by the standard deviation.

The mean and standard deviation as found from observed data are only estimates of the true parameters of the curve. We have seen in the previous chapter how a sample of individuals drawn from a population whose characteristics are known can, and indeed must, as a result of the process of random sampling, show departures from these ideal features, realizable only with infinitely large numbers. Thus the estimated mean and standard deviation will not have the exact values of μ and σ. They will be just as much subject to sampling error as the number of fern-leaved plants in a segregating family. It is necessary, therefore, to distinguish carefully between the parameters characterizing the population from which our sample is drawn, and the estimates of these parameters calculated from our limited data. One way of emphasizing this distinction, suggested by Fisher, is to denote the parameters by Greek letters and their estimates by corresponding Latin letters. Thus the estimated mean should be denoted by m, and the estimated standard deviation by s. This practice will be followed as far as possible throughout this book, but one great exception must be made. It is, and has long been, customary to denote the mean of a series of observed values, $x_1 x_2 x_3 \ldots x_j$, by the symbol $\bar{x}$, and this well-established custom will be followed, even though it conflicts with Fisher's system of notation. The symbol m is thus released for use in another connexion.

10. FITTING THE NORMAL CURVE

Details of the arithmetical process of estimating the mean and standard error can best be illustrated by a numerical example.

Example 2. In Table 5 are given the heights, in decimeters, of 530 maize plants (Emerson and East's data). We have seen that such a character as height is determined by the action of a large number of different factors, just as the mean number of individuals of a given kind in a segregating family is determined by the joint behaviour of a number of factors, viz. the number of individuals in the family, each of which may, or may not, fall into the category in question. So each height measurement corresponds to a family in the genetical examples of the previous chapter. Now the chance of obtaining a family of a given kind could be calculated from theory, but it could also have been found experimentally by the process of raising a large

TABLE 5

Distribution of the Heights of Maize Plants (in Decimeters) and the Calculation of $\bar{x}$ and s^2 using a Working Mean (Emerson and East)

Height of plant in dms. (x) [class centre]	Deviation from the working mean $(x_m = 15$ dms.$)$	Frequency observed (a)	$a(x-x_m)$	$a(x-x_m)^2$
7	−8	1	− 8	64
8	−7	3	− 21	147
9	−6	4	− 24	144
10	−5	12	− 60	300
11	−4	25	−100	400
12	−3	49	−147	441
13	−2	68	−136	272
14	−1	95	− 95	95
15	0	96	0	0
16	1	78	78	78
17	2	53	106	212
18	3	26	78	234
19	4	16	64	256
20	5	3	15	75
21	6	1	6	36
Total		530	−244	2,754

$$\bar{x} = 15 - \frac{244}{530} = 14\cdot5396 \text{ dms.}$$

$$S(x-\bar{x})^2 = 2{,}754 - \frac{244^2}{530} = 2{,}641\cdot6679$$

$$N = 529$$

$$V_x = \frac{S(x-\bar{x})^2}{N} = 4\cdot9936 - 0\cdot0833 \text{ [Sheppard's correction]}$$

$$= 4\cdot9103$$

$$s_x = \sqrt{V_x} = 2\cdot2159$$

number of families of the size in question and observing how many fell into the classes with 0, 1, &c., of the particular kind of individual. The frequency distribution obtained in this way is an estimate of the probability distribution of families of the size in question. Just in the same way the frequency distribution of the heights of the maize plants is, within the limits of sampling error, a model of the probability distribution of such heights. The observed frequency of a given class is an estimate of the probability of obtaining a plant of that kind. The frequency distribution may thus be used as material for the estimation of the characteristics of the distribution of probabilities of plants with the various heights.

In the data given in Table 5 the exact height of each plant is not given, the plants being grouped into classes whose central values are at 7, 8, 9, &c., decimeters. This can be done by measuring to the nearest decimeter, or, at a later stage, by grouping all plants with heights between 6·5 and 7·5 decimeters into the 7-dm. class, and so on. This process is a great convenience as it simplifies calculation. When finding the mean, for example, instead of adding a large number of single values, we can do the major part of the work by multiplying together the frequency of each class and the central class value, subsequently summing the relatively small number of products obtained in this way. Tedious additions are replaced by rapid multiplications. Grouping does, however, have certain undesirable consequences. These follow from the fact that the true data are really being replaced by fictitious results when the process of grouping is applied. In replacing the plants whose heights fall between, say, 8·5 and 9·5 dms. by an equal number of fictitious individuals, all of height 9 dms., the spread of the frequency distribution is spuriously increased, since if the true heights follow a normal curve the number of plants between 8·5 and 9 dms. is less than that between 9 and 9·5 dms. Thus the average of the true plants is nearer to the centre of the curve than is 9 dms. On the other side of the curve the fictitious plants have too great a height, as the average of the actual plants in the class, in being nearer to the centre, is lower than the value assigned to the fictitious individuals.

Grouping does not bias our estimate of μ because, as will be seen from the foregoing remarks, the discrepancies between the fictitious plants and the ones they replace are of opposite sign on opposite sides of the curve. The normal curve is symmetrical and so the discrepancies cancel out. The estimate of the standard deviation is, however, markedly biased by grouping, as the discrepancies are all deviations from the mean and so will be summed in the process of calculating this quantity. The estimate arrived at from grouped data will thus be spuriously large. Fortunately, due allowance can be made for this bias, as will be shown below.

The best estimate of μ is the average plant height. It is found, of course, by summing the heights of the plants and dividing the total so obtained by the number of individuals measured. This is expressed algebraically by the formula $\bar{x} = \frac{1}{n} S(x)$, where n is the number of individuals measured and

S means 'the sum of'. The obvious way of doing this in our example is to find $(7×1)+(8×3)+(9×4)+(10×12)+ \ldots +(20×3)$ $+(21×1)$ and divide by 530. This gives $\bar{x}=\dfrac{7{,}706}{530}=14\cdot5396$ dms. The numbers involved in this calculation are somewhat too large to allow of easy manipulation unless a calculating machine is used, so the device of the working mean is to be recommended. This is usually most conveniently taken at the value of the class with the greatest frequency, which in the present case is 15 dms. The various classes are then regraduated, using the working mean as the origin. Thus the 14-dm. class becomes −1, the 13-dm. class −2, while 16 dms. and 17 dms. are replaced by 1 and 2 respectively (Column 2, Table 5). We then find $(-8×1)+(-7×3)$ $+(-6×4)+ \ldots +(4×16)+(5×3)+(6×1)$. The sum of these fourteen quantities is −244, which when divided by 530 gives −0·4604. Hence our estimate of the true mean is 15−0·4604 or 14·5396, as found earlier by the heavier method.

The next operation is that of estimating the standard deviation, for which purpose it is necessary to find the squared deviations from the mean and to take the square root of their average. Expressing this algebraically:

$$s^2=\dfrac{1}{n-1}S[(x-\bar{x})^2]$$

In order to find the sum of the squared deviations we could regraduate all the classes in terms of their deviations from 14·5396. The 14-dm. class would become −0·5396, and the 13-dm. class −1·5396, while 15 dms. would be replaced by 0·4604 and 16 by 1·4604. The sum of squares of deviations is then

$[(-7\cdot5396)^2×1]+[(-6\cdot5396)^2×3]+[(-5\cdot5396)^2×4]+ \ldots$
$+[(4\cdot4604)^2×16]+[(5\cdot4604)^2×3]+[(6\cdot4604)^2×1]$

This is an extremely cumbersome calculation and is never attempted in practice, as the device of the working mean offers an easier and more exact method. Let us denote the working mean by x_m. The deviation of any x, say x_1, from the true mean $\bar{x}$ can be expressed as the difference of two quantities, one a deviation of x_1 from x_m and the other the difference between x_m and $\bar{x}$. Thus

$$(x_1-\bar{x})=(x_1-x_m)-(\bar{x}-x_m)$$
and
$$(x_1-\bar{x})^2=(x_1-x_m)^2-2(x_1-x_m)(\bar{x}-x_m)+(\bar{x}-x_m)^2$$

Summing the n items of this kind, obtained by squaring each of the deviations of the n different x values observed, we find

$$S(x-\bar{x})^2=S(x-x_m)^2-2S[(x-x_m)(\bar{x}-x_m)]+S(\bar{x}-x_m)^2$$
$$=S(x-x_m)^2-2(\bar{x}-x_m)S(x-x_m)+n(\bar{x}-x_m)^2$$

as $\bar{x}$ and x_m are constant.

But
$$n(\bar{x}-x_m) = n\bar{x}-nx_m$$
$$= S(x)-nx_m \quad \text{by definition of } \bar{x}$$
$$= S(x-x_m)$$

and so
$$S(x-\bar{x})^2 = S(x-x_m)^2 - \frac{2}{n}S^2(x-x_m) + \frac{1}{n}S^2(x-x_m)$$

$$= S(x-x_m)^2 - \frac{1}{n}S^2(x-x_m)$$

where S^2 stands for 'the square of the sum of'.

Thus we obtain the sum of squares of deviations from the true mean by first finding the sum of squares of deviations from the working mean and subtracting from it a quantity which is the squared sum of deviations from the working mean divided by the number of observations.

In the maize example the working mean already used is at $x_m = 15$ dms. Then the sum of squares of deviations from this working mean is easily found as

$$[(-8)^2 \times 1] + [(-7)^2 \times 3] + [(-6)^2 \times 4] + \ldots + [4^2 \times 16] + [5^2 \times 3] + [6^2 \times 1]$$

which is 2,754. The sum of deviations from the working mean has earlier been found to be -244 and the number of observations, n, is 530.

The sum of squares of deviations from the true mean is thus

$$2{,}754 - \frac{(-244)^2}{530}$$

$$= 2{,}754 - 112 \cdot 3321 = 2{,}641 \cdot 6679$$

The square of the standard deviation is then

$$2{,}641 \cdot 6679 \div 529 = 4 \cdot 9936$$

It was pointed out earlier that grouping of the data would lead to a spuriously high value for the standard error. Sheppard's correction for the error of grouping may be applied to rectify this, before taking the square root; it consists of subtracting $\frac{1}{12}$ of the unit of grouping. In the present case the grouping unit is 1 dm. and so 0·0833 is subtracted from 4·9936 to leave 4·9103 as the square of the standard deviation, which is itself then found to be 2·2159.

The square of the standard deviation, which it will be noted must always be found as part of the calculation of the standard deviation, is termed the variance (V), or, when estimated, the mean square. The mean and standard deviation are linear quantities expressible in our example in decimeters, but the variance is a quadratic quantity expressible in square decimeters.

In obtaining the variance, the sum of squares, 2,641·6679,

was divided not by n, but by $n-1$, i.e. 529, which is termed the number of degrees of freedom (N). The choice of $n-1$ instead of n as the divisor can be justified by a simple consideration. The standard deviation and variance are measures of the ' spread ' of the curve and as such are based on the magnitudes of differences. The greater the spread of the curve the greater will be the average difference between the individual x values and the mean; hence the greater also will be the average difference between any two individual x values. In other words, at least two values are required to afford any idea of the spread of the curve and any two values will supply but one difference. Just as two values give one difference, three values give two independent differences and in general n values give $n-1$ independent differences. If the mean is fixed by hypothesis the difference between this theoretical mean and that actually observed will contribute an nth difference. But in our example the mean was not fixed by hypothesis, and so the n observations together contribute only $n-1$ independent differences, or degrees of freedom, to the estimation of the standard error.

This justification of the use of $n-1$ as the divisor may be completed by considering the case of only one observation. If the mean were fixed by hypothesis this single observation would supply one difference for the estimation of σ. Where, however, the mean must be calculated from the data, as it must in the majority of instances, the observation is itself the best estimate of the mean and hence the deviation of observation from the mean will inevitably be 0. If $n-1$ is used as the divisor the variance is found to be $\frac{0}{0}$, which is indeterminate—a very reasonable result. But if n is used as the divisor the variance would be $\frac{0}{1}$, which is clearly ridiculous. It will be observed that it is the fitting of the mean which reduces the number of degrees of freedom from n to $n-1$. The principle that a degree of freedom is lost every time a parameter is estimated is highly important and will be considered in detail later.

Reverting for a moment to the use of the working mean in finding the sum of squares of deviations from the true mean, it must be emphasized that the working mean need not necessarily be chosen near to the true mean. It has been shown that the true mean can be found when the working mean is taken at $x_m=0$ and the sum of squares can be found by using the same value. The appropriate formula then reduces to

$$S(x-\bar{x})^2 = S(x^2) - \frac{1}{n}S^2(x)$$

In the present example this calculation is made as follows:
$S(x^2) = (7^2 \times 1) + (8^2 \times 3) + (9^2 \times 4) + \ldots$
$$+ (19^2 \times 16) + (20^2 \times 3) + (21^2 \times 1) = 114{,}684.$$
$S(x)$ has early been found to be 7,706, so
$$S(x-\bar{x})^2 = 114{,}684 - \frac{7{,}706^2}{530} = 114{,}684 - 112{,}042 \cdot 3321$$
$$= 2{,}641 \cdot 6679$$
as before.

When $x_m = 0$ the calculation is heavy, and so unless a calculating machine is available it is better to take a value near to the true mean. For machine calculation, however, the value of 0 is preferable, since large numbers present little difficulty and the labour of finding deviations from the working mean is obviated.

The use of a working mean involves no approximation in

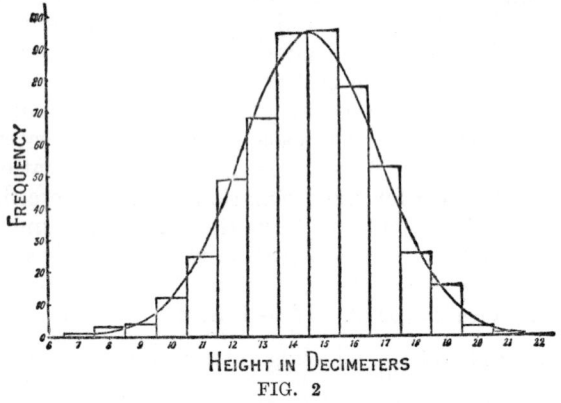

FIG. 2

Frequency histogram of Emerson and East's maize heights and the normal distribution fitted to them

finding the sum of squares. It leads to a fully accurate value. In fact, the results obtained in this way are often more accurate than those obtained by squaring and summing deviations from the true mean, because the latter process involves multiplication of indefinite decimal fractions, whereas the working mean necessitates only the squaring of whole numbers.

Having estimated μ and σ, their numerical values may be substituted in the general formula of the normal curve. This gives the particular expression which best fits the maize data. The formula obtained in this way is

$$m = \frac{1}{2 \cdot 2159 \sqrt{2\pi}} e^{-\frac{(x - 14 \cdot 5396)^2}{2 \times 2 \cdot 2159^2}}$$

and the corresponding curve is plotted in Fig. 2 together with the original data. It will be seen that the agreement between observation and expectation is quite good.

11. SKEWNESS AND KURTOSIS

Fitting the normal curve depends on calculating μ and σ, which are termed respectively the first and second moments of the data. Higher moments can be calculated, in particular the third and fourth which depend, as might be expected, on $S(x-\bar{x})^3$ and $S(x-\bar{x})^4$ respectively.

The third moment is of interest in that it affords a test of the skewness of the distribution. Where this is symmetrical, as in the case of the normal curve, the third moment is 0. A positive value of the sum of cubes of deviations indicates that the curve has a long tail to the right and its mode to the left of the mean. This is positive skewness. When the long tail is to the left and the mode to the right, the sum of cubes is negative and the skewness is said to be negative.

A curve may be symmetrical and yet not normal, in that it shows kurtosis, which means that, relative to the shoulders, the centre and tails have too many or too few values for normality. Kurtosis is detected by the use of the fourth moment. Negative kurtosis implies that the shoulders are excessive and positive kurtosis that the centre and tails contain too many observations. Examples of such curves are given in Fig. 1.

In practice, moments of order higher than the second are not often used. It is occasionally necessary to test for skewness by using third-degree statistics, but such needs are rare. Kurtosis is very seldom considered. Practically the whole of present-day statistical analysis depends on the comparison of variances and co-variances, i.e. on the use of second-degree statistics. It is nearly always assumed that the data fall on a normal distribution, and, though the fact that skew curves are not too uncommon shows that this assumption is not generally justified, the errors introduced into second-degree calculations by such departures from normality are small and may be neglected. Actual data have been analysed by Eden and Yates and the insignificance of these errors has been fully demonstrated.

12. THE POISSON SERIES

A binomial distribution approaches normality as k in the formula $(p+q)^k$ increases, provided that both p and q are of an order larger than $\frac{1}{k}$. Where, however, p or q is of the magnitude $\frac{1}{k}$ the limit approached by the binomial as k increases is not the continuous normal curve but the discontinuous Poisson series, whose formula is

$$e^{-\mu}(1,\ \mu,\ \frac{\mu^2}{2!},\ \frac{\mu^3}{3!},\ \ldots,\ \frac{\mu^j}{j!},\ \ldots)$$

where μ is the mean. The chief characteristic of this distribution is that its variance equals its mean, i.e. $\mu = \sigma^2$.

Data on the frequency of a given event are expected to fall on a Poisson series when the probability of the event happening on any one occasion is very small but when the number of occasions is sufficiently large for the event to be observed not too infrequently. One example, quoted by R. A. Fisher, is that of deaths of soldiers as a result of mule kicks. The chance of any one soldier being killed in any one year in this way is small, but where a whole army corps is exposed to the risk a number will sometimes be killed. Bortkewitch records that when 10 Prussian corps were exposed to mule kicks over a period of 20 years, the following frequency distribution of deaths per corps per year was obtained:

Deaths per corps per year	0	1	2	3	4	Total
Frequency	109	65	22	3	1	200

Various biological problems involve the use of this distribution, notably those arising when estimating the density of cells or organisms by haemacytometer counts or by the plating method. The same situation is encountered when measuring the density of plants in the wild by the use of quadrat counts. If a quadrat of appropriate size is used the chance that any one plant in a given one of its squares will be of the species under investigation is small, but a sufficient number of plants are included to ensure that a small number of this species are in fact found.

Example 3. The following data on the density of *Eryngium maritimum* were collected by Blackman. In all, 147 counts were made and 0, 1, 2, 3, &c., plants of this species were found in a square of the quadrat with the frequencies shown in Table 6. The table also includes details of the estimation of the mean and variance using a working mean of 0. It will be seen that $\bar{x} = \frac{293}{147} = 1\cdot 9931$. The sum of squares of deviations from the mean is $851 - 584\cdot 0068 = 266\cdot 9932$, and since there are 146 degrees of freedom or independent differences on which the sum of squares is based

$$s^2 = \frac{266\cdot 9932}{146} = 1\cdot 8287$$

Since the data were not artificially grouped, Sheppard's correction is not used.

TABLE 6
The density of Eryngium maritimum (*Blackman's data*)
Number of Plants per Quadrat Squares

Number of plants per quadrat square (x)	Frequency (a)	ax	ax^2	Frequency expected (mn)
0	16	0	0	20·03
1	41	41	41	39·93
2	49	98	196	39·79
3	20	60	180	26·44
4	14	56	224	13·17
5	5	25	125	5·25
6	1	6	36	1·74
7	1	7	49	0·50
8 and over	0	0	0	0·15
Total . .	147	293	851	147·00

$$\bar{x} = \frac{293}{147} = 1 \cdot 9931$$

$$S(x-\bar{x})^2 = 851 - \frac{293^2}{147} = 266 \cdot 9932$$

$$N = 146$$

$$V = s^2 = \frac{S(x-\bar{x})^2}{N} = 1 \cdot 8287$$

The estimates of mean and variance agree reasonably well. Perfect agreement is not to be expected, for though the true mean and true variance are equal, sampling error will cause slight discrepancies between their estimated values.

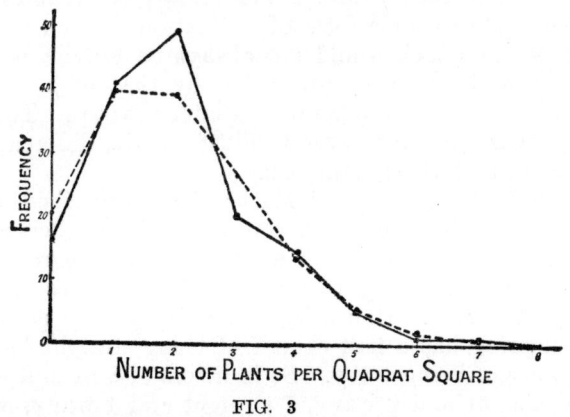

FIG. 3

Frequency polygons of the number of *Eryngium* plants observed by Blackman to fall into quadrat squares (solid line) and the Poisson series fitted to the data (broken line)

The numerical value found for $\bar{x}$ can be substituted in the general formula and gives as the expected frequencies

$$e^{-1\cdot9931}\left[1,\ 1\cdot9931,\ \frac{1\cdot9931^2}{2!},\ \frac{1\cdot9931^3}{3!},\ \ldots\right]$$

for the classes 0, 1, 2, &c. These expectations are given in Table 6, and are also plotted together with the observed values in Fig. 3. The close agreement of the data with a Poisson distribution is well illustrated by both table and figure.

13. THE MEAN AND VARIANCE OF THE BINOMIAL DISTRIBUTION

In both the Normal and Poisson distributions the mean and variance are usually estimated from the data themselves. The necessity for this arises from the fact that these distributions are used to replace binomials when information about p and k is lacking. Now clearly if the values of these latter quantities are given the distribution is known exactly and there is no need to estimate μ and σ from the data. The mean and variance would in fact be calculable from p and k, irrespective of the magnitude of the latter, i.e. whether a normal distribution could be assumed or not. The appropriate formulae are:

$$\mu = p \quad \text{and} \quad \sigma = \sqrt{\frac{pq}{k}}$$

These formulae give the theoretical values of the parameters and do not merely lead to estimates of them. Estimates could of course be made from the observed data, but they would not be so valuable as the values expected, unless it could be shown that the data did not agree with expectation, in which case the initial premise that p and k are known is invalid and resort must be made to some form of estimation. Even in such cases the proper approach would not always be by the estimation of the mean and variance, but rather by that of p and k. This will be discussed in more detail in a later chapter. The following example will, however, serve to illustrate the difference between parameters and their estimates.

Example 4. Fisher and Mather have described a genetical experiment with mice which consisted of a backcross in which the gene Wv, wv (straight—wavy hair) was segregating. The females were all wavy (wv wv) and the males heterozygous straight (Wv wv). Hence by mendelian theory each mouse in their offspring has a half chance of being straight haired and a half chance of being wavy. So in litters of 8 mice it is expected that 8 straight and 0 wavy, 7 straight and 1 wavy, &c., will be found with relative frequencies given by the expansion of $(\frac{1}{2}+\frac{1}{2})^8$, i.e. $p=q=\frac{1}{2}$ and $k=8$. The theoretical mean proportion of straight-haired mice, μ, is equal to p, i.e. is $\frac{1}{2}$. The variance of the distribution is $\frac{pq}{k}$, i.e. $\frac{1}{2} \times \frac{1}{2} \times \frac{1}{8}$, which is $\frac{1}{32}$ or 0·03125. The standard deviation is thus $\sqrt{0 \cdot 03125}$ or 0·1796. But we may also estimate the mean and variance from the actual experimental data.

TABLE 7

Segregation for Straight—Wavy in Litters of Eight Mice (Fisher and Mather)

Proportion of straight-haired mice (x)	Frequency observed (a)	ax	ax^2	Number of straight-haired mice (x)	ax	ax^2
0·000	0	0·000	0·000000	0	0	0
0·125	1	0·125	0·015625	1	1	1
0·250	2	0·500	0·125000	2	4	8
0·375	4	1·500	0·562500	3	12	36
0·500	12	6·000	3·000000	4	48	192
0·625	6	3·750	2·343750	5	30	150
0·750	5	3·750	2·812500	6	30	180
0·875	2	1·750	1·531250	7	14	98
1·000	0	0·000	0·000000	8	0	0
Total	32	17·375	10·390625	Total	139	665

$$\bar{x} = \frac{17 \cdot 375}{32} = 0 \cdot 542969 \qquad \bar{x} = \frac{139}{32} = 4 \cdot 34375$$

$$S(x-\bar{x})^2 = 10 \cdot 390625 - \frac{17 \cdot 375^2}{32} \qquad S(x-\bar{x})^2 = 665 - \frac{139^2}{32}$$

$$= 0 \cdot 956543 \qquad = 61 \cdot 21875$$

$$N = 31 \qquad N = 31$$

$$s^2 = V = \frac{S(x-\bar{x})^2}{N} = 0 \cdot 03086 \qquad s^2 = V = \frac{S(x-\bar{x})^2}{N} = 1 \cdot 9748$$

$$\mu = p = 0 \cdot 5 \qquad \mu = pk = 4 \cdot 0$$

$$\sigma^2 = \frac{pq}{k} = 0 \cdot 03125 \qquad \sigma^2 = pqk = 2 \cdot 0$$

Table 7 gives the segregation observed in 32 such litters. The type of litter is denoted by the proportion, x, of straight-haired mice that it contains. Thus a litter with seven straight and one wavy has 0·875 of its mice straight. The second column shows the observed frequency (a) of such litters. The third and fourth columns show ax and ax^2, which are necessary for the calculation of the estimates. The working mean is taken at 0 for this purpose. $S(x)$ is 17·375, so the estimate of μ, viz. $\bar{x}$, is 0·542969. The sum of squares of deviations from the mean is

10·390625−9·434082, which reduces to 0·956543. Since there are 32 observations the sum of squares is based on 31 degrees of freedom, so the estimate of the variance, s^2, is 0·03086, and, by taking the square root, the standard deviation is estimated at 0·1757.

The estimates of the mean and the standard error differ from their theoretical values, though the deviations are not large. This is to be expected, since the theoretical values are based on the properties of a hypothetical population including an infinite number of litters, whereas the experimental data comprised only 32 litters. The estimates are thus subject to sampling errors. A closer approximation to the expected values would be anticipated if more families were used as material for estimation.

A further important point may be illustrated by these data. So far the measure of x used has been the proportion of straight-haired mice in the litter. Instead, we might equally well have used the number of such mice. The corresponding estimations of the mean and variance are carried out in the second part of Table 7, and we find that $\bar{x}$ is now 4·34375, while s^2 is 1·9748. These are respectively 8 and 64 times as big as the values obtained when the proportion of mice was used as the measure. The standard deviation will, of course, be 8 times the earlier value, just as was the mean. It is, in fact, a general rule that if the scale of x is increased by a factor C the mean and standard deviation will be multiplied by C and the variance by C^2.

The same rule holds good for the expected mean and variance. Thus taking x as the number of straight-haired mice in the litter is equivalent to using the expansion of $(4+4)^8$. Then μ is equal to 4 and σ^2 is $\frac{4\times 4}{8}=2$. It will be observed that these values are respectively k and k^2 times as big as the figures obtained earlier. The formulae can then be written in terms of the original p and k as $\mu=pk$ and $\sigma^2=pqk$. These formulae are appropriate to the analysis of the observed numbers of individuals in the various classes, while the earlier ones are used for the analysis of the proportions of individuals observed to fall into the two groups.

REFERENCES

BLACKMAN, G. E. 1935. A study by statistical methods of the distribution of species in grassland associations. *Ann. Bot.*, **49**, 749–77.

EDEN, T., and YATES, F. 1933. On the validity of Fisher's z test when applied to an actual example of non-normal data. *J. Agr. Sci.*, **33**, 6–17.

EMERSON, R. A., and EAST, E. M. 1913. Inheritance of quantitative characters in maize. *Neb. Exp. Sta. Res. Bul.* 2.

FISHER, R. A., and MATHER, K. 1936. A linkage test with mice. *Ann. Eugen.*, **7**, 265–80.

CHAPTER IV

TESTS OF SIGNIFICANCE

14. THE NORMAL DEVIATE

ANY observed quantity is likely to deviate from its expected value for either of two reasons. In the first place it may deviate because of sampling error arising from the necessary use of finite numbers of observations; and, secondly, it may depart from expectation because the premises on which the expectation is based are invalid. The purpose of a test of significance is to effect a distinction between these two sorts of deviation.

We have already seen, in Section 6, how such a test of significance works in the case of observations relating to an hypothesis on the basis of which probabilities are obtained by the expansion of a binomial expression. The operations involved are the same for all tests of significance. It is first necessary to determine, from the hypothesis to be tested, the distribution of probabilities of obtaining the various observable values; and, secondly, to assess from this distribution the probability of obtaining, as a result of sampling error, as bad or worse fit with hypothesis than that shown by observations in question. If this probability is sufficiently small it is then assumed that the hypothesis is incapable of explaining the data, or, in other words, that the deviation of observation from expectation is significant.

In the genetical example of Section 6 it was easy to evaluate the probabilities of all possible types of family. It was then possible to arrive at the probability of obtaining as bad or worse fit by the simple process of picking out all the types of family which fell into this category and summing their probabilities.

It is, however, obvious that this technique is applicable only when the number of observable types is limited. Where, for example, the observation in question is one concerning a character such as plant height, which by hypothesis can have any value between wide limits, the probabilities of the various heights following a normal curve, a different approach is necessary.

In Example 2 it has been shown that the frequency distribution of heights of 530 maize plants agrees well with a normal curve of mean 14·5396 and standard deviation 2·2159. From this we infer that the probability (m) of any plant of the population from which these 530 were taken will have a height of x dms. is given by the formula

$$m = \frac{1}{2 \cdot 2159 \sqrt{2\pi}} e^{-\frac{(x-14 \cdot 5396)^2}{2 \times 2 \cdot 2159^2}}$$

or, more precisely, the probability dm of any plant having a height falling within the small range dx is

$$dm = \frac{1}{2 \cdot 2159 \sqrt{2\pi}} e^{-\frac{(x-14 \cdot 5396)^2}{2 \times 2 \cdot 2159^2}} dx$$

This probability is greatest when $x = 14 \cdot 5396$ and gets progressively smaller as $x - 14 \cdot 5396$, which we may denote as d, increases, irrespective of sign. Thus the best agreement with the hypothesis that a given plant is a member of this population is obtained when the plant in question is $14 \cdot 5396$ dms. tall, and the fit gets worse as the plant is found to be further from this height. So in order to find the probability of obtaining at least as bad a fit with hypothesis it is necessary to sum the probabilities of all heights which deviate from the mean by at least d dms. These probabilities together constitute the two tails of the distribution, as shown in Fig. 1.

The normal curve is continuous. So it is impossible to find the probability which the tails of the curve represent by summing the individual probabilities of the various possible heights included in these tails, because the number of such heights is theoretically infinite. What must be done is to find the area of the tails by integrating the curve from $-\infty$ to $14 \cdot 5396 - d$ and from $14 \cdot 5396 + d$ to $+\infty$. Since the curve is symmetrical this is the same as finding twice the integral from $-\infty$ to $14 \cdot 5396 - d$ (see Fig. 1). The integration is itself a cumbersome operation and need not be carried through here. It results in the finding that the area of the tails cut off by lines at the distance d from the mean is a function of $\frac{d}{\sigma}$. Thus for any normal curve the deviation $c\sigma$ has a probability dependent only on c, which is called the normal deviate. Tables have been prepared relating this probability to the value of c. So in order to determine the significance of any deviation, d, it is only necessary to find $c = \frac{d}{\sigma}$ and look up the corresponding probability in a table of normal deviates such as that given in Table I at the end of this book. An example of the calculation will be given later.

15. THE t DISTRIBUTION

The normal deviate, c, is defined as the ratio of the deviation, d, to the standard deviation, σ. But, as we have already seen, the exact value of σ is not always known. The best figure which is available is most commonly an estimate, s, of σ. Now the estimate s is itself subject to sampling error and will depart more or less widely from the true standard deviation, the accuracy of the estimate increasing as the number of degrees of freedom, on which it is based, increases. When this number of degrees of freedom is reasonably large, say thirty or more, the error to which s is subject becomes sufficiently small to be neglected with safety. In such cases s may be used to replace σ without serious inaccuracy resulting. But if s is estimated from a small number of comparisons, its departure from σ may be very wide, and to use it in the calculation of a normal deviate would be to invite serious trouble. The test of significance in such cases requires a knowledge of the distribution of $\dfrac{d}{s}$ rather than $\dfrac{d}{\sigma}$. This distribution was calculated in 1908 by 'Student' and is known as the t distribution. It is unnecessary to give the details of its derivation, but its formula is quite a simple one.

$$dm = \frac{\dfrac{N-1}{2}!}{\dfrac{N-2}{2}!\sqrt{\pi}} \cdot \frac{dt}{\left(1+\dfrac{t^2}{N}\right)^{\frac{1}{2}(N+1)}}$$

Two points should be noted concerning this quantity. In the first place it is expressed solely in terms of t which is found as d/s. σ does not enter into the formula, and so t is a quantity exactly calculable from observational data and involves no assumptions about the unknown parameter. In other words, it affords an exact test of significance for use when the true standard deviation is unknown. Secondly, the t distribution takes into account the number of degrees of freedom (N) * on which the estimate s is based. This is to be expected as the sampling error of s depends on N. Table II at the end of the book shows t tabulated against the probability of getting at least as bad a fit (i.e. as big a value for t) as the one observed. It will be seen that the table of t is two-dimensional where the normal deviate was tabulated in one dimension. The second dimension in the case of t is N, which must be known before any value can be entered in the table. Thus to use t we must find d, s and N. t is the ratio of d to s and is entered in Table II in the row corresponding to whatever value is found for N. Any given level of probability is reached by smaller and smaller values of t as N increases.

Since the sampling error of s becomes zero as N becomes infinitely large, t reaches the normal deviate, c, as a limit under these circumstances. So the normal deviate is a special example

* N will be used to denote the number of degrees of freedom, in order to avoid confusion with the sample size, n. It should, however, be noted that Fisher frequently uses n for the number of degrees of freedom. Fisher and Yates also follow this practice in their book of tables.

of t and may be tabulated in a single dimension solely because it is really a single row of the two-dimensional t table.

16. THE z DISTRIBUTION

The use of both t and c is limited to cases where the significance of a single deviation is in question. It is, however, clear that such cases are only special examples of the general situation in which the joint significance of a number of deviations is at issue. The appropriate general tests can be derived from a consideration of the nature of c and t.

Consider for a moment a t for one degree of freedom. The numerator, d, is a single deviation or difference. The denominator s is a standard deviation based on one degree of freedom, i.e. is also a single difference. The two parts of the fraction are exactly similar in nature, and so the numerator can be considered as a standard deviation based on one degree of freedom. As the number of degrees of freedom of t increases, the denominator becomes the root mean square of a number of differences, though all t's have a single difference as their numerator. There is, however, no reason why the numerator should not be a root mean square just as the denominator can be, and, as such, be based on any number of degrees of freedom. Such a ratio of two root mean squares, characterized by two numbers of degrees of freedom, that of the numerator, N_1, and that of the denominator, N_2, is the generalization of t.

This general distribution was first found by R. A. Fisher, who, however, did not use the ratio of the two root mean squares as his variable, but chose instead the natural logarithm of this ratio. This he termed z, and the formula of his z distribution is

$$dm = 2 \frac{\frac{N_1+N_2-2}{2}!}{\frac{N_1-2}{2}! \cdot \frac{N_2-2}{2}!} N_1^{\frac{1}{2}N_1} N_2^{\frac{1}{2}N_2} \frac{e^{N_1 z} dz}{(N_1 e^{2z}+N_2)^{\frac{1}{2}(N_1+N_2)}}$$

The transformation into logarithms has certain advantages for interpolation in a table of z, but the direct use of the ratio of the root mean squares, or of the ratio of two mean squares from which the roots are derived, has much to recommend it. Various of these forms of z have been tabulated. Fisher and Yates's book of tables include z and the variance, or mean square, ratio. This latter has also been tabulated under the symbol F by Snedecor, while Tedin has given the table of the root mean square ratio. Table IV at the end of this book gives the Variance Ratio. This will be found sufficient for all practical purposes. Simple transformation will give any other forms in which it is desirable to represent a z value.

In the calculation of z or the variance ratio, just as in the case of t, estimated standard deviations and variances are used. The probability distributions of z and the variance ratio are independent of the two true standard deviations or variances of which estimates are being used. Hence z and the variance ratio afford exact tests of significance of observed data.

Each value of z, just like each value of c and t, corresponds to some definite probability of finding at least as bad a fit, or, in other words, at least as large a value of z, as that actually obtained. In order to use z for the purpose of finding this sampling error probability it is necessary to know the number of degrees of freedom appertaining to both numerator and denominator. Any given level of probability is reached by smaller values of z as both N_1 and N_2 increase, although these two numbers of degrees of freedom do not have an equal effect on the relation between z and its probability.

There is never any ambiguity as to which is the numerator and which the denominator in the case of t, since the former must always be a single difference. In the case of z, on the other hand, this simple method of decision is not available and ambiguity may arise. The rule which covers all cases is, however, quite a simple one. The numerator is always the larger mean square or root mean square. This usually, but not always, has the smaller number of degrees of freedom. Confusion is sometimes caused by a failure to realize that it is the magnitude of the mean square or root mean square, and not that of its number of degrees of freedom, which determines whether it will go into the numerator or the denominator.

The tabulation of z or of the variance ratio causes some difficulty as it requires a three-dimensional table. The table of normal deviates has only one dimension, viz. the probability. The table of t has a second dimension, the number of degrees of freedom of the denominator. The table of z has still another dimension, the number of degrees of freedom of the numerator. Now a three-dimensional table is impracticable and so it is customary to give a series of two-dimensional tables in its place. Each such table corresponds to a given probability level, the two dimensions used in the table being N_1 and N_2, the two numbers of degrees of freedom. The probability levels for which tables of z and the variance ratio have been prepared are $P=0.2$, 0.05, 0.01 and 0.001 (Table IV). It should always be remembered that these are only slices from a three-dimensional whole.

The use of the variance ratio in analysis will be fully illustrated in later chapters.

17. THE χ^2 DISTRIBUTION

The relation of χ^2 to the variance ratio is like the relation of c to t. χ^2 is the special case of the variance ratio where the denominator is fixed by hypothesis, i.e. it is the ratio of an observed variance, or, more correctly, sum of squares, to another fixed by hypothesis. It might equally be said the χ^2 is a generalized c^2, just as the variance ratio is a generalized t^2. The numerator of χ^2 differs from that of c^2 by being based on any number of differences, and so is characterized by a number of degrees of freedom. The denominators of χ^2 and c^2 are equivalent.

The χ^2 table has two dimensions like the t table, one margin being the probability and the other the number of degrees of freedom to which the value corresponds. It cannot, however, be over-emphasized that whereas the degrees of freedom of t are those appertaining to the denominator, the degrees of freedom of χ^2 are those appertaining to the numerator. t is characterized by the N_2 of z while χ^2 is characterized by the N_1 value.

A χ^2 is seldom obtained directly as the ratio of two variances or sums of squares. It is usually found in the form for which it was first calculated by Karl Pearson, viz. as a test of goodness of fit of observed with expected frequencies. The formula for the calculation of χ^2 observed in this way is

$$\chi^2 = S\left[\frac{(a-mn)^2}{mn}\right]$$

where a is the observed class frequency, m the proportion expected in that class, n the number of observations and S indicating summation over all classes. The appropriate number of degrees of freedom is found as the number of classes to which values may be assigned arbitrarily.

The probability distribution of χ^2 is

$$dm = \frac{1}{\frac{N-2}{2}!}(\tfrac{1}{2}\chi^2)^{\frac{1}{2}(N-2)} e^{-\frac{1}{2}\chi^2} d(\tfrac{1}{2}\chi^2)$$

Its various uses will be illustrated by later examples. A table of χ^2 will be found at the end of this book (Table III).

18. THE INTERRELATIONS OF c, t, χ^2 AND z AND THEIR USE IN ANALYSIS

The four exact tests of significance, c, t, χ^2 and z, were developed by different mathematicians for widely different purposes at different times. It is not then surprising that their interrelations have tended to be obscured. They are all essentially ratios of two variances, or alternatively of two standard deviations, though these ratios may be subjected to various simple transformations. The most general form, and the last to be calculated, is z. The other three are best understood as special cases of z.

It has already been noted that a z table is three-dimensional, the three dimensions being N_1, N_2 and P, the probability. Such a table is shown diagrammatically in Fig. 4, where the two numbers of degrees of freedom are marked along the sides of the face of the figure. The probability is marked along the receding dimension. t^2 is a variance ratio whose numerator has always one degree of freedom (i.e. $N_1=1$). Therefore the t table is derived from the leftmost vertical side of the z table. χ^2 is a variance ratio whose denominator is fixed by hypothesis, which

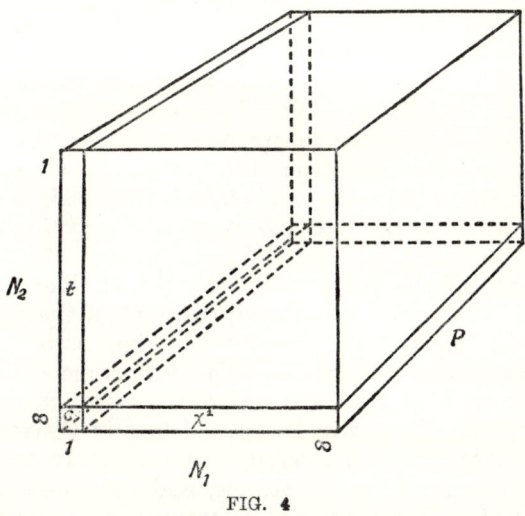

FIG. 4
The three-dimensional z table showing the interrelations of c, t, χ^2 and z

is equivalent to its having ∞ degrees of freedom ($N_2=\infty$). Therefore the χ^2 table is obtained from the under-surface of the z table. c has a numerator with one degree of freedom and a denominator fixed by hypothesis. So c is a special case of both t and χ^2. Actually it is the lower left receding corner of the solid.

Thus the four probability distributions are simply related and the choice of one of them for use in a particular problem depends solely on the nature of the data. The whole of the analysis of data really consists of their reduction to a state in which the question at issue can be formulated in terms of the ratio of two mean squares, or correspondingly of two root mean squares. This will be better appreciated from the examples and discussion of later chapters.

It is of course clear that z or its transformation, the variance ratio, could be used in all cases, and that t or χ^2 could be used to replace c wherever that quantity is relevant. The reason for the use of the various special cases of z is simply that they are tabulated more easily and fully than the general quantity. Thus the table of c given at the end of this book is somewhat fuller and distinctly less cumbersome than the tables of t and χ^2, which in their turn are fuller and less cumbersome than the table of z.

The use of the c, t, χ^2 and z distributions forms the last stage of the statistical analysis of a set of data. The preceding operations are concerned with reducing the data to a state in which the question at issue can be answered by means of a comparison between observed and expected deviations, in the way made possible by the test distributions. These preceding operations, however, usually involve more varied and heavier computation than does the actual test towards which the whole analysis is directed. In consequence the discussion of the preparatory calculations will be much longer and more complex than that of the test distributions themselves. It is, however, necessary always to bear in mind that, in general, these calculations exist only to reduce the data to the state necessary for the actual test.

The form of the preparatory calculation, like that of the actual test distribution to be used, depends on the type of data for analysis. There are, broadly speaking, two such types, measurements and frequencies. The former generally involve the use of estimated variances and so the test is made with t or z distributions. These will be treated first in Chapters V–VII. Frequencies, on the other hand, can commonly be compared with variances fixed by hypothesis, and so require the use of c and χ^2 tests. Their analysis is treated in Chapter XI with the exception of one simple example in Chapter V. The joint analysis of two or more variates almost always involves estimated variances and so is handled by extensions of the methods of Chapters V–VII. Hence, though mathematically more complex than some of the frequency analyses, regression and correlation are discussed before frequencies in Chapters VIII–X. Some problems of estimation are treated in connexion with the use of tests of significance, but the general discussion of estimation and its relation to significance tests is somewhat heavy and so is deferred to the last chapter.

Before leaving the consideration of these four quantities it must be emphasized once again that they are exact in the sense that each of them is calculated from exactly known constituents, and involves no approximation. This, of course, presupposes the correct use of the quantities. Thus a t which was mistakenly used as a c would not be exact. The inexactitude here, however, lies with the user and not with the t distribution.

The importance of the exact nature of these four distributions depends on the fact that in drawing conclusions from them no assumptions are made about those parameters of the population which are not given by hypothesis. Estimates of these parameters are used and the distributions make the proper allowance for the sampling error of the estimates. Thus rigorous inferences may be reached from observational data alone, without involving any assumptions about the parent populations.

REFERENCES

AITKIN, A. C., 1940. *Statistical Mathematics.* Oliver and Boyd, Edinburgh.

FISHER, R. A., and YATES, F. 1943. *Statistical Tables for Biological, Agricultural and Medical Research.* Oliver and Boyd. Edinburgh. 2nd ed.

SNEDECOR, G. W. 1934. *Calculation and Interpretation of Analysis of Variance and Covariance.* Ames. Iowa.

NOTE.—In this chapter $n!$ is used in a new way, viz. when n is not an integer. In such cases $n!$ is defined as the Eulerian integral

$$\int_0^\infty x^n e^{-x} dx$$

which gives

$$(-\tfrac{1}{2})! = \sqrt{\pi}$$
$$(\tfrac{1}{2})! = \tfrac{1}{2}\sqrt{\pi}$$
$$(\tfrac{3}{2})! = \tfrac{3}{2} \cdot \tfrac{1}{2}\sqrt{\pi}$$

and so on.

CHAPTER V

THE SIGNIFICANCE OF SINGLE OBSERVATIONS, SUMS, DIFFERENCES AND MEANS

19. SINGLE OBSERVATIONS

IN the last chapter we examined the principles on which tests of significance are based and discussed the distributions which are used in assessing significance. The application of these principles and distributions must be considered next.

The normal deviate, c, may strictly speaking be used only when hypothesis fixes the variance of the distribution involved. Actually it may be used in place of t without serious error whenever the number of degrees of freedom on which the variance is based is reasonably large, say 30 or more. Thus the ratio of an observed deviation to the standard deviation of the maize distribution calculated in Section 10 could be treated as a normal deviate because the number of degrees of freedom is 529.

It is the exception rather than the rule for the variance to be fixed by hypothesis, but cases are not uncommon, especially in genetical experiments. A genetical example will be chosen to illustrate the method of testing the significance of single observations and sums.

Example 5. The gene P, p determines flower colour in *Datura stramonium*, PP and Pp plants having anthocyanin pigmentation, while pp individuals are white. On self-pollinating heterozygous Pp plants a 3 : 1 ratio for coloured to white is expected, and Sirks obtained an actual segregation of 59 coloured to 14 white. Does this agree with expectation?

The frequencies with which families of 73 individuals containing 0, 1, 2 . . . whites are expected are given by the expansion of the binomial

$$(\tfrac{3}{4}+\tfrac{1}{4})^{73}$$

i.e. $p=\tfrac{1}{4}$, $q=\tfrac{3}{4}$ and $k=73$.

Then the number of white plants expected, pk, is $\tfrac{1}{4}\times 73$ or 18·25. The number observed is 14, so that d, the deviation of observation from expectation, is 4·25.

The variance of the distribution obtained when the binomial expression is expanded may be found as $V=pqk$, which in the present case is $\dfrac{3\times 73}{16}$ or 13·6875. The standard deviation, or standard error, σ, is obtained as the square root of the variance, so being 3·6997. The normal deviate, c, is the ratio of d to σ

and so in the present case is $\dfrac{4\cdot 2500}{3\cdot 6997}$ or 1·149. Table I shows that a c of this magnitude is equalled or exceeded as a result of random sampling in about 25% of cases. The deviation could thus reasonably be ascribed to sampling error and the fit with expectation passes as sufficiently good.

The use of the normal deviate as a test of significance in this case requires some comment. Strictly speaking, the method is applicable only to data which may be supposed to fall on a normal distribution. The binomial approaches normality as k increases and when, as in the present case, $k=73$, the error introduced by the assumption of normality is not large. This error largely results from the fact that, while the binomial distribution is discontinuous in that the variate can only take certain values, in the present case 0, 1, 2, &c., the assumption of normality presupposes that variation is continuous. A correction can be applied in order to reduce this error. Yates's Correction for Continuity, as it is called, consists of reducing the deviation, d, by 0·5 before calculating the normal deviate. Thus in the above example we should take $d=4\cdot25-0\cdot5=3\cdot75$, which gives $c=\dfrac{3\cdot 7500}{3\cdot 6997}=1\cdot014$, with a probability of 30% instead of the 25% found when an uncorrected deviate is used. Actually Yates's correction is rather too drastic, and while the original calculation overestimates the significance of the result, the corrected result is an underestimate, though much nearer to the true value. The true value can be found by expanding the binomial distribution and summing the tails as shown in Section 6, but this is far too cumbersome a process to be undertaken as a regular measure and so the quick approximate normal deviate method is used instead.

Another family of 126 plants was later raised by Sirks by self-pollinating Pp individuals in the same pedigree. On this second occasion he obtained a segregation of 103 coloured to 23 white. The expectation on the basis of 3 : 1 is that 31·5 whites will be found in a family of this size. The deviation observed is thus 8·5. The standard deviation for a family of 126 is $\sqrt{\tfrac{3}{4}\times\tfrac{1}{4}\times 126}$ or 4·8606, and so $c=\dfrac{8\cdot 500}{4\cdot 8606}=1\cdot 749$, with a probability of about 8%. Even this result is reasonably ascribable to chance variation when considered by itself. Yet both families show a marked deviation in the same direction, so encouraging the belief that, though neither is significant when alone, taken together the deviations might be too large to attribute to random sampling. A method of testing the joint significance is needed, and it is not difficult to see how this should be done.

The two families are separated because they were obtained by pollinating different parent plants. These parents are, however, of the same genetical constitution (Pp) on our hypothesis, and in consequence their progenies may be combined and treated as one large family. There is a special test of the legitimacy of such addition, but it must be reserved for later discussion (Section 48).

Combining the two families gives a total of 199 plants consisting of 162 coloured and 37 white, where the expectations are 149·25 and 49·75 respectively. The deviation of observation from expectation is thus 12·75. The standard deviation is $\sqrt{\frac{3}{4} \times \frac{1}{4} \times 199}$, i.e. 6·1084, giving $c = \frac{12 \cdot 7500}{6 \cdot 1084} = 2 \cdot 087$, with a probability of between 0·03 and 0·04. This must be judged to be at least highly suspicious, and so in the absence of further information the departure is taken to be too large to be reasonably attributed to sampling error. There is evidence of a real discrepancy between observation and hypothesis.

20. THE VARIANCE OF SUMS, DIFFERENCES AND MEANS

In the last example the two families were combined by simple addition of the observed segregations and the treatment of the resultant as a single large family. The observed deviation and the standard deviation were obtained by the application of the ordinary binomial formula. This question can, however, be approached in a different and more instructive way, viz. by attempting to find a method of combining the observed deviations and standard deviations directly rather than by adding the observed families.

The deviations of the two individual families were 4·25 and 8·50 in the same direction. On adding, these give 12·75, which was the deviation found from the combined data. The two individual standard deviations were 3·6997 and 4·8606, while that from the combined data was 6·1084. Simple addition clearly does not apply in this case. But it does apply to the squares of the standard deviations, i.e. to the variances. These were found to be 13·6875 and 23·6250 for the separate families and 37·3125 for the combined data. The first two values give the third by simple addition.

It can easily be shown that these results hold true for all similar cases of the binomial expansion. Let x_1 and x_2 be the numbers of white individuals observed in the two families which contain in all k_1 and k_2 individuals respectively. The values of p and q are clearly the same for both families. Then the numbers of whites expected are pk_1 and pk_2 in the two families, giving

THE VARIANCE OF SUMS, DIFFERENCES AND MEANS 53

as the observed deviations pk_1-x_1 and pk_2-x_2. The two variances are $\frac{3k_1}{16}$ and $\frac{3k_2}{16}$. Adding the two families, we find x_1+x_2 whites out of a total of k_1+k_2. The deviation and variance of the combined data are $p(k_1+k_2)-(x_1+x_2)$ and $\frac{3(k_1+k_2)}{16}$ respectively. These two values are clearly the sums of corresponding quantities obtained from the individual families, since they may be written as $(pk_1-x_1)+(pk_2-x_2)$ and $\frac{3k_1}{16}+\frac{3k_2}{16}$.

Thus the variance of the sum of two single observations, x_1 and x_2, is the sum of the separate variances of x_1 and x_2 for the binomial expansion. This rule is in fact of wider application, being true of all independent observations and applying to the sum of any number of observations. It may be written as

$$V_{(x_1+x_2+\ldots+x_j)} = V_{x_1}+V_{x_2}+\ldots+V_{x_j}$$

where V_{x_1} indicates the variance of the distribution on which the observation x_1 is presumed to fall.

It is important to notice that the rule applies to the sums of independent observations. A further analysis of the situation is of interest since it will help to clarify the mathematical meaning of this term 'independent'. Let us consider a sample of size n of each of a pair of measurements, x and y, which are both normally distributed. Then the variance of the distribution of x will be $\frac{S(x-\bar{x})^2}{n-1}$ and that of y will be $\frac{S(y-\bar{y})^2}{n-1}$. Similarly the variance of their sum will be $\frac{S[x+y-\overline{(x+y)}]^2}{n-1}$. It should be noted that

$$\overline{x+y} = \frac{S(x+y)}{n} = \frac{S(x)}{n}+\frac{S(y)}{n} = \bar{x}+\bar{y}.$$

Hence

$$\frac{1}{n-1}S[x+y-\overline{(x+y)}]^2 = \frac{1}{n-1}S[(x-\bar{x})+(y-\bar{y})]^2$$

$$= \frac{1}{n-1}S(x-\bar{x})^2+\frac{2}{n-1}S[(x-\bar{x})(y-\bar{y})]+\frac{1}{n-1}S(y-\bar{y})^2$$

or $$V_{(x+y)} = V_x+\frac{2}{n-1}S[(x-\bar{x})(y-\bar{y})]+V_y$$

Now a value of y which deviates by d_y from the mean $\bar{y}$ is as likely to occur as a corresponding value which deviates by $-d_y$. Furthermore, if the value of x is not determined by that of y, the deviation d_y is just as likely to accompany any value of x as is $-d_y$. So no matter how many pairs of observations are classified on the basis of x, the mean of the y values in any class determined by x will be $\bar{y}$ within the limits of sampling error. Thus for any value of $(x-\bar{x})$ the mean value of $(y-\bar{y})$ will be $(\bar{y}-\bar{y})$ or in other words 0, and so the value of $\frac{2}{n-1}S[(x-\bar{x})(y-\bar{y})]$ will be 0 within the limits of sampling error. Hence if x and y are distributed independently in the sense that the value of y is not determined by the value of x or vice versa

$$V_{(x+y)} = V_x + V_y$$

If, on the other hand, the distributions are not independent and a large value of x is preponderantly accompanied by a large value of y, $(y-\bar{y})$ will be positive more often than not when $(x-\bar{x})$ is positive, and negative more often than not when $(x-\bar{x})$ is negative. In other words, $\frac{2}{n-1}S[(x-\bar{x})(y-\bar{y})]$ will be positive. When the situation is reversed and a large value of x is most frequently accompanied by a small value of y, $\frac{2}{n-1}S[(x-\bar{x})(y-\bar{y})]$ will clearly be negative. In either case the magnitude of this term will increase as the interdependence of x and y becomes more pronounced.

So the sign and magnitude of this term afford a measure of the closeness and nature of the relations between the two quantities concerned. It is in fact the mathematical measure of dependence and is very widely used as such. $\frac{1}{n-1}S[(x-\bar{x})(y-\bar{y})]$ is called the covariance of x and y, being written W_{xy}. $S[(x-\bar{x})(y-\bar{y})]$ is known as the sum of cross products of x and y.

Then, in general, $V_{(x+y)} = V_x + V_y + 2W_{xy}$, which reduces to $V_{(x+y)} = V_x + V_y$ for the case of independence.

Similarly, $V_{(x-y)} = V_x + V_y - 2W_{xy}$, which again reduces to $V_{(x-y)} = V_x + V_y$ when x and y are independent.

One further special case is worthy of note. Suppose we wish to find the variance of $2x$ by this method.

$$V_{2x} = V_x + V_x + 2W_{xx}$$

But $S[(x-\bar{x})(x-\bar{x})] = S(x-\bar{x})^2$, and so $W_{xx} = V_x$. Hence

$$V_{2x} = V_x + V_x + 2V_x = 4V_x,$$

which is the rule that has already been found empirically in Section 13.

It is now possible to find the formula for the variance of a mean. Consider a sample consisting of n observations of the variate x. These n observations are independent in that they are made on different individuals or at different times, as for

SIGNIFICANCE OF MEANS AND DIFFERENCES 55

example the 530 maize observations were independent inasmuch as they were taken from different plants. Each observation will be subject to a variance V_x, so that from the argument developed above their sum will have a variance of nV_x. The mean is found by dividing the sum of the observations by n and we have seen that $V_{nx}=n^2V_x$. Similarly $V_{S(x)}=n^2V_{\bar{x}}$, since $S(x)=n\bar{x}$, or, by a rearrangement of the various components,

$$V_{\bar{x}} = \frac{V_{S(x)}}{n^2} = \frac{nV_x}{n^2} = \frac{V_x}{n}$$

Thus the variance of the distribution of the mean of n observations is the variance of a single observation divided by n.

21. THE SIGNIFICANCE OF MEANS AND DIFFERENCES OF MEANS

The method of testing the significance of single observations and of the sum of two observations has been illustrated in Example 5. The next example will give the procedure appropriate to testing means and differences of means.

Example 6. Table 8 gives the yields, over a certain period of time, of ten plants of each of two tomato varieties (Crane and Mather's unpublished data). The results are expressed in kilograms of ripe fruit. Now these two strains, together with others, were grown in a lean-to greenhouse in which the lighting conditions were far from uniform. So it was deemed necessary to design the experiment in such a way that each variety had plants in corresponding positions relative to the light, paths and other features. Thus each variety had one plant in position 1, and another in position 2, and so on.

First take the individual yields of the two varieties. We might, for example, ask whether either could be considered to be giving an average yield of over 1 Kg. per plant during the period over which records were taken. To answer this question it is necessary, first, to calculate the mean yield of each variety, and next, the standard deviation of the distribution which this mean supposedly follows. The necessary calculations are set out in Table 8. In variety A the ten plants together gave 13·253 Kg. of ripe fruit (Sx), which corresponds to a mean yield of 1·3253 per plant ($\bar{x}$). The variance of the yield of single plants must be estimated from the data, as the hypothesis under consideration, viz. that the mean yield per plant is 1 Kg., supplies no expected variance. To estimate the variance we find that the sum of squares of yields (Sx^2) is 18·521355. From this must be subtracted a correction term to reduce it to the sum of squares of deviation from the mean (Section 10). This correction is $\dfrac{S^2(x)}{n} = \dfrac{13\cdot253^2}{10}$, i.e. 17·564201, leaving $S(x-\bar{x})^2 = 18\cdot521355$

−17·564201=0·957154. There are 10−1 comparisons involved in the estimate of the sum of squares, as the mean has already been found from the data, and so

$$V_x = \frac{S(x-\bar{x})^2}{N} = \frac{0\cdot957154}{9} = 0\cdot106350$$

But the variance of the distribution of the mean of n observations is $\frac{1}{n}$th the variance of the distribution of single observations, and so

$$V_{\bar{x}} = \frac{V_x}{n} = \frac{0\cdot106350}{10} = 0\cdot010635$$

Taking the square root, we find that the standard deviation, $s_{\bar{x}} = 0\cdot103126$.

TABLE 8
The Yields of Two Varieties of Tomato (Crane and Mather)

Position	Yields of varieties A	Yields of varieties B	A−B
1	1·375	1·033	0·342
2	1·407	1·217	0·190
3	1·068	0·984	0·084
4	1·752	1·615	0·137
5	1·773	1·693	0·080
6	1·201	0·673	0·528
7	0·779	0·840	−0·061
8	1·042	0·842	0·200
9	1·223	1·252	−0·030
10	1·633	1·217	0·416
$S(x)$	13·253	11·367	1·886
$\bar{x}$	1·3253	1·1367	0·1886
$S(x)^2$	18·521355	13·909499	0·681750
$\frac{1}{n}S^2(x)$	17·564201	12·920869	0·355700
$S(x-\bar{x})^2$	0·957154	0·988630	0·326050
V_x	0·106350	0·109848	0·036228
$V_{\bar{x}}$	0·010635	0·010985	
$s_{\bar{x}}$	0·103126	0·104811	
d	0·1886		0·1886
V_d	0·021620		0·003623
s_d	0·147036		0·060189
t	1·283		3·133
N	18		9
P	0·3–0·2		0·02–0·01

SIGNIFICANCE OF MEANS AND DIFFERENCES

Thus on our hypothesis we expect that the yield of the ten plants will be distributed about a mean of 1 Kg. with a standard error of 0·103126 Kg. It is assumed that distribution is normal. The distribution of the mean tends to normality even when that of the single observation departs widely from this form. In any case, as pointed out in Section 11, the assumption of normality leads to no serious error.

The observed mean shows a deviation of 0·3253 from that expected, and so $t_{[9]} = \dfrac{d}{s} = \dfrac{0\cdot 3253}{0\cdot 103126} = 3\cdot 154$. The standard error has been estimated from the data and so the ratio of deviation to standard deviation is a t, not a c (Section 15). This t will have 9 degrees of freedom, the standard deviation having been estimated on the basis of 9 independent comparisons. The number of degrees of freedom is denoted by the subscript 9 attached to the t above. This device, though not in standard use, is very convenient. On consulting the table of t it is found that a value of 3·154 when based on 9 degrees of freedom has a probability slightly greater than 1% of being equalled or exceeded as a result of sampling error. This is very small, so the variety A must be supposed to have a yield greater than 1 Kg. per plant.

A similar calculation for variety B gives $\bar{x} = 1\cdot 1367$, $V_x = 0\cdot 109848$, $V_{\bar{x}} = 0\cdot 010985$, $s_{\bar{x}} = 0\cdot 104811$, $d = 0\cdot 1367$ and $t_{[9]} = \dfrac{0\cdot 1367}{0\cdot 104811} = 1\cdot 304$ with a probability of between 0·2 and 0·3. Thus though the mean of variety A differs significantly from 1 Kg. per plant, that of variety B does not do so.

The next question which may be considered is whether there exists a real difference in yield between the two varieties. The two means have already been found and the difference between them ($\bar{d}$) is 0·1886 Kg. The variance of this difference will be the sum of the variances of the two separate means since the measurements of the two varieties might be supposed to be independent. Hence $V_{\bar{d}} = V_{\bar{x}_A} + V_{\bar{x}_B} = 0\cdot 010635 + 0\cdot 010985 = 0\cdot 021620$. Then $s_{\bar{d}} = \sqrt{V_{\bar{d}}} = 0\cdot 147036$, and as $\bar{d} = 0\cdot 1886$, $t_{[18]} = \dfrac{0\cdot 1886}{0\cdot 1470} = 1\cdot 283$. It will be observed that the variance of the average difference is compounded from the variance of the average yield of variety A and that of variety B. Each of these two variances was based on 9 degrees of freedom, and so the variance of the difference is derived ultimately from 18 comparisons. Hence the t takes 18 degrees of freedom. A t of value 1·283 for 18 degrees of freedom has a probability of between 0·2 and 0·3. We must therefore judge that the difference between the yields of the two varieties may be acccunted for by sampling error and that there is no reason to suppose that a real difference in productivity exists.

The test of significance between the mean yields may, however, be attempted in another way. In Table 8 the yields of plants of the varieties growing in similar positions in the greenhouse are listed side by side. Now if there is no real difference between the two varieties the mean difference between plants growing in corresponding positions should be zero, within the limits of sampling error. This hypothesis can be tested.

The fourth column of Table 8 gives the ten differences and shows the calculation of the test of significance. The sum of the differences, taking sign into account, is 1·886, and so the mean difference is 0·1886 Kg. The sum of squares of the differences is 0·681750, from which must be subtracted the correction term $\frac{1\cdot886^2}{10}$ or 0·355700, leaving 0·326050 as the sum of squares of deviations from the mean. Then the variance of the distribution of differences (V_d) is estimated as $\frac{0\cdot326050}{9}$, i.e. 0·036228, as there are 9 degrees of freedom between the 10 values, after the mean has been calculated. The variance of the distribution on which the mean difference ($\bar{d}$) falls is $\frac{V_d}{n} = \frac{0\cdot036228}{10} = 0\cdot003623$. So $s_{\bar{d}} = \sqrt{V_{\bar{d}}} = \sqrt{0\cdot003623} = 0\cdot060189$ and $t_{[9]} = \frac{0\cdot1886}{0\cdot06019} = 3\cdot133$. The probability of such a t is less than 0·02 and the mean difference cannot be considered to be 0 within the limits of sampling error. This test, unlike the previous one, tells us that there is a real difference in productivity between the two varieties. Why do the tests disagree?

The t's used in the two tests differed in two respects. First of all, though having the same numerator, 0·1886, they had different denominators. The standard deviation, or alternatively the variance, of the mean difference was different in the two tests. In the second place it will be remembered that in the first test t had 18 degrees of freedom, while in the second test t had only 9 degrees of freedom. The variance in the first test was based on 18 comparisons between 20 individuals, while in the second test only 9 of these comparisons were used. Thus in the second test 9 comparisons were rejected as not contributing relevant information, and the remaining 9 taken as giving the appropriate measure of sampling variance.

It is not difficult to see how this came about. In the first test no account was taken of the position of each plant in the greenhouse, while in the later test comparisons were made only

SIGNIFICANCE OF MEANS AND DIFFERENCES

between plants in like positions. Thus in the second test 9 degrees of freedom were found to be concerned with differences in position and as such were rejected. That this really accounts for the difference between the two tests can be shown by taking differences between plants in unlike positions. In Table 9 the 10 yields of variety B are rearranged in a random order, while those of variety A are as before. The technique of the second test is then applied to the data of Table 9. The mean difference is

TABLE 9

Rearranged Tomato Data

Yields of varieties		A−B	
A	B		
1·375	1·217	0·158	$S(d)=1·886$
1·407	1·217	0·190	$\bar{d}=0·1886$
1·068	0·842	0·226	$S(d^2)=1·985842$
1·752	0·840	0·912	$\frac{1}{n}S^2(d)=0·355700$
1·773	1·693	0·080	$S(d-\bar{d})^2=1·630142$
1·201	1·253	−0·052	$V_d=0·181127$
0·779	0·984	−0·205	$V_{\bar{d}}=0·018113$
1·042	1·615	−0·573	$s_{\bar{d}}=0·134585$
1·223	0·673	0·550	$t=1·401$
1·633	1·033	0·600	$N=9$
			$P=0·2-0·1$

again 0·1886, but the variance of the distribution is now 0·181127, giving as the standard deviation of the mean difference $\sqrt{0·018113}$, i.e. 0·13459. Then $t_{[9]}=\dfrac{0·1886}{0·1346}=1·401$, which has a probability of between 0·2 and 0·1. The difference is no longer significant when the positions of the plants in the greenhouse are rearranged. In other words, the wrong 9 degrees of freedom have been chosen for use in the test. If position had played no part in determining the yields, i.e. if conditions had been constant all over the greenhouse, then this test would have given the same result as the other two, which would, of course, have agreed with each other. It is solely the effect of position which makes it profitable to distinguish between the various degrees of freedom. This may be expressed in another way, viz. that, since position affects the yields of the plants, the observations of the varieties are not wholly independent and the calculation of the variance of the mean difference by summing the variances of the two means is not legitimate. When the dependence due to position effect has been removed, as in the second calculation, the ten observations used are really independent and the test of significance is valid.

This result clearly implies that degrees of freedom can have special individual properties and that, on the basis of these individual properties, some may be rejected from use and others chosen as appropriate to the test in hand. This isolation of degrees of freedom is of immense importance in statistical analysis and must next be examined in greater detail.

REFERENCES

SIRKS, M. J. 1929. Mendelian factors in *Datura, III. Genetica,* **11,** 257–66.

CHAPTER VI
DEGREES OF FREEDOM AND THE ANALYSIS OF VARIANCE

22. THE INDIVIDUALITY OF DEGREES OF FREEDOM

IN discussing degrees of freedom we may start with the simplest case, viz. that of two observations. Assuming that the mean and variance are not fixed by hypothesis, there will be one comparison left for the purpose of estimating the variance once the mean has been calculated. Let the two observed values be a_1 and a_2 respectively. Then the mean is clearly $\frac{1}{2}(a_1+a_2)$. The sum of squares of deviations from the mean may be found from the formula $S(a^2) - \frac{S^2(a)}{n}$, which applied to the present case gives

$$S.S. = a_1^2 + a_2^2 - \tfrac{1}{2}(a_1+a_2)^2 = \tfrac{1}{2}(a_1^2 - 2a_1 a_2 + a_2^2) = \tfrac{1}{2}(a_1-a_2)^2$$

where $S.S.$ stands for the 'sum of squares'. Thus the sum of squares corresponding to the single degree of freedom is based on the rather obvious comparison afforded by the difference between a_1 and a_2.

The next simplest case is that of three observations, a_1, a_2 and a_3. The mean of the three is $\frac{1}{3}(a_1+a_2+a_3)$ and their sum of squares of deviations from the mean is

$$a_1^2 + a_2^2 + a_3^2 - \tfrac{1}{3}(a_1+a_2+a_3)^2 = \tfrac{2}{3}(a_1^2 + a_2^2 + a_3^2 - a_1 a_2 - a_1 a_3 - a_2 a_3)$$

Now this sum of squares is based on two comparisons, and it has been shown already that the comparison between a_1 and a_2 corresponds to a sum of squares of $\frac{1}{2}(a_1-a_2)^2$. Hence the remaining comparison is $\tfrac{2}{3}(a_1^2+a_2^2+a_3^2-a_1 a_2-a_1 a_3-a_2 a_3) - \tfrac{1}{2}(a_1-a_2)^2$

$$= \tfrac{1}{6}(4a_1^2 + 4a_2^2 + 4a_3^2 - 4a_1 a_2 - 4a_1 a_3 - 4a_2 a_3 - 3a_1^2 - 3a_2^2 + 6a_1 a_2)$$
$$= \tfrac{1}{6}(a_1^2 + a_2^2 + 4a_3^2 + 2a_1 a_2 - 4a_1 a_3 - 4a_2 a_3) = \tfrac{1}{6}(a_1+a_2-2a_3)^2$$

This is clearly a simple comparison between the third observation and the mean of the other two. Thus the two degrees of freedom have quite distinct meanings. One is concerned with the comparison of a_1 and a_2. The other is concerned with the comparison of a_3 and the other two taken jointly. It should, however, be noted that other possibilities exist for separating the 2 degrees of freedom, e.g. the first comparison could be made between a_1 and a_3 or between a_2 and a_3, instead of between a_1 and a_2. The three ways of partitioning the sum of squares implied by these three choices of the first comparison are

(i) $\tfrac{1}{2}(a_1-a_2)^2$ and $\tfrac{1}{6}(a_1+a_2-2a_3)^2$
(ii) $\tfrac{1}{2}(a_1-a_3)^2$ and $\tfrac{1}{6}(a_1-2a_2+a_3)^2$
(iii) $\tfrac{1}{2}(a_2-a_3)^2$ and $\tfrac{1}{6}(-2a_1+a_2+a_3)^2$

A great number of further less obvious and generally less useful partitions could also be devised.

Cases of four observations offer a still greater variety of useful partitions. The mean is $\frac{1}{4}(a_1+a_2+a_3+a_4)$ and the total sum of squares $a_1^2+a_2^2+a_3^2+a_4^2-\frac{1}{4}(a_1+a_2+a_3+a_4)^2$
$$=\tfrac{1}{4}(3a_1^2+3a_2^2+3a_3^2+3a_4^2-2a_1a_2-2a_1a_3-2a_1a_4-2a_2a_3-2a_2a_4-2a_3a_4)$$

Continuing along the line of the previous analyses the first two comparisons, between a_1 and a_2, and between a_1, a_2 and a_3, have a joint sum of squares of $\frac{2}{3}(a_1^2+a_2^2+a_3^2-a_1a_2-a_1a_3-a_2a_3)$, leaving as the sum of squares for the third comparison

$$\tfrac{1}{12}(9a_1^2+9a_2^2+9a_3^2+9a_4^2-6a_1a_2-6a_1a_3-6a_1a_4-6a_2a_3-6a_2a_4-6a_3a_4$$
$$-8a_1^2-8a_2^2-8a_3^2+8a_1a_2+8a_1a_3+8a_2a_3)$$
$$=\tfrac{1}{12}(a_1^2+a_2^2+a_3^2+9a_4^2+2a_1a_2+2a_1a_3-6a_1a_4+2a_2a_3-6a_2a_4-6a_3a_4)$$
$$=\tfrac{1}{12}(a_1+a_2+a_3-3a_4)^2$$

This is a comparison between a_4 and the mean of the first three observations.

Just as there were three possible partitions of the 2 degrees of freedom from three observations, there are twelve possibilities of this type with four observations, viz.:

$$
\begin{array}{llll}
\text{(i)} & \tfrac{1}{2}(a_1-a_2)^2, & \tfrac{1}{6}(a_1+a_2-2a_3)^2, & \tfrac{1}{12}(a_1+a_2+a_3-3a_4)^2 \\
\text{(ii)} & \tfrac{1}{2}(a_1-a_2)^2, & \tfrac{1}{6}(a_1+a_2-2a_4)^2, & \tfrac{1}{12}(a_1+a_2-3a_3+a_4)^2 \\
\text{(iii)} & \tfrac{1}{2}(a_1-a_3)^2, & \tfrac{1}{6}(a_1-2a_2+a_3)^2, & \tfrac{1}{12}(a_1+a_2+a_3-3a_4)^2 \\
\text{(iv)} & \tfrac{1}{2}(a_1-a_3)^2, & \tfrac{1}{6}(a_1+a_3-2a_4)^2, & \tfrac{1}{12}(a_1-3a_2+a_3+a_4)^2 \\
\text{(v)} & \tfrac{1}{2}(a_1-a_4)^2, & \tfrac{1}{6}(a_1-2a_2+a_4)^2, & \tfrac{1}{12}(a_1+a_2-3a_3+a_4)^2 \\
\text{(vi)} & \tfrac{1}{2}(a_1-a_4)^2, & \tfrac{1}{6}(a_1-2a_3+a_4)^2, & \tfrac{1}{12}(a_1-3a_2+a_3+a_4)^2 \\
\text{(vii)} & \tfrac{1}{2}(a_2-a_3)^2, & \tfrac{1}{6}(-2a_1+a_2+a_3)^2, & \tfrac{1}{12}(a_1+a_2+a_3-3a_4)^2 \\
\text{(viii)} & \tfrac{1}{2}(a_2-a_3)^2, & \tfrac{1}{6}(a_2+a_3-2a_4)^2, & \tfrac{1}{12}(-3a_1+a_2+a_3+a_4)^2 \\
\text{(ix)} & \tfrac{1}{2}(a_2-a_4)^2, & \tfrac{1}{6}(-2a_1+a_2+a_4)^2, & \tfrac{1}{12}(a_1+a_2-3a_3+a_4)^2 \\
\text{(x)} & \tfrac{1}{2}(a_2-a_4)^2, & \tfrac{1}{6}(a_2-2a_3+a_4)^2, & \tfrac{1}{12}(-3a_1+a_2+a_3+a_4)^2 \\
\text{(xi)} & \tfrac{1}{2}(a_3-a_4)^2, & \tfrac{1}{6}(-2a_1+a_3+a_4)^2, & \tfrac{1}{12}(a_1-3a_2+a_3+a_4)^2 \\
\text{(xii)} & \tfrac{1}{2}(a_3-a_4)^2, & \tfrac{1}{6}(-2a_2+a_3+a_4)^2, & \tfrac{1}{12}(-3a_1+a_2+a_3+a_4)^2 \\
\end{array}
$$

But these do not end the simple ways of partitioning the four observations. When the first comparison is of a_1 with a_2, the second degree of freedom might not be calculated as $\frac{1}{6}(a_1+a_2-2a_3)^2$, but might rest instead on the comparison $\frac{1}{2}(a_3-a_4)^2$. The third degree of freedom will then have as its sum of squares

$$\tfrac{1}{12}(9a_1^2+9a_2^2+9a_3^2+9a_4^2-6a_1a_2-6a_1a_3-6a_1a_4-6a_2a_3-6a_2a_4-6a_3a_4)$$
$$-\tfrac{1}{2}(a_1^2+a_2^2-2a_1a_2)-\tfrac{1}{2}(a_3^2+a_4^2-2a_3a_4)$$

which reduces to

$$\tfrac{1}{12}(3a_1^2+3a_2^2+3a_3^2+3a_4^2+6a_1a_2-6a_1a_3-6a_1a_4-6a_2a_3-6a_2a_4+6a_3a_4)$$
$$=\tfrac{1}{4}(a_1+a_2-a_3-a_4)^2$$

This is the comparison between the sums, or means, of the first two observations, themselves compared in the first degree of freedom, and of the last two observations, compared in the second degree of freedom. There are clearly three partitions of this kind:

(i) $\frac{1}{2}(a_1-a_2)^2$, $\quad \frac{1}{2}(a_3-a_4)^2$, $\quad \frac{1}{4}(a_1+a_2-a_3-a_4)^2$
(ii) $\frac{1}{2}(a_1-a_3)^2$, $\quad \frac{1}{2}(a_2-a_4)^2$, $\quad \frac{1}{4}(a_1-a_2+a_3-a_4)^2$
(iii) $\frac{1}{2}(a_1-a_4)^2$, $\quad \frac{1}{2}(a_2-a_3)^2$, $\quad \frac{1}{4}(a_1-a_2-a_3+a_4)^2$

There is still another valuable partition in which all the 3 degrees of freedom rest on comparisons involving the four observations. In this case the sums of squares are

$$\tfrac{1}{4}(a_1+a_2-a_3-a_4)^2, \quad \tfrac{1}{4}(a_1-a_2+a_3-a_4)^2, \quad \tfrac{1}{4}(a_1-a_2-a_3+a_4)^2$$

That these expressions together equal the total sum of squares may be shown by expansion and addition. Though this is not perhaps such an obvious method of partition it is, as will be seen in later sections, the one most used in analysis.

23. THE PRINCIPLES OF PARTITION

The components into which a sum of squares can be divided are very simple. Indeed, it is not difficult to write down a set of them for the partition of any given sum of squares. They have, however, special properties which must be ascertained before such rapid partition is, in general, possible.

It will be observed that each component has two parts, the initial fraction and the squared portion, which determines the comparison on which the item is based. Thus for the comparison between a_1 and a_2 the sum of squares is $\frac{1}{2}(a_1-a_2)^2$, the initial fraction being $\frac{1}{2}$ and the squared portion resting on the comparison (a_1-a_2).

Now the comparisons are always linear functions of a_1, a_2, a_3, &c., that is to say, they always involve a_1 rather than a_1^2 or a_1^3, &c. So we may write down a general form to include all sets of comparisons:

$$x_1 = k_{11}a_1 + k_{12}a_2 + k_{13}a_3 + \ldots + k_{1n}a_n$$
$$x_2 = k_{21}a_1 + k_{22}a_2 + k_{23}a_3 + \ldots + k_{2n}a_n$$
$$\vdots$$
$$x_{(n-1)} = k_{(n-1)1}a_1 + k_{(n-1)2}a_2 + k_{(n-1)3}a_3 + \ldots + k_{(n-1)n}a_n$$

as there are $n-1$ different independent comparisons possible with n observations. The important parts of these formulae are the k's—the coefficients by which the a values are multiplied to give the comparison used. Thus in the simple case of two observations we have seen that the contribution to the sum of squares is based on (a_1-a_2). Then $k_{11}=1$ and $k_{12}=-1$. Taking the case of three observations, one possible method of partition is into components based on (a_1-a_2) and $(a_1+a_2-2a_3)$. Here we have

$$k_{11}=1 \quad k_{12}=-1 \quad k_{13}=0$$
and
$$k_{21}=1 \quad k_{22}=1 \quad k_{23}=-2$$

With four observations, where the partition is on the basis of $x_1=a_1-a_2$, $x_2=a_1+a_2-2a_3$, $x_3=a_1+a_2+a_3-3a_4$ the k values are

$k_{11}=1 \quad k_{12}=-1 \quad k_{13}=0 \quad k_{14}=0$
$k_{21}=1 \quad k_{22}=1 \quad k_{23}=-2 \quad k_{24}=0$
$k_{31}=1 \quad k_{32}=1 \quad k_{33}=1 \quad k_{34}=-3$

One characteristic property of the k values is immediately obvious, viz. that in any comparison they add up to 0, or

$$S(k)=0$$

This is easily shown for the three comparisons of the preceding paragraph.

1st comparison $\quad S(k)=1-1+0+0=0$
2nd   ,, $\quad S(k)=1+1-2+0=0$
3rd   ,, $\quad S(k)=1+1+1-3=0$

The second characteristic is not so obvious. It relates to the cross products of k's in pairs of comparisons. Now it has continually been emphasized that the various comparisons of a set must be independent of one another or, as it is often called, orthogonal, if a successful partition is to be achieved; and it will be remembered (Section 20) that the test of independence of any two quantities is that their cross product should be zero within the limits of sampling error. The way in which this cross-product test is applied to a pair of x functions (or comparisons) is to multiply the two k's, one from each function, associated with a_1, also the two associated with a_2, and so on, and add the products together. If the functions are orthogonal this sum is 0.

Taking the three functions used above for showing that $S(k)=0$, the k values give as their cross products

x_1x_2; $\quad k_{11}k_{21}=1, \quad k_{12}k_{22}=-1, \quad k_{13}k_{23}=0, \quad k_{14}k_{24}=0; \quad S(k_1k_2)=0$
x_1x_3; $\quad k_{11}k_{31}=1, \quad k_{12}k_{32}=-1, \quad k_{13}k_{33}=0, \quad k_{14}k_{34}=0; \quad S(k_1k_3)=0$
x_2x_3; $\quad k_{21}k_{31}=1, \quad k_{22}k_{32}=1, \quad k_{23}k_{33}=-2, \quad k_{24}k_{34}=0; \quad S(k_2k_3)=0$

The sums of all three cross products are 0 and the comparisons are independent. Such a set of independent comparisons is often spoken of as a set of orthogonal functions.

The comparison term of the sum of squares formula has occupied our attention so far, but there still remains the question of the initial fraction to be considered. This, too, is dependent on the k values of the orthogonal functions. Turning once more to the three comparisons

$$(a_1-a_2), \quad (a_1+a_2-2a_3), \quad (a_1+a_2+a_3-3a_4)$$

between four observations, we have, it will be remembered, $\frac{1}{2}$, $\frac{1}{6}$ and $\frac{1}{12}$ as the initial fractions to the formulae. In every case the numerator is 1 and the denominator is $S(k^2)$. In x_1; $k_{11}=1$, $k_{12}=-1$, $k_{13}=k_{14}=0$ and $S(k^2)=1+1+0+0=2$, so giving $\frac{1}{2}$ as the fraction. In x_2; $k_{21}=k_{22}=1$, $k_{23}=-2$, $k_{24}=0$ so that $S(k^2)=1+1+4+0=6$. Similarly for the third component $k_{31}=k_{32}=k_{33}=1$, $k_{34}=-3$ and $S(k^2)=1+1+1+9=12$, the initial fraction being $\frac{1}{12}$.

24. THE ANALYSIS OF VARIANCE

We have now found the three characteristics of the components of a sum of squares, viz. (a) $S(k)=0$ for each comparison, (b) $S(k_1k_2)=0$ for all pairs of comparisons, and (c) $\dfrac{1}{S(k^2)}$ as the initial fraction of any component of sum of squares. By using these characteristics it is possible to partition the sum of squares in any way which seems appropriate to the analysis in hand.

It is clear, however, that although the separation of every individual degree of freedom is possible, such a complete partition is seldom necessary. As a case to point, consider an experiment of the type discussed in Section 21. The problem was, it will be remembered, that of testing a possible difference in yield between two varieties of tomato, when the different plants of each variety grow in positions of varying fertility.

As a simple case for discussion, consider two plants of each variety. There will be four plants in all, that of variety A in position 1 and that of variety A in position 2, that of variety B in position 1 and that of variety B in position 2. The initial, or null, hypothesis is that all varieties have the same yield, and we wish to determine whether the observed results agree with this view, within the limits of sampling error. A low probability will indicate that sampling error is incapable of explaining the departures from equality of yield, and in consequence one type must be supposed to be more prolific than the other.

The yields of the four individual plants will be denoted as a_{A1}, a_{A2}, a_{B1} and a_{B2} where the subscripts A and B refer to variety and 1 and 2 to position. There are 3 degrees of freedom between the four observations. Of these, 2 can be related to comparisons of obvious interest, viz. the differences between plants of the two varieties and between plants in the two different positions. The former is a comparison of A with B and so must be based on the expression $(a_{A1}+a_{A2})-(a_{B1}+a_{B2})$. Similarly the position comparison will be $(a_{A1}+a_{B1})-(a_{A2}+a_{B2})$. The third degree of freedom necessary for the completion of the analysis can be found by the methods of Section 22 to be $(a_{A1}+a_{B2})-(a_{A2}+a_{B1})$. It will be observed that these constitute a set of orthogonal functions as $S(k)=0$ for each expression and $S(k_1k_2)=0$ for each pair of expressions. Furthermore, each comparison gives $S(k^2)=4$, and so the initial fraction will in all cases be $\frac{1}{4}$. The three contributions to the sum of squares are thus:

(i) $\frac{1}{4}(a_{A1}+a_{A2}-a_{B1}-a_{B2})^2$
(ii) $\frac{1}{4}(a_{A1}-a_{A2}+a_{B1}-a_{B2})^2$
(iii) $\frac{1}{4}(a_{A1}-a_{A2}-a_{B1}+a_{B2})^2$

Now these three comparisons are of very different importance for our purpose. The first one obviously depends on the difference whose significance is our central problem. The second one concerns the positional difference in fertility and hence is irrelevant. The third one, like the first, is of importance but in a different way. It will be observed that just as the first comparison may be written $(a_{A1}-a_{B1})+(a_{A2}-a_{B2})$, the third one can be made to take the form $(a_{A1}-a_{B1})-(a_{A2}-a_{B2})$. So the first represents total difference in varietal yield while the third is the difference of this varietal difference in the two positions. It is in fact a measure of the variation in the varietal difference, and hence gives information necessary for the calculation of the mean square measuring uncontrolled variation, i.e. the error mean square with which the mean square between varieties must be compared in order that its probability may be assessed.

When there are three plants the analysis is a simple extension of that given above. There are 5 degrees of freedom to be accounted for. One is obviously dependent on the total varietal difference, and is based on the comparison

$$(a_{A1}+a_{A2}+a_{A3})-(a_{B1}+a_{B2}+a_{B3}).$$

As there are now three positions, two degrees of freedom are assignable to the comparisons between them. A typical partition would be into the elements $(a_{A1}+a_{B1})-(a_{A2}+a_{B2})$ and

$$(a_{A1}+a_{B1})+(a_{A2}+a_{B2})-2(a_{A3}+a_{B3}),$$

but the precise method of decomposition is not important since these comparisons are only picked out in order that they may be rejected as irrelevant to our purpose. The two remaining degrees of freedom are $(a_{A1}-a_{B1})-(a_{A2}-a_{B2})$ and

$$(a_{A1}-a_{B1})+(a_{A2}-a_{B2})-2(a_{A3}-a_{B3})$$

if the position comparisons are partitioned as above. All comparisons satisfy the criteria of orthogonal functions. The calculation of $S(k^2)$ for each of them shows that the contributions to the sum of squares will be:

Varieties: $\frac{1}{6}[(a_{A1}-a_{B1})+(a_{A2}-a_{B2})+(a_{A3}-a_{B3})]^2$

Positions: $\begin{cases} \frac{1}{4}[(a_{A1}+a_{B1})-(a_{A2}+a_{B2})]^2 \\ \frac{1}{12}[(a_{A1}+a_{B1})+(a_{A2}+a_{B2})-2(a_{A3}+a_{B3})]^2 \end{cases}$

Error: $\begin{cases} \frac{1}{4}[(a_{A1}-a_{B1})-(a_{A2}-a_{B2})]^2 \\ \frac{1}{12}[(a_{A1}-a_{B1})+(a_{A2}-a_{B2})-2(a_{A3}-a_{B3})]^2 \end{cases}$

As in the simpler example, there are three types of comparisons, and these three have exactly the same importance as before for our purpose. The position comparisons may be pooled and rejected together. In just the same way the two error comparisons can and should be used jointly in estimating the sampling error to which the varietal difference is subject. So even if the position comparisons are found separately they will ultimately be summed, and even if the error comparisons are found separately they will be summed too. Hence a direct method of finding the joint sum of squares would be advantageous in each case.

Taking the two position comparisons first, it will be seen that

$$\tfrac{1}{4}[(a_{A1}+a_{B1})-(a_{A2}+a_{B2})]^2+\tfrac{1}{12}[(a_{A1}+a_{B1})+(a_{A2}+a_{B2})-2(a_{A3}+a_{B3})]^2$$

$$=\tfrac{1}{4}[(a_{A1}+a_{B1})^2-2(a_{A1}+a_{B1})(a_{A2}+a_{B2})+(a_{A2}+a_{B2})^2]$$
$$+\tfrac{1}{12}[(a_{A1}+a_{B1})^2+(a_{A2}+a_{B2})^2+4(a_{A3}+a_{B3})^2+2(a_{A1}+a_{B1})(a_{A2}+a_{B2})$$
$$-4(a_{A1}+a_{B1})(a_{A3}+a_{B3})-4(a_{A2}+a_{B2})(a_{A3}+a_{B3})]$$

$$=\tfrac{1}{12}[4(a_{A1}+a_{B1})^2+4(a_{A2}+a_{B2})^2+4(a_{A3}+a_{B3})^2-4(a_{A1}+a_{B1})(a_{A2}+a_{B2})$$
$$-4(a_{A1}+a_{B1})(a_{A3}+a_{B3})-4(a_{A2}+a_{B2})(a_{A3}+a_{B3})]$$

$$=\tfrac{1}{12}[6(a_{A1}+a_{B1})^2+6(a_{A2}+a_{B2})^2+6(a_{A3}+a_{B3})^2]-\tfrac{1}{12}[2(a_{A1}+a_{B1})^2$$
$$+2(a_{A2}+a_{B2})^2+2(a_{A3}+a_{B3})^2+4(a_{A1}+a_{B1})(a_{A2}+a_{B2})+4(a_{A1}+a_{B1})(a_{A3}+a_{B3})$$
$$+4(a_{A2}+a_{B2})(a_{A3}+a_{B3})]$$

$$=\tfrac{1}{2}[(a_{A1}+a_{B1})^2+(a_{A2}+a_{B2})^2+(a_{A3}+a_{B3})^2]-\tfrac{1}{6}(a_{A1}+a_{B1}+a_{A2}+a_{B2}+a_{A3}+a_{B3})^2$$

This is the form of the familiar calculation of the sum of squares from a series of observed values, except that there is a fraction $\tfrac{1}{2}$ in the first term. Such a divisor is characteristically the number of observations summed to give the item which is squared. In the present case each position total is obtained by summing the yields of two plants. Hence to find the sum of squares for all the position comparisons taken together, the three position totals are squared, divided by 2 and summed. The correction term, $\dfrac{1}{n}S^2(a)$, is then deducted. In the present case there are six observations in all, and so n is 6 in the calculation of this correction. It will be seen that this agrees with the general rule about divisors, viz. that any square is divided by the number of observations which have been summed to give the item which is squared.

In the same way it can be shown that the total sum of squares of the error comparisons is given by

$$\tfrac{1}{2}[(a_{A1}-a_{B1})^2+(a_{A2}-a_{B2})^2+(a_{A3}-a_{B3})^2]-\tfrac{1}{6}[a_{A1}-a_{B1}+a_{A2}-a_{B2}+a_{A3}-a_{B3}]^2$$

This resembles the sum of squares for position except that $(a_{A1}-a_{B1})$ replaces $(a_{A1}+a_{B1})$, and so on. Here the correction term is itself the sum of squares for varietal difference.

In the tomato experiment described in Example 6, plants of each of two varieties were grown in ten positions. There are thus 19 degrees of freedom in all. By analogy with the simpler cases already considered, these 19 degrees of freedom are subdivisible into three groups, (a) 1 for the comparison between varieties, (b) 9 for differences between the fertilities of the different positions and (c) 9 for variation of the varietal difference in the ten positions, i.e. for error. The calculation of the sums of squares appropriate to each of these groups can be made by extending that used in the case of three positions. The data are set out for the calculation in Table 8.

First of all the comparison of the yields of the two varieties will be $(a_{A1}+a_{A2}+ \ldots +a_{A10})-(a_{B1}+a_{B2}+ \ldots +a_{B10})$. This gives $S(k^2)=20$, and so the sum of squares is

$$\tfrac{1}{20}[(a_{A1}+a_{A2}+ \ldots +a_{A10})-(a_{B1}+a_{B2}+ \ldots +a_{B10})]^2$$

Arithmetically this becomes $\tfrac{1}{20}(13 \cdot 253-11 \cdot 367)^2=0 \cdot 177850$. We may note in passing that this value could have been found in a somewhat different way analogous to that used for the position total. Putting $a_{A1}+a_{A2}+ \ldots +a_{A10}=a_A$ and

$$a_{B1}+a_{B2}+ \ldots + a_{B10}=a_B$$

we can rewrite the formula for the sum of squares, for

$$\tfrac{1}{20}(a_A-a_B)^2 = \tfrac{1}{20}(a_A^2 - 2a_A a_B + a_B^2)$$
$$=\tfrac{1}{20}[2a_A^2+2a_B^2-(a_A+a_B)^2]=\tfrac{1}{10}(a_A^2+a_B^2)-\tfrac{1}{20}(a_A+a_B)^2$$

It will be seen that the correction term is the same as that used in the calculation of the position sum of squares. The first term consists of the sum of squares of the two varietal totals divided by the number of plants on which each total is based, i.e. 10. Arithmetically this is

$$\tfrac{1}{10}(13 \cdot 253^2+11 \cdot 367^2)-\tfrac{1}{20}(24 \cdot 620)^2=30 \cdot 485070-30 \cdot 307220=0 \cdot 177850$$

as before.

The sum of squares for position is found from the summed yields of each position. These numbers are squared and their squares summed. Each is based on two plant yields, and so the sum of squares will be divided by 2. The correction term is as above, viz. the square of the total yield divided by the number of plants. So arithmetically we find the position sum of squares to be

$$\tfrac{1}{2}(2 \cdot 408^2+2 \cdot 624^2+ \ldots +2 \cdot 850^2)-\tfrac{1}{20}(24 \cdot 620)^2$$
$$=32 \cdot 035979-30 \cdot 307220=1 \cdot 728759$$

Lastly, we must calculate the sum of squares due to positional variation in the varietal difference. As already shown, this calculation is just the same as that for positions, but the differences between the yields of the two plants in each position are used instead of their sums. So the sum of squares is

$$\tfrac{1}{2}(0\cdot 342^2 + 0\cdot 190^2 + \ldots 0\cdot 416^2) - \tfrac{1}{20}(1\cdot 886)^2$$
$$= 0\cdot 340875 - 0\cdot 177850$$
$$= 0\cdot 163025.$$

Table 10 gives these results in the form of what is termed an analysis of variance. The sums of squares are found in the second column, while the third column gives the numbers of degrees of freedom (N). The ratio of a sum of squares to its corresponding number of degrees of freedom gives the mean square as shown in the fourth column. It will be recalled that a mean square is an estimated variance, and the term is extensively used in connexion with the type of analysis now under discussion.

TABLE 10
Analysis of Variance of Tomato Yields

Item	Sum of Squares (S.S.)	Degrees of Freedom (N)	Mean Square (S.S./N)	t	Probability
Varieties	0·177850	1	0·177850	3·133	0·02–0·01
Positions	1·782759	9	0·198084		
Varieties-Positions (Error)	0·163025	9	0·018114		
Total	2·123634	19			

At this stage the test of significance, towards which the whole analysis has been leading, becomes possible. We are interested in the varietal difference whose mean square is based on one comparison, so a t test is suitable for our purpose. The denominator of t is clearly to be found by taking the square root of the error mean square. Then

$$t_{[9]} = \sqrt{\frac{0\cdot 177850}{0\cdot 018114}} = \sqrt{9\cdot 8184} = 3\cdot 133$$

The probability of finding such a poor fit by chance is very small (0·02–0·01). The varieties must be supposed to have genuinely different yields.

The value of t found by the analysis of variance is exactly the same as that found by a slightly different method in Example 6; though it will be observed that the two root mean squares whose ratio gives t are different in the two calculations. In Section 21 the numerator of t was found as the difference between the mean yields of the varieties, i.e. as $\tfrac{1}{10}(a_A - a_B)$ where a_A is the summed yield of A plants and a_B that of B plants. Similarly the denominator of t was $\sqrt{\tfrac{1}{90}S(a_A - a_B)^2}$ where $S(a_A - a_B)^2$ is the sum of squares of the difference in yields of A and B plants in corresponding positions. The analysis of variance provides $\sqrt{\frac{1}{20}(a_A-a_B)^2}$ as the numerator of t and $\sqrt{\frac{1}{18}S(a_A-a_B)^2}$ as its denominator. Thus both numerator and denominator as found in Section 21 have $\frac{1}{\sqrt{5}}$ times the value of those given by the analysis of variance. The two methods of analysis give results differing by a constant fraction which cancels out when the test of significance is performed.

Before leaving this example a further computational point may be noted. There are 20 observed yields and a total sum of squares for 19 degrees of freedom may be found directly from these 20 values. This is clearly the total sum of squares of the whole experiment and so represents the number which has been partitioned in the analysis. Therefore, when correctly calculated, the three components already found should agree with this total on summing. Arithmetically the total sum of squares is $(1 \cdot 375^2 + 1 \cdot 407^2 + \ldots + 1 \cdot 223^2 + 1 \cdot 633^2 + 1 \cdot 033^2 + 1 \cdot 217^2 + \ldots + 1 \cdot 252^2 + 1 \cdot 217^2) - \frac{1}{20}(24 \cdot 620)^2 = 2 \cdot 123634$, which tallies with the total of the three components. Thus we can determine any one of the three components by finding the total and subtracting from it the other two component items; this is the method normally used for the calculation of the error sum of squares, which is not always so easy to find directly as in the present example.

25. INTERACTIONS BETWEEN MAIN EFFECTS

Two main effects were recognized in the tomato example. These were the difference between the varieties and the differences due to position in the greenhouse. In addition, a third term appeared in the analysis, depending on the effect of position on the varietal difference. This item was used as an estimate of error, in that it was taken as a measure of the fluctuation of yield differences due to factors over which no experimental control could be exercised, though of course it is a valid estimate only if the effects of position and variety are additive. In such a case the varietal difference in any position is independent of the position effect.

If there were any other method of estimating the error variance in the tomato experiment it would be possible to use the third term of the analysis for the specific purpose of testing the additive nature of the two main effects, or finding out whether they 'interacted' to a significant extent. In general, terms of this kind are recognized in the analysis of variance and are called interactions. The one under consideration would be described as a first-order interaction between variety and position.

As the number of recognizable main effects increases the

number of interactions increases even more rapidly, and some of them will be of an order higher than the one in the tomato analysis. Suppose, for example, we have an experiment in which observations are made on eight individuals, the first of which had been subjected to treatments A, B, and C, the second to A and B, the third to A and C, the fourth to B and C, the fifth to A alone, the sixth to B alone, the seventh to C alone, and the eighth to no treatment at all. There are three main effects due to the three treatments A, B, and C. Their sums of squares will be derived from the comparisons

$$(a_{ABC}+a_{AB}+a_{AC}+a_A)-(a_{BC}+a_B+a_C+a_1)$$
$$(a_{ABC}+a_{AB}+a_{BC}+a_B)-(a_{AC}+a_A+a_C+a_1)$$
$$(a_{ABC}+a_{AC}+a_{BC}+a_C)-(a_{AB}+a_A+a_B+a_1)$$

where a_{ABC} represents the observation made on the individual who receives all three treatments, and so on, a_1 being that from the untreated individual. There are 4 more degrees of freedom to be accounted for, and these will be interactions of various sorts. They can be assigned to particular comparisons in the following way, which is due to R. A. Fisher.

The treatment A is denoted by that letter while its absence is denoted by 1. Similar symbolism is used for the other two treatments, so that any combination of the three may be noted by a corresponding combination of A, B, C, and 1. The k coefficients assigned to the eight individual observations in the comparison giving the main effect of A can then be found by expanding the expression $(A-1)(B+1)(C+1)$ into the form $ABC+AB+AC+A-BC-B-C-1$ as already used. The main effects of B and C are similarly found from the expansions of

$$(A+1)(B-1)(C+1) \quad \text{and} \quad (A+1)(B+1)(C-1) \quad \text{respectively.}$$

It will be seen that the factor whose effect is being considered is represented by a bracket containing a difference, while those whose effects are not under consideration are used as sums. It is not difficult to see how the expressions giving the interaction comparisons are found. A first-order interaction depends on the interplay of two main effects, the third being left out of consideration. The corresponding expression thus contains two brackets with differences and one with a sum. The first-order interaction of A and B will then be the expansion of

$$(A-1)(B-1)(C+1) \quad \text{giving} \quad ABC+AB+C+1-AC-BC-A-B$$

In this case $k_{ABC}=k_{AB}=k_C=k_1=1$ and $k_{AC}=k_{BC}=k_A=k_B=-1$. The other two first-order interactions are $(A-1)(B+1)(C-1)$ and $(A+1)(B-1)(C-1)$ respectively.

The seventh degree of freedom is then seen to be a second-order interaction of A, B, and C, and will be derivable from the expression $(A-1)(B-1)(C-1)$. For this comparison

$$k_{ABC}=k_A=k_B=k_C=1 \text{ and } k_{AB}=k_{AC}=k_{BC}=k_1=-1.$$

The k coefficients obtained in this way are set out in Table 11, from which it is readily shown that the comparisons are orthogonal and that the divisor is 8 in each case.

TABLE 11

k *Coefficients of 7 Orthogonal Functions for the Analysis of 3 Treatments each at 2 Levels*

		ABC	AB	AC	BC	**A**	B	C	1	$S(k)$	$S(k^2)$
Main Effects	A	1	1	1	−1	1	−1	−1	−1	0	8
	B	1	1	−1	1	−1	1	−1	−1	0	8
	C	1	−1	1	1	−1	−1	1	−1	0	8
1st-order interactions	AB	1	1	−1	−1	−1	−1	1	1	0	8
	AC	1	−1	1	−1	−1	1	−1	1	0	8
	BC	1	−1	−1	1	1	−1	−1	1	0	8
2nd-order interaction	ABC	1	−1	−1	−1	1	1	1	−1	0	8

Though these coefficients are not applicable to cases with more than 1 degree of freedom for each main effect and interaction, the method of calculation of the sum of squares corresponding to the various comparisons is suggested by these formulae. The main effect of A will be obtainable from the totals found by summing over the various B and C classes. The corresponding C classes will be summed for the determination of the interaction between A and B. This will leave a two-way table having three kinds of degrees of freedom, one being the main A effect obtainable from one margin, a second kind from the other margin being the main B effect, and lastly a third type for interaction of A and B. This last group can be found as the difference of the total sum of squares of the table and the two main effects calculated from the margins.

The application of these methods of calculation to a more complex case may be illustrated by the following results taken from an analysis of barley yields, in bushels per three acres, published by Immer, Hayes and Powers.

Example 7. Data on the yields of five varieties when grown at each of six places in the State of Minnesota during the years 1931 and 1932 are given in Table 12. There are 5×6×2 observations in all, and so the total analysis will contain 59 degrees of freedom. The first task is that of partitioning these degrees of freedom into the components appropriate to the various comparisons which might be interesting.

TABLE 12
Barley Yields in Bushels per Three Acres (Immer, Hayes, and Powers)

Place and Year	Varieties				
	Manchuria	Svansota	Velvet	Trebi	Peatland
1 { 1931	81·0	105·4	119·7	109·7	98·3
1932	80·7	82·3	80·4	87·2	84·2
2 { 1931	146·6	142·0	150·7	191·5	145·7
1932	100·4	115·5	112·2	147·7	108·1
3 { 1931	82·3	77·3	78·4	131·3	89·6
1932	103·1	105·1	116·5	139·9	129·6
4 { 1931	119·8	121·4	124·0	140·8	124·8
1932	98·9	61·9	96·2	125·5	75·7
5 { 1931	98·9	89·0	69·1	89·3	104·1
1932	66·4	49·9	96·7	61·9	80·3
6 { 1931	86·9	77·1	78·9	101·8	96·0
1932	67·7	66·7	67·4	91·8	94·1

We first of all note that summation of the yields of each variety over places and year leaves five varietal totals, which will supply 4 degrees of freedom for varietal differences. A similar procedure, but summing over varieties and years, gives six place totals with 5 degrees of freedom for differences between places. Finally, summing over varieties and places gives two annual totals with 1 degree of freedom for the difference between the two years. So 10 degrees of freedom are accounted for by the main effects.

To obtain the material for calculating the first-order interaction of varieties and places, it is necessary to sum over years. Adding the 1931 and 1932 yields of each variety in each place leaves a table with thirty entries (5×6). Of the 29 degrees of freedom which it contains, 9 are assignable to main effects, viz. 4 to varieties and 5 to places. These are found from the row and total columns in the two margins of the table. The remaining 20 degrees of freedom, obtained by subtracting these 9 from the total of 29, relate to the first-order interaction under consideration.

A 5×2 table is obtained when summation is made over places. Of the 9 degrees of freedom which this contains, 4 are attributable to varietal differences and 1 to years, leaving 4 for the first-order interaction of variety and year. Finally, with summation over varieties a 6×2 table containing 11 degrees of freedom is left. Deduction of the 5 place and 1 year degrees of freedom gives

5 for interaction of place and time. The three first-order interactions have together taken up 29 degrees of freedom. With the 10 for main effects this leaves 20 to be accounted for by the second-order interaction of variety with time and place.

There is a very simple rule for determining the number of degrees of freedom appertaining to any interaction. The varieties take 4 and the places 5 degrees of freedom. Then their interaction takes 4×5. Similarly, years take 1, so the variety-year interaction will have 4 and the place-year interaction 5 degrees of freedom. The second-order interaction has 4×5×1 or 20 degrees of freedom assignable to it.

So we reach the analysis of degrees of freedom shown in Table 15. The calculation of the corresponding sums of squares proceeds along much the same lines.

TABLE 13
A. *Varietal Total Yields of Barley*

Manchuria	Svansota	Velvet	Trebi	Peatland	Total
1,132·7	1,093·6	1,190·2	1,418·4	1,230·5	6,065·4

B. *Place total yields of Barley*

1	2	3	4	5	6	Total
928·9	1,360·4	1,053·1	1,089·0	805·6	828·4	6,065·4

C. *Year total yields of Barley*

1931	1932	Total
3,271·4	2,794·0	6,065·4

The varietal sum of squares is found by summation over places and years (Table 13A). Each total is composed of 12 values, and so after squaring and summing the result must be reduced to $\frac{1}{12}$. The term correcting for the use of 0 as a working mean is, of course, found by dividing the square of the grand total by the number of observations, viz. 60. Thus the sum of squares for varieties is:

$$\tfrac{1}{12}(1{,}132{\cdot}7^2 + 1{,}093{\cdot}6^2 + 1{,}190{\cdot}2^2 + 1{,}418{\cdot}4^2 + 1{,}230{\cdot}5^2) - \tfrac{1}{60}(6{,}065{\cdot}4)^2$$

or 5,309·9723 for 4 degrees of freedom.

Table 13B shows the place totals obtained by summing over varieties and years. Each total comprises 10 values, and so the divisor of the squared values will be 10. The correction term is as before. This gives

$$\tfrac{1}{10}(928{\cdot}9^2 + 1{,}360{\cdot}4^2 + \ldots + 828{\cdot}4^2) - \tfrac{1}{60}(6{,}065{\cdot}4)^2 = 21{,}220{\cdot}9040$$

as the sum of squares in question. Table 13C supplies the material for calculating the "years" sum of squares. The divisor is 6×5, i.e. 30, and using the same correction term the result of the calculation is 3,798·5126.

TABLE 14

A. Variety-Place Classification of Yield in Barley

Place \ Variety	Manchuria	Svansota	Velvet	Trebi	Peatland	Place total
1	161·7	187·7	200·1	196·9	182·5	928·9
2	247·0	257·5	262·9	339·2	253·8	1,360·4
3	185·4	182·4	194·9	271·2	219·2	1,053·1
4	218·7	183·3	220·2	266·3	200·5	1,089·0
5	165·3	138·9	165·8	151·2	184·4	805·6
6	154·6	143·8	146·3	193·6	190·1	828·4
Variety total	1,132·7	1,093·6	1,190·2	1,418·4	1,230·5	6,065·4

B. Variety-Year Classification of Yield in Barley

Year \ Variety	Manchuria	Svansota	Velvet	Trebi	Peatland	Year total
1931	615·4	612·2	620·8	764·4	658·5	3,271·4
1932	517·2	481·4	569·4	654·0	572·0	2,794·0
Variety total	1,132·7	1,093·6	1,190·2	1,418·4	1,230·5	6,065·4

C. Place-Year Classification of Yield in Barley

Year \ Place	1	2	3	4	5	6	Year total
1931	514·1	776·5	458·9	630·8	450·4	440·7	3,271·4
1932	414·8	583·9	594·2	458·2	355·2	387·7	2,794·0
Place total	928·9	1,360·4	1,053·1	1,089·0	805·6	828·4	6,065·4

Turning next to the first-order interactions between varieties and places, we sum over years to get Table 14A, in which each entry is the sum of two observed values. The sum of squares calculated from this table corresponds to 29 degrees of freedom. The divisor is 2 and the correction term as before; so the sum of squares is

$\frac{1}{2}(161 \cdot 7^2 + 247 \cdot 0^2 + \ldots + 154 \cdot 6^2 + 187 \cdot 7^2 + \ldots + 190 \cdot 1^2) - \frac{1}{60}(6,065 \cdot 4^2)$,
i.e. 30,963·8940

But this includes the variety and place main effects as well as their interaction. Deducting the main effect sums of squares, as already found, leaves 30,963·8940−5,309·9723−21,220·9040, i.e. 4,433·0177 for the interaction.

The variety-year interaction is found in the same way from Table 14B. The divisor is 6, as summation has been over 6 places. The total sum of squares is found to be

$$\tfrac{1}{6}(615\cdot4^2+517\cdot2^2+612\cdot2^2+ \ldots +572\cdot0^2)-\tfrac{1}{60}(6{,}065\cdot4^2)$$

from which deduction of the two main effect items, for varieties and years, leaves 291·8124 for the interaction.

The last interaction of this order, that between places and years, is found from Table 14C, in which each entry is the sum of 5 items. The divisor is 5 and the sum of squares 31,913·3180. Subtraction of the place and year sums of squares gives 6,893·9014 for the interaction.

The full table of 60 items has 59 degrees of freedom corresponding to a sum of squares of

$$(81\cdot0^2+80\cdot7^2+ \ldots +67\cdot7^2+105\cdot4^2+ \ldots +94\cdot1^2)-\tfrac{1}{60}(6{,}065\cdot4)^2,$$

i.e. 44,732·3540

The main effects and first-order interactions between them have been shown to take up 5,309·9723+21,220·9040+3,798·5126 +4,433·0177+291·8124+6,893·9014, or 41,948·1204 of this total, leaving the difference of 2,784·2336 for the 20 degrees of freedom of the second-order variety-place-time interaction.

The various sums of squares found in this way are entered opposite their degrees of freedom in Table 15 and the division of each sum of squares by the number of degrees of freedom gives the mean square or variance appropriate to each of the sets of comparisons.

This method of analysis, of both the degrees of freedom and the sums of squares, can obviously be extended to more complex cases. The main effects are found first by means of the various one way tables. The first-order interactions are obtained from the two way tables by subtraction of the main effects. The three way tables give second-order interactions after the corresponding main and first order deductions have been made. Four way tables contain main effects and first- and second-order interactions together with a third-order type which will be left when the other items found from the lower order tables have been subtracted. Five way and higher tables are analysed by extension of this process.

The question of the significance of the various items of Table 15 remains. The second-order interaction is the most appropriate measure of sampling error in this case, it being usual to take the highest order interaction for this purpose, unless some

TABLE 15
Analysis of Variance of Barley Yields

Item	Sum of Squares (S.S.)	Degrees of Freedom (N)	Mean Square $\left(\frac{S.S.}{N}\right)$	Variance Ratio*	Probability
Main effects { Varieties	5,309·9723	4	1,327·4931	9·536	less than 0·001
Places	21,220·9040	5	4,244·1808	30·487	less than 0·001
Years	3,798·5126	1	3,798·5126	27·286	less than 0·001
First-order interactions { Varieties-Places	4,433·0177	20	221·6509	1·592	0·20–0·05
Varieties-Years	291·8124	4	72·9531	—	—
Places-Years	6,893·9014	5	1,378·7803	9·904	less than 0·001
Second-order interaction Varieties-Places-Years (Error)	2,784·2336	20	139·2117		
Total	44,732·3540	59			

* Where the item in question has $N = 1$, the Variance Ratio $= t^2$.

other is specially indicated by the results. This has a mean square of 139·2117 based on 20 degrees of freedom. Only the main effect of years may be tested by the calculation of a t, as this is the sole item based on 1 degree of freedom. This component has a mean square of 3,798·5126, giving

$$t_{[20]} = \sqrt{\frac{3,798 \cdot 5126}{139 \cdot 2117}} = \sqrt{27 \cdot 286} = 5 \cdot 234$$

with a probability of less than 0·001. Such a departure cannot reasonably be attributed to sampling error, and it must be supposed that the barley gave different yields in the two years.

The other items are tested by means of z or the variance ratio. The varieties comparisons give a variance ratio of 9·536 for $N_1=4$ and $N_2=20$. (N_1=degrees of freedom of larger variance, N_2 of smaller variance, in this case the error mean square.) This has a probability of less than 0·001, so showing that there are real differences in yield between the varieties. The other variance ratios and their probabilities are given in the table of analysis of variance. The 6 different places at which tests were conducted are clearly shown to have different fertilities and they also differ in their reactions to the varying climatic conditions of the two years, as the significant place-year interaction shows. The interactions of varieties with places and years may reasonably be attributed to sampling error; indeed, the latter has a mean square smaller than that which is being used as the estimate of sampling error. No variance ratio is given in this case. It cannot be calculated in a way parallel to that of the other items because in determining a z or variance ratio the smaller mean square must always be used as the denominator. (See Section 16.)

As these two interactions, variety-place and variety-year, are not significant, they could be combined with the second-order interaction to give a joint estimate of error, which would, of course, be known with greater accuracy in that it would be based on 44 degrees of freedom. Division gives this new error mean square as 170·6605. In the present case there is little to be gained by this procedure, as the increase in precision is small and is offset by an increase in the mean square. Where, however, a smaller number of degrees of freedom is concerned, this practice may be of great value.

Finally we may consider the question of the standard error of the various yields. The sampling error variance per plot is 139·2117, so that the standard error of a single plot yield is $\sqrt{139 \cdot 2117}$, i.e. 11·7992 bushels per acre. The variance of the total yield of a variety based on 12 plots is 139·2117×12, i.e. 1,670·5404, and the standard error is 40·8718. The total yield of the variety Manchuria is, for example, $1{,}132{\cdot}7 \pm 40{\cdot}8718$. The mean yield of each variety will have a variance of $\dfrac{139 \cdot 2117}{12}$ or $11 \cdot 6010$, and a standard error of $3 \cdot 4060$. The mean yield of Manchuria is thus $94 \cdot 3917 \pm 3 \cdot 4060$ bushels per acre. Lastly, the variance of the differences between two means is $11 \cdot 6010 + 11 \cdot 6010$ or $23 \cdot 2020$, the standard error being $4 \cdot 8169$. So Velvet and Trebi show a difference of $19 \cdot 0167 \pm 4 \cdot 8169$—a difference which clearly cannot be attributed to sampling error and must be judged real.

Standard errors can be found in the same way for the place and year means. The mean yield of the 1931 crop is, for example, based on 30 plots. So its variance will be $\dfrac{139 \cdot 2117}{30}$ or $4 \cdot 6404$, and the standard error $2 \cdot 1542$. The variance of the difference between the means of the 1931 and 1932 crops would then be $4 \cdot 6404 \times 2$, i.e. $9 \cdot 2808$, and the standard error $3 \cdot 0464$.

26. INCOMPLETE ANALYSIS

In the two examples of analysis of variance so far considered, classification of the data was complete. The tomatoes, for example, could be classified for variety no matter what position they were grown in, and the position was classifiable no matter what variety was placed in it. In the same way every barley observation could be assigned to its proper variety, place, and year. Such complete classification is, however, not always possible.

Suppose, for example, that twenty plants, ten of each variety, A and B, were grown in no special order in a greenhouse. There would be 20 yields recorded, giving 19 degrees of freedom, of which one would be assignable to the varietal difference; but the remaining 18 would not be further subdivisible, because there would be no correspondence in position between the plants of the different varieties. There would be no way of separating the main effect of position from the variety-position interaction. The analysis of variance would be incomplete owing to the short-comings of the design and classification.

This particular example of incomplete analysis is perhaps artificial, but somewhat similar situations are often met with in practice. In such cases it is necessary, though not always easy, to ascertain the extent to which the analysis is incomplete, by determining which classes, theoretically distinguishable, must be grouped as a result of the limitations of classification. An example of this is provided by Mather and Dobzhansky's data on the number of teeth in the sex-combs of the male *Drosophila pseudo-obscura*.

Example 8. This species of *Drosophila* comprises two races which give nearly sterile hybrids on inter-crossing. A number of strains of each race were examined in order to determine whether they showed any characteristic morphological differences. In particular, counts were made of the number of teeth in the proximal sex comb of the male. The experiment under consideration included 4 strains of each race, A and B, and all the strains were raised at two different temperatures, viz. 17·5° C. and 24·5° C. Twenty-five males of each strain raised at each temperature were counted, the results being set out in Table 16. There were 25×2×4×2 or 400 counts in all, giving a total of 399 degrees of freedom. How far can this be analysed ?

Let us first consider what the complete classification would have given (see Table 17). There are 2 races, and hence 1 degree of freedom for racial differences. The 4 strains contribute 3 degrees of freedom for strain differences, and as 4 strains of each race were raised, there will be 3 degrees of freedom for race-strain interaction. Two temperatures were used, so giving 1 degree of freedom for temperature effects, 1 degree of freedom for race-temperature interaction, 3 degrees of freedom for strain-temperature interaction, and 3 degrees of freedom for the second-order interaction between races, strains and temperatures. Lastly, there are 25 individuals with 24 degrees of freedom for differences between individuals, 24 for race-individual interaction, 72 for strain-individual interaction, 72 for race-strain-individual interaction, 24 for temperature-individual interaction, 72 for strain-temperature-individual interaction, 24 for race-temperature-individual interaction, and finally, 72 for the third order race-strain-temperature-individual interaction. It is, however, clear that many of these categories cannot be distinguished.

There are four strains of each race, but there is no way of linking up the strains of opposite races into what might be termed homologous pairs. Each strain is unique. Hence of the 7 degrees of freedom from the 8 strains, 1 will be assignable to races, but the remaining 6 must be grouped together as strain differences. The analysis cannot separate the strain main effect from the race-strain interaction. Turning to temperature differences, the main effect can be picked out, as can the interactions of temperature with race ; but there will be a group of 6 degrees of freedom for strain-temperature interaction which in the complete analysis would fall into two parts, viz. strain-temperature first-order interaction and race-strain-temperature second-order interaction, each with 3 degrees of freedom.

Lastly, there are obviously no relations between the single individuals of the different samples, in the way that a plant of variety A in a given position can be related to a plant of variety

TABLE 16

Number of Teeth in the Proximal Sex-combs of Drosophila pseudo-obscura *Males (Mather and Dobzhansky)*

Race	Strain	\multicolumn{6}{c}{Temperature 17·5°}			\multicolumn{6}{c}{24·5°}			\multicolumn{6}{c}{Total}		17·5°–24·5°
		\multicolumn{5}{c}{Number of teeth}	Total teeth		\multicolumn{6}{c}{Number of teeth}	Total teeth	\multicolumn{6}{c}{Number of teeth}	Total teeth	
		4	5	6	7	8	9		4	5	6	7	8	9		4	5	6	7	8	9		
A	Wawona—6			6	19			169		4	7	18			168		4	13	37			337	1
	Pikes Peak—4			11	13	1		165			19	2			148			30	15	1		313	17
	Treeline—3				17	7	1	184			12	12	1		164			12	29	8	1	348	20
	Santa Rita—1			4	15	6		177			15	10			160			19	25	6		337	17
	Total			21	64	14	1	695		4	53	42	1		640		4	74	106	15	1	1,335	55
B	Sequoia—5		1	24				149		7	18				143		8	42				292	6
	Reedsport—2		4	21	3			146		13	12				137		17	33				283	9
	Campbell River		1	21				152		7	17	1			144		8	38	4			296	8
	Cowichan—6		16	9				134	11	14					114	11	30	9				248	20
	Total		22	75	3			581	11	41	47	1			538	11	63	122	4			1,119	43
	Grand Total		22	96	67	14	1	1,276	11	45	100	43	1		1,178	11	67	196	110	15	1	2,454	98

The entries in the table are frequencies of flies falling into the class distinguished by the number of teeth shown in the column heading, except in the column labelled 'total teeth', where the entries are numbers of teeth.

B in the same, rather than in any other, position. It is quite clear that the only comparison for which any individual can be used is that made with the mean of the sample in which this individual is contained. Hence the 25 individuals of each sample will contribute 24 degrees of freedom to a general pool. This pool must include the degrees of freedom for the main comparison of individuals and all the interactions of individuals with the other main effects as classified in the complete analysis. Thus the estimate of variance due to sampling error in this analysis will be of a highly composite nature. The only possible subdivision of this group would be into 16 sub-groups each from a different sample; but unless there is reason to suspect an effect of race, strain or temperature on individual variability, such a subdivision would carry no advantage.

Turning next to the calculation of the sums of squares it should be noted that, as before, the method of partitioning the degrees of freedom points the way to the analysis of the sum of squares. First of all there is the race comparison. Race A has in all 1,335 teeth and race B 1,119 (see Table 16). Each total is the sum of 200 items, the grand total of 2,454 teeth being based on 400 flies. Hence the sum of squares for race is

$$\tfrac{1}{200}(1,335^2+1,119^2)-\tfrac{1}{400}(2,454^2)=15,171 \cdot 93-15,055 \cdot 29=116 \cdot 64$$

The main effect of temperature is similarly

$$\tfrac{1}{200}(1,276^2+1,178^2)-\tfrac{1}{400}(2,454^2)=24 \cdot 01$$

Next, summation over strains and individuals gives a 2×2 table of temperature by race from which the total sum of squares for 3 degrees of freedom is

$$\tfrac{1}{100}(695^2+640^2+581^2+538^2)-\tfrac{1}{400}(2,454^2)=141 \cdot 01$$

Subtraction of the main temperature and race effects, as already found, then leaves 0·36 for the race-temperature interaction.

The eight strain totals, summed over individuals and temperatures, are each the sum of 50 observations. Hence the 7 degrees of freedom between them will have a sum of squares of

$$\tfrac{1}{50}(337^2+313^2+ \ldots +337^2+292^2+ \ldots +248^2)-\tfrac{1}{400}(2,454)^2$$

or 158·39. But this will include the main item for race, deduction of which leaves 41·75 for the 6 degrees of freedom depending on strain differences. We have now accounted for 9 of the 15 degrees of freedom between the 16 sample totals. The remaining 6 form the strain-temperature interaction item. The sum of squares can be found in either of two ways. It may be obtained directly by the calculation of the sum of squares for the 15 comparisons between sample totals and the subsequent deduction of the four

INCOMPLETE ANALYSIS

items already calculated. The sample totals give a sum of squares of

$$\tfrac{1}{25}(169^2+165^2+ \ldots +149^2+ \ldots +134^2+168^2+ \ldots +114^2)-\tfrac{2{,}454^2}{400}$$
$$=189{\cdot}59$$

from which the race, strain, temperature, and race-temperature items of 116·64, 41·75, 24·01, and 0·36 are deducted, to leave 6·83 for the strain-temperature interaction.

The second way of finding the interaction in question is based on the use of the eight differences in teeth number of the eight strains grown at two temperatures. Thus at 17·5° C., Wawona—6 has 169 teeth, while at 24·5° C. it has 168 teeth, so giving a difference of 1 tooth. The other similar items are shown in the last column of Table 16. Each figure is based on 50 flies, being the difference between two samples of 25, and so the total sum of squares for the eight comparisons is

$$\tfrac{1}{50}(1^2+17^2+ \ldots +17^2+6^2+ \ldots +20^2)=31{\cdot}2$$

No correction term is involved when such differences are squared (see Section 24). These 8 comparisons include the main temperature effect and all the temperature-race and temperature-strain interactions. The first of the items may be found by squaring the total difference, i.e. 98 teeth, and dividing the square by 400, to give 24·01 as already obtained in a different way. We next use the racial totals of the differences, viz. 55 and 43, each based on 200 flies, to give $\tfrac{1}{200}(55^2+43^2)$ or 24·37 as the sum of the temperature and race-temperature effects. Deduction of the temperature effect leaves 0·36, as previously found, for the race-temperature interaction. Deduction of the temperature and race-temperature items from the total of 31·2 leaves 6·83 for strain-temperature interaction.

The last sum of squares to be found is that corresponding to the individual or error item of 384 degrees of freedom. It is most easily found as a difference. The sum of squares of all 400 single counts is $15{,}388-\tfrac{1}{400}(2{,}454)^2$, i.e. 283·71. Of the 399 degrees of freedom on which this total is based, 15 are accounted for by differences between sample totals. The remaining 384 form the item under consideration. These 15 degrees of freedom have already been shown to take a sum of squares of 189·59, so leaving 283·71−189·59, i.e. 94·12 for the error item.

The analysis of variance is set out in Table 17, the mean squares having been found as usual by dividing the degrees of freedom into the sums of squares. In calculating the variance ratios given in the column next to the mean squares, the error or individual mean square was used as the denominator. A *t* for 384 degrees of freedom may be used for the race, temperature

TABLE 17

Analysis of Variance of Teeth in Drosophila Sex-combs

Item		Sum of Squares	N Full analysis	N Incomplete analysis	Mean Square	Variance Ratio—1*	Probability	Variance Ratio—2*	Probability
Full analysis	Incomplete analysis								
Races (R)	Races	116·64	1	1	116·6400	475·853	less than 0·001	16·763	0·01–0·001
Temperatures (T)	Temperatures	24·01	1	1	24·0100	97·953	less than 0·001	0·316	0·70–0·50
R–T	Race-Temperature	0·36	1	1	0·3600	1·469	greater than 0·2		
Strains (S)	Strains	41·75	3	6	6·9583	28·388	less than 0·001		
S·R			3						
T·S			3						
T·R·S	Temperature-Strain	6·83	3	6	1·1383	4·644	less than 0·001		
Individuals (I)			24						
R·I			24						
T·I			24						
S·I	Individual (Error)	94·12	72	384	0·2451				
R·T·I			24						
R·S·I			72						
T·S·I			72						
R·T·S·I			72						
Total		283·71	399						

Variance Ratio—1 is obtained when the error term is used.
Variance Ratio—2 is obtained by comparison with some appropriate term other than error.
* A Variance Ratio for 1 degree of freedom $= t^2$.

and race-temperature items and such a t is for all practical purposes a normal deviate (c). The interaction of both race and temperature may safely be attributed to sampling error, though both main effects are clearly significant on this test.

An examination of the strain and strain-temperature interaction puts a somewhat different light on these results, however. These two items are tested by the use of z or variance ratio tables. It is found that both are highly significant, having a probability of less than 0·001. (It may be noted that in using the variance ratio table 384 degrees can be considered to be ∞.) Now if there is a large strain effect, the race difference could be significant when tested against the error variance and yet still be imaginary in the sense that it was simply a reflexion of the large strain differences. So the individual mean square must be rejected as an estimate of the error to which race totals are subject and replaced by the strain mean square. When this is done a t of 4·095 for 6 degrees of freedom is obtained and found to have a probability of 0·01–0·001. So even this more stringent test shows that the racial difference is real and not merely an outcome of variation between strains of a race.

Similarly, the race-temperature interaction should be compared with the strain-temperature interaction. The former is much lower than the latter and so the question arises as to whether it is significantly lower. The t of 0·562 has, however, a probability of less than 0·70 and there is no reason to suspect a subnormal value.

So the main conclusions derived from the analysis are unambiguous. Strains differ from one another in tooth number and also in their reactions to temperature change. Races also differ from one another, and to a greater degree than do strains ; but they do not show any interaction with temperature. The choice of the proper error variance is essential to the rigorous testing of these various items. Failure to make use of the proper variance could result in seriously faulty conclusions.

REFERENCES

FISHER, R. A. 1937. *The Design of Experiments*. Oliver and Boyd. Edinburgh. 2nd ed.

—— and YATES, F. 1943. *Statistical Tables for Biological, Agricultural and Medical Research*. Oliver and Boyd. Edinburgh. 2nd ed.

IMMER, F. R., HAYES, H. K., and POWERS, L. R. 1934. Statistical determination of barley varietal adaptation. *J. Amer. Soc. Agron.*, **26**, 403–19.

MATHER, K., and DOBZHANSKY, TH. 1939. Morphological differences between the ' races ' of *Drosophila pseudo-obscura*. *Amer. Nat.*, **73**, 5–25.

CHAPTER VII

PLANNING EXPERIMENTS

27. THE FACTORIAL EXPERIMENT

THE development of the analysis of variance has profoundly affected the planning of experiments, for two reasons. In the first place the full advantage of this technique can only be obtained if the data fulfil certain requirements; and secondly, more complex and informative experiments are made possible by the separation of particular comparisons in the analysis of variance. The new technique of experimentation has been developed and discussed at length by Fisher in his book *The Design of Experiments*. His main principles may be illustrated quite simply.

Suppose it is desired to test the effect on growth of feeding two substances, A and B, to some animal, say the rat. The traditional way of doing the experiment would be to divide the available rats into three groups, using one, to which neither A nor B was fed, as a control, and giving one of the remaining two groups the control diet with the addition of A and the other the control diet with the addition of B. Since it would be expected that the individual response to any treatment would vary, large numbers of rats would be used in each group and some precaution might be taken with a view to equalizing the distribution of animals of the various ages and sizes among the groups. A likely variant of this procedure would be to investigate the effects of A and B in two separate experiments. A control group would be used on each occasion so that twice as many rats would receive this treatment as either of the others.

The logic of this technique is not difficult to follow. Uncontrollable variation will be encountered and so everything must be done to make the effects of A and B, respectively, as striking as possible in order that the error variation will not obscure them. Thus it would be bad policy to mix up A and B as the former treatment would increase the apparent variability of the B experiment and make its effect more difficult to establish, and *vice versa*. Then again, large numbers of rats would be used without paying too much regard to their origin, as increase in numbers reduces the variability of the mean response. Lastly, the animals might be assigned to the treatments in some particular way to reduce the error to a minimum. Thus the emphasis is laid throughout on the reduction of variability by whatever means are available. It would probably also be maintained that the A and B tests must be separated, since a joint test would give no means of determining their individual effects.

Fisher's approach differs in two fundamental respects. In the first place he lays stress on the estimation of the uncontrollable, or error, variation rather than on its minimization; though any device, and he has developed several, which reduces this error without invalidating the measurement of the residuum, is to be adopted. Secondly, he emphasizes the benefits of including as many as possible of the factors, whose effects are to be determined, in a single experiment. There are three such advantages, viz. (a) greater precision of comparison is obtained for the expenditure of a given amount of labour or space, (b) information is obtained on more points than the older type of experiment can possibly give, and (c) there is a wider inductive basis for any conclusion which might be reached as a consequence of the experiment.

Let us consider these various points in more detail. First of all there is the question of error variation. Once it has been shown that any error variation occurs at all, the problem of testing whether any apparent effect of a specific treatment is real or only illusory, in that it arises from the error variation, reduces to that of deciding whether the differences could reasonably be attributed to random fluctuation or not. In other words, a test of significance, of the kind we have discussed earlier, is involved; and such a test of significance demands the use of an unbiased estimate of sampling error variation. No matter how large or small the error may be, it can be used if, and only if, its magnitude is known. Any device which reduces the error variation is clearly of value, but it must not invalidate the estimate of residual error. The older idea of stressing the necessity of reducing error variation to a minimum clearly assumes the necessity for taking this variance into account when judging the effect of a treatment; but it misses the real requirement of providing a means of making this judgement, viz. the necessity for the provision of an estimate of the error's magnitude.

Next we may turn to the method of applying the treatments in an experiment. Fisher advocates the use of what he terms the factorial experiment, i.e. the division of the material into a sufficiently large number of groups for every combination of treatments to be applied to some fixed number of these groups. Certain restrictions of the combinations may be imposed without destroying the factorial nature of the experiment, as will be seen later, but in principle all combinations of treatments are used.

In the rat experiment, detailed above, there are four combinations of treatments, A and B used together, A alone, B alone, and O, i.e. no treatment. So at least four groups of experimental animals would be required, though, of course, any multiple of four would do equally well. One of the four groups would receive each of the four treatment combinations. The effect of A will be found as $(AB-B)+(A-O)$, where AB is the effect of the double treatment, A that of A alone, B that of B alone and O that of using neither substance. The B comparison would similarly be $(AB-A)+(B-O)$. These are clearly comparisons which can be used in the analysis of variance, provided that the number of animals assigned to each group is equal. It might be added that such equality in numbers is presupposed in the whole design, as otherwise the comparisons given would obviously fail to measure the effect desired. When regarded from the standpoint of the analysis of variance it is apparent that we can also take out an interaction comparison $(AB-A-B+O)$ which is independent of the A and B items and gives information as to the additive nature of the two effects.

Every animal is used in the formulation of each of these three comparisons, so that the experiment has full efficiency for each of the main effects and also for their interaction. This is in marked contradistinction to the type of experiment outlined earlier, which has at most only $\frac{2}{3}$ efficiency for the main effects of A and B and supplies no information on their interaction. It might be noted that as the number of treatments increases, more and more information is to be extracted from the factorial experiment, as more and more interactions are calculable. The older experiment, on the other hand, gives less and less information, as more groups must be sacrificed for new treatments. In fact, the case of two treatments shows this type of experiment at its best, and how good that best is when compared with Fisher's factorial design has already been seen.

The information about treatment interactions is of immense importance in exploratory experiments where no earlier information is available. In later experiments, when interactions may be known to be of less importance, they can be sacrificed for the purpose of still further increasing the precision of the main comparisons. It will also be seen that by using all the combinations of treatments the effects of A and B are tested in a wider variety of circumstances and so the experiment provides a broader inductive basis for any conclusions which may be drawn. Any statements about the effect of, say, A will take into account its interaction with B and with C, D, &c., as well, if more treatments are used.

The factorial experiment is intimately bound up with the analysis of variance; indeed, the whole success of the factorial design depends on the separation of comparisons in the way made possible by the analysis of variance. This potentiality may also be used for the partial control of error. Suppose, for example, that, in the rat experiment, animals were available from a number of litters. There is likely to be more variation in response to treatment between animals from different litters than between animals of the same litter. Now if, say, four animals are used from each litter, one receiving each of the four treatment combinations, a series of comparisons may be isolated in the analysis of variance for the differences between litter responses. These will probably have larger mean squares than the remaining comparisons within litters and the error variation will be correspondingly reduced.

Consideration of a number of actual experiments carried out along these lines will show how the principles of the factorial design are applied in practice.

28. AN EXPERIMENT WITH THREE FACTORS

Example 9. The following results are taken from a larger experiment on the effect of environment on callus formation in apple cuttings, conducted by Shippy. The whole experiment was not in fact completely factorial though the portion used here is of this kind.

The principal object of the experiment was to discover whether temperature had any effect on the rate of callus formation, but two other variables could conveniently be introduced, viz. (a) the difference between scion cuttings of the variety Yellow Transparent and seedlings of a certain winter hardy northern strain and (b) the time factor in callus formation. Both kinds of material were cut back and their callus allowed to develop at 20° C. and at 32° C., the growth being determined at intervals of 5 and 7 days after cutting. The amount of growth was measured as the diameter, in units of one-quarter millimeter, of the callus roll on lip, base, and sides of the cut surface. These measurements require a considerable time to make, and so it was impossible to use more than one cutting of each kind at each temperature. To increase the number of observations, two series were started, the second a few days after the first.

Eight cuttings were used in all, four in each of the two series. Two in each series were Yellow Transparent scions, while the other two were hardy stock cuttings, and these were kept one at each temperature. Each cutting had its callus measured twice, once after 5 days and once after 7 days, so there were 16 observations in all, as set out in Table 18.

There are 15 degrees of freedom in the whole analysis, and these can be subdivided into components testing various effects. If we sum like observations of the two series there will result eight totals separable in the basis of (a) temperature, (b) variety, and (c) time of observation. Each variety is observed at each temperature at each time. So there will be four totals (i.e. eight observations) at each temperature and the temperature totals will be independent of both variety and time (and also, of course, of series), since all combinations of variety and time are included equally, viz. twice, in each temperature. Similarly four totals are recorded for each variety, and the varietal effect is independent of temperature and time. Finally a time comparison can be made independently of variety and temperature in the same way.

TABLE 18
The Growth of Callus by Apple Cuttings (Shippy)

Time of observation and series	Temperature and variety	20° C. Scion	20° C. Stock	32° C. Scion	32° C. Stock	Total
Series 1	5 days	3	3	9	7	22
	7 days	9	9	19	7	44
Series 2	5 days	3	2	7	3	15
	7 days	8	5	5	3	21
Total		23	19	40	20	102

Scion = Yellow Transparent. Stock = Hardy northern strain.

There are two varieties, two temperatures, and two times, so that these three main effects will each take 1 degree of freedom. The remaining 4, of the 7 degrees of freedom between the eight treatment totals, are ascribable to interactions, one of the first order between temperature and varieties, one of the first order between temperatures and times, one of the first order between varieties and times and one of the second order between all three treatments.

So 7 of the 15 degrees of freedom are accounted for by treatment comparisons of various kinds. The remaining 8 depend on differences between the duplicate observations of eight treatment combinations in the two series. These can be profitably subdivided still further. One is assignable to the total difference between series 1 and series 2, being independent of treatments since these were equally represented in the two series. The remaining 7 are interactions of the treatment effects with the series comparison. They need not be isolated, but can be jointly used to give an estimate of error variation.

It should be noticed that this analysis has depended throughout on the factorial nature of the experiment. The effect of temperature, for example, can be separated from those of variety and time only because each temperature includes exactly equal numbers of observations on each variety at each time. For every observation at 20° C. there is one of an exactly similar nature at 32° C. If one or more observations were omitted, or replaced by others of a different status with respect to variety or time or both, this balance would be upset and the comparisons would no longer be independent. Thus the experiment must be carried out with scrupulous care or its whole value will be forfeited. If the various treatment comparisons are tested by the method of Section 23 it will be seen that they answer to all the requirements of orthogonality if, but only if, the factorial design is adopted.

TABLE 19
Analysis of Variance of Apple Callus Growth

Item	Sum of Squares	N	Mean Square	t	Probability
Temperatures (T)	20·25	1	20·25	1·444	0·2–0·1
Variety (V)	36·00	1	36·00	1·914	0·1–0·05
Time (D)	49·00	1	49·00	2·234	0·1–0·05
TV interaction	16·00	1	16·00	1·276	0·3–0·2
TD „	9·00	1	9·00		
VD „	6·25	1	6·25		
TVD „	2·25	1	2·25		
Series	56·25	1	56·25		
Error	68·75	7	9·8214		
Total	263·75	15			

The analysis of variance is given in Table 19. The three main effects and the four interactions of temperature, variety and time are found by the methods of Chapter VI. The correction term is $\frac{102^2}{16}$, i.e. 650·25. The temperature sum of squares is $\frac{1}{8}(42^2+60^2)-650\cdot25$, that for varieties $\frac{1}{8}(63^2+39^2)-650\cdot25$, and that for times $\frac{1}{8}(37^2+65^2)-650\cdot25$. In each case the divisor is 8, because each number which is squared is the sum of eight single observations. These sums of squares could equally have been found by direct utilization of the comparison formulae (Section 25 and Table 11) as

$\frac{1}{16}(60-42)^2$, $\frac{1}{16}(63-39)^2$ and $\frac{1}{16}(65-37)^2$ respectively.

The divisor is now 16 as this number of observations is involved, once each, in every quantity to be squared, or in other words, $S(k^2)=16$.

Two way tables give the material for finding the first-order interactions. That for temperature and variety contains four values, 23, 19, 40, and 20, so the total sum of squares for three degrees of freedom is $\frac{1}{4}(23^2+19^2+40^2+20^2)-650\cdot25$, from which are deducted the main temperature and variety items to give 16·00 for the interaction degree of freedom. The second-order interaction is found similarly from the three way table, by deduction of the three main and three first-order interaction effects.

There remain 8 degrees of freedom for which sums of squares are to be found. The total of the whole 15 can be obtained by squaring the 16 single observations and deducting the correction term. It is 263·75. The 7 degrees of freedom already accounted for take a sum of squares of 138·75 between them, leaving 125·00 for the 8 degrees of freedom under discussion. The totals of the two series are 66 and 36 respectively, so that an item corresponding to 1 degree of freedom can be found and isolated from the total of 8 degrees of freedom just calculated. This sum of squares is $\frac{1}{16}(66-36)^2$, i.e. 56·25, leaving 125·0−56·25 or 68·75 for the 7 error degrees of freedom. The analysis is now complete (Table 19).

After the mean squares have been found a t can be calculated to test the significance of any of the 8 individual items which have been separated. All the three main effects have rather large mean squares, though not one of them is significant at the 5% level. With the exception of one, the interactions are subnormal in size. The experiment is thus inconclusive, but it suggests that either a larger experiment, or one in which the error variation was more carefully controlled by the removal of further factors, in the way the series difference was eliminated, would give significant results for the three main factors, though probably not for their interactions.

Three main points stand out clearly from the analysis. In the first place the elimination of the series difference contributed materially to increasing the precision of the experiment. This elimination is made possible by careful design. A faulty design would not permit the isolation of the main series difference, which would then be included in the error variance, with the result that the latter would be almost twice the value found above. In that case the experiment would be of considerably less value.

Secondly, though temperature and time differences are observed and trend in the direction which would be expected *a priori*, they are not significant when compared with the error variance. The use of a proper experimental technique has allowed of their being adequately tested and has introduced the proper caution into the interpretation of the results.

Lastly, the results show quite clearly that other unisolated error factors are having a marked influence on callus formation. Hence it may be concluded that a full analysis of this process will require a considerable amount of further exploratory research. The two series differed so profoundly that a study of the conditions which varied between them might lead to some enlightenment on this point.

These implications are only realizable because of the adoption of the factorial design, and of the care taken in providing a valid estimate of error variation. This question of the control and estimation of error must be given a more detailed consideration.

29. THE CONTROL OF ERROR

When considering the handling of undesirable variation it is inevitable that the discussion will centre on agricultural field trials, since modern experimental technique was initiated and has reached its greatest elaboration in this realm. It is to field trial designs that we must now turn to see how error can be controlled.

It has been shown that a special item of uncontrollable variation can be estimated and removed from the error term. Two questions next arise: (a) Can more than one item be so removed? and (b) What precautions must be taken to prevent this process from invalidating the estimate of error? Clearly the first question turns largely on the second one.

In order to reach an answer to this second question it is necessary to recall the principles of a test of significance. The deviation of the observation to be tested is compared with the estimated variance, or with the standard deviation, of a frequency distribution representing the effects of the variables which, though present, are not being controlled in the experiment. In order to estimate this error variance a number of observations are made of individuals from the distribution, and these individuals must be taken at random from the population of which they form part. If this is not done the estimate of variance will be biased in one direction or another and so will lead to spuriously large or small probabilities when used in the test of significance, for the whole analysis is, as we have seen, based on the assumption that sampling is a random process.

Now suppose that one of the several variables determining the magnitude of the individuals in the population is recognizable. The population can then be divided into two parts containing respectively the individuals showing the action of one phase of this variable and those showing the action of the other phase. Provided that these two sub-populations are then sampled at random the variance of each will be estimated without bias, or, as is more commonly done, the sum of squares of deviations from the means of both sub-populations will, on pooling, give an unbiased estimate of the variance of the two distributions taken together. So the prerequisite for the successful isolation of one cause of variation, while retaining the possibility of estimating the residual error, is that the various observations shall be made at random within the two groups separated by the variable to be isolated. It is then clearly possible to go further and say that any number of error variables may be isolated without affecting the validity of the estimate of error, provided always that the observations are made at random within the sub-populations distinguished by these means. This will also be true if the means of separating the sub-populations is a controlled treatment rather than an observable, but uncontrollable, variable. That which holds for one type of separation also holds for the other.

The necessary and sufficient condition for the correct estimation of error is the random sampling within such groups as may be distinguished in the experiment. Now the way that the controlled treatments are applied to the material of the experiment may have a considerable effect on this sampling. Suppose that, in a replicated experiment, we are applying two alternative treatments A and O, having a difference in effect of a, to two different individuals who differ to the extent x as a result of uncontrolled variation. If A is always applied to the individual which is larger as a result of the effect x the observable difference between the two individuals will be $a+x$ in all replications. If A is applied to the lesser individual the difference will always be $a-x$. If A and O are assigned to the individuals at random the estimate of a will be unaffected by x and the estimate of x be unaffected by a. Furthermore, no systematic allocation of A or O can be used, because although the two individuals are here formally distinguished into greater and lesser, in practice it is impossible to predict which of the two will be the larger and which the smaller. Furthermore, they will not always differ by the exact amount x in all replications. Random assignment of the treatments is the only way of overcoming these difficulties.

A little reflection will show that the absolute magnitudes of the individuals in each replication need not be fixed. The two quantities a and x are estimated from differences between the individuals of the same replication. This method of estimation is always successful provided that the treatments are disposed equally in the replications, i.e. provided that the design is factorial, and that the treatments are allocated at random within the replication. This rule provides the key to the successful design and conduct of all experiments. Furthermore, no matter what restraints are applied in arranging the replications, a valid estimate of error is always obtainable if the different restraints affect both one another and the treatments equally, i.e. if they are orthogonal both to one another and to the treatments.

The application of this principle is well shown by the two simplest designs used in agricultural trials. These are known respectively as the Randomized Block and Latin Square arrangements. In a simple randomized block trial each block is a full replication containing one plot of each treatment or treatment combination, these being assigned at random to the various plots in the block. The apple callus experiment of Example 9 is an experiment of this kind. Each of the two series was a 'block' containing all the treatment combinations. If the experiment had consisted of two series each containing single individuals of eight varieties, as in a variety trial, it would still have been a randomized block arrangement, but the degrees of freedom for treatment comparisons would have had different meanings. In other words, the operation of the restraint introduced by arrangement into two equal series is unaffected by the interrelations of the treatments themselves. The estimate of error is the same in all cases, being dependent on the variation of the different treatment comparisons from block to block.

The Latin square is more instructive to consider in detail. It contains a double restraint in layout, as compared with the single restraint of the randomized block. The latter merely demands that a given treatment combination shall occur once in each block and, as a result, one item for block differences is removed from the error in the analysis of variance. The Latin square has n^2 plots arranged in n rows each of n plots. A square of 9 plots would be arranged as 3 rows of 3 plots thus:

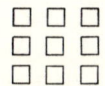

☐ ☐ ☐
☐ ☐ ☐
☐ ☐ ☐

It will be seen that this arrangement can also be regarded equally well as 3 columns each of 3 plots. If a row is considered as a block the whole experiment can be designed as 3 blocks each with 3 treatment combinations, but exactly the same result can be reached if the columns are considered as blocks. So if the three treatments are made to occur once in each row and once in each column, a double restraint is brought into operation and two items can be isolated from the error component in the analysis of variance, one for row differences and the other for column differences.

A sample 3×3 square is

   A B C
   C A B
   B C A

where A, B and C represent the three treatment comparisons. This design conforms to the necessary conditions since groups are separable on the basis of either columns or rows, the remaining restraint and also the treatments, indicated by letters, being equally represented in all of them. Rows, columns and treatments are orthogonal to one another. If the layout were

   A B C A
   C A B
   B C

the restraints and the treatments would not be orthogonal and the design would be unsound.

One further point must be taken into account in laying out a Latin square. Within the limits of the restraints the assignments of treatments to plots must be at random. There are 12 possible ways of laying out a 3×3 square, as shown in Table 20, and the random allocation of treatments to plots means the random selection of one of these twelve designs. In this case 12 squares are all obtainable from one another by rearrangement of the order of rows and columns; but this cannot be done with all sizes of square. A 4×4 square may be of any of 4 standard types, which cannot be converted into one another by reshuffling rows and columns. With higher squares still more standard types are obtained.

TABLE 20
The Twelve 3×3 Latin Squares

A B C	A C B	B C A	B A C
B C A	B A C	C A B	C B A
C A B	C B A	A B C	A C B
C B A	C A B	A B C	A C B
A C B	A B C	C A B	C B A
B A C	B C A	B C A	B A C
B C A	B A C	C B A	C A B
A B C	A C B	B A C	B C A
C A B	C B A	A C B	A B C

In planning experiments where the Latin square design is used it may be very tedious making up a square for the purpose. Certainly the process is rendered much more rapid if the various types of square of a given size are catalogued. This cataloguing has now been done up to and including the 7×7 square, of which there are 61,428,210,278,400 types. Whether any higher ones will be catalogued is, however, doubtful, as the labour required will be very great even for the 8×8 size. Many sample squares of high order are given in Fisher and Yates's tables.

The analysis of the results obtained from a Latin square experiment presents no great difficulty, as the following example taken from the Rothamsted Report of 1931 will show.

Example 10. It was desired to determine whether sulphate of potash and superphosphate would affect the yield of 'Arran Chief' potatoes grown at a place in the Eastern Counties. Furthermore, the phosphatic manure was to be tested at three levels in order to obtain some idea of the most economic dressing to use.

Superphosphate was applied at the levels of 0 cwt. (P_0), 5 cwts. (P_1) and 10 cwts. (P_2) per acre, and the sulphate of potash at the two levels of 0 cwt. (K_0) and 2 cwts. (K_1) per acre. There are six possible combinations of these treatments, and so a 6×6 Latin square was used. In addition, certain plots received a nitrogenous dressing, but this will be disregarded as it apparently had no effect and complicates both design and analysis. Each of the plots was $\frac{1}{70}$ acre in size. The detailed arrangement was as shown in Table 21, which also gives the yield, in lbs., of the various plots. The different treatment combinations were, of course, assigned at random within the restraints of the experiment. The margins show the summed yields of rows and columns, while the summed yields of the different treatment combinations are given in the subsidiary table at the bottom.

The analysis of variance is given in Table 22. The correction term is $\frac{8,729^2}{36}$, i.e. 2,116,540·0278, as the total yield of 36 plots is 8,729 lbs. The total sum of squares for all 36 plots is found to be 2,184,663−2,116,540·0278, i.e. 68,122·9722.

The six row totals are based on 6 plots and so the sum of squares for row differences becomes

$\frac{1}{6}(1,430^2+1,411^2+1,486^2+1,356^2+1,558^2+1,488^2)-2,116,540 \cdot 0278$
$=4,170 \cdot 1389$

Similarly the column sum of squares is 40,481·1389. Lastly, the sum of squares for treatment differences is calculated from the six entries in the subsidiary table. Each of these is the sum of 6 observations made on plots receiving treatments as indicated by the headings in the left margin and top row. The calculation is

$\frac{1}{6}(1,286^2+1,317^2+1,419^2+1,540^2+1,511^2+1,656^2)-2,116,540 \cdot 0278$
$=16,610 \cdot 4722$

TABLE 21
The Yield of 'Arran Chief' Potatoes in a Fertilizer Trial
(Rothamsted Report)

The fertilizer treatment is given above and the yield in lbs. below in each plot of the 6×6 Latin Square

K_1P_0 186	K_0P_2 187	K_0P_0 208	K_0P_1 222	K_1P_1 296	K_1P_2 331	Row totals 1,430
K_1P_1 213	K_0P_0 134	K_1P_2 296	K_0P_2 265	K_0P_1 250	K_1P_0 253	1,411
K_0P_1 198	K_1P_0 155	K_0P_2 272	K_1P_2 290	K_0P_0 261	K_1P_1 310	1,486
K_1P_2 233	K_1P_1 184	K_0P_1 218	K_1P_0 234	K_0P_2 248	K_0P_0 239	1,356
K_0P_2 245	K_1P_2 233	K_1P_1 282	K_0P_0 248	K_1P_0 247	K_0P_1 303	1,558
K_0P_0 196	K_0P_1 228	K_1P_0 242	K_1P_1 255	K_1P_2 273	K_0P_2 294	1,488
Column totals 1,271	1,121	1,518	1,514	1,575	1,730	Grand total 8,729

Treatment Totals

	P_0	P_1	P_2	$P_0+P_1+P_2$	P_2-P_0	$P_2-2P_1+P_0$
K_0	1,286	1,419	1,511	4,216	225	−41
K_1	1,317	1,540	1,656	4,513	339	−107
K_1+K_0	2,603	2,959	3,167	8,729	564	−148
K_1-K_0	31	121	145	297	114	−66

TABLE 22
Analysis of Variance of the Potato Yields

Item	Sum of Squares	N	Mean Square	Variance Ratio	t	Probability
Rows	4,170·1389	5	834·0278	2·431		0·20–0·05
Columns	40,481·1389	5	8,096·2278	23·600		very small
K	2,450·2500	1	2,450·2500		2·673	0·02–0·01
P_1	13,254·0000	1	13,254·0000		6·215	very small
P_2	304·2222	1	304·2222		0·942	0·40–0·30
KP_1	541·5000	1	541·5000		1·257	0·30–0·20
KP_2	60·5000	1	60·5000		0·420	0·70–0·60
[Treatments (total)	16,610·4722	5	3,322·0944	9·684		very small]
Error	6,861·2222	20	343·0611			
Total	68,122·9722	35				

The three items, rows, columns and treatments, account for 5 degrees of freedom each, leaving, out of the total of 35, 20 degrees of freedom for the estimation of error. The error sum of squares is found by subtracting the row, column and treatment sums of squares from the total, to give

68,122·9722−(4,170·1389+40,481·1389+16,610·4722)=6,861·2222

This completes the first analysis and it will be seen that after finding the mean squares and, from them, the variance ratios, the column and treatment items are significant. The row item is just not significant at the 5% level. In spite of this, however, the double restraint was most probably justified as the row mean square is fairly large and, in any case, a randomized block experiment, unless very fortunately arranged, would not have removed the full soil effect shown by the columns, with a consequent loss in efficiency.

If the six treatment combinations had been unrelated, or dependent on varietal differences, no further analysis would be possible; but in the present case a more searching inquiry into the effects of the different fertilizers can be made. Full analysis is possible as the design incorporates all possible combinations of K_0, K_1 and P_0, P_1 and P_2 equally.

There are 5 degrees of freedom for differences between the six combinations. One of these is ascribable to the main effect of sulphate of potash and will be calculated from the (K_1-K_0) differences. Three such differences exist, distinguished by the presence of P_2, P_1 or P_0 in the plots from which they are found. The whole comparison may be represented as:

$$(K_1P_0-K_0P_0+K_1P_1-K_0P_1+K_1P_2-K_0P_2)$$

The six k coefficients are all 1 in this expression, but as each item is the sum of six observations the divisor must be 6(1+1+1+1+1+1) if the sum of squares is to be placed on the basis of single plots. This may be expressed somewhat differently by saying that the divisor is 36 as the number to be squared is compounded of 36 observations used once each. Arithmetically this sum of squares is found as

$$\tfrac{1}{36}(1,317-1,286+1,540-1,419+1,656-1,511)^2, \text{ i.e. } 2,450\cdot2500$$

This could, of course, equally have been found as

$$\tfrac{1}{18}(4,216^2+4,513^2)-\frac{8,729^2}{36}$$

There are three phosphate treatments and so there will be 2 degrees of freedom for differences between them. The total sum of squares corresponding to these two degrees of freedom can be obtained from the P_2, P_1 and P_0 totals summed over

K_1 and K_0 as shown in the third line of the subsidiary Table 21. This gives

$$\tfrac{1}{12}(2,603^2+2,959^2+3,167^2)-\frac{8\,729^2}{36} \text{ or } 13,558\cdot 2222$$

There still remain 2 degrees of freedom for the interaction of K and P. Subtraction of the main K and P items from the total sum of squares for treatments leaves 602·0000 for this interaction sum of squares. It could also have been found from the (K_1-K_0) values in the bottom line of the subsidiary table, by taking

$$\tfrac{1}{12}(31^2+121^2+145^2)-\frac{297^2}{36}$$

This calculation is strictly analogous to that of the main P sum of squares from the (K_1+K_0) sums of the line above.

The analytical possibilities do not stop here. The 2 degrees of freedom for the main effect of P and the 2 degrees of freedom for the KP interaction may be separated into their components. We might expect that if P has any effect at all the treatment P_2 will have twice the effect of the treatment P_1. This suggests the subdivision of the P effect into single items based on the comparisons (P_2-P_0) and $(P_2-2P_1+P_0)$ respectively. The first one tests whether phosphates are effective manures, while the second tests the linearity of the response, if any. The sums of squares are found from the formulae:

$$\tfrac{1}{24}(K_1P_2+K_0P_2-K_1P_0-K_0P_0)^2$$
$$\tfrac{1}{72}(K_1P_2+K_0P_2-2K_1P_1-2K_0P_1+K_1P_0+K_0P_0)^2$$

These are easily shown to be independent comparisons. Indeed, the only point about them requiring comment is the determination of the divisors. The first one presents little difficulty, as the number to be squared is based on 24 observations each used once. The second is a little more troublesome because 12 plots are used twice each in addition to the 24 used once. Section 23 shows that the divisor must be $S(k^2)$. In this case $k=1$ for 24 entries and $k=2$ for the remaining twelve, and so $S(k^2)$ is

$$(24\times 1)+(12\times 4)=72$$

The two sums of squares are then

$$\tfrac{1}{24}(1,656+1,511-1,317-1,286)^2=13,254\cdot 0000$$
and $\tfrac{1}{72}(1,656+1,511-2\times 1,540-2\times 1,419+1,317+1,286)^2=304\cdot 2222$

which together equal the joint sum of squares found earlier.

The analysis of the KP interaction is conducted similarly, except that it is based on the (K_1-K_0) differences instead of on the (K_1+K_0) sums used in the calculation of the main effects of P. The divisors are just as before, so that the two sums of squares are:

$$\tfrac{1}{24}(145-31)^2=541{\cdot}5000$$

and $$\tfrac{1}{72}(145-\overline{2\times121}+31)^2=60{\cdot}50000$$

The analysis of variance has now been taken to its limit. The significance of the five separate treatment effects may be determined by the use of t's because each is based on one degree of freedom. Each t will have, of course, 20 degrees of freedom as this number of comparisons was used in the estimation of error. The main effect of potash, marked K in the analysis, and also the item testing the effect of phosphate, marked P_1, are highly significant. The potatoes respond to both manures. The item P_2 testing for departure from a linear response to phosphate is not significant. So it would appear that a double dose of phosphate has twice the effect of a single dose. Neither of the potash-phosphate interactions is significant and so there is no evidence that the response to one manure is affected by the presence or absence of the other.

The main points to be observed about the design of this experiment are (a) the retention of the factorial design, which allows of fine analysis of the treatment effects, while a double restraint is applied to reduce the error variance, and (b) the method of obtaining a valid estimate of error when a doubly restrained design is used.

Squares afford the possibility of applying more than two restraints to the design. In a 3×3 square, for example, we can assign three Greek letters in such a way that each occurs once in every row, once in every column and once with every Latin letter, thus:

$$\begin{matrix} A_\gamma & B_\beta & C_\alpha \\ C_\beta & A_\alpha & B_\gamma \\ B_\alpha & C_\gamma & A_\beta \end{matrix}$$

Not all Latin squares are capable of being turned into Graeco-Latin squares of this type. Of the four standard types of 4×4 squares only one gives a Graeco-Latin design, viz.

$$\begin{matrix} A_\alpha & B_\beta & C_\gamma & D_\delta \\ B_\gamma & A_\delta & D_\alpha & C_\beta \\ C_\delta & D_\gamma & A_\beta & B_\alpha \\ D_\beta & C_\alpha & B_\delta & A_\gamma \end{matrix} \quad \text{or} \quad \begin{matrix} A_\alpha & B_\beta & C_\gamma & D_\delta \\ B_\delta & A_\gamma & D_\beta & C_\alpha \\ C_\beta & D_\alpha & A_\delta & B_\gamma \\ D_\gamma & C_\delta & B_\alpha & A_\beta \end{matrix}$$

These two Graeco-Latin squares cannot be mutually transformed by reshuffling rows and columns or even letters, and so they are distinct standard types. A single type of Latin square may give several types of Graeco-Latin square in this way, and the number of possibilities with higher-order squares becomes very large.

In practice, however, examples where three or more restraints have been used are seldom encountered. Perhaps this is because such designs have not been used widely outside agricultural work, where a third restraint would do little to help the reduction of soil error variation. In other types of work it is likely that multiple restraints would be advantageous, though they should obviously be used with care sufficient to obviate any loss of precision by the immoderate reduction of the number of error degrees of freedom.

30. CONFOUNDING

Whatever restraints are applied with a view to reducing error variation, the factorial design of the treatment combinations must be retained if the experiment is to be efficient. In all the cases considered so far this has been achieved by the equal use of all possible treatment combinations in every replication. Fisher has shown, however, that this is not necessary for maintaining the factorial nature of the design. Certain limitations of the treatment combinations, which allow the use of more stringent restraints to reduce error variation without affecting the calculation of the treatment effects, are possible.

In order to see how this can happen, let us consider the case of two treatments, A and B, each used at two levels, A_1 and A_0, and B_1 and B_0. A simple randomized block experiment would have four plots to the block, one taking each of the four treatment combinations. There would then be 3 degrees of freedom for differences between treatments and single comparisons could be isolated for the main effects of A and B and for their first-order interaction. With n such blocks the analysis of variance would be:

TABLE 23

Item	N
Blocks	$n-1$
A main effect	1
B main effect	1
AB interaction	1
Error	$3n-3$
Total	$4n-1$

The sums of squares for the three treatment items would be found from the formulae

$$A \quad \frac{1}{4n}(A_1B_1+A_1B_0-A_0B_1-A_0B_0)^2$$

$$B \quad \frac{1}{4n}(A_1B_1-A_1B_0+A_0B_1-A_0B_0)^2$$

$$AB \quad \frac{1}{4n}(A_1B_1-A_1B_0-A_0B_1+A_0B_0)^2$$

The independence of the main effect of A and block differences will be ensured by placing A_1B_1 in the same block as A_0B_1, and A_1B_0 in the same block as A_0B_0, though these two pairs, on the other hand, need not be in the same block. For suppose that A_1B_1 and A_0B_1 are in a block with fertility x, while A_1B_0 and A_0B_0 are in a second block with fertility y, the sum of squares then becomes

$$\tfrac{1}{4}[(A_1B_1+x)+(A_1B_0+y)-(A_0B_1+x)-(A_0B_0+y)]^2$$

This reduces to the original form because the x and y items cancel out. The same result could be achieved by having A_1B_1 and A_0B_0 in block X and A_1B_0 and A_0B_1 in block Y. This is perhaps less obviously true than is the case of the first arrangement, but a little reflection will show that block differences cancel out as before. The rule is apparently that the comparisons can be made free of block differences provided that the two plots of a block have opposite signs in the formula from which the sum of squares is calculated.

The B comparison may also be found independently of block differences if the treatments are paired in either of the two ways

	Block X			Block Y	
(a)	A_1B_1 and A_1B_0			A_0B_1 and A_0B_0	
(b)	A_1B_1 and A_0B_0			A_0B_1 and A_1B_0	

Similarly, pairs which will give an unbiased estimate of the interaction item are:

	Block X			Block Y	
(a)	A_1B_1 and A_1B_0			A_0B_1 and A_0B_0	
(b)	A_1B_1 and A_0B_1			A_1B_0 and A_0B_0	

These various arrangements are collected together in Table 24, together with the comparisons from which the three sums of squares are calculated. There are three arrangements of pairs in

TABLE 24
Confounding Arrangements

Comparisons		
Main effect A	$A_1B_1+A_1B_0-A_0B_1-A_0B_0$
Main effect B	$A_1B_1-A_1B_0+A_0B_1-A_0B_0$
Interaction AB	$A_1B_1-A_1B_0-A_0B_1+A_0B_0$

Pairs of plots in block		Comparisons	
X	Y	Recoverable	Confounded
A_1B_1 A_1B_0	A_0B_1 A_0B_0	B and AB	A
A_1B_1 A_0B_1	A_1B_0 A_0B_0	A and AB	B
A_1B_1 A_0B_0	A_1B_0 A_0B_1	A and B	AB

two blocks and each arrangement permits the isolation of two of the three treatment comparisons independently of block differences. The third comparison is inextricably mixed up with the differences in fertility between the two blocks and cannot be recovered. It is said to be 'confounded' with block differences.

So by sacrificing one of the three treatment comparisons the number of plots per block is halved and the number of blocks can be doubled. This may be of great value where either the number of 'plots' per 'block' is limited, as in twin research or feeding experiments with animals, or where it is necessary to keep the block size small in order to reap the full benefit which local control gives in the reduction of error variation.

Confounding would probably not often be practised in such a simple case as that outlined, but the same principles apply to more complex experiments such as the one on asparagus described by Wishart.

Example 11. Table 25 gives the yield in lbs. per plot of asparagus which had been subjected to all combinations of the three fertilizers, nitrogen (N), phosphate (P) and potash (K) each at two levels. Eight blocks each of four plots were used. Four of the blocks had one plot each with dressings of nitrogen alone (N), phosphate alone (P), potash alone (K) and all three together (NPK). The other four blocks each had one plot with no fertilizer (O), with nitrogen and phosphate together (NP), with nitrogen and potash together (NK), and with phosphate and potash together (PK).

The design involves confounding, as each block carries but four of the eight possible treatment combinations, though all eight have been used equally when the whole experiment is taken into account. Our first task, then, is to determine which comparison or comparisons have been sacrificed to increase the local control of error variation.

There are seven treatment comparisons whose sums of squares are calculated from the formulae

Main effects
$$\begin{cases} N & \tfrac{1}{32}(NPK-PK+NP-P+NK-K+N-O)^2 \\ P & \tfrac{1}{32}(NPK+PK+NP+P-NK-K-N-O)^2 \\ K & \tfrac{1}{32}(NPK+PK-NP-P+NK+K-N-O)^2 \end{cases}$$

First-order interactions
$$\begin{cases} NP & \tfrac{1}{32}(NPK-PK+NP-P-NK+K-N+O)^2 \\ NK & \tfrac{1}{32}(NPK-PK-NP+P+NK-K-N+O)^2 \\ PK & \tfrac{1}{32}(NPK+PK-NP-P-NK-K+N+O)^2 \end{cases}$$

Second-order interaction NPK $\tfrac{1}{32}(NPK-PK-NP+P-NK+K+N-O)^2$

The divisor is 32 as all comparisons involve, once each, the sums of the four plots, receiving each of the various treatments, there being eight treatments in all.

TABLE 25
Yields of Asparagus in a Fertilizer Trial (Wishart)
The fertilizers are shown above and the yields in lbs. below

Block	Type of block	Plots				Block total
1	X	NPK 12·0	K 16·2	P 14·6	N 12·7	55·5
2	Y	NK 10·2	NP 12·8	PK 13·8	O 13·9	50·7
3	Y	O 14·7	NP 9·3	NK 8·8	PK 9·0	41·8
4	X	N 10·8	P 8·9	K 8·3	NPK 10·3	38·3
5	Y	PK 13·0	O 12·7	NK 11·3	NP 10·3	47·3
6	X	K 13·3	P 15·2	N 12·1	NPK 11·5	52·1
7	X	NPK 11·4	K 10·4	P 11·7	N 9·3	42·8
8	Y	NP 9·1	O 10·5	NK 8·2	PK 13·5	41·3

Treatment Totals

Block X					Block Y					Grand Total
NPK	N	P	K	Group Total	NP	NK	PK	O	Group Total	
45·2	44·9	50·4	48·2	188·7	41·5	38·5	49·3	51·8	181·1	369·8

A comparison of these formulae with the layout adopted shows that in the first six formulae half the plots with a plus sign occur in each of the two types of block, as do those with a minus sign. Thus in the first one, the main N comparison, one type of block contains NPK, N, P and K which have the signs +, +, −, − respectively, while the other type of block contains NP, NK, PK and O with signs +, +, −, −. So the first six comparisons can be recovered free of block differences. The seventh comparison is the one which is confounded. The types of plot with a + sign all occur in one kind of block and those taking a − sign in the comparison are found together in the other kind of block. This comparison cannot be separated from the difference between the two kinds of block.

Having decided which comparison is confounded, the analysis of variance is easy. There are 31 degrees of freedom in all, of which 7 are taken up by block differences, and 6 by unconfounded treatment comparisons. This leaves 18 degrees of freedom for error.

The correction term is $\dfrac{369 \cdot 8^2}{32}$, i.e. 4,273·5013, and the total sum of squares for 31 degrees of freedom is found from the 32 individual observations to be 145·4787. The blocks each contain four plots and so, in the calculation of the block sum of squares, the divisor is 4. This sum of squares is then found in the usual way to be 65·0237. The treatment sum of squares cannot, however, be found in quite the normal fashion, because the 8 treatments yield only 6 degrees of freedom.

If the treatment totals are separated into two groups of four, according to whether they are found from one type of block or the other, there are 3 degrees of freedom within each group. The seventh degree of freedom, that between the groups, is the one which has been confounded and which has already been determined as part of the block difference item. The sum of squares corresponding to the 3 degrees of freedom for treatment comparisons from the first type of block is found as

$$\tfrac{1}{4}(44 \cdot 9^2 + 50 \cdot 4^2 + 48 \cdot 2^2 + 45 \cdot 2^2) - \frac{188 \cdot 7^2}{16}$$

the correction term being derived from the total yield of this group of results. The other set of treatment is similarly obtained as $\tfrac{1}{4}(51 \cdot 8^2 + 41 \cdot 5^2 + 38 \cdot 5^2 + 49 \cdot 3^2) - \dfrac{181 \cdot 1^2}{16}$, giving with the first group a joint sum of squares of 34·8638 for treatments. The error variance is obtained by subtraction from the total sum of squares. The resulting analysis of variance is set out in Table 26, from which it will be seen that while the block item is highly significant that for treatments could reasonably be ascribed to sampling error.

TABLE 26
Analysis of Variance of Asparagus Yields

Item	Sum of Squares	N	Mean Square	Variance Ratio		Probability
Blocks	65·0237	7	9·2891	3·668		0·01
N	27·3800	1	27·3800		3·289	0·01–0·001
P	0·2813	1	0·2813		0·333	0·80–0·70
K	1·7112	1	1·7112		0·822	0·50–0·40
NP	0·4050	1	0·4050		0·400	0·70–0·60
NK	0·1250	1	0·1250		0·222	0·90–0·80
PK	4·9613	1	4·9613		1·400	0·20–0·10
[Treatments (total)	34·8638	6	5·8106	2·294		0·20–0·05]
Error	45·5912	18	2·5328			
Total	145·4787	31				

The next part of the analysis is the decomposition of the treatment comparisons, and the formulae used earlier for the detection of the confounded component can be used for this purpose. The individual items are then found to have the values shown in the analysis of variance. Comparison with the error item by means of t tests shows that the main effect of nitrogen is highly significant, but that all other items fail to show any real departure from expectation. Nitrogen is the only fertilizer which affects the yield. It might be noted that its effect on yield is curious in that the addition of nitrogen decreases, rather than increases, the amount of asparagus harvested.

Taken together, the six treatment items have a barely significant mean square, but when they are decomposed one of them, the main effect of nitrogen, is found to be highly significant. The nitrogen effect was masked by the other five components, but decomposition brings out the relative importance of the various items.

In this example the second-order interaction was completely lost, but a slight modification would have allowed of its recovery though with reduced precision, and at the expense of decreasing the precision of other comparisons. Suppose that the eight blocks are grouped in pairs, each block consisting of an X block and a Y block. Then consider what would have been recoverable if the various X and Y blocks were not alike but had had the following contents:

	Block X	Block Y
1.	NPK, N, P, K	NP, NK, PK, O
2.	NPK, PK, N, O	NK, NP, K, P
3.	NPK, NK, P, O	PK, NP, K, N
4.	NPK, NP, K, O	PK, NK, P, N

The first group is of the type already examined and has the second-order interaction NPK confounded. If group 2, however, is analysed by means of the comparison formulae, it is found to have the first-order interaction of P and K confounded. Similarly, the first-order interactions NK and NP are confounded in groups 3 and 4 respectively. So, such an experiment would give estimates of the three main effects, N, P and K, from all four groups and estimates of each of the interactions from three of the four groups. All treatments are recoverable, but the four interactions have only $\frac{3}{4}$ the precision of the main effects.

Where soil heterogeneity is very marked the use of such a 'partially confounded' design may, by doubling the number of blocks, so reduce the error variance that the $\frac{3}{4}$ precision of the partially confounded comparisons may even be greater than the full precision obtained with half as many blocks each including the full range of treatment combinations. Partial confounding is a very valuable device in the application of complex series of treatments to limited experimental material and has been used with great success by Yates in designing experiments for a large number of different purposes.

There are, however, limitations to the use of confounding. In some cases the confounding of one comparison may automatically mean the confounding of another, and potentially more interesting, item. Reference should be made to accounts given by Fisher and Yates for a more detailed discussion of the scope and limitations of confounding designs. These designs are worth attention as they are likely to be of great value in many kinds of biological experimentation.

REFERENCES

FISHER, R. A. 1937. *The Design of Experiments*. Oliver and Boyd. Edinburgh. 2nd ed.
—— and YATES, F. 1943. *Statistical Tables for Biological, Agricultural and Medical Research*. Oliver and Boyd. Edinburgh. 2nd ed.
Report of the Rothamsted Experimental Station. 1931.
SHIPPY, W. B. 1930. Influence of environment on callusing of apple cuttings and grafts. *Contr. Boyce Thompson Inst.*, **2**, 351–88.
WISHART, J. 1940. *Field Trials : Their Lay-out and Statistical Analysis*. Imperial Bureau of Plant Breeding and Genetics.
YATES, F. 1937. *The Design and Analysis of Factorial Experiments*. Imperial Bureau of Soil Science.

CHAPTER VIII

THE INTERRELATIONS OF TWO VARIABLES

31. LINEAR REGRESSION

IT often happens that in an experiment or series of observations interest centres on the relations holding between two or more measurements made on the same individual, family or occasion. The determination of growth rate, for example, depends on finding the relation between measurements of time and size; the study of heredity demands observations on at least two members of each family, and so on. The statistical reduction of such data is achieved by the use of regression and correlation techniques, of which the former class is much the more widely applicable and so will be considered first.

The law relating the values of two variables to each other may be written algebraically in the form $y=f(x)$, where $f(x)$ represents a function of x of any degree of complexity. It often happens, however, that a simple manipulation or transformation of the data may be used to reduce a complex $f(x)$ to a relatively simple form, so leading to a considerable reduction in the labour of calculation. Thus the compound interest law of growth is often written in the form

$$y = y_0 e^{kx}$$

where x is the time at which the size y is attained, y_0 a constant depending on the size at time 0, and k a constant which is called the efficiency index. Such a formula would be troublesome to handle statistically. But if y is transformed into its logarithm the operations are much simpler, as

$$\log y = \log y_0 + kx$$

This is an expression of the general form $y=a+bx$, which is the equation of a straight line. When faced with the analyses of two variables likely to show a complex relation a search should always be made for a transformation of this kind with a view to reducing the work involved.

The simplest relation between x and y from the statistical point of view is that of the straight line $y=a+bx$, and in consequence this is the most widely used in statistical analysis. The statistical problem which presents itself is that of estimating the constants a and b from data provided by a series of double observations $(x_1 y_1)$, $(x_2 y_2)$, &c. In the case of the growth formula given above, the data would be the size y_1 at time x_1, size y_2 at time x_2, and so on. We could then by logarithmic transformation recast the data into a new series of double observations ($\log y_1$, x_1), ($\log y_2$, x_2) . . ., and so have the material for the estimation of the two constants, $\log y_0$ and k.

If neither x nor y was subject to any uncontrolled, or error, variation the problem would be easy of solution; for it would only be necessary to have two double observations to give the values of the constants.

$$b = k = \frac{\log y_1 - \log y_2}{x_1 - x_2} \quad \text{and} \quad a = \log y_0 = \log y_1 - x_1 \left(\frac{\log y_1 - \log y_2}{x_1 - x_2} \right)$$

Both x and y may, however, be subject to error variation of various kinds and degrees. The estimation of the two constants is then less obvious, and the actual method used will be dependent on the types of error to which each variable is subject. When it is desired to determine a growth law, for example, the size of the individual, y, will be subject to marked variation as a result of genetic, dietetic, climatic or other uncontrolled factors; but the time, x, at which the size observation is made will be known with reasonable exactitude. Now the size, y, of a number of individuals at time x may be considered to be normally distributed about the mean $\bar{y}$. So long as an unbiased estimate of $\bar{y}$ is obtainable, as it will be if the population of individuals is sampled at random in making an observation, the relation of y to x can be fairly determined. Thus error variation in y does not invalidate the calculation provided that no selection is exercised.

The situation with regard to x may be of a very different kind. A serious error in the determination of the time, x, in a growth relation will invalidate the whole calculation, as x is not normally distributed about a mean $\bar{x}$. It will not be subject to the usual treatment of error variation. But it should be noted that any value of x may be chosen for making the corresponding assessment of size, y, without spoiling the data, for there is no question of taking random samples from a large population of times. The time x must be determined accurately, but its values may be selected in such a case.

Where these differences in the type of variation are present, x is called the 'independent variate' and y the 'dependent variate'. The distinction is very important, as the determination of the regression of y on x is a valid statistical operation, while the calculation of the regression of x on y may be vitiated by the wrong assumptions made about the nature of the variation to which the two quantities are subject.

Sometimes, however, x may be subject to error variation like y, in which case selection of the data should not be practised. When x and y are exactly of the same nature, both being subject to error variation, either regression may be calculated with equal validity. Even in this case, however, the two regressions will not be the same. The differences between the regression of y on x and that of x on y will be better appreciated after some concrete cases have been considered.

Where the regression of y on x is linear, i.e. the relation of y to x is representable geometrically as a straight line, the value of y corresponding to any value of x can be found, once the constants a and b are known in the equation $y=a+bx$.* Estimates of a and b could be obtained in any number of ways from a set of double observations, though when the calculated line and the observed points were plotted on a graph some would obviously not be so good as others. It would not, however, always be clear from such inspection which of any two formulae gave the better fit. How, then, should the constants be evaluated?

To answer this question it is necessary to consider the measurement of discrepancy between observed values of y and those expected on the basis of any given formula. In the absence of any information about x, the variability of y, as we have seen in an earlier chapter, would be measured by finding the sum of squares of deviations of y from its mean $\bar{y}$. This would be equivalent to finding the sum of squares of deviations of y from the line $y=\bar{y}$ which, as shown in Fig. 5, is parallel to the x axis of the graph. The sum of squares of departures from any other such line, parallel to the abscissa, would be larger than that found when using $\bar{y}$ as it would include an item representing the square of the difference in position between this new line and the line $y=\bar{y}$. To use such a second line would be equivalent to calculating the sum of squares of deviations from a working mean y_m. We have seen in Section 10 that

$$S(y-\bar{y})^2 = S(y-y_m)^2 - \frac{1}{n}S^2(y-y_m)$$

The last term must be positive as it is a perfect square, and so

$$S(y-y_m)^2 \geqslant S(y-\bar{y})^2$$

Hence, in the absence of information about x, the line best representing the observations is found by minimizing the magnitude of the sums of squares from the value of y which it represents. The best value, $\bar{y}$, gives the smallest sum of squares.

As soon as knowledge of x is introduced it is possible to arrive at expected values of y closer to those observed, for the straight line need no longer be parallel to the abscissa. When y alone was considered, the line could vary in position but not slope. Now it can slope at any angle depending on the constant b, and this slope can bring about a reduction in the sum of

* The determination of the regression of x on y would involve the calculation of the constants a' and b' in the equation $x=a'+b'y$.

squares of deviations from the expectations derived from the line. The sum of squares of y is, in fact, being separated into two parts, one representing departures from the regression line and the other the difference in slope between the regression line and that line parallel to the abscissa through $\bar{y}$. Clearly, then, the best fitting regression line will be the one which maximizes the item attributable to the slope of the line and hence minimizes

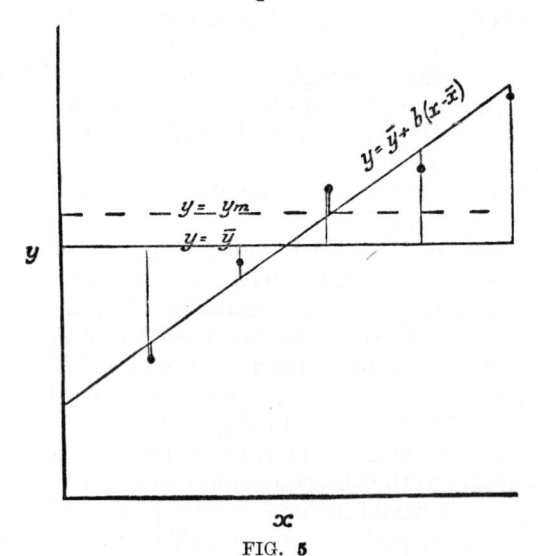

FIG. 5

The relations of the lines $y=y_m$, $y=\bar{y}$ and $y=\bar{y}+b(x-\bar{x})$ to observed points, to show how the deviations of the latter are progressively reduced. Deviations from $y=\bar{y}$ are marked by thin uprights and deviations from $y=\bar{y}+b(x-\bar{x})$ by thick uprights

that attributable to the departure of observation from the linear expectation.

Let x, for convenience' sake, be measured from its mean $\bar{x}$, and let the expected value of y be denoted as Y. Then

$$Y=a+b(x-\bar{x})$$

which gives a deviation of

$$(y-Y)=y-a-b(x-\bar{x})$$

when compared with the observed value y. The sum of squares of such deviations is

$$S(y-Y)^2=S[y-a-b(x-\bar{x})]^2$$
$$=S(y^2)+S(a^2)+S[b(x-\bar{x})]^2-2S(ay)-2S[yb(x-\bar{x})]+2S[ab(x-\bar{x})]$$

which, since a and b are constants and $S(x-\bar{x})=0$, may be written as

$$S(y-Y)^2=S(y^2)+na^2+b^2S(x-\bar{x})^2-2aS(y)-2bS[y(x-\bar{x})]$$

where n is the number of double observations.

THE SAMPLING ERROR OF REGRESSION CONSTANTS 113

We require the values of a and b which will make this sum of squares a minimum. These may be found by partially differentiating with respect to a and b, equating the expressions so obtained to 0 and solving for a and b.

$$\frac{\partial}{\partial a}S(y-Y)^2 = 2an - 2S(y) = 0 \quad \cdot \quad \cdot \quad \cdot \quad \cdot \quad \text{(i)}$$

$$\frac{\partial}{\partial b}S(y-Y)^2 = 2bS(x-\bar{x})^2 - 2S[y(x-\bar{x})] = 0 \quad \cdot \quad \cdot \quad \text{(ii)}$$

From (i) $\qquad a = \dfrac{S(y)}{n} = \bar{y}$

From (ii) $\qquad b = \dfrac{S[y(x-\bar{x})]}{S(x-\bar{x})^2}$ *

This method of finding a and b is referred to as the method of least squares and is basic to the theory of regression. It is a special case of the method of maximum likelihood discussed in Chapter XII.

The formulae for the evaluation of a and b are not surprising. The constant a fixes the position of the regression line and b, which is itself called the regression coefficient, fixes its slope. Now when $x=\bar{x}$, i.e. when x is out of the picture, $y=a=\bar{y}$, as would be expected from the consideration of the case when knowledge of x is lacking. The formula for b bears an obvious resemblance to that used in finding the standard deviation of a distribution (Section 10). The other possibility that b is evaluated as the ratio of the sums of deviations of y and x from their means, neglecting sign, resembles the calculation of the mean deviation rather than the standard deviation of a distribution, and the mean deviation is not so informative a measure as the standard deviation.

32. THE SAMPLING ERROR OF REGRESSION CONSTANTS

Having found a and b, it is next necessary to determine the sampling errors to which they are subject. These are dependent on the residual variation of y about the regression line. We have found that $a=\bar{y}$ and $b=\dfrac{S[y(x-\bar{x})]}{S(x-\bar{x})^2}$. In each case the greater the error variance of y the greater the possible random fluctuation in a and b. So the first step is to calculate the sampling variance of y itself. This is dependent on the sum of squares of deviations of y from the regression line and can always be found by squaring and summing these deviations. There is, however, an easier

---

* $S[y(x-\bar{x})] = S[(y-\bar{y})(x-\bar{x})]$ since $S[(y-\bar{y})(x-\bar{x})] = S[y(x-\bar{x}) - \bar{y}(x-\bar{x})]$
$\qquad = S[y(x-\bar{x})] - \bar{y}S(x-\bar{x})$ and $S(x-\bar{x}) = 0$.

calculation which will give the same results. Substituting for a and b in the general regression formula we find

$$S(y-Y)^2 = S\left[y-\bar{y}-(x-\bar{x})\frac{S[y(x-\bar{x})]}{S(x-\bar{x})^2}\right]^2$$

$$= S\left[y^2+\bar{y}^2-2y\bar{y}+(x-\bar{x})^2\frac{S^2[y(x-\bar{x})]}{S^2(x-\bar{x})^2}-2y(x-\bar{x})\frac{S[y(x-\bar{x})]}{S(x-\bar{x})^2}\right.$$
$$\left.-2\bar{y}(x-\bar{x})\frac{S[y(x-\bar{x})]}{S(x-\bar{x})^2}\right]$$

$$= S(y^2)+n\bar{y}^2-2\bar{y}S(y)+\frac{S(x-\bar{x})^2 S^2[y(x-\bar{x})]}{S^2(x-\bar{x})^2}$$
$$-\frac{2S^2[y(x-\bar{x})]}{S(x-\bar{x})^2}-\frac{2\bar{y}S(x-\bar{x})S[y(x-\bar{x})]}{S(x-\bar{x})^2}$$

which, since $S(y)=n\bar{y}$ and $S(x-\bar{x})=0$, gives

$$S(y-Y)^2 = S(y^2) - \frac{S^2(y)}{n} - \frac{S^2[y(x-\bar{x})]}{S(x-\bar{x})^2}$$

The various terms of this expression are easily recognized. The second is the usual correction for a working mean of 0, i.e. for not using a $\bar{y}$ as the origin in measuring y, and so constitutes a deduction depending on the value of a. The third and last term is $-bS[y(x-\bar{x})]$ and is the correction for the sum of squares removed by the slope of the regression line. It bears the same relation to b, i.e. to $\frac{S[y(x-\bar{x})]}{S(x-\bar{x})^2}$, as the correction for the mean, viz. $\frac{S^2(y)}{n}$, does to the mean itself. In this way the sum of squares of deviations of y from its mean is partitioned into parts attributable to regression and residual error.

As a sum of squares can be attributed to the effect of fitting a regression coefficient b, there must be a corresponding partition of the degrees of freedom. Where one value of y is observed there will be one comparison with any theoretically fixed mean; but if the mean is to be estimated from the data the value itself will provide the best estimate of this parameter. So there will be no degree of freedom for the estimation of the variance. This is, it will be remembered, the reason for the use of $n-1$ as the number of degrees of freedom in calculating the variance of y. Since $a=\bar{y}$ the calculation of a from the data is accommodated by the use of $N=n-1$.

When there are two observations, fitting the mean will still leave one comparison available for the estimate of the variance. But a straight line can be drawn through any two points on a graph showing the relation of y to x. Hence the calculation of b removes the single remaining degree of freedom. Then clearly with n observations, $n-2$ degrees of freedom remain after a and

THE SAMPLING ERROR OF REGRESSION CONSTANTS 115

b have both been fitted. It is another example of the loss of one degree of freedom when a parameter has been estimated from the data.

The analysis of variance of y obtained in this way is

Item	Sum of Squares	N
Regression	$\dfrac{S^2[y(x-\bar{x})]}{S(x-\bar{x})^2}$	1
Remainder or error	$S(y^2) - \dfrac{S^2(y)}{n} - \dfrac{S^2[y(x-\bar{x})]}{S(x-\bar{x})^2}$	$n-2$
Total	$S(y^2) - \dfrac{S^2(y)}{n}$	$n-1$

The test of significance of b is now obvious. The two mean squares are found and their ratio is a t for $n-2$ degrees of freedom, which will test whether the calculation of b has removed a significantly large sum of squares, i.e. whether b differs significantly from 0. If b does not differ significantly from 0 then, so far as the observations go, y is unrelated to x. If b is significant it constitutes the best estimate of the change in y for each unit change in x.

The standard errors of a and b are not difficult to find when the sampling error of y is known. The variance of y, V_y, is, from the analysis given above,

$$\frac{1}{n-2}\left[S(y^2) - \frac{S^2(y)}{n} - \frac{S^2[y(x-\bar{x})]}{S(x-\bar{x})^2} \right]$$

Now a is the mean of y and so from Section 20

$$V_a = V_{\bar{y}} = \frac{1}{n}V_y = \frac{1}{n(n-2)}\left[S(y^2) - \frac{S^2(y)}{n} - \frac{S^2[y(x-\bar{x})]}{S(x-\bar{x})^2} \right]$$

It was also shown in Section 20 that if y is multiplied by any given quantity, the variance of y is multiplied by the square of the quantity. So

$$V_{y_1(x_1-\bar{x})} = (x_1-\bar{x})^2 V_{y_1}$$

and
$$V_{S[y(x-\bar{x})]} = (x_1-\bar{x})^2 V_{y_1} + (x_2-\bar{x})^2 V_{y_2} + \ldots$$
$$= V_y[(x_1-\bar{x})^2 + (x_2-\bar{x})^2 + \ldots] = V_y S(x-\bar{x})^2$$

as
$$V_{y_1} = V_{y_2} = \ldots = V_y$$

But
$$b = \frac{1}{S(x-\bar{x})^2}(S[y(x-\bar{x})])$$

and so
$$V_b = \frac{1}{S^2(x-\bar{x})^2} V_{S[y(x-\bar{x})]} = \frac{S(x-\bar{x})^2}{S^2(x-\bar{x})^2} V_y = \frac{V_y}{S(x-\bar{x})^2}$$
$$= \frac{1}{(n-2)S(x-\bar{x})^2}\left[S(y^2) - \frac{S^2(y)}{n} - \frac{S^2[y(x-\bar{x})]}{S(x-\bar{x})^2} \right]$$

Example 12. The application of this analysis to the interpretation of experimental data may be illustrated by Steward and Harrison's results on the rate of uptake of rubidium ions by potato slices. Table 27 gives the number of milligram equivalents per 1,000 gms. of water in the potato tissue after immersion in a solution of rubidium bromide for various numbers of hours. What is the relation of Rb ion content to the length of time of immersion?

TABLE 27

The Uptake of Rb and Br ions by Potato Slices (Steward and Harrison)

Time of immersion (x)	mg. equivalents per 1,000 gms. of water in the tissue	
	Rb(y_R)	Br(y_B)
21·7	7·2	0·7
46·0	11·4	6·4
67·0	14·2	9·9
90·2	19·1	12·8
95·5	20·0	15·8
Total 320·4	71·9	45·6

$S(x)=320\cdot4$ $S(y_R)=71\cdot9$ $S(y_B)=45\cdot6$
$\bar{x}=64\cdot08$ $\bar{y}_R=14\cdot38$ $\bar{y}_B=9\cdot12$
$S(x-\bar{x})^2=3{,}800\cdot948$ $S(y_R-\bar{y}_R)^2=114\cdot328$ $S(y_B-\bar{y}_B)^2=137\cdot068$

$S[y_R(x-\bar{x})]=657\cdot508$ $\qquad$ $S[y_B(x-\bar{x})]=714\cdot302$
$b_R=0\cdot172985$ $\qquad$ $b_B=0\cdot187927$
Error sum of $\qquad$ Error sum of
squares $=0\cdot5888$ $\qquad$ squares $=2\cdot8311$
$V_{y_R}=0\cdot1963$ $\qquad$ $V_{y_B}=0\cdot9437$
$V_{b_R}=0\cdot000051645$ $\qquad$ $V_{b_B}=0\cdot000248280$
$s_{b_R}=0\cdot007186$ $\qquad$ $s_{b_B}=0\cdot015757$

$d=b_R-b_B=0\cdot014942$
$s_d=0\cdot017315$

Clearly time must be the independent variate, x, and Rb content the dependent variate, y, as the latter is subject to normal error variation while the former is not. Furthermore, the times have been selected as convenient to the experimenters, while there is no reason to suspect any selection in the choice of potato slices for analysis at any given time. So the regression to be determined is that of Rb content on time.

From Table 27 $n=5$, $S(x)=320\cdot 4$, and $S(y)=71\cdot 9$.

$$S(x-\bar{x})^2 = S(x^2) - \frac{S^2(x)}{n} = 24{,}332\cdot 180 - 20{,}531\cdot 232 = 3{,}800\cdot 948$$

$$S(y-\bar{y})^2 = S(y^2) - \frac{S^2(y)}{n} = 1{,}148\cdot 250 - 1{,}033\cdot 922 = 114\cdot 328$$

The calculation of $S[y(x-\bar{x})]$, or the identical $S[(y-\bar{y})(x-\bar{x})]$, requires a word of explanation. It could, of course, be found by multiplying together each y value and the corresponding $(x-\bar{x})$ and subsequently summing. But it is more conveniently found in a way analogous to that used in computing the sum of squares of x or y. For

$$S[y(x-\bar{x})] = S(xy) - S(y\bar{x}) = S(xy) - \bar{x}S(y) = S(xy) - \frac{S(x)S(y)}{n}$$

Then in the present case $S[y(x-\bar{x})] = 5{,}264\cdot 860 - \dfrac{320\cdot 4 \times 71\cdot 9}{5} = 657\cdot 508$

So $\quad a = \bar{y} = \dfrac{71\cdot 9}{n} = 14\cdot 38$ and $b = \dfrac{S[y(x-\bar{x})]}{S(x-\bar{x})^2}$

$$= \frac{657\cdot 508}{3{,}800\cdot 948} = 0\cdot 172985$$

The linear regression of y on x is thus given by the formula

$$Y = 14\cdot 38 + 0\cdot 172985(x-\bar{x})$$

The content of Rb in the potato increases by 0·172985 mg. equivalents per 1,000 gms. of water each hour.

To find the standard deviation of b the variance of y must first be analysed. The total sum of squares has already been found to be 114·328, for, of course, 4 degrees of freedom. The regression of y on x takes from this total a sum of squares of $\dfrac{S^2[y(x-\bar{x})]}{S(x-\bar{x})^2}$ for 1 degree of freedom. $S[y(x-\bar{x})]=657\cdot 508$ and $S(x-\bar{x})^2 = 3{,}800\cdot 948$, and so the sum of squares for regression is $\dfrac{657\cdot 508^2}{3{,}800\cdot 948}$ or 113·7392. The full analysis becomes

Item	Sum of Squares	N	Mean Square
Regression	113·7392	1	113·7392
Error	0·5888	3	0·1963
Total	114·3280	4	

The significance of the regression coefficient can then be calculated by the calculation of $t_{[3]} = \sqrt{\dfrac{113\cdot 7392}{0\cdot 1963}} = 24\cdot 071$, which has a very small probability. The coefficient is very significant.

A t test is used as the error variance is estimated on the basis of three comparisons from the data.

The variance of b is given by the formula $V_b = \dfrac{1}{S(x-\bar{x})^2} V_y$ and so arithmetically is $\dfrac{0\cdot 1963}{3{,}800\cdot 948} = 0\cdot 000051645$ and $s_b = \sqrt{V_b} = 0\cdot 007186$. If the departure of b from 0 is compared with this estimated standard deviation, $t_{[3]} = \dfrac{0\cdot 172985}{0\cdot 007186} = 24\cdot 071$, as already found by the analysis of variance of y. This is not surprising because the two tests differ only in the method of arriving at t, just as when the difference of two means was tested in Sections 21 and 24.

The standard deviation of a is found as $\sqrt{\dfrac{V_y}{n}} = \sqrt{\dfrac{0\cdot 1963}{5}} = 0\cdot 1981$.

It is sometimes of interest to know whether the regression line passes through some point with which it might theoretically be expected to agree, within the limits of sampling error. This can be tested quite easily. When $x = x_1$ and $Y_1 = a + b(x_1 - \bar{x})$, $V_{Y_1} = V_a + (x_1 - \bar{x})^2 V_b$. The derivation of this formula follows from the principles developed in Section 20. The statistics a and b are orthogonal. Hence the variance of a compound of a and b is the sum of the variances of the two parts which are dependent on a and b respectively. In the calculation of Y_1, a takes the coefficient 1 and so contributes $1^2 \times V_a$ to the variance of Y_1, but b has a coefficient of $(x_1 - \bar{x})$ and so V_b is multiplied by $(x_1 - \bar{x})^2$. Hence V_{Y_1} is the sum of V_a and $(x_1 - \bar{x})^2 V_b$. The deviation of Y_1, from the value with which it is to be compared, has a standard error of $\sqrt{V_a + (x_1 - \bar{x})^2 V_b}$, and its significance may be tested by the calculation of $t_{[n-2]} = \dfrac{v - Y_1}{\sqrt{V_a + (x_1 - \bar{x})^2 V_b}}$ for a number of degrees of freedom equal to that for the estimation of V_y. This allocation of the degrees of freedom may not appear obvious at first sight, but it follows from the fact that

$$V_{Y_1} = V_a + (x_1 - \bar{x})^2 V_b = \dfrac{V_y}{n} + \dfrac{(x_1 - \bar{x})^2 V_y}{S(x-\bar{x})^2} = V_y\left[\dfrac{1}{n} + \dfrac{(x_1-\bar{x})^2}{S(x-\bar{x})^2}\right]$$

It is now clear that V_{Y_1} is derived from V_y by the use of a multiplier itself independent of y. Hence V_{Y_1} has the same number of degrees of freedom as V_y.

In the case of Steward and Harrison's data it is of some interest to know whether the regression line may be considered to pass through the origin, i.e. the point (0.0). Substituting 0 or x_1, 64·08 for $\bar{x}$, and 14·38 for a, we find

$$Y_1 = 14\cdot 38 + 0\cdot 172985(0 - 64\cdot 08)$$
$$= 14\cdot 38 - 11\cdot 0849 = 3\cdot 2951$$

Since the value expected is 0 the deviation, d, is 3·2951.

$$V_d = V_{Y_1} = V_a + (-64·08)^2 V_b$$
$$= 0·03926 + (-64·08)^2 \times 0·000051645 = 0·251327$$

and $\quad s_d = \sqrt{V_d} = 0·50133$

Then $t_{[3]} = \dfrac{d}{s_d} = 6·573$, which has a probability of less than 0·01. The line cannot reasonably be supposed to pass through the origin. Since, however, at time 0 the Rb content of the potatoes was presumably 0 also, this result must mean that the regression was not linear for the whole time preceding the first measurement at 21·7 hours. The absorption of Rb ions must have been more rapid in the early stages than it was later in the experiment.

33. THE DIFFERENCE BETWEEN TWO REGRESSION COEFFICIENTS

It is often necessary to test the agreement of two regression coefficients, and this may be done in either of two ways, which, however, lead ultimately to the same test. In the first place the difference of the two coefficients may be compared with its standard error by means of a t test. The standard error is found, as might be expected, by taking the square root of the sum of the variances of the two coefficients, provided, of course, that they were, as is usually the case, independently determined. Thus if

$$d = b_1 - b_2$$
$$V_d = V_{b_1} + V_{b_2} \quad \text{and} \quad s_d = \sqrt{V_{b_1} + V_{b_2}}$$

Then $\quad t = \dfrac{d}{s_d} = \dfrac{b_1 - b_2}{\sqrt{V_{b_1} + V_{b_2}}}$

and will have a number of degrees of freedom equal to the sum of the numbers available for the estimation of V_{b_1} and V_{b_2}.

The second way of testing the agreement of b_1 and b_2 is by the use of the analysis of variance. Each of the two regression coefficients accounts for a characteristic sum of squares in the analyses of variance of the separate sets of y data. Now if, apart from sampling error, b_1 is really equal to b_2, we can put $b_1 = b_2 = b$ and calculate the value of b from the pooled sums of squares of x and sums of cross-products of x and y as derived from the two sets of data. A regression coefficient found in this way will account for a characteristic sum of squares in the joint analysis of variance. This sum of squares for b must be less than the pooled sum of squares for b_1 and b_2, and will have 1 degree of freedom, whereas the latter pool will have 2 degrees of freedom. The difference between the pooled sum of squares for b_1 and b_2 and the sum of squares for b corresponds to the remaining degree of freedom and may be used as a test of significance of b_1-b_2, since it is the sum of squares remaining when the best joint regression coefficient has been found. This approach can be extended to test the homogeneity of three or more regression coefficients and is of wider application than the simple use of a t test.

Example 13. Steward and Harrison immersed their potato discs in a solution of rubidium bromide and estimated the Br content at the same times as the Rb content. The Br figures are given in Table 27 together with the Rb data. Is the rate of uptake the same for both kinds of ion?

The regression line of the Rb content on time has already been found as:

$$Y_R=14\cdot38+0\cdot172985(x-\bar{x})$$

The regression of Br content on time can be found in exactly the same way. The same observation times were used and so $\bar{x}=64\cdot08$ and $S(x-\bar{x})^2=3{,}800\cdot948$ as before. But $\bar{y}_B=\dfrac{45\cdot6}{5}=9\cdot12$

and
$$S(y_B-\bar{y}_B)^2=552\cdot940-\dfrac{45\cdot6^2}{5}=137\cdot068$$

$$S[y_B(x-\bar{x})]=3{,}636\cdot350-\dfrac{320\cdot4\times45\cdot6}{5}=714\cdot302$$

Then
$$b_B=\dfrac{714\cdot302}{3{,}800\cdot948}=0\cdot187927$$

This regression accounts for a sum of squares of $\dfrac{714\cdot302^2}{3{,}800\cdot948}$, i.e. $134\cdot2369$ out of the total $137\cdot068$, leaving $2\cdot8311$ as the portion corresponding to the three error degrees of freedom. Then

$$V_{Y_B}=\dfrac{2\cdot8311}{3}=0\cdot9437$$

and
$$V_{b_B}=\dfrac{V_y}{S(x-\bar{x})^2}=\dfrac{0\cdot9437}{3{,}800\cdot948}=0\cdot000248280$$

Thus $\quad d=b_B-b_R=0\cdot187927-0\cdot172985=0\cdot014942$

and $\quad s_d=\sqrt{V_{b_R}+V_{b_B}}=\sqrt{0\cdot000051645+0\cdot000248280}=0\cdot017315$

$$t_{[6]}=\dfrac{0\cdot014942}{0\cdot017315}=0\cdot863$$

This t has $(3+3)$ degrees of freedom, as V_{b_R} and V_{b_B} were each estimated from 3 comparisons. The difference, d, is less than its standard error and hence the two rates of uptake are in good agreement.

To test the significance of b_B-b_R by means of the analysis of variance it is necessary to calculate a joint regression coefficient.

This can be done from the material already available. The joint sum of cross-products, like the joint sum of squares of x, is equal to the sum of the two separate items. So

$$S[y(x-\bar{x})] = 657 \cdot 508 + 714 \cdot 302 = 1,371 \cdot 810$$
and $$S(x-\bar{x})^2 = 3,800 \cdot 948 + 3,800 \cdot 948 = 7,601 \cdot 896.$$

Then $b = \dfrac{1,371 \cdot 810}{7,601 \cdot 896} = 0 \cdot 180456$. The sum of squares accounted for by this joint regression is $\dfrac{1,371 \cdot 810^2}{7,601 \cdot 896} = 247 \cdot 5518$.

The two separate regressions accounted for 113·7392 and 134·2369 of the sum of squares of y_R and y_B respectively, leaving 0·5888 and 2·8311 for the two error items. Taking y_R and y_B together, this means that 247·9761 was taken out by the two regressions for 2 degrees of freedom in all, while there remained 3·4199 corresponding to the 6 error degrees of freedom. Of the 247·9761 for the two regressions, we have found that 247·5518 is attributable to the best fitting regression coefficient, leaving 0·4243 as the sum of squares for the difference between b_B and b_R. These results are set out in the form of an analysis of variance in Table 28 which also gives the mean squares. Two t's may be calculated, one to test the significance of the joint regression and the other to test the difference between b_R and b_B. The result of the former test is not in question as it will obviously be very large. The second test, that of the difference between b_R and b_B, gives $t_{[6]} = \sqrt{\dfrac{0 \cdot 4243}{0 \cdot 5700}} = 0 \cdot 863$ with a probability, as before, of between 0·5 and 0·4. There is no evidence that the uptakes of Rb and Br ions proceed at different rates.

TABLE 28

Analysis of Variance of Uptake of Rb and Br Ions by Potato Slices

Item	Sum of Squares	N	Mean Square	t	Probability
Joint regression	247·5518	1	247·5518		
Difference between regressions	0·4243	1	0·4243	0·863	0·5–0·4
Difference between means	69·1690	1	69·1690	11·014	very small
Error	3·4199	6	0·5700		
Total	320·5650				

One further item is included in the analysis of variance in Table 28. Those already considered account for 8 degrees of freedom but, when the two series are considered together, there are ten observations with 9 degrees of freedom between them. The ninth degree of freedom is that for differences between the means of y_B and y_R. This clearly has been omitted from the analysis so far since all the sums of squares have been taken about the separate means of y_B and y_R in the two series. The last item can be found as $\frac{1}{10}[S(y_R)-S(y_B)]^2$, the divisor being 10 because each observation is used once in obtaining the number to be squared. From Table 27 the calculation becomes

$$\tfrac{1}{10}[71\cdot 9 - 45\cdot 6]^2 = 69\cdot 1690.$$

As this sum of squares corresponds to one degree of freedom, the mean square is also 69·1690 and comparison with error gives

$$t_{[6]} = \sqrt{\frac{69\cdot 1690}{0\cdot 5700}} = 11\cdot 014.$$ The two means definitely differ.

The two series of observations, the one on the Rb content and the other on the Br content, were made at exactly the same

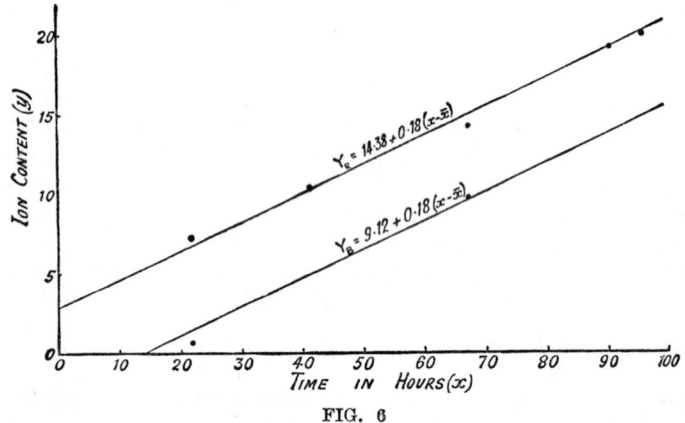

FIG. 6

Steward and Harrison's observations, on the rate of uptake of Rb and Br ions by potato slices, in relation to the calculated regression lines. The two regression lines, though parallel over the period of observation, pass on either side of the origin when projected, so showing that the rates of uptake must have differed prior to the first observation

times and, as $b_B = b_R$, the difference between their means indicates that the regression lines differ in position. They are plotted, together with the observed points, in Fig. 6, from which it will be seen that whereas the rate of uptake of Rb must have been higher before 21·7 hours than it was afterwards, the rate of uptake of Br must have been lower before this time than it was later. The two kinds of ion show the same behaviour after the initial observation but differed in the early stages of the experiment, Rb starting rapidly and Br slowly.

34. THE USE OF CONCOMITANT OBSERVATIONS

Before leaving the subject of linear regression for the consideration of more complex situations, one further and very important use must be mentioned, viz. the incorporation of concomitant measurements into a statistical analysis. The value of this technique is most easily shown by consideration of a concrete example.

Example 14. There is reason to suspect that trout fry raised in swiftly running streams respire more actively than others whose life has been spent in slowly moving water. Washbourn conducted an experiment to test this expectation. His results were expressed in cubic millimetres of oxygen consumed per gram of fish per hour, but for our purpose it is necessary to reconstruct the actual amounts of oxygen used per hour by the fish in the various experiments. These data are given in Table 29, together with the wet weights of the fish themselves.

TABLE 29

Oxygen Consumption in Cubic Millimetres per Hour of Trout Fry (Washbourn)

Series	Wet weight of fish (x)	Total oxygen consumption (y) (reconstructed)	Oxygen consumption per gm. wet weight
Swift water	7·1	766·8	108
	7·0	854·0	122
	7·5	1,080·0	144
	7·4	954·6	129
	7·5	802·5	107
	7·5	862·5	115
	4·4	501·6	114
	4·3	417·1	97
	6·2	595·2	96
	8·2	1,033·2	126
Total	67·1	7,867·5	1,158
Slow water	7·2	612·0	85
	6·2	942·4	152
	4·4	365·2	83
	4·0	276·0	69
	7·7	731·5	95
	5·6	487·2	87
	5·2	369·2	71
	5·3	498·2	94
	5·6	464·8	83
	7·1	667·4	94
Total	58·3	5,413·9	913
Grand total	125·4	13,281·4	2,071

The experiment was quite a simple one. Newly hatched trout fry were separated into two groups, one being raised in swiftly running and the other in slowly moving water. The source of the water and its temperature were controlled so that each sample of fish was subjected as nearly as possible to the same conditions, apart from the speed of flow. The rate of respiration of the fish, when of a convenient size, was measured by finding their oxygen consumption. Parallel tests of the two groups were conducted, ten assays from each set being made in all. The total weight of the ten fish used in each assay was also recorded. These weights were somewhat variable, the individuals used from the swiftly running water having a higher mean than those from the other group. Though interest centres on the oxygen consumption, the concomitant measurement of fish weight is clearly of importance in interpreting the results, as any difference in respiration rate between fish from two different habitats could perhaps be ascribed to weight discrepancies. How should the weights be used in the analysis of respiration rate?

Two courses are open. Either some arbitrary correction of the oxygen consumption can be made to allow for variation in weight, or the data can be used to supply their own correction. If the former method is adopted the correction may be based on previous experience or on *a priori* reasoning. In either case, objections may be raised as the experiment under consideration may differ from others in which a correction could be calculated, and *a priori* arguments are very dangerous guides in such cases. No exception can, on the other hand, be taken to a correction based on the data of the experiment itself and such a correction is not difficult to calculate.

Ten tests were made on individuals from each habitat, the weights of the fish varying from test to test. The ten tests thus supply all the information necessary for determining the regression of oxygen consumption on fish weight. The problem of testing the effect of water speed then resolves itself into testing whether the two regressions of respiration on weight, one from the slow and the other from the fast water, are in fact different. This test would offer no difficulties if treated by the methods of the previous section, but the analysis would be somewhat laborious, because, by the very nature of the experiment, the same fish weights do not occur in the two series of observations. An alternative method, known as the analysis of covariance, may be adopted if it is desired only to perform the test of significance, without calculating the actual regression formulae.

The null hypothesis to be tested is that the rate of respiration of equally heavy fish is the same whether they are raised in slow or fast water. We thus assume that the regression of respiration rate on weight is the same in fish from both habitats. When this is not true, the hypothesis will be as much disproved as if the corrected means were different. So the regression coefficient can be estimated from the two series jointly, and the method is exactly the same as that used for the uptake of Rb and Br ions in the last example. The sums of squares of x and cross-products of x and y are found from each series separately, using the series, and not the general, means, and the data are pooled before calculating b. In such a calculation both the sum of squares of x and the sum of cross-products of x and y are in reality being split up into two parts, the sum within series and the sum between series, though this latter does not appear explicitly in the analysis. The process may, then, be cast in the form of an analysis of variance of x and of the covariance of x with y.

For all of the 20 observations $S(x)=125\cdot4$, where x is the wet weight of the fish, and $S(x-\bar{x})^2 = 819\cdot64 - \dfrac{125\cdot4^2}{20} = 33\cdot382$. The two series totals, 67·1 and 58·3, are each based on 10 observations, and so the sum of squares of x between series is

$$\tfrac{1}{10}(67\cdot1^2+58\cdot3^2) - \dfrac{125\cdot4^2}{20} = 3\cdot872$$

which on being subtracted from the total sum of squares already found leaves 29·510 for the item within series. Of the total 19 degrees of freedom, 1 is accounted for by the difference between series, leaving 18 for differences within series.

The analysis of the cross-products is made in the same way. $S(x)=125\cdot4$ and $S(y)=13{,}281\cdot4$. Then

$$S[y(x-\bar{x})] \text{ is } 88{,}459\cdot62 - \dfrac{125\cdot4\times13{,}281\cdot4}{20} = 5{,}185\cdot242$$

The cross-product between series is

$$\tfrac{1}{10}(67\cdot1\times7{,}867\cdot5+58\cdot3\times5{,}413\cdot9) - \dfrac{125\cdot4\times13{,}281\cdot4}{20} = 1{,}079\cdot584$$

leaving 4,105·658 as the sum of cross-products within series. The degrees of freedom are partitioned as in the case of the analysis of x.

Though not wanted immediately, it is convenient to analyse the variance of y, the oxygen consumption, at this stage. The total sum of squares is 1,101,071·422 and the sum of squares between series 301,007·648, leaving 800,063·774 within series. The three analyses, of x^2, xy and y^2, are set out in Table 30.

The regression coefficient of respiration on weight would normally be found from the line of Table 30 giving the items

TABLE 30
Analysis of Covariance of Oxygen Consumption of Trout Fry

Item	N	x^2	xy	y^2	Correction for regression of y on x
Between series	1	3·872	1,079·584	301,007·648	
Within series	18	29·510	4,105·658	800,063·774	571,210·695
Total	19	33·382	5,185·242	1,101,071·422	805,426·116

Analysis of Variance of y after Correction

Item	Sum of Squares	N	Mean Square	t	Probability
Between series	66,792·227	1	66,792·227	2·227	0·05–0·02
Within series	228,853·079	17	13,461·946		
Total	295,645·306	18			

within series. The cross-products item is 4,105·658 and the sum of squares of x, 29·510. So $b=\dfrac{4,105·658}{29·510}=139·1277$. The sum of squares for y for which this regression accounts is $\dfrac{4,105·658^2}{29·510}$ or 571,210·695, leaving 228,853·079 for the 17 error degrees of freedom of y.

The regression coefficient calculated in this way can be used to make a direct correction for weight differences between series. When a test of significance is wanted, however, this is not the best procedure as it leads to a slightly biased result through failing to take account of the effect of sampling error in the estimation of b. The exact test is given by a slightly different procedure. A correction for regression is calculated from the total sums of squares and cross-products, in exactly the same way as that already found from the items within series. This correction is clearly $\dfrac{5,185·242^2}{33·382}=805,426·116$, which on subtraction leaves 295,645·306 as the corrected total sum of squares of y.

Each of the two regression corrections, obtained from the total sums and from the sums within series respectively, accounts for 1 degree of freedom, leaving 18 for the corrected 'total' and 17 for the corrected 'within series' sums of squares of y. If, when due allowance has been made for weight differences, there is no difference in the oxygen consumption of fish from the two habitats, the two corrections are equivalent within the limits of sampling error. Then the subtraction of the corrected sum of squares of y within series from the corrected total sum of squares of y will leave a corrected sum of squares of y between series, so giving an analysis of variance of corrected y values. This is shown in the lower part of Table 30. The item between series in this corrected analysis will have 1 degree of freedom as before, since the corrected total has 18, and the corrected item within series has 17, degrees of freedom. The mean squares are found by division of the sums of squares by N and a t is used to compare the item between series with that within series.

$$t_{[17]} = \sqrt{\frac{66{,}792 \cdot 227}{13{,}461 \cdot 946}} = \sqrt{4 \cdot 9616} = 2 \cdot 227$$

which has a probability of between 0·05 and 0·02. The difference between the two series is suggestively large.

Before leaving this example it will be of interest to compare the results obtained by the analysis of covariance with those which would have been found if no correction was made for the effect of weight and also with those which would have followed the use of an obvious arbitrary correction.

The analysis of variance of uncorrected y is to be found in Table 30 and this is, of course, the analysis which would be used to test the significance of water speed if no allowance were to be made for weight difference. The mean square between series is 301,008 and that within series 44,448. The test of significance is thus $t_{[18]} = \sqrt{\dfrac{301{,}008}{44{,}448}} = 2 \cdot 602$, which has a probability of less than 0·02. The significance of the difference shown by this analysis is greater than that obtained when corrections are made. The neglect of the weight variation has led to a misleading exaggeration of the significance. In other experiments the result could of course go the other way, viz. the significance could be underestimated by neglect of the concomitant measurement. In either case the test of significance would be misleading.

The most obvious arbitrary correction for weight difference is that of using the oxygen consumption per unit weight of fish, rather than the oxygen consumption itself, as the variate. There are some theoretical arguments against the use of such a correction, but none is so strong as the objection which becomes apparent when the result of this analysis is compared with that of the analysis of covariance. The oxygen consumption per unit weight is given in Table 29 for each of the 20 tests. The analysis of variance of these data follows exactly the same lines as that for total oxygen consumption. The mean square between series is found as 3,001·250, while that within series is 378·761. Then

$$t_{[18]} = \sqrt{\frac{3{,}001 \cdot 250}{378 \cdot 761}} = 2 \cdot 815$$ with a probability of only just over 0·01. The arbitrary correction has not, in fact, made a proper allowance for the weight difference. On the contrary, it has magnified the already misleadingly high significance obtained when the uncorrected total oxygen consumptions are analysed. The dan-

gers of arbitrary correction are clearly very large. Where concomitant observations are involved the analysis of covariance should be used, and the experiment allowed to supply its own correction formula. When designing an experiment in which concomitant observations will be made, care should be taken that the results will be susceptible to analysis by the covariance method.

This example is a very simple one and the use of the correction did not make a very large difference, though, since the probability was in the 0·05–0·02 region, the effect was important. In many cases, however, the results are completely obscure until an analysis of covariance has been made. The correction need not just be that appropriate to linear regression. Polynomial and multiple regression corrections can be used, provided that sufficient degrees of freedom are available to supply an estimate of error after their deduction.

REFERENCES

STEWARD, F. C., and HARRISON, J. A. 1939. The absorption and accumulation of salts by living plant cells—IX. *Ann. Bot. N.S.*, **3**, 427–54.

WASHBOURN, R. 1936. Metabolic rates of trout fry from swift and slow running waters. *J. exp. Biol.*, **13**, 145–7.

CHAPTER IX

POLYNOMIAL AND MULTIPLE REGRESSIONS

35. TESTING LINEARITY OF REGRESSIONS

THE most common type of regression calculated in statistical analysis is the straight line having the formula $Y=a+b(x-\bar{x})$. Other cases in which the relation of Y to x is better represented by a line of higher order are, however, not infrequent. The equation may be quadratic, $Y=a+b_1(x-\bar{x})+b_2(x-\bar{x})^2$, cubic, $Y=a+b_1(x-\bar{x})+b_2(x-\bar{x})^2+b_3(x-\bar{x})^3$, or indeed of any power of x. Fitting such polynomial regressions clearly involves more computational labour than a straight regression line, and this naturally would not be undertaken unless necessary. So it is desirable to have a method of testing the adequacy of straight regression lines for the description of the relations existing between x and y. A rigorous test of this point is not always possible, but where replicated experiments, or their equivalents, are used as the source of data the fit given by a straight-line regression can be tested by a simple adaptation of the analysis of variance.

Example 15. Table 31 gives the results of an experiment conducted by Ashby to find the growth rate of a certain variety of tomato. The plants were grown, together with certain other varieties, in four replications or blocks. Two samples were taken from each block at the ages of 10 days, 17 days, 24 days, 31 days, 38 days and 45 days. The dry weights of the samples were determined. Since the growth curve was expected to be of the form $y=y_0 e^{kx}$ where y is the dry weight and x the time, the logarithm of the dry weight was used as the variate in order that a straight-line relationship between x and y should be calculated (see Section 31). Do the results justify the expectation that the regression of the logarithm of dry weight on time is linear?

There are 48 observations in all, so the analysis of variance of y, the logarithm of the dry weight, will include 47 degrees of freedom. Of these, 3 are dependent on block differences, 5 on differences between the samples taken at different times, and 15 on the interaction of blocks and times. The remaining 24 are not further separable as they are dependent on differences between the two samples taken each time from each block. The analysis is, in fact, incomplete (Section 26).

The sum of all the observations, $S(y)$, is 112·898 and so

TABLE 31

The Growth of Tomato Plants in Units of the Logarithm of Dry Weight (Ashby)

y = logarithm of dry weight. Two samples from each of four blocks

Sampling time in days	x	I		II		III		IV		Total of eight samples
10	0	0·748	0·763	0·845	0·672	0·881	0·785	0·580	0·663	5·937
17	1	1·279	1·732	1·398	1·591	1·342	1·799	1·580	1·398	12·119
24	2	2·117	2·290	2·452	2·097	2·170	2·236	2·243	2·164	17·769
31	3	2·857	3·004	2·839	2·806	2·964	2·886	2·935	2·732	23·023
38	4	3·230	3·390	3·487	3·167	3·367	3·358	3·236	3·217	26·452
45	5	3·602	3·477	3·204	3·447	3·556	3·519	3·362	3·431	27·598
Block totals		28·489		28·005		28·863		27·541		112·898

TABLE 32

Analysis of Variance of Tomato Data

Item		Sum of Squares	N	Mean Square	Variance Ratio	Probability
Blocks	. . .	0·082750	3	0·027583		
Times {Regression	. . .	43·768585	1	43·768585	22·730	very small
{Remainder	. . .	1·849606	4	0·462402	46·385	very small
Interaction	. . .	0·087938	15	0·005863		
Error	. . .	0·488239	24	0·020343		
Total	. . .	46·277118	47			

the correction term used in determining the sum of squares is $\frac{112\cdot 898^2}{48}$, i.e. $265\cdot 540800$

$S(y^2)=311\cdot 817918$, so giving $S(y-\bar{y})^2=46\cdot 277118$. The block totals each include 12 observations, and so the sum of squares for block differences is

$$\tfrac{1}{12}(28\cdot 489^2+28\cdot 005^2+28\cdot 863^2+27\cdot 541^2)-\frac{112\cdot 898^2}{48}=0\cdot 082750$$

Similarly, as 8 samples are taken on each of the six occasions, the sum of squares for sampling times is

$$\tfrac{1}{8}(5\cdot 937^2+12\cdot 119^2+ \ldots +27\cdot 598^2)=\frac{112\cdot 898^2}{48}, \text{ i.e. } 45\cdot 618191$$

To find the item for interaction between blocks and times, the two samples from each block are added together, so giving a 6×4 table. The entries of this table are squared and the squares summed and divided by 2, after which the deduction of the correction term leaves the sums of squares for the 23 degrees of freedom which include the items for blocks, times and their interaction. The first two items have already been found and may be deducted from this total to leave the interaction sum of squares. Numerically the calculation is

$\tfrac{1}{2}(1\cdot 511^2+3\cdot 011^2+ \ldots +7\cdot 079^2+1\cdot 517^2+ \ldots +6\cdot 793^2)$
$\qquad -265\cdot 540800-0\cdot 082750-45\cdot 618191=0\cdot 087938$

Finally, the sums of squares between like samples, which may be used to supply the error variance, is found as the remainder after deducting the block, time and interaction items, already calculated, from the total sum of squares.

Before proceeding further with the analysis of variance, which is set out in Table 32, it should be observed that though the 'times' mean square is highly significant, the other mean squares, for blocks and interaction, are subnormal when compared with the error. Indeed, the interaction is significantly below the value of the error mean square as it gives a variance ratio of $3\cdot 4697$ with $N_1=24$ and $N_2=15$. The probability of such a result is just less than $0\cdot 01$. There is no obvious reason why this should be so, but in view of the low probability, the interaction item will not be pooled with error to give a new error mean square based on 39 degrees of freedom, as would have been legitimate if no significant difference existed.

Of the 5 degrees of freedom for time difference, 1 can be used for the calculation of a linear regression relating log dry weight (y) to time of sampling (x). The six sample times are separated by a constant interval of 7 days, so the labour of calculation can be reduced by assigning the x values 0, 1, 2, 3, 4 and 5 to the sampling times 10, 17, 24, 31, 38 and 45 days respectively. Now 8 samples were taken on each occasion, viz. two from each of four blocks, so that each x value is used 8 times. Hence

and
$$S(x)=8(0+1+2+3+4+5)=120\cdot 0$$
$$S(x^2)=8(0^2+1^2+2^2+3^2+4^2+5^2)=440\cdot 0$$

Then $\quad S(x-\bar{x})^2=440-\dfrac{120^2}{48}=140$

$S(xy)=(0\times 5\cdot 937)+(1\times 12\cdot 119)+(2\times 17\cdot 769)+(3\times 23\cdot 023)$
$\qquad\qquad\qquad +(4\times 26\cdot 452)+(5\times 27\cdot 598)=360\cdot 524$

and the correction term necessary to reduce this to $S[y(x-\bar{x})]$ is

$$\dfrac{120\times 112\cdot 898}{48}=282\cdot 245$$

Hence $\quad S[y(x-\bar{x})]=360\cdot 524-282\cdot 245=78\cdot 279$

This gives $b=\dfrac{78\cdot 279}{140\cdot 0}=0\cdot 559136$, i.e. the log dry weight of each sample increases, on the average, by 0·559136 over each period of seven days. The sum of squares of y for which this regression accounts is $\dfrac{78\cdot 279^2}{140\cdot 0}$, i.e. 43·768585. The analysis of variance now takes its final form of Table 32. The linear regression is highly significant, but we are more interested in the mean square for 'times' remaining after the regression item has been subtracted. This is $\dfrac{1\cdot 849606}{4}=0\cdot 462402$, which when divided by the error mean square gives a variance ratio of 22·730 for 4 and 24 degrees of freedom. The probability of a fit as bad or worse with the hypothesis of linear regression is shown to be very small, and it must be concluded that the straight line is inadequate for describing the relation of dry weight to time of sampling. A regression of higher order must be used.

36. THE CHOICE OF ORDER OF A POLYNOMIAL

Having concluded that a regression of order higher than the first is needed, it is next necessary to decide just how high the order must be.

If n points are available to show the relation between x and y, a curve of order $n-1$ can be found to give a perfect fit with these points. Thus two points can be joined by a straight line which is, of course, a curve of the first order, and has the general formula $Y=a+b_1(x-\bar{x})$. With three observations a quadratic curve, $Y=a+b_1(x-\bar{x})+b_2(x-\bar{x})^2$, will pass through all points. With four points a cubic, $Y=a+b_1(x-\bar{x})+b_2(x-\bar{x})^2+b_3(x-\bar{x})^3$, is necessary, and so on.

It will be seen that the order of the curve necessary to give a perfect fit in all cases is the same as the number of degrees of freedom available for differences between the observations. We have seen that the calculation of a first order or linear regression can be used to take out a sum of squares of y, the dependent variate, for 1 degree of freedom. So it might be expected that the calculation of a second order or quadratic regression term would take out an additional sum of squares for a second degree of freedom, and so on. The calculation of $n-1$ regression coefficients would then remove $n-1$ items from the sum of squares, each for 1 degree of freedom. In this way the degrees of freedom would all be accounted for; but if the process is equally to account for the whole of the sum of squares, each of the $n-1$ items must be orthogonal to the rest. When this criterion is not satisfied the various items cannot be incorporated in the same analysis of variance. Now orthogonality is not obtained if regression items of the form $b_1(x-\bar{x})$, $b_2(x-\bar{x})^2$, $b_3(x-\bar{x})^3$ are used, but this difficulty can be overcome by a modification of procedure.

It has already been shown that in Ashby's experiment the first-order regression coefficient, b, is 0·559136 and the mean of all the log dry weights is 2·352042. So the first-order regression equation is:

$$Y=2\cdot352042+0\cdot559136(x-\bar{x})$$

where $\bar{x}=2\cdot5$. Now the two portions of this equation take out independent sums of squares in the partition of $S(y^2)$ as discussed in Section 32. But we can rewrite the formula as

$$Y=2\cdot352042+0\cdot559136(x-2\cdot5)$$
$$=2\cdot352042-(2\cdot5\times0\cdot559136)+0\cdot559136x$$
$$=1\cdot102160+0\cdot559136x$$

In this last equation the two parts do not take out independent items in the partition of $S(y^2)$. Yet it is only another form of the first equation in which the two portions were orthogonal. The difference between the two lies in the fact that in the latter equation the second term is concerned solely with x, while in the former version, which represents the usual type of linear regression equation, the second term includes items based on both x and $\bar{x}$, the latter being a constant for any set of data.

In the same way a second-order regression coefficient, b_2, need not be concerned solely with x^2, but can control any term of the form $(\alpha+\beta x+x^2)$ and the values of α and β can be chosen to make this term orthogonal to any other term in the regression equation. So instead of calculating the coefficients b_1, b_2, &c., in the equation

$$Y = a + b_1(x-\bar{x}) + b_2(x-\bar{x})^2 + b_3(x-\bar{x})^3 \ldots$$

we find b_1', b_2', b_3', &c., in

$$Y = a + b_1'\xi_1 + b_2'\xi_2 + b_3'\xi_3 \ldots$$

where ξ_1 is of the form $\alpha_1 + x$
ξ_2 is of the form $\alpha_2 + \beta_2 x + x^2$
ξ_3 is of the form $\alpha_3 + \beta_3 x + \gamma_3 x^2 + x^3$, &c.

and ξ_1, ξ_2 and ξ_3 are chosen to be orthogonal to one another. Each successive regression coefficient will then represent an independent sum of squares in the analysis of variance of y.

In this way it is possible to find, first, the sum of squares removed by a linear regression involving ξ_1, second, the additional sum of squares accounted for by the introduction of the quadratic item ξ_2, third, the item removed by ξ_3, which is cubic in x, and so on. The sum of squares between n observations is thus partitioned into $n-1$ items, each for 1 degree of freedom and each of which corresponds to a regression component of characteristic order in x. When this is done the choice of order of a polynomial adequately representing the relation of y to x is made easy.

In order to specify the exact relation between the various ξ's and x it is necessary to know the values of α_1, α_2, β_2, α_3, β_3, γ_3, &c. These can be found by a consideration of the properties of orthogonal functions as developed in Section 23. First let us take the case of three double observations $(x_1 y_1)$, $(x_2 y_2)$ and $(x_3 y_3)$, the x values being 0, 1 and 2. There are 2 degrees of freedom between the three values of y, and so a quadratic regression of y on x will give a perfect fit with all three points on the graph relating y to x. The complete analysis will thus involve two ξ functions. The first, ξ_1, will be linear with respect to x and the second, ξ_2, will be quadratic in x.

In the analysis of variance of y each of these functions will take out a sum of squares of $\dfrac{1}{S(k^2)}[k_1 y_1 + k_2 y_2 + k_3 y_3]^2$, where k_1 is the value of ξ when x_1 is substituted for x in the general formula, k_2 the value of ξ when x_2 is substituted for x, and k_3 the value of ξ when x_3 is substituted for x. A comparison of this formula for the sum of squares removed by each ξ function with the formula for the sum of squares removed by a simple regression coefficient shows that $(x-\bar{x})$ in the latter is replaced by the various k values in the former. The formula is, in fact, merely re-written in the form with which we have become familiar from the discussion of the analysis of variance.

Now if the various sums of squares are to be independent,

THE CHOICE OF ORDER OF A POLYNOMIAL

two conditions must be satisfied. These are that $S(k)=0$ for each function and $S(k_1k_2)=0$ for each pair of functions. In our example of three double observations, in which the x values are 0, 1 and 2 respectively, $\xi_1 = \alpha_1 + x$ and so $k_{11} = \alpha_1 + x_1$, $k_{12} = \alpha_1 + x_2$, and $k_{13} = \alpha_1 + x_3$. Then $S(k_1) = 3\alpha_1 + S(x) = 0$. Hence $\alpha_1 = -\dfrac{S(x)}{3} = -\bar{x}$. So $\xi_1 = x - \bar{x}$, and $k_{11} = -1$, $k_{12} = 0$ and $k_{13} = 1$ as $\bar{x} = 1$.

The second ξ function is quadratic with respect to x and has the general formula $\xi_2 = \alpha_2 + \beta_2 x + x^2$. Substituting the three specific values for x in this formula we have

$$k_{21} = \alpha_2 + \beta_2 x_1 + x_1^2, \quad k_{22} = \alpha_2 + \beta_2 x_2 + x_2^2 \quad \text{and} \quad k_{23} = \alpha_2 + \beta_2 x_3 + x_3^2$$

Then $\qquad S(k_2) = 3\alpha_2 + \beta_2 S(x) + S(x^2) = 0$

But we can obtain a second equation from the fact that $S(k_1k_2)$ must also equal 0. We already know that

$$k_{11} = x_1 - \bar{x}, \quad k_{12} = x_2 - \bar{x} \quad \text{and} \quad k_{13} = x_3 - \bar{x}$$

Then $\quad S(k_1 k_2) = -3\bar{x}\alpha_2 + (\alpha_2 - \beta_2 \bar{x})S(x) + (\beta_2 - \bar{x})S(x^2) + S(x^3) = 0$

These equations may be simplified by substituting 0, 1 and 2 for x_1, x_2 and x_3. $S(x) = 3$, $S(x^2) = 5$ and $S(x^3) = 9$, with $\bar{x} = 1$. Hence

$$S(k_2) = 3\alpha_2 + 3\beta_2 + 5 = 0 \quad . \quad . \quad . \quad . \quad \text{(i)}$$

and $\qquad S(k_1 k_2) = -3\alpha_2 + 3(\alpha_2 - \beta_2) + 5(\beta_2 - 1) + 9$

$$= 2\beta_2 + 4 = 0 \quad . \quad . \quad . \quad . \quad \text{(ii)}$$

From (ii) $\qquad \beta_2 = -\tfrac{4}{2} = -2$

Substituting in (i) $\qquad 3\alpha_2 - 6 + 5 = 0$

and $\qquad \alpha_2 = \tfrac{1}{3}$

So $\qquad \xi_2 = \tfrac{1}{3} - 2x + x^2$

and substitution for x in this general formula gives

$$k_{21} = \tfrac{1}{3} - 2x_1 + x_1^2 = \tfrac{1}{3} - 0 + 0 = \tfrac{1}{3}$$
$$k_{22} = \tfrac{1}{3} - 2x_2 + x_2^2 = \tfrac{1}{3} - 2 + 1 = -\tfrac{2}{3}$$
$$k_{23} = \tfrac{1}{3} - 2x_3 + x_3^2 = \tfrac{1}{3} - 4 + 4 = \tfrac{1}{3}$$

We now have the two orthogonal functions which will partition the sum of squares of y into two parts dependent respectively for their values on the first order, or linear, and on the second order, or quadratic, regressions of y on x, as determined from the three double observations $(x_1 y_1)$, $(x_2 y_2)$, $(x_3 y_3)$ when $x_1 = 0$, $x_2 = 1$ and $x_3 = 2$. It may be noted, too, that as the second component of the sum of squares, viz.

$$\frac{1}{S(k_2^2)}[k_{21}y_1 + k_{22}y_2 + k_{23}y_3]^2 = \frac{3}{2}\left(\frac{y_1}{3} - \frac{2y_2}{3} + \frac{y_3}{3}\right)^2$$

can be re-written as

$$\tfrac{1}{6}(y_1 - 2y_2 + y_3)^2$$

the k values can be made integral * thus
$$k_{21}=1 \quad k_{22}=-2 \quad k_{21}=1$$
the general formula becoming $\xi_2=1-6x+3x^2$. A glance back to Section 29 will show that these ξ's are, in fact, the two functions already used in the analysis of the effects of phosphatic manure when applied at the three levels 0, 1 and 2.

One further point should be noticed about these ξ functions. ξ_1 is already in the form $(x-\bar{x})$, but ξ_2 has been found as $\tfrac{1}{3}-2x+x^2$. We know that $\bar{x}=1$ and so

$$\begin{aligned}\xi_2 &= \tfrac{1}{3}-2x+x^2 \\ &= 1-\tfrac{2}{3}-2x+x^2 \\ &= \bar{x}^2-\tfrac{2}{3}-2x\bar{x}+x^2 = (x^2-2x\bar{x}+\bar{x})^2-\tfrac{2}{3} \\ &= (x-\bar{x})^2-\tfrac{2}{3}\end{aligned}$$

Thus both ξ's can be written in terms of the deviation of x from its mean. So, provided that $(x_1-x_2)=(x_2-x_3)=-1$, the same k's will be obtained no matter what the absolute values of x_1, x_2 and x_3 may be.

Ashby's data can be treated in exactly the same way as this relatively simple case of three observations. Six sampling times were used, and these have already been denoted as $x_1 \ldots x_6$, where $x_1=0$, $x_2=1$, $x_3=2$, &c. Now $\xi_1=\alpha_1+x$, and so $k_{11}=\alpha_1+x_1$, &c. Hence $S(k_1)=6\alpha_1+S(x)=0$ and $\alpha_1=-\bar{x}$. In this case $\bar{x}=2\tfrac{1}{2}$ and so $k_{11}=-2\tfrac{1}{2}$, $k_{12}=-1\tfrac{1}{2}$, $k_{13}=-\tfrac{1}{2}$, $k_{14}=\tfrac{1}{2}$, $k_{15}=1\tfrac{1}{2}$ and $k_{16}=2\tfrac{1}{2}$. These coefficients may be multiplied by 2 to make them integral, whereupon they become -5, -3, -1, 1, 3 and 5. Then
$$S(k_1{}^2)=(25+9+1+1+9+25)=70$$
and the sum of squares accounted for by linear regression is
$$\tfrac{1}{70}(-5y_1-3y_2-y_3+y_4+3y_5+5y_6)^2$$

Turning to the quadratic regression $\xi_2=\alpha_2+\beta_2 x+x^2$
and $\quad k_{21}=\alpha_2+\beta_2 x_1+x_1{}^2$, &c.
Hence $\quad S(k_2)=6\alpha_2+\beta_2 S(x)+S(x^2)$
and $\quad S(k_1 k_2)=-6\alpha_2\bar{x}+(\alpha_2-\beta_2\bar{x})S(x)+(\beta_2-\bar{x})S(x^2)+S(x^3)=0$
Now $\quad S(x)=15$, $S(x^2)=55$ and $S(x^3)=225$, with $\bar{x}=2\tfrac{1}{2}$
So $\quad S(k_2)=6\alpha_2+15\beta_2+55=0$
and $\quad S(k_1 k_2)=-15\alpha_2+15(\alpha_2-\tfrac{5}{2}\beta_2)+55(\beta-\tfrac{5}{2})+225=0$

The solution of these equations is easily found to be
$$\alpha_2=3\tfrac{1}{3} \quad \text{and} \quad \beta_2=-5$$
so making $\quad \xi_2=3\tfrac{1}{3}-5x+x^2$

---

* Integral in the sense that each value is a whole number and does not include any fractions.

The k values are then obtained by substituting the various numerical values for x in this formula and

$$k_{21}=3\tfrac{1}{3}, \quad k_{22}=-\tfrac{2}{3}, \quad k_{23}=-2\tfrac{2}{3}, \quad k_{24}=-2\tfrac{2}{3}, \quad k_{25}=-\tfrac{2}{3}, \quad k_{26}=3\tfrac{1}{3}$$

These coefficients require multiplication by $\tfrac{3}{2}$ to make them integral in the form

$$k_{21}=5, \quad k_{22}=-1, \quad k_{23}=-4, \quad k_{24}=-4, \quad k_{25}=-1, \quad k_{26}=5$$

It is then seen that $S(k_2^2)=84$ and the sum of squares of y accounted for by the quadratic regression item is

$$\tfrac{1}{84}(5y_1-y_2-4y_3-4y_4-y_5+5y_6)^2$$

The expression in x of ξ_3, the cubic regression, and of the corresponding k coefficients can be found in the same way. It will be of the general form

$$\xi_3=\alpha_3+\beta_3 x+\gamma_3 x^2+x^3$$

and the three simultaneous equations necessary for evaluating the constants will be derived from the relations

$$S(k_3)=S(k_1 k_3)=S(k_2 k_3)=0$$

If the operation is carried through it will be found that

$$\xi_3=-3+13\cdot 7x-7\cdot 5x^2+x^3$$
$$k_{31}=-3+0-0+0=-3$$
$$k_{32}=-3+13\cdot 7-7\cdot 5+1=4\cdot 2$$
$$k_{33}=-3+27\cdot 4-30+8=2\cdot 4$$
$$k_{34}=-3+41\cdot 1-67\cdot 5+27=-2\cdot 4$$
$$k_{35}=-3+54\cdot 8-120+64=-4\cdot 2$$
$$k_{36}=-3+68\cdot 5-187\cdot 5+125=3$$

If these are all multiplied by $\tfrac{5}{3}$ they become -5, 7, 4, -4, -7 and 5 respectively and $S(k_3^2)=180$. The sum of squares accounted for by cubic regression is thus

$$\tfrac{1}{180}(-5y_1+7y_2+4y_3-4y_4-7y_5+5y_6)^2$$

The calculation of ξ_3 in this way is, however, rather laborious, and the calculations of ξ_4 and ξ_5 will be even more so. An alternative method is offered by the use of the recurrence formula

$$\xi_{r+1}=\xi_r\xi_1-\frac{r^2(n^2-r^2)\xi_{r-1}}{4(4r^2-1)}$$

where n is the number of double observations, in this case 6. This formula can only be used to give the original k coefficients, i.e. it will not apply after the k's have been multiplied through by some constant to make them integral. Thus we must use $\xi_1=x-\bar{x}$ and $\xi_2=3\tfrac{1}{3}-5x+x^2$ in order to derive ξ_3. If $\xi_2=5-\dfrac{15}{2}x+\dfrac{3}{2}x^2$ were employed a wrong answer would be obtained.

Let us consider the derivation of k_{31}, knowing that k_{11} is $-2\frac{1}{2}$ and k_{21} is $3\frac{1}{3}$. In this case $n=6$ and $r+1=3$. Hence

$$k_{31} = k_{11}k_{21} - \frac{2^2(6^2-2^2)}{4(4\times 2^2-1)}k_{11}$$

which on substituting for k_{11} and k_{21} gives

$$k_{31} = (-2\tfrac{1}{2}\times 3\tfrac{1}{3}) - \left[\frac{4(36-4)}{4(16-1)}\times(-2\tfrac{1}{2})\right] = -\frac{50}{6} + \frac{320}{60} = -3$$

as already found by the other method.
Similarly

$$k_{32} = [(-1\tfrac{1}{2})\times(-\tfrac{2}{3})] - [\tfrac{32}{15}\times(-1\tfrac{1}{2})] = \tfrac{15}{15} + \tfrac{48}{15} = 4\cdot 2$$

k_{33}, k_{34}, &c., can be found in the same way.

Next, turning to the calculation of the coefficients necessary for finding the sum of squares due to the quartic regression, $r+1=4$ and so

$$k_{41} = k_{11}k_{31} - \frac{9(36-9)}{4(36-1)}k_{21}$$

$$= [(-2\tfrac{1}{2})\times(-3)] - [\tfrac{243}{140}\times 3\tfrac{1}{3}]$$

$$= \frac{1{,}050}{140} - \frac{810}{140} = \frac{12}{7}$$

and k_{42}, &c., can be derived similarly.

This process is repeated until all the k's of ξ_3, ξ_4 and ξ_5 have been found. The integral k values corresponding to those found by the use of the recurrence formula, which are, of course, non-integral, are given in Table 33, together with the multipliers used to make them integral and the values of $S(k^2)$ obtained from the integral values. The use of the multipliers can be seen from an example. k_{41} is given in the table as 1, and the multiplier appropriate to ξ_4 is given as $\tfrac{7}{12}$. Then the non-integral value originally found for k_{41} was $\tfrac{12}{7}$, which gave on multiplication $\tfrac{12}{7}\times\tfrac{7}{12}=1$. It might be noted that the multiplier is also the coefficient of the highest power of x in the general form of the ξ function to which it belongs. Thus the multiplier given for ξ_2 is $\tfrac{3}{2}$, and so we know that the coefficient of x^2, the highest power of x, in that form of ξ_2 which gives the values of k shown in the table, is $\tfrac{3}{2}$. It will be remembered that the full formula has been established as

$$\xi_2 = 5 - \tfrac{15}{2}x + \tfrac{3}{2}x^2$$

The material necessary for the analysis of variance of y in relation to its polynomial regression on x has now been obtained for the case of six observations in which x takes the values 0, 1, 2 ... 5. It may be mentioned that similar sets of coefficients are given by Fisher and Yates for the analysis of all cases up to $n=52$, though they confine their attention to the first five ξ functions for the cases where $n=6$ or more.

TABLE 33
Orthogonal Polynomials for the Analysis of Six Double Observations

x	0	1	2	3	4	5	Sum of squares of k	Multiplication factor
ξ_1	-5	-3	-1	1	3	5	70	2
ξ_2	5	-1	-4	-4	-1	5	84	$\frac{3}{2}$
ξ_3	-5	7	4	-4	-7	5	180	$\frac{5}{3}$
ξ_4	1	-3	2	2	-3	1	28	$\frac{7}{12}$
ξ_5	-1	5	-10	10	-5	1	252	$\frac{21}{10}$

In Ashby's experiment, eight samples were taken at each time and so each x corresponds to eight y values. Thus each k will be used eight times, once on each of the eight values corresponding to the same x. So the $S(k^2)$ used in finding any sum of squares will be eight times the value given opposite the appropriate k values in Table 33. The arithmetic is simplified by remembering that the sum of the cross-products of k_{11} and the eight separate y's is the same as the cross-product of k_{11} and the sum of the eight y values. Thus in the calculation of the linear regression sum of squares $k_{11}=-5$. This corresponds to the eight observations 0·748, 0·763, 0·845, 0·672, 0·881, 0·785, 0·580 and 0·663, of which the sum is 5·937 (Table 31). So instead of performing eight separate multiplications and afterwards summing the products, we merely multiply 5·937 by -5. The sums of y, corresponding to each of the six sampling times, are given in Table 31 and these are multiplied by the k's of Table 33. The sum of squares for linear regression so obtained is

$$\frac{1}{70\times 8}[(-5\times 5\cdot 937)+(-3\times 12\cdot 119)+(-1\times 17\cdot 769)+(1\times 23\cdot 023)$$
$$+(3\times 26\cdot 452)+(5\times 27\cdot 598)]^2 = \frac{156\cdot 558^2}{560}=43\cdot 768585$$

as obtained in the previous section by a different method.

The sum of squares for quadratic regression is found similarly, but using ξ_2, to be

$$\frac{1}{84\times 8}[(5\times 5\cdot 937)+(-1\times 12\cdot 119)+(-4\times 17\cdot 769)+(-4\times 23\cdot 023)$$
$$+(-1\times 26\cdot 452)+(5\times 27\cdot 598)]^2=\frac{(-34\cdot 064)^2}{672}=1\cdot 726720$$

The remainder of the five orthogonal items are calculated in just the same way and the results are shown in Table 34. Their sum is 45·618191, as found in the original analysis of variance of Table 32. This provides an arithmetic check of the success of the partition.

TABLE 34

Decomposition of the "Times" in the Analysis of Variance of y

Regression item	$S(\xi^2)$	$S(y\xi)$	b'	Sum of squares		Probability	Remainder sum of Square	N	Remainder mean square
Linear (ξ_1)	560	156·558	0·279568	43·768585	46·385	very small	1·849606	4	0·462402
Quadratic (ξ_2)	672	−34·064	−0·050690	1·726720	9·213	very small	0·122886	3	0·040962
Cubic (ξ_3)	1,440	−13·042	−0·009057	0·118121	2·409	0·05–0·02	0·004765	2	0·002383
Quartic (ξ_4)	224	−0·594	−0·002652	0·001575	0·278	0·80–0·70	0·003190	1	0·003190
Quintic (ξ_5)	2,016	2·536	0·001258	0·003190	0·396	0·70–0·60	—	—	—

These five items each correspond to 1 degree of freedom, and so may be compared with the error variance of the experiment, as given in Table 32, by means of a t test. The test of the linear item has already been made in the previous section. The quadratic item gives $t_{[24]}=\sqrt{\dfrac{1 \cdot 726720}{0 \cdot 020343}}=9 \cdot 213$ with a very small probability. There is a significant quadratic term in the regression of y on x. The cubic item is suggestively large, with a probability of less than 0·05, and so will be worth including in the regression analysis, but the mean squares due to the quartic and quintic terms are subnormal. Hence these items may be omitted from the regression equation. This could actually have been shown to be the case without calculating the quartic and quintic items separately, as the sum of squares remaining when the linear, quadratic and cubic items have been isolated is subnormal. In either case it is clear that a cubic regression equation will adequately represent the relation of y to x.

In this example it has been possible to use an error variance provided by the replication of the experiment, but even if this mean square had not been available it would still have been possible to make a partial analysis of the regression. The sum of squares remaining after deduction of the items under consideration would then have formed the estimate of error. Thus linear regression removes from the 'times' item a sum of squares of 43·768585 for 1 degree of freedom, leaving a remainder of 1·849606 for 4 degrees of freedom. This gives a mean square of 0·462402, against which the linear regression mean square is highly significant. The next deduction is 1·726720 for the quadratic regression, which leaves a remainder of 0·122886 for 3 degrees of freedom. The remainder mean square is thus 0·040962 and the quadratic item is again significant. This process is continued, but it does not provide a very good test of the cubic and quartic items as the number of degrees of freedom in the remainder is getting very small. There is, of course, no test at all of the quintic regression term since no error mean square remains. It will be seen then that the provision of an error variance by replication is greatly to be desired, even though its omission may not be fatal to the analysis.

37. THE CALCULATION OF A POLYNOMIAL REGRESSION

It is now known that a cubic curve is necessary to express y in terms of x in Ashby's experiment. The next and last part of the analysis is that of finding the formula of this curve.

The calculation of the various coefficients in the polynomial regression of the form
$$Y=a+b_1(x-\bar{x})+b_2(x-\bar{x})^2+b_3(x-\bar{x})^3 \ldots$$

is a special case of the much wider question of finding the regression of y on two or more variates, which may themselves be non-independent. The degree of dependence of these variates must have an effect on the regression coefficients. If they are independent of one another every variate is capable of supplying further information for the prediction of Y, while if the dependence is complete the second and all later variates supply no information not already obtained from the first one. In such a case the calculation of the regression of y on any but the first variate is a waste of time.

There is a general treatment of regression on a number of variates, which may not be mutually independent, but this will be reserved for discussion in the next section. In the case of polynomial regression there exists a special way of overcoming the difficulties, which depends on the use of the ξ functions already developed.

The difficulty of fitting the regression coefficients in the polynomial

$$Y = a + b_1(x-\bar{x}) + b_2(x-\bar{x})^2 + b_3(x-\bar{x})^3$$

depends entirely on the fact that $(x-\bar{x})$, $(x-\bar{x})^2$, &c., are correlated, i.e. not independent. If independent, the various regression coefficients could be found without reference to one another, just as b is found in the case of a linear regression. But we have already seen that the polynomial can, by use of the ξ functions, be recast in a form where each term is independent of the rest. Hence the use of these functions affords a way of surmounting the difficulties of estimation, in exactly the same way and for the same reason as it enabled the sum of squares of y to be partitioned in the analysis of variance. Instead of estimating b_1, b_2, &c., in the polynomial regression already given, we estimate b_1', b_2', &c., in the equivalent

$$Y = a + b_1'\xi_1 + b_2'\xi_2 + b_3'\xi_3 \ldots$$

When these have been found they can be used to reconstruct the first polynomial equation, since the relations of ξ_1, ξ_2, &c., to x, x^2, &c., are known (see Table 33).

Each of the regression coefficients b_1', b_2', &c., can be calculated independently of the rest, as ξ_1, ξ_2, &c., are mutually independent. So we can put

$$b_1' = \frac{S(\xi_1 y)}{S(\xi_1^2)}, \quad b_2' = \frac{S(\xi_2 y)}{S(\xi_2^2)}, \quad b_3' = \frac{S(\xi_3 y)}{S(\xi_3^2)}$$

In every case $\bar{\xi} = 0$ as $S(k) = 0$, so that ξ itself replaces the term $(x-\bar{x})$ in the commoner type of regression equation. In the case of Ashby's data it is necessary to remember that there are eight y observations corresponding to each time, x. So $S(\xi^2)$

will have eight times the value of the sum of squares given in Table 33.

The arithmetic is very simple. From Tables 31 and 33
$S(\xi_1 y) = S(k_1 y) = [(-5 \times 5 \cdot 937) + (-3 \times 12 \cdot 119) + (-1 \times 17 \cdot 769)$
$$+ (1 \times 23 \cdot 023) + (3 \times 26 \cdot 452) + (5 \times 27 \cdot 598)] = 156 \cdot 558$$
and from Table 33
$$(S\xi_1^2) = S(k_1^2) = 8 \times 70 = 560$$
Hence $b_1' = \dfrac{156 \cdot 558}{560} = 0 \cdot 279568$. This regression coefficient is the one appertaining to the linear regression of y on x. But we found in Section 35 that the linear regression coefficient was $0 \cdot 559136$, i.e. exactly double the value now reached. The reason for this is not difficult to see. ξ_1 was originally found as $(x - \bar{x})$, but it was multiplied by 2 in order to make the k values integral. Hence ξ_1 now is $2(x - \bar{x})$, and so the regression coefficient should be half that found when $(x - \bar{x})$ is used as the independent variate.

$b_2' = \dfrac{S(\xi_2 y)}{S(\xi_2^2)} = \dfrac{S(k_2 y)}{S(k_2^2)}$

$= \dfrac{1}{84 \times 8}[(5 \times 5 \cdot 937) + (-1 \times 12 \cdot 119) + (-4 \times 17 \cdot 769) + (-4 \times 23 \cdot 023)$
$$+ (-1 \times 26 \cdot 452) + (5 \times 27 \cdot 598)]$$

$= \dfrac{-34 \cdot 064}{672} = -0 \cdot 050690$

$b_3' = \dfrac{S(\xi_3 y)}{S(\xi_3^2)} = \dfrac{S(k_3 y)}{S(k_3^2)}$

$= \dfrac{1}{180 \times 8}[(-5 \times 5 \cdot 937) + (7 \times 12 \cdot 119) + (4 \times 17 \cdot 769) + (-4 \times 23 \cdot 023)$
$$+ (-7 \times 26 \cdot 452) + (5 \times 27 \cdot 598)]$$

$= \dfrac{-13 \cdot 042}{1{,}440} = -0 \cdot 009057$

To complete the calculation we note that, as in the case of simple linear regression, $a = \bar{y} = 2 \cdot 352042$.

Hence $Y = 2 \cdot 352042 + 0 \cdot 279568 \xi_1 - 0 \cdot 050690 \xi_2 - 0 \cdot 009057 \xi_3$.

It will have been observed that all the material needed for the estimation process was available from the partition of the sum of squares of y. Whichever is undertaken first, the partition of the variance of y, or the estimation of b_1', b_2', &c., the material for the other calculation is automatically available and little extra work is required to complete the analysis.

The regression equation of y on ξ_1, ξ_2, and ξ_3 can be used directly for the calculation of the numerical values of Y when $x = 0, 1, 2, 3, 4$ and 5. Furthermore, this equation can be used to observe the progression in goodness of fit of expectation with observation, when the various terms are added one by one. When

$x=x_1=0$, $\xi_1=-5$, $\xi_2=5$, $\xi_3=-5$. Then the best-fitting linear regression
$$Y_1=a+b_1'\xi_1$$
$$=2\cdot352042+0\cdot279568\xi_1$$
gives $\quad Y_{11}=2\cdot352042+0\cdot279568\times(-5)$
$$=0\cdot954202$$
The best-fitting quadratic
$$Y_2=a+b_1'\xi_1+b_2'\xi_2$$
$$=2\cdot352042+0\cdot279568\xi_1-0\cdot050690\xi_2$$
gives $\quad Y_{21}=0\cdot954202-(5\times0\cdot050690)$
$$=0\cdot700752.$$
The best-fitting cubic
$$Y_3=a+b_1'\xi_1+b_2'\xi_2+b_3'\xi_3$$
$$=2\cdot352042+0\cdot279568\xi_1-0\cdot050690\xi_2-0\cdot009057\xi_3$$
gives $\quad Y_{31}=0\cdot700752-(-5\times0\cdot009057)$
$$=0\cdot746037$$

The eight values of y observed when $x=0$ totalled 5·937, so their mean was 0·742125. The approach of expectation to this observed value as term after term of the regression equation is added is very clear. The mean values of y observed at the six sampling times are compared with their linear, quadratic and cubic expectations in Table 35, and are shown graphically in Fig. 7.

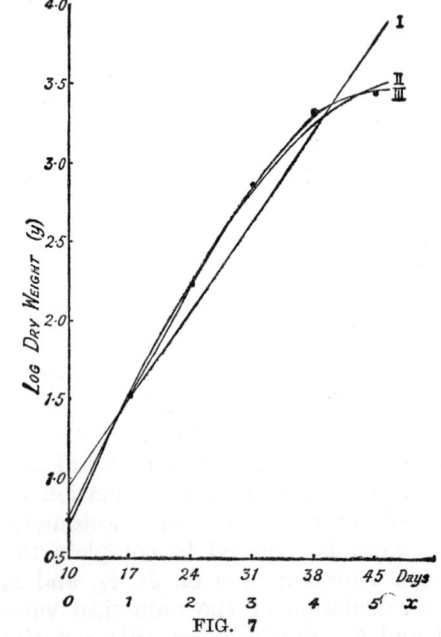

FIG. 7

Six points on the growth curve of maize, observed by Ashby, compared with linear (I), quadratic (II), and cubic (III) regressions, to show the progressive improvement in fit

TABLE 35

Agreement of Maize Observations with Expectations from Linear, Quadratic, and Cubic Regressions

x	0	1	2	3	4	5
Observed y	0·742125	1·514875	2·221125	2·877875	3·306500	3·449750
Expected { Linear Y_1	0·954202	1·513338	2·072474	2·631610	3·190746	3·749882
Quadratic Y_2	0·700752	1·564028	2·275234	2·834370	3·241436	3·496432
Cubic Y_3	0·746037	1·500629	2·239006	2·870598	3·304835	3·451147

The polynomial
$$Y = a + b_1(x-\bar{x}) + b_2(x-\bar{x})^2 + b_3(x-\bar{x})^3$$
can be reconstructed from the equation relating Y, ξ_1, ξ_2 and ξ_3. From the previous section $\xi_1 = 2(x-\bar{x})$ and, since $\bar{x} = 2\cdot 5$,

$$\xi_2 = \tfrac{3}{2}(x^2 - 5x + 3\tfrac{1}{3}) = \tfrac{3}{2}[(x-\bar{x})^2 - 2\cdot 91\dot{6}] = 1\cdot 5(x-\bar{x})^2 - 4\cdot 3750$$
and $\quad\xi_3 = \tfrac{5}{3}(x^3 - 7\cdot 5x^2 + 13\cdot 7x - 3) = \tfrac{5}{3}[(x-\bar{x})^3 - 5\cdot 05(x-\bar{x})]$
$\quad\quad\quad = 1\cdot \dot{6}(x-\bar{x})^3 - 8\cdot 41\dot{6}(x-\bar{x})$

Then $\quad b_1'\xi_1 = 0\cdot 5591(x-\bar{x}), \quad b_2'\xi_2 = 0\cdot 2218 - 0\cdot 0760(x-\bar{x})^2$
and $\quad b_3'\xi_3 = 0\cdot 0762(x-\bar{x}) - 0\cdot 0151(x-\bar{x})^3$
So $\quad Y_1 = a + b_1'\xi_1 = 2\cdot 3520 + 0\cdot 5591(x-\bar{x})$
$\quad\quad Y_2 = a + b_1'\xi_1 + b_2'\xi_2 = 2\cdot 5738 + 0\cdot 5591(x-\bar{x}) - 0\cdot 0760(x-\bar{x})^2$
$\quad\quad Y_3 = a + b_1'\xi_1 + b_2'\xi_2 + b_3'\xi_3 = 2\cdot 5738 + 0\cdot 6353(x-\bar{x}) - 0\cdot 0760(x-\bar{x})^2$
$$-0\cdot 0151(x-\bar{x})^3$$

The effect of the correlations between x, x^2 and x^3 is obvious from the way that the addition of the term involving $(x-\bar{x})^2$ changes the term independent of x, and the way that the addition of $(x-\bar{x})^3$ increases the coefficient of $(x-\bar{x})$ from $0\cdot 5591$ to $0\cdot 6353$. The utility of the ξ functions depends on the fact that the addition or subtraction of any term has no effect on the rest of the regression equation.

38. REGRESSION ON TWO OR MORE VARIATES

Polynomial regressions are special cases of the calculation of regressions on two or more variates which may not be independent of one another. The general solution to this problem has been found and is described under the name of Multiple Regression.

Let us consider the regression of y on two variates x_1 and x_2, which may be mutually dependent. We wish to find a, b_1 and b_2 in the regression equation
$$Y = a + b_1(x_1 - \bar{x}_1) + b_2(x_2 - \bar{x}_2)$$
from n triple observations of the kind (y, x_1, x_2). The method of least squares can be employed for this purpose.

$(y-Y) = y - a - b_1(x_1 - \bar{x}) - b_2(x_2 - \bar{x}_2)$
$(y-Y)^2 = [y - a - b_1(x_1 - \bar{x}_1) - b_2(x_2 - \bar{x}_2)]^2$
$\quad = y^2 - 2ay + a^2 + b_1^2(x_1 - \bar{x}_1)^2 + b_2^2(x_2 - \bar{x}_2)^2 + 2b_1b_2(x_1 - \bar{x}_1)(x_2 - x_2)$
$$-2[b_1(x_1 - \bar{x}_1) + b_2(x_2 - \bar{x}_2)][y - a]$$

and since a, b_1 and b_2 are constants

$S(y-Y)^2 = S(y^2) - 2aS(y) + na^2 + b_1^2 S(x_1 - \bar{x}_1)^2 + b_2^2 S(x_2 - \bar{x}_2)^2$
$\quad\quad + 2b_1 b_2 S[(x_1 - \bar{x}_1)(x_2 - \bar{x}_2)] - 2b_1 S[y(x_1 - \bar{x}_1)]$
$\quad\quad\quad - 2b_2 S[y(x_2 - \bar{x}_2)] + 2a[b_1 S(x_1 - \bar{x}_1) + b_2 S(x_2 - \bar{x}_2)]$

and the last term vanishes as $S(x_1 - \bar{x}_1) = S(x_2 - \bar{x}_2) = 0$.

This sum of squares of deviations of y from the expected Y

is next minimized by partially differentiating with respect to a, b_1 and b_2, equating to 0 and solving.

$$\frac{\partial}{\partial a}S(y-Y)^2 = 2na - 2S(y) = 0$$

$$\frac{\partial}{\partial b_1}S(y-Y)^2 = 2b_1 S(x_1-\bar{x}_1)^2 + 2b_2 S[(x_1-\bar{x}_1)(x_2-\bar{x}_2)] - 2S[y(x_1-\bar{x}_1)] = 0$$

$$\frac{\partial}{\partial b_2}S(y-Y)^2 = 2b_1 S[(x_1-\bar{x}_1)(x_2-\bar{x}_2)] + 2b_2 S(x_2-\bar{x}_2)^2 - 2S[y(x_2-\bar{x}_2)] = 0$$

Then, as before, $a = \bar{y}$ and b_1 and b_2 are the solutions of the equations
$$b_1 S(x_1-\bar{x}_1)^2 + b_2 S[(x_1-\bar{x}_1)(x_2-\bar{x}_2)] = S[y(x_1-\bar{x}_1)]$$
$$b_1 S[(x_1-\bar{x}_1)(x_2-\bar{x}_2)] + b_2 S(x_2-\bar{x}_2)^2 = S[y(x_2-\bar{x}_2)]$$

The covariance of x_1 and x_2 enters into the estimation of b_1 and b_2. Thus the necessary adjustments for any mutual dependence of x_1 and x_2 are automatically made. Where x_1 and x_2 are independent, $S[(x_1-\bar{x}_1)(x_2-\bar{x}_2)]$ will be 0 within the limits of sampling error. The equations then reduce to:
$$b_1 S(x_1-\bar{x}_1)^2 = S[y(x_1-\bar{x}_1)]$$
$$b_2 S(x_2-\bar{x}_2)^2 = S[y(x_2-\bar{x}_2)]$$

These are recognizable as the types used in calculating the regressions on ξ_1 and ξ_2 in the last example, ξ_1 and ξ_2 having been deliberately chosen to be independent of one another.

The solutions to the general equations of estimation found above are easily shown to be

$$b_1 = \frac{S[y(x_2-\bar{x}_2)]S[(x_1-\bar{x}_1)(x_2-\bar{x}_2)] - S[y(x_1-\bar{x}_1)]S(x_2-\bar{x}_2)^2}{S^2[(x_1-\bar{x}_1)(x_2-\bar{x}_2)] - S(x_1-\bar{x}_1)^2 S(x_2-\bar{x}_2)^2}$$

$$b_2 = \frac{S[y(x_1-\bar{x}_1)]S[(x_1-\bar{x}_1)(x_2-\bar{x}_2)] - S[y(x_2-\bar{x}_2)]S(x_1-\bar{x}_1)^2}{S^2[(x_1-\bar{x}_1)(x_2-\bar{x}_2)] - S(x_1-\bar{x}_1)^2 S(x_2-\bar{x}_2)^2}$$

If these are then substituted in the expression found for $S(y-Y)^2$, simple but tedious algebraic manipulation will show that the sum of squares of y removed by the two regressions when taken together is

$$b_1 S[y(x_1-\bar{x}_1)] + b_2 S[y(x_2-\bar{x}_2)]$$

so that $\quad S(y-Y)^2 = S(y^2) - \dfrac{S^2(y)}{n} - b_1 S[y(x_1-\bar{x}_1)] - b_2 S[y(x_2-\bar{x}_2)]$

Though this sum of squares due to regression is expressible as the sum of two terms which seem to be ascribable to the relations between y and x_1 and y and x_2 respectively, it is not, in fact, capable of being so subdivided unless x_1 and x_2 are independent. When this is not the case, the joint sum of squares incorporates the necessary allowance for the non-independence of x_1 and x_2, and it is clear that the sum of squares is not divisible. Two

parameters have been estimated and so the sum of squares due to regression corresponds to 2 degrees of freedom. Hence
$$V_y = \frac{S(y-Y)^2}{n-3}$$

In order to find the variance and standard error of b_1 we note that $b_1 = \frac{N}{D}$ where

$$N = S[y(x_2-\bar{x}_2)]S[(x_1-\bar{x}_1)(x_2-\bar{x}_2)] - S[y(x_1-\bar{x}_1)]S(x_2-\bar{x}_2)^2$$
and $\quad D = S^2[(x_1-\bar{x}_1)(x_2-\bar{x}_2)] - S(x_1-\bar{x}_1)^2 S(x_2-\bar{x}_2)^2$

Now, as we have shown in Section 32
$$V_{S[y(x_1-\bar{x}_1)]} = S(x_1-\bar{x}_1)^2 V_y$$
$$V_{S[y(x_2-\bar{x}_2)]} = S(x_2-\bar{x}_2)^2 V_y$$
and the covariance of $S[y(x_1-\bar{x}_1)]$ and $S[y(x_2-\bar{x}_2)]$ is
$$V_y S[(x_1-\bar{x}_1)(x_2-\bar{x}_2)]$$

Hence
$$V_N = V_y\{(S(x_2-\bar{x}_2)^2 S^2[(x_1-\bar{x}_1)(x_2-\bar{x}_2)] - 2S(x_2-\bar{x}_2)^2 S^2[(x_1-\bar{x}_1)(x_2-\bar{x}_2)] \\ + S(x_1-\bar{x}_1)^2 S^2(x_2-\bar{x}_2)^2]\}$$

the second term depending on the covariance. This reduces to
$$V_N = V_y S(x_2-\bar{x}_2)^2 \{S(x_1-\bar{x}_1)^2 S(x_2-\bar{x}_2)^2 - S^2[(x_1-\bar{x}_1)(x_2-\bar{x}_2)]\}$$

Then, since D is independent of y, $V_{b_1} = \frac{V_N}{D^2}$

$$= \frac{V_y S(x_2-\bar{x}_2)^2}{S(x_1-\bar{x}_1)^2 S(x_2-\bar{x}_2)^2 - S^2[(x_1-\bar{x}_1)(x_2-\bar{x}_2)]}$$

Similarly $\quad V_{b_2} = \dfrac{V_y S(x_1-\bar{x}_1)^2}{S(x_1-\bar{x}_1)^2 S(x_2-\bar{x}_2)^2 - S^2[(x_1-\bar{x}_1)(x_2-\bar{x}_2)]}$

A very convenient method of estimating b_1 and b_2 which at the same time considerably eases the calculation of V_{b_1} and V_{b_2} has been introduced by Fisher.

The equations of estimation of b_1 and b_2 are
$$b_1 S(x_1-\bar{x}_1)^2 + b_2 S[(x_1-\bar{x}_1)(x_2-\bar{x}_2)] = S[y(x_1-\bar{x}_1)]$$
$$b_1 S[(x_1-\bar{x}_1)(x_2-\bar{x}_2)] + b_2 S(x_2-\bar{x}_2)^2 = S[y(x_2-\bar{x}_2)]$$

Now if we set up two new pairs of equations like these but with 1 and 0 in the first pair, and 0 and 1 in the second pair, substituted on the right-hand sides we can find

$$c_{11} = -\frac{1}{D} S(x_2-\bar{x}_2)^2 \qquad c_{12} = \frac{1}{D} S[(x_1-\bar{x}_1)(x_2-\bar{x}_2)]$$

$$c_{21} = \frac{1}{D} S[(x_1-\bar{x}_1)(x_2-\bar{x}_2)] \qquad c_{22} = -\frac{1}{D} S(x_1-\bar{x}_1)^2$$

where $D = S^2[(x_1-\bar{x}_1)(x_2-\bar{x}_2)] - S(x_1-\bar{x}_1)^2 S(x_2-\bar{x}_2)^2$, c_{11} and c_{12} being the values of b_1 and b_2 in the first pair of equations and c_{21} and c_{22} being the values of b_1 and b_2 in the second pair of equations.

A comparison of c_{11} and c_{21} with the value of b_1 found by solving the true equations of estimation shows that
$$b_1 = c_{11}S[y(x_1-\bar{x}_1)] + c_{21}S[y(x_2-\bar{x}_2)]$$
and, similarly,
$$b_2 = c_{12}S[y(x_1-\bar{x}_1)] + c_{22}S[y(x_2-\bar{x}_2)]$$
Furthermore, when c_{11} is compared with V_{b_1} it is seen that $V_{b_1} = c_{11}V_y$ and similarly $V_{b_2} = c_{22}V_y$.

It may be added that this method of estimation holds distinct advantages for the treatment of complex cases of regression on several variates in that it makes easy the omission of a variate, if this should be deemed necessary. Reference should be made to Fisher's account of multiple regression for a further discussion of this operation.

Example 16. Buck's data (Table 36) on the dependence of the time of the first flash of male fireflies on the intensity of light and on temperature provide a case which can be analysed by the method of multiple regression. The time of first flash, y, is given as minutes after 6.40 p.m., the temperature, x_2, in degrees Centigrade and the light intensity, x_1, in metre-candles. To what extent do the temperature and light intensity influence the onset of flashing?

TABLE 36

The Time of First Flash of Male Fireflies in relation to Temperature and Light Intensity (Buck)

Light-intensity in metre-candles (x_1)	Temperature in °C. (x_2)	Time of flash in minutes after 6.40 p.m. (y)
26	21·1	35
35	23·9	30
40	17·8	48
41	22·0	40
45	22·3	21
55	22·3	42
55	23·3	0
55	20·5	44
56	25·5	28
70	21·7	30
75	26·7	18
79	25·0	28
84	26·7	19
87	24·4	26
100	22·3	26
100	22·3	5
100	25·5	36
110	26·7	30
130	25·5	21
140	26·7	30

From the table we find that

$S(x_1)=1{,}483 \cdot 000$, $\quad S(x_1^2)=129{,}409 \cdot 000$, $\quad S(x_1-\bar{x}_1)^2=19{,}444 \cdot 550$
$S(x_2)=473 \cdot 200$, $\quad S(x_2^2)=11{,}308 \cdot 720$, $\quad S(x_2-\bar{x}_2)^2=112 \cdot 808$
$S(y)=557 \cdot 000$, $\quad S(y^2)=18{,}237 \cdot 000$, $\quad S(y-\bar{y})^2=2{,}724 \cdot 550$

$S(x_1 x_2)=35{,}983 \cdot 200$, $\quad S[(x_1-\bar{x}_1)(x_2-\bar{x}_2)]=895 \cdot 420$
$S(x_1 y)=39{,}213 \cdot 000$, $\quad S[y(x_1-\bar{x}_1)]=-2{,}088 \cdot 550$
$S(x_2 y)=12{,}857 \cdot 700$, $\quad S[y(x_2-\bar{x}_2)]=-320 \cdot 920$

Then we write down as the equations for the calculation of c_{11}, c_{12}, c_{21} and c_{22}:

$$b_1 19{,}444 \cdot 550 + b_2 895 \cdot 420 = 1,\ 0$$
$$b_1 895 \cdot 420 + b_2 112 \cdot 808 = 0,\ 1$$

giving as the solutions:

$c_{11}=0 \cdot 000081056 \quad c_{12}=-0 \cdot 000643389$
$c_{21}=-0 \cdot 000643389 \quad c_{22}=0 \cdot 013971556$

It should be noted that the relation $c_{21}=c_{12}$ provided a check on the arithmetic of the solution.

Then $b_1 = c_{11} S[y(x_1-\bar{x}_1)] + c_{21} S[y(x_2-\bar{x}_2)]$
$ = -(0 \cdot 000081056 \times 2{,}088 \cdot 550) + (0 \cdot 000643389 \times 320 \cdot 920)$
$ = 0 \cdot 037186$

and $\quad b_2 = c_{12} S[y(x_1-\bar{x}_1)] + c_{22} S[y(x_2-\bar{x}_2)]$
$ = (0 \cdot 000643389 \times 2{,}088 \cdot 550) - (0 \cdot 013971556 \times 320 \cdot 920)$
$ = -3 \cdot 140002$

$S(y-Y)^2 = S(y-\bar{y})^2 - b_1 S[y(x_1-\bar{x}_1)] - b_2 S[y(x_2-\bar{x}_2)]$
$ = 2{,}724 \cdot 550 + (0 \cdot 037186 \times 2{,}088 \cdot 550) - (3 \cdot 140002 \times 320 \cdot 920)$
$ = 1{,}794 \cdot 5254$

There are 20 sets of observations in all, so that 17 degrees of freedom remain after the estimation of b_1 and b_2.

Then $V_y = \dfrac{1{,}794 \cdot 5254}{17} = 105 \cdot 56032$

$s_{b_1} = \sqrt{V_{b_1}} = \sqrt{c_{11} V_y} = \sqrt{0 \cdot 000081056 \times 105 \cdot 56032} = 0 \cdot 092501$
$s_{b_2} = \sqrt{V_{b_2}} = \sqrt{c_{22} V_y} = \sqrt{0 \cdot 013971556 \times 105 \cdot 56032} = 1 \cdot 214433$

The significance of the departure of b_1 from the value of 0, which would indicate independence of the time of flash and light intensity, can be tested by finding $t_{[17]} = \dfrac{b_1 - 0}{s_{b_1}}$. This t must have 17 degrees of freedom, as the sampling variance of y is determined on the basis of 17 comparisons.

$t_{[17]} = \dfrac{0 \cdot 037186}{0 \cdot 092501} = 0 \cdot 402$ with a probability of $0 \cdot 7 - 0 \cdot 6$

Similarly to test the significance of b_2.

$t_{[17]} = \dfrac{b_2 - 0}{s_{b_2}} = \dfrac{3 \cdot 140002}{1 \cdot 214433} = 2 \cdot 586$ with a probability of less than $0 \cdot 02$

The time of flashing is thus demonstrably dependent on temperature but not on light intensity over the range available at this time of day.

Now if the simple regression of y on x_1 is found without reference to x_2 it can be shown that the test of significance of dependence of y on x_1 is given by $t_{[18]}=1{\cdot}266$ with a probability of just over 0·2. Even in this case significance is not obtained, but the probability is much lower than that of 0·7–0·6 found when x_2 is included in the analysis. The non-independence of x_1 and x_2 results in a spuriously large apparent dependence of y on x_1 unless the relations holding between x_1 and x_2 are taken into account, as by the use of the method of multiple regression.

Before leaving this subject the general formulae for the calculation of multiple regressions of y on j different variates may be given. They are derived by an extension of the analysis given above for the case of x_1 and x_2. There are j equations:

$$b_1 S(x_1-\bar{x}_1)^2 + b_2 S[(x_1-\bar{x}_1)(x_2-\bar{x}_2)] + \ldots + b_j S[(x_1-\bar{x}_1)(x_j-\bar{x}_j)] = S[y(x_1-\bar{x}_1)]$$

$$b_1 S[(x_1-\bar{x}_1)(x_2-\bar{x}_2)] + b_2 S(x_2-\bar{x}_2)^2 + \ldots + b_j S[(x_2-\bar{x}_2)(x_j-\bar{x}_j)] = S[y(x_2-\bar{x}_2)]$$

$$\vdots$$

$$b_1 S[(x_1-\bar{x}_1)(x_j-\bar{x}_j)] + b_2 S[(x_2-\bar{x}_2)(x_j-\bar{x}_j)] + \ldots + b_j S(x_j-\bar{x}_j)^2 = S[y(x_j-\bar{x}_j)]$$

which may be replaced by j sets each of j equations with the right sides altered to:

$$\begin{matrix} 1, & 0 & \ldots & 0 \\ 0, & 1 & \ldots & 0 \\ & \vdots & & \vdots \\ 0, & 0 & \ldots & 1 \end{matrix}$$

giving as solutions for b_1, b_2, &c.

$c_{11}, c_{12} \ldots c_{1j}$ $b_1 = c_{11} S[y(x_1-\bar{x}_1)] + c_{21} S[y(x_2-\bar{x}_2)] + \ldots + c_{j1} S[y(x_j-\bar{x}_j)]$

$c_{21}, c_{22} \ldots c_{2j}$ $b_2 = c_{12} S[y(x_1-\bar{x}_1)] + c_{22} S[y(x_2-\bar{x}_2)] + \ldots + c_{j2} S[y(x_j-\bar{x}_j)]$

and

$\vdots$

$c_{j1}, c_{j2} \ldots c_{jj}$ $b_j = c_{1j} S[y(x_1-\bar{x}_1)] + c_{2j} S[y(x_2-\bar{x}_2)] + \ldots + c_{jj} S[y(x_j-\bar{x}_j)]$

Checks on the arithmetic are provided by the fact that $c_{12}=c_{21}$, $c_{hj}=c_{jh}$, and so on.

$$S(y-Y)^2 = S(y-\bar{y})^2 - b_1 S[y(x_1-\bar{x}_1)] - b_2 S[y(x_2-\bar{x}_2)] - \cdots$$
$$- b_j S[y(x_j-\bar{x}_j)]$$

and since j parameters have been fitted

$$V_y = \frac{1}{n-1-j} S(y-Y)^2$$

The variances of the regression coefficients are obtained from the formulae

$$V_{b_1} = c_{11} V_y$$
$$V_{b_2} = c_{22} V_y$$
$$\vdots \quad \vdots$$
$$V_{b_j} = c_{jj} V_y$$

It will be observed that since x_1 can bear any relation to x_2, x_3, &c., without invalidating the calculation, we can take $x_2 = x_1^2$, $x_3 = x_1^3$, &c. The calculation of polynomial regressions may thus be undertaken by the use of the multiple regression technique. The recalculation of Ashby's data by this method may be made as an exercise.

39. DISCRIMINANT FUNCTIONS

A new device introduced by Fisher closely resembles the technique of multiple regression in some ways, though it is designed for the solution of a rather different class of problem. This is the calculation of so-called discriminant functions. A number of uses have already been found for these, ranging from anthropometric classification of skulls to parent selection in plant breeding and to the choice of speciality salesmen, but the most common use will perhaps be found in the handling of taxonomic data. We shall discuss discriminants in this connexion; their use in the solution of problems in other fields of research involves the same statistical analysis.

Suppose we have a number of individuals of two species or varieties from which certain measurements have been taken. It may be difficult to distinguish the species or variety to which an individual belongs. We might then wish to find that linear compound of the available measurements which will give the smallest possible frequency of misclassification when used as a means of discrimination. Such a linear compound is termed a discriminant function of the measurements.

Let us call the two species or varieties A and B respectively and, for the sake of simplicity, confine our attention to the case where two measurements, x_1 and x_2, are available from each of equal numbers of individuals of two groups. If we call the linear

compound X, the problem is to find those values of λ_1 and λ_2 in the expression
$$X = \lambda_1 x_1 + \lambda_2 x_2$$
which will minimize the misclassification of A and B when X is used as the means of discrimination. We may denote the value of $\bar{X}$ in species A as $\bar{X}_A$ and that in species B as $\bar{X}_B$. The difference between $\bar{X}_A$ and $\bar{X}_B$ will be called D.

Then $\quad \bar{X}_A = \lambda_1 \bar{x}_{1A} + \lambda_2 \bar{x}_{2A}$
and $\quad \bar{X}_B = \lambda_1 \bar{x}_{1B} + \lambda_2 \bar{x}_{2B}$
and $\quad D = \lambda_1 d_1 + \lambda_2 d_2$
where $\quad d_1 = \bar{x}_{1A} - \bar{x}_{1B} \quad$ and $\quad d_2 = \bar{x}_{2A} - \bar{x}_{2B}$

Misclassification will increase when the sampling error of X_A or X_B becomes larger as compared with the difference between A and B. The minimization of misclassification, therefore, involves making D as large as possible with respect to the sampling variance of X_A and X_B, by adjustment of λ_1 and λ_2. The variance of X must be partitioned in such a way that the mean square attributable to D is at a maximum, the remainder at a minimum. It is not, however, actually necessary to maximize the ratio of the mean square of X between species to that within species. Maximization of any ratio proportional to this one will serve equally well.

The mean square between species will be proportional to D^2, and as $\quad X = \lambda_1 x_1 + \lambda_2 x_2$
so making $\quad V_X = \lambda_1^2 V_{x_1} + 2\lambda_1 \lambda_2 W_{x_1 x_2} + \lambda_2^2 V_{x_2}$
the mean square within species will be proportional to
$$T = \lambda_1^2 S(x_1 - \bar{x}_1)^2 + 2\lambda_1 \lambda_2 S[(x_1 - \bar{x}_1)(x_2 - \bar{x}_2)] + \lambda_2^2 S(x_2 - \bar{x}_2)^2$$
the deviations of x_1 and x_2 being taken from the specific means, not from the general mean. So the maximization of $\dfrac{D^2}{T}$ will give the values of λ_1 and λ_2 in the compound X. This maximization can be accomplished by partially differentiating $\dfrac{D^2}{T}$ with respect to λ_1 and λ_2, equating to 0 and solving the two simultaneous equations that are so obtained.

$$\frac{\partial}{\partial \lambda_1}\left(\frac{D^2}{T}\right) = \frac{1}{T^2}\left(2DT\frac{\partial D}{\partial \lambda_1} - D^2 \frac{\partial T}{\partial \lambda_1}\right) = 0$$

$$\frac{\partial}{\partial \lambda_2}\left(\frac{D^2}{T}\right) = \frac{1}{T^2}\left(2DT\frac{\partial D}{\partial \lambda_2} - D^2 \frac{\partial T}{\partial \lambda_2}\right) = 0$$

Hence $\quad \dfrac{1}{2} \dfrac{\partial T}{\partial \lambda_1} = \dfrac{T}{D} \dfrac{\partial D}{\partial \lambda_1}$

and $\quad \dfrac{1}{2} \dfrac{\partial T}{\partial \lambda_2} = \dfrac{T}{D} \dfrac{\partial D}{\partial \lambda_2}$

Since $\dfrac{T}{D}$ is common to both equations it may be removed to give two new equations whose solutions will themselves be proportional to the solutions of the two equations obtained by the maximization process.

Now $T = \lambda_1^2 S(x_1-\bar{x}_1)^2 + 2\lambda_1\lambda_2 S[(x_1-\bar{x}_1)(x_2-\bar{x}_2)] + \lambda_2^2 S(x_2-\bar{x}_2)^2$
and $\quad D = \lambda_1 d_1 + \lambda_2 d_2$

So
$$\frac{\partial T}{\partial \lambda_1} = 2\lambda_1 S(x_1-\bar{x}_1)^2 + 2\lambda_2 S[(x_1-\bar{x}_1)(x_2-\bar{x}_2)],$$
$$\frac{\partial D}{\partial \lambda_1} = d_1$$
$$\frac{\partial T}{\partial \lambda_2} = 2\lambda_1 S[(x_1-\bar{x}_1)(x_2-\bar{x}_2)] + 2\lambda_2 S(x_2-\bar{x}_2)^2$$
$$\frac{\partial D}{\partial \lambda_2} = d_2$$

Thus the equations of estimation become
$$\lambda_1 S(x_1-\bar{x}_1)^2 + \lambda_2 S[(x_1-\bar{x}_1)(x_2-\bar{x}_2)] = d_1$$
$$\lambda_1 S[(x_1-\bar{x}_1)(x_2-\bar{x}_2)] + \lambda_2 S(x_2-\bar{x}_2)^2 = d_2$$
which are of the familiar multiple regression type and may be solved in the same way as multiple regression equations. Putting 1 and 0, and 0 and 1 respectively for d_1 and d_2 gives two pairs of equations whose solutions are

$$\begin{matrix} c_{11} & c_{12} \\ c_{21} & c_{22} \end{matrix}$$

from which $\quad \lambda_1 = c_{11} d_1 + c_{21} d_2 \quad$ and $\quad \lambda_2 = c_{12} d_1 + c_{22} d_2$

As in the case of multiple regression
$$V_{\lambda_1} = c_{11} V_X \quad \text{and} \quad V_{\lambda_2} = c_{22} V_X$$

To find the value of V_X an analysis of variance of X is necessary. The partition of the sum of squares of X offers no difficulty. The sum of squares between species can be found from $S(X_A) - S(X_B)$ which is, of course, equal to nD, where n is the number of individuals of each species to be measured. This quantity is a compound of $2n$ observations each used once, and so the divisor used in finding the sum of squares will be $2n$. The sum of squares between species then becomes:
$$\frac{1}{2n}[S(X_A) - S(X_B)]^2 = \frac{1}{2n} n^2 D^2 = \frac{n}{2} D^2$$

The sum of squares within species has already been used under the symbol T. Hence the partition of the sum of squares takes the form

Between species	$\dfrac{n}{2} D^2$
Within species	$T = D$
Total	$D\left(1 + \dfrac{n}{2} D\right)$

It will be observed that T is put equal to D. This is true, because if we multiply the two equations of estimation of λ_1 and λ_2 by λ_1 and λ_2 respectively, we find

$$\lambda_1^2 S(x_1-\bar{x}_1)^2 + \lambda_1\lambda_2 S[(x_1-\bar{x}_1)(x_2-\bar{x}_2)] = \lambda_1 d_1$$
$$\lambda_1\lambda_2 S[(x_1-\bar{x}_1)(x_2-\bar{x}_2)] + \lambda_2^2 S(x_2-\bar{x}_2)^2 = \lambda_2 d_2$$

which, on summing, gives

$$\lambda_1^2 S(x_1-\bar{x}_1)^2 + 2\lambda_1\lambda_2 S[(x_1-\bar{x}_1)(x_2-\bar{x}_2)] + \lambda_2^2 S(x_2-\bar{x}_2)^2 = \lambda_1 d_1 + \lambda_2 d_2$$

i.e. $$T = D$$

The next task is that of assigning the appropriate numbers of degrees of freedom to these two sums of squares. The total number will clearly be $2n-1$ as there are $2n$ values of X in all. The partition of these $2n-1$ between the two items is not obvious until the analogy with multiple regression has been pursued a little further.

Suppose that we assigned some arbitrary value to each individual of the two species such that all the individuals of one species received the same value, and that the sum of all these values was 0. Where, as in the case we have been considering, equal numbers of the two species have been measured, the values of 1 for each individual of species A and -1 for each of species B would be suitable. If the arbitrary values are then treated as dependent variates their multiple regression on x_1 and x_2 can be found. This would give for each individual of each species an expectation

$$Y = a + b_1(x_1-\bar{x}_1) + b_2(x_2-\bar{x}_2)$$

where $a=\bar{y}=0$ and $\bar{x}_1$ and $\bar{x}_2$ are the general, not, as above, the specific means.

There are only two species involved and so the mean difference between the species will be fully accounted for by the regression and the only differences between y and Y will exist within species. Now $S(y-Y)^2$ is, by definition of multiple regression, at a minimum. Hence the fitting of b_1 and b_2 is exactly equivalent in its effect on the mean squares to the calculation of λ_1 and λ_2. Indeed, it can be shown that b_1 and b_2 are proportional to λ_1 and λ_2.

We have already seen in the last section that a multiple regression on two independent variates x_1 and x_2 take up 2 degrees of freedom in the analysis of variance of y. The remainder of the sum of squares has $2n-3$ degrees of freedom when n individuals of each species are involved. The discriminant leads to the same partition of the sum of squares and so the partitions of the degrees of freedom must be alike in the two cases. The analysis of variance of the discriminant function X will thus be:

	Sum of Squares	N
Between species	$\frac{n}{2}D^2$	2
Within species	D	$2n-3$
Total	$D\left(1+\frac{n}{2}D\right)$	$2n-1$

The significance of the specific difference can be tested by means of a z or variance ratio, using the mean square within species as the error variance.

Example 17. The two races, A and B, of the fly *Drosophila pseudo-obscura* are not easily distinguishable morphologically, but when the numbers of teeth in the sex-combs of the males are counted it is found that race A shows a greater mean than race B. There are two sex-combs on each foreleg of the male, the proximal comb and distal comb respectively, and the numbers of teeth in the two are not fully correlated. The mean numbers of teeth in each comb in 11 different strains of each race are shown in Table 37. What compound of x_p and x_d will maximize the racial difference and to what extent will this improve the racial classification of males?

TABLE 37

Mean Numbers of Teeth in the Male Sex-combs of Eleven Strains in each Race of Drosophila pseudo-obscura (*Mather and Dobzhansky*)

Race A			Race B		
Proximal comb (x_p)	Distal comb (x_d)	X	Proximal comb (x_p)	Distal comb (x_d)	X
6·36	5·24	2·546	6·00	4·88	2·394
5·92	5·12	2·402	5·60	4·64	2·245
5·92	5·36	2·434	5·64	4·96	2·299
6·44	5·64	2·623	5·76	4·80	2·313
6·40	5·16	2·547	5·96	5·08	2·409
6·56	5·56	2·647	5·72	5·04	2·333
6·64	5·36	2·644	5·64	4·96	2·299
6·68	4·96	2·602	5·44	4·88	2·231
6·72	5·48	2·682	5·04	4·44	2·056
6·76	5·60	2·710	4·56	4·04	1·863
6·72	5·08	2·629	5·48	4·20	2·152

$$X = 0·291174 x_p + 0·132507 x_d$$

DISCRIMINANT FUNCTIONS

For the purpose of finding the discriminant
$$X=\lambda_p x_p+\lambda_d x_d$$
It is necessary to calculate
$$d_p=\bar{x}_{pA}-\bar{x}_{pB}=6\cdot465454-5\cdot530909=0\cdot934545$$
$$d_d=\bar{x}_{dA}-\bar{x}_{dB}=5\cdot323636-4\cdot720000=0\cdot603636$$
$$S(x_p-\bar{x}_p)^2 \text{ within races}=7\cdot431927-4\cdot803563=2\cdot628364$$
$$S(x_d-\bar{x}_d)^2 \text{ within races}=3\cdot752727-2\cdot004072=1\cdot748655$$
$$S[(x_p-\bar{x}_p)(x_d-\bar{x}_d)] \text{ within races}=4\cdot380073-3\cdot102691=1\cdot277382$$
Then
$$2\cdot628364\lambda_p+1\cdot277382\lambda_d=0\cdot934545$$
$$1\cdot277382\lambda_p+1\cdot748655\lambda_d=0\cdot603636$$
which gives $\lambda_p=0\cdot291174$ and $\lambda_d=0\cdot132507$
So
$$X=0\cdot291174 x_p+0\cdot132507 x_d$$
and
$$D=\bar{X}_A-\bar{X}_B=\lambda_p d_p+\lambda_d d_d=(0\cdot291174\times0\cdot934545+0\cdot132507\times0\cdot603636)$$
$$=0\cdot352101$$

The number of strains of each race used in the calculation, i.e. n, is 11. The analysis of variance of X may now be written down.

Item	Sum of Squares	N	Mean Square	Variance Ratio	Probability
Between races	0·681863	2	0·340932	18·397	Very small
Within races	0·352101	19	0·018532		
Total	1·033964	21			

The sum of squares of X between races is
$$\frac{n}{2}D^2=\frac{11}{2}(0\cdot352101)^2$$
$=0\cdot681863$ and the sum of squares within races is $D=0\cdot352101$.

The calculation of the mean squares and variance ratios proceeds as usual, and the probability is found to be very small when the table of variance ratios is consulted. There is a good racial difference in the value of our discriminant X.

Misclassification of a strain will occur when its departure from the racial mean is greater than half the racial difference, provided that the departure occurs in the right direction; for in such a case the strain mean will fall nearer to the mean of the race to which it does not belong.

The racial difference in X is 0·352101 and the estimated standard deviation of X within races is $\sqrt{0\cdot018532}=0\cdot13613$. A deviation of $\dfrac{D}{2}=\dfrac{0\cdot352101}{2}=0\cdot17605$ will cause misclassification, and such a deviation is $\dfrac{0\cdot17605}{0\cdot13613}$, i.e. 1·293 times the standard deviation, as estimated from the 19 degrees of freedom. Now a $t_{[19]}$ equals or exceeds the value 1·293 by chance in just over 20% of cases. But for misclassification to occur the deviation must be in one given direction. Hence, although such a t value may be exceeded in about 20% of cases, misclassification will occur in about 10% of cases only. The other 10% of cases represents the occasions on which the departure of the strain mean from the race mean is over half the size of the racial difference but is in the direction away from that which causes misclassification.

The misclassification rate of the strains of Table 37 agrees reasonably well with this expectation. $\bar{X}_A = 2·58799$ and $\bar{X}_B = 2·23589$. Therefore anything greater than 2·41194 will be attributed to race A and anything less to race B. This results in 1 out of the 22 strains being misclassified where 2·2 are expected to be placed wrongly. We should note also that two other strains deviate from the mean by more than 0·17605 in the direction of not causing misclassification, 2·2 being expected to show such a deviation.

The same analysis may be made on the data for proximal and distal combs separately. With the proximal comb the racial difference is 0·934545 and the mean square within races $\dfrac{2·628364}{20} = 0·131418$. Note that here there are 20 degrees of freedom within races in contrast to the 19 of the discriminant analysis. Then $t_{[20]} = \dfrac{0·934545}{2} \div \sqrt{0·131418} = 1·289$, which has a probability almost equal to that of the discriminant's t with misclassification about 10%. The discriminant enjoys but little advantage over the proximal comb used alone.

The distal comb alone is not so discriminative as either the proximal comb or the discriminant X. The racial difference is 0·603636 and the standard deviation within races

$$\sqrt{\dfrac{1·748655}{20}} = 0·59138$$

So $t_{[20]} = \dfrac{0·603636}{2 \times 0·59138} = 1·021$ with a probability of 30% and hence a misclassification frequency of 15%.

The frequency of misclassification can be found exactly if t values are used, as the t distribution makes due allowance for sampling errors in the estimation of the standard deviation. The use of the normal deviate for this purpose would not accommodate such sampling errors and hence would lead to underestimation of the misclassification frequency.

If the discriminant is to be used frequently in practice it is better to put

$$X' = 3\cdot 43437 X = x_p + 0\cdot 4551 x_d$$

The first-order quantities, such as mean and standard deviation, will then all be $3\cdot 43437$ times the values obtained when X was used and the quadratic quantities, like the variance and sums of squares, will be $(3\cdot 43437)^2$, i.e. $11\cdot 7949$ times the value given by X.

A further modification might be considered for very extensive use of the discriminant. We could take a new X equal to $x_p + \frac{1}{2} x_d$. This would not cause much loss of precision and would materially lessen the arithmetic. In order to use this compound a fresh standard deviation would be necessary and it could be found from the sum of squares within races obtained as

$$S(x_p - \bar{x}_p)^2 + 2(\tfrac{1}{2}) S[(x_p - \bar{x}_p)(x_d - \bar{x}_d)] + (\tfrac{1}{2})^2 S(x_d - \bar{x}_d)^2$$

all deviations being from the racial means.

In the present example the extensive use of the discriminant would hardly be justified as the proximal comb alone supplied nearly as much information about racial differences. In other cases, however, this is not true and the discriminant has been found to give much greater precision of classification than any single measurement. Such a case is described in the genus *Iris*, where three species were involved, by Fisher, and should be consulted for further details of the application of discriminant functions to taxonomic problems.

REFERENCES

ASHBY, E. 1937. Studies in the inheritance of physiological characters —III. *Ann. Bot. N.S.*, **1**, 11–41.

BUCK, J. B. 1937. Studies on the firefly—I. *Physiol. Zool.*, **10**, 45–58.

FISHER, R. A. 1944. *Statistical Methods for Research Workers.* Oliver and Boyd. Edinburgh. 9th ed.

—— 1936. The use of multiple measurements in taxonomic problems. *Ann. Eugen.*, **7**, 87–104.

—— and YATES, F. 1943. *Statistical Tables for Biological, Agricultural and Medical Research.* Oliver and Boyd. Edinburgh. 2nd ed.

MATHER, K., and DOBZHANSKY, TH. 1939. Morphological differences between the 'races' of *Drosophila pseudo-obscura*. *Amer. Nat.*, **73**, 5–25.

CHAPTER X

CORRELATION

40. INTER-CLASS CORRELATION

IN the calculation of a regression coefficient the parts played by the dependent variate, y, and the independent variate, x, are very different. Hence the regression of y on x is quite distinct from the regression of x on y. This difference is reflected in the conditions which must be fulfilled by the variates in order that the regression calculation shall be valid.

It is, however, not infrequently the case that x and y are similarly distributed, whereupon the regression of x on y has as much relevance to the problem as has the regression of y on x. One example of this is afforded by the coincident measurement of some physical character, e.g. stature, in fathers and sons, both the fathers and sons being sampled at random from the population. With such data it is possible to use the correlation coefficient for the purpose of summarization and analysis.

The correlation coefficient has occupied a very important place in statistics, but its use is gradually dying, as the method of regression will always offer as good a solution to a problem and is very frequently much better. This is especially true where x, the independent variate, is not normally distributed, as in the case of the analyses shown in Examples 12, 13 and 15. The use of the correlation coefficient for such analyses would be incorrect. Correlation is still used fairly extensively, chiefly in the analysis of observations made on non-experimental material, and so some account of its application must be given. In general, however, the method of regression is much to be preferred.

When a variable, x, is normally distributed about the mean μ with a standard deviation σ, the frequency curve may be represented by the formula

$$m_x = \frac{1}{\sigma\sqrt{2\pi}} e^{\frac{-(x-\mu)^2}{2\sigma^2}} \quad . \quad . \quad . \quad . \quad (1)$$

m_x being the frequency expected in the class showing measurement x. Similarly, when the two variables, x and y, are each normally distributed with standard deviations σ_x and σ_y about the means μ_x and μ_y, the frequency surface is representable by

$$m_{xy} = \frac{1}{2\pi\sigma_x\sigma_y\sqrt{1-\rho^2}} e^{-\frac{1}{2(1-\rho^2)}\left[\frac{(x-\mu_x)^2}{\sigma_x^2} - \frac{2\rho(x-\mu_x)(y-\mu_y)}{\sigma_x\sigma_y} + \frac{(y-\mu_y)^2}{\sigma_y^2}\right]} \quad . \quad (2)$$

m_{xy} being the expected frequency of the double observation (x, y).

This formula contains a new quantity ρ which is called the inter-class correlation coefficient of x and y.

The following properties of ρ are not difficult to deduce mathematically from the formula (2). Suppose that $(x-\mu_x)$ takes the value x_1. Then from formula (1) $m_1 = \dfrac{1}{\sigma_x \sqrt{2\pi}} e^{-\dfrac{x_1^2}{2\sigma_x^2}}$ and

from (2) $\quad m_{1y} = \dfrac{1}{2\pi\sigma_x\sigma_y(1-\rho^2)} e^{-\dfrac{1}{2(1-\rho^2)}\left[\dfrac{x_1^2}{\sigma_x^2} - \dfrac{2\rho x_1(y-\mu_y)}{\sigma_x\sigma_y} + \dfrac{(y-\mu_y)^2}{\sigma_y^2}\right]}$

So, when $x-\mu_x=x_1$, the frequency distribution of y is representable as
$$m_y = \frac{m_{1y}}{m_1} = \frac{1}{\sigma_y\sqrt{2\pi(1-\rho^2)}} e^{-\dfrac{1}{2(1-\rho^2)\sigma_y^2}\left[y-\mu_y-\dfrac{\rho x_1 \sigma_y}{\sigma_x}\right]^2}$$

Thus no matter what particular value x may take, y is always normally distributed, and when $(x-\mu_x)$ has the value x_1 the mean value of y is $\mu_y + \rho\dfrac{x_1\sigma_y}{\sigma_x}$. This relation may be re-written as

$$\bar{y} = \mu_y + \rho\frac{\sigma_y}{\sigma_x}(x-\mu_x)$$

which is clearly the formula to a straight regression line with

$$b_y = \rho\frac{\sigma_y}{\sigma_x}$$

By substituting for y it can equally well be shown that x is normally distributed when y takes any special value and that the regression of x on y is linear with $b_x = \rho\dfrac{\sigma_x}{\sigma_y}$. On comparing the two regression coefficients, that of y on x and that of x on y, it becomes obvious that ρ is the geometrical mean of the two. It can then be shown that ρ must lie within the range $+1$ to -1.

One further conclusion remains to be drawn. When x takes a particular value the variance of y becomes $\sigma_y^2(1-\rho^2)$, i.e. is independent of x. So we may say that the correlation of y with x accounts for a proportion ρ^2 of the variance of y, the remaining portion $(1-\rho^2)$ being independent of x.

Example 18. A typical example of data to which the correlation approach is often applied is afforded by the results of Roberts and Griffiths's comparison of two methods of assessing the intelligence of all children born in Bath during the period 13 to 31 January 1922.

Examination was by means of both the Binet and the Otis tests, the former giving an I.Q. and the latter an I.B. value for each child. The results of testing these 65 children by both methods are given in Table 38.

TABLE 38
The I.Q. and I.B. scores of 65 Bath children (Roberts and Griffiths)

I.Q. (x)	I.B. (y)	I.Q. (x)	I.B. (y)	I.Q. (x)	I.B. (y)
67	36	91	91	108	91
70	28	91	129	108	111
72	34	92	92	108	115
74	28	92	98	109	134
75	48	94	115	110	113
76	50	95	80	110	124
77	62	96	96	110	129
78	22	96	108	110	140
81	82	96	146	112	145
82	84	97	118	113	147
83	64	97	121	114	126
83	77	99	106	114	132
83	82	100	79	115	142
84	92	101	103	115	157
85	91	101	113	116	126
86	65	101	118	116	138
86	75	101	119	123	149
86	76	101	141	126	142
87	68	103	115	126	164
89	80	103	131	127	172
89	110	103	139	135	156
91	72	107	102	Total 6,366	6,739

If we wished to find the regression of I.B., which may be called y, on I.Q., which may be called x, we should calculate

$$b_y = \frac{S[y(x-\bar{x})]}{S(x-\bar{x})^2} = \frac{S[(x-\bar{x})(y-\bar{y})]}{S(x-\bar{x})^2}$$

Similarly, the regression of x on y would be found as

$$b_x = \frac{S[x(y-\bar{y})]}{S(y-\bar{y})^2} = \frac{S[(x-\bar{x})(y-\bar{y})]}{S(y-\bar{y})^2}$$

Our estimate, r, of the correlation coefficient ρ is the geometric mean of b_x and b_y, so that

$$r = \sqrt{\frac{S[(x-\bar{x})(y-\bar{y})]}{S(x-\bar{x})^2} \cdot \frac{S[(x-\bar{x})(y-\bar{y})]}{S(y-\bar{y})^2}} = \frac{S[(x-\bar{x})(y-\bar{y})]}{\sqrt{S(x-\bar{x})^2 S(y-\bar{y})^2}}$$

On dividing both numerator and denominator by the number of degrees of freedom it is apparent that the equation of estimation may also be written

$$r = \frac{W_{xy}}{s_x s_y}$$

where W_{xy} is the covariance of x and y and s_x and s_y are the estimates of the two standard deviations.

Thus the calculation of r necessitates our knowing the sums of squares and the sum of cross-products of x and y. From Table 38 we find

$$S(x)=6,366 \qquad S(y)=6,739$$

Then
$$S(x-\bar{x})^2 = S(x^2) - \frac{S^2(x)}{n} = 638,650\cdot0000 - 623,476\cdot2462$$
$$= 15,173\cdot7538$$
$$S(y-\bar{y})^2 = S(y^2) - \frac{S^2(y)}{n} = 781,685\cdot0000 - 698,678\cdot7846$$
$$= 83,006\cdot2154$$
$$S[(x-\bar{x})(y-\bar{y})] = S(xy) - \frac{S(x)S(y)}{n} = 691,449\cdot0000 - 660,007\cdot2923$$
$$= 31,441\cdot7077$$

and
$$r = \frac{S[(x-\bar{x})(y-\bar{y})]}{\sqrt{S(x-\bar{x})^2 \cdot S(y-\bar{y})^2}} = \frac{31,441\cdot7077}{\sqrt{15,173\cdot7583 \times 83,006\cdot2154}}$$
$$= \frac{31,441\cdot7077}{35,489\cdot6587}$$
$$= 0\cdot885940$$

We may note that the regression of x on y is
$$b_x = \frac{31,441\cdot7077}{83,006\cdot2154} = 0\cdot378787$$

And the regression of y on x
$$b_y = \frac{31,441\cdot7077}{15,173\cdot7538} = 2\cdot072111$$

As a check on the arithmetic
$$r = \sqrt{b_x b_y} = \sqrt{0\cdot378787 \times 2\cdot072111} = 0\cdot885940$$

Taken together, the two regressions give more information than does the correlation coefficient. When $b_x = 0\cdot378787$ we know that for every unit advance in I.B. an advance of $0\cdot378787$ may be expected in I.Q.; and when $b_y = 2\cdot072111$ we know that for every unit advance in I.Q. an advance of $2\cdot072111$ is to be expected in I.B. Such forecasting is not possible when only the correlation coefficient is given.

With r of moderate or small size and the size of sample, n, large, r is distributed normally about the parameter ρ of which it is an estimate. Its variance, V_r, is $\frac{(1-\rho^2)^2}{n-1}$ in such cases. This is not, however, to be recommended as a basis for the calculation of a test of significance using a normal deviate, as n is seldom sufficiently large and r may not be small or even moderate in size. A t test may be employed instead, with $s_r = \sqrt{V_r} = \sqrt{\frac{(1-r^2)}{n-2}}$ as the denominator, t having $n-2$ degrees of freedom. Thus to test the significance of the deviation of r from 0, the value expected if x and y are unrelated,

$$t_{[n-2]} = \frac{r\sqrt{n-2}}{\sqrt{1-r^2}}$$

In the data of Table 38, $r = 0.885940$ and so $r^2 = 0.784890$, $1-r^2 = 0.215110$ and $\sqrt{1-r^2} = 0.463800$. Furthermore,

$$\sqrt{n-2} = \sqrt{63} = 7.9373$$

So $t_{[63]} = \frac{r\sqrt{n-2}}{\sqrt{1-r^2}} = \frac{0.8859 \times 7.9373}{0.4638} = \frac{7.0140}{0.4638} = 15.162$ and the probability of obtaining such a value by random sampling of an uncorrelated population is very small.

Fisher has devised another method of testing the significance of a correlation coefficient. It involves the use of what is called a transformed correlation, as it depends on the properties of z where

$$z = \tfrac{1}{2}[\log_e (1+r) - \log_e (1-r)]$$

When the two variates x and y are independent in distribution, $z = r = 0$. When x and y are fully correlated, i.e. $r = \pm 1$, z is very large. No matter what its value, z is very nearly normally distributed for all values of n, its standard deviation being $\frac{1}{\sqrt{n-3}}$. This is the true standard deviation σ_z, not the estimate s_z, as it is not found from the sum of squares of z in the data. Consequently the ratio of the deviation of z, from any expected value, to its standard deviation is a normal deviate, c, not a t, and may be tested by use of the table of normal deviates.

In the case of Roberts and Griffiths's data $r = 0.8859$. So

and
$$\begin{aligned}
1+r &= 1.8859, \quad \log_{10}(1+r) = 0.2756 \\
1-r &= 0.1141, \quad \log_{10}(1-r) = \bar{1}.0573 \\
\log_{10}(1+r) &- \log_{10}(1-r) = 1.2183 \\
z &= \tfrac{1}{2}[\log_e(1+r) - \log_e(1-r)] \\
&= 1.1513 [\log_{10}(1+r) - \log_{10}(1-r)] \\
&= 1.4026
\end{aligned}$$

$$n = 65, \text{ so } \sigma_z = \sqrt{V_z} = \sqrt{\frac{1}{65-3}} = \frac{1}{7.8740}$$

and $c = \dfrac{z}{\sigma_z} = 1.4026 \times 7.8740 = 11.044$ with a very small probability.

The normal deviate given by z is 11.044 while t, which for

63 degrees of freedom is almost the same as a normal deviate, is 15·162. The two methods of testing the same hypothesis do not give exactly the same result. Clearly the two tests are not exactly equivalent, but each is testing the hypothesis in its own characteristic way. The discrepancy between the two is not difficult to explain. The hypothesis has been rendered unlikely by both of the tests of significance. Now the two are testing the hypothesis in different ways, and so if the hypothesis is untrue their connecting link disappears. Hence when the hypothesis is rendered unlikely two such tests are not expected to give similar results. Where, however, the hypothesis in question is not rendered improbable by the tests, the two should give closely approximating results. Departure from hypothesis and discrepancy between valid tests of significance go hand-in-hand. A different example of this same phenomenon has been recorded by Mather in connexion with the χ^2 test of significance.

41. THE COMBINATION OF INTER-CLASS CORRELATION COEFFICIENTS

The transformed correlation coefficient, z, is of value in another way, viz. in combining two or more correlation coefficients.

Example 19. Roberts and Griffiths also give data on the I.Q.s and I.B.s of children born in Bath in the months of January 1923 and January 1924. In the following discussion the 1922 children will be referred to as Group 1, the 1923 children as Group 2 and the 1924 children as Group 3. Table 39 gives the correlation coefficients, r, and also the transformed correlations, z, for the three groups. As z is nearly normally distributed it may be used for combining these three estimates of ρ to give the best joint estimate.

TABLE 39
The Combination of Correlation Coefficients (Roberts and Griffiths)

Group of Children	r	z	n	I_z ($=n-3$)	$I_z z$
1	0·8859	1·4026	65	62	86·9612
2	0·9257	1·6274	60	57	92·7618
3	0·8749	1·3537	67	64	86·6368
			Total	183	266·3598

$$\hat{z} = \frac{S(I_z z)}{S(I_z)} = 1\cdot 4555$$
$$\hat{r} = 0\cdot 8968$$
$$V_{\hat{z}} = \frac{1}{S(I_z)} = \frac{1}{183}$$

Now the three groups contain different numbers of individuals so that the precisions of the three estimates are different. This clearly must affect the procedure of combination, because an estimate of greater precision will be of more value in pointing to the best estimate. It must be given a greater weight in the calculation. This raises the problem of the measure of precision of an estimate.

As the variance of any distribution decreases, the chance of finding a deviation from the mean of any given magnitude decreases, too. In other words, the precision of our knowledge of the distribution has increased and we can predict the behaviour of single observations with greater accuracy. So the precision must obviously be related to the variance. Indeed, the reciprocal of the variance immediately suggests itself as a measure of precision. But it is equally true to say that as the standard deviation of the distribution decreases, the precision of our knowledge of the behaviour of a single observation also increases. Thus we might, on the face of it, suppose that the reciprocal of the standard deviation also provided a good measure of precision. How are we to decide between these two possible measures?

Let us consider a specific case, viz. the estimation of a mean. The variance of the mean of a distribution is obtained as the ratio of the distribution's variance to the number of observations. When the number of observations is doubled the variance of their mean is, on the average, halved. The standard error of the mean, on the other hand, is divided by $\sqrt{2}$. Now if the reciprocal of the variance is taken as the measure of precision, the precision value characteristic of the mean x based on n_1 observations will be $\frac{n_1}{V_x}$, i.e. the reciprocal of $\frac{V_x}{n_1}$, where V_x is the variance of the distribution whose mean is $\bar{x}$. The precision of a mean based on n_2 observations is similarly $\frac{n_2}{V_x}$ and that of the mean of n_1+n_2 observations $\frac{n_1+n_2}{V_x}$. The precision of the joint mean is equal to the sum of the precisions of the two individual means.

Where, however, precision is measured by the reciprocal of the standard deviation this simple additive rule does not hold, as the three precisions would clearly be in the ratio
$$\sqrt{n_1} : \sqrt{n_2} : \sqrt{n_1+n_2}$$
Hence the reciprocal of the variance is a much more convenient measure. When used in this way the reciprocal of the variance, or invariance, is called the amount of information and is denoted by the letter I. The choice of this measure of precision will be

discussed in more detail in relation to the theory of estimation in a later chapter.

The amounts of information about the three z values of Table 39 are easily found from the reciprocals of the variances of each of the z's. $V_z = \dfrac{1}{n-3}$ and so $I_z = \dfrac{1}{V_z} = n-3$. These, then, are the weights to be applied to the z's in calculating the best joint estimate, which will be found in the form of what is commonly called a weighted mean of the three values. Each z is multiplied by its characteristic weight and the three products are summed, due weight thus being given to each estimate in the joint sum. Supposing, however, that all the estimates had been identical. Then the best joint estimate would also be the same as each of the three individuals. Now if we had arrived at a weighted sum in the above way it would clearly be necessary to divide the sum by the sum of the weights in order to recover this best estimate. This is also the correct procedure in the case where the three individual estimates are not all alike. Thus the formula for finding a weighted mean, $\hat{z}$, is

$$\hat{z} = \frac{S(I_z z)}{S(I_z)}$$

In our case $I_z z = (n-3)z$ and $S(I_z z) = (62 \times 1 \cdot 4026) + (57 \times 1 \cdot 6274)$
$$+ (64 \times 1 \cdot 3537) = 266 \cdot 3598$$
$$S(I_z) = 62 + 57 + 64 = 183$$

So
$$\hat{z} = \frac{266 \cdot 3598}{183} = 1 \cdot 4555$$

and
$$\hat{r} = \frac{(e^{2\hat{z}} - 1)}{(e^{2\hat{z}} + 1)} = 0 \cdot 8968$$

The variance of $\hat{z}$ is also found from the amounts of information. It will be recalled from our discussion of the precision of a mean that information, as defined in our present way, is additive. Hence

$$I_{\hat{z}} = S(I_z) = 183 \text{ and so } V_{\hat{z}} = \tfrac{1}{183}$$

42. PARTIAL CORRELATION

It has already been shown that correlation is a modification of linear regression and in consequence we may reasonably expect that any operation involving linear regression analysis will have a counterpart in the correlation method. So we should anticipate that multiple, or, as it is often called, partial regression, can be reproduced in the correlation technique, and indeed this is so. The method in question is termed partial correlation.

Suppose that we have taken three measurements w, x and y, on each of n individuals. A correlation coefficient relating any pair can be found. There will be three such quantities, r_{xy}, r_{xw} and r_{yw}. From these three the partial correlation coefficient, $r_{xy.w}$, which measures the correlation between x and y when due allowance is made for the effect of w, can be found by using the formula

$$r_{xy.w} = \frac{r_{xy} - r_{xw} r_{yw}}{\sqrt{(1-r_{xw}^2)(1-r_{yw}^2)}}$$

The method can be extended to cases involving more than three variables, but the arithmetic labour increases enormously as the number of variates becomes larger.

The significance of partial correlation is tested in exactly the same way as that used for simple correlation coefficients, but with an additional degree of freedom deducted for every variate eliminated. In the example with three variates, considered above, one degree of freedom would be lost when the variate w was eliminated. Thus if there were n observations, t testing $r_{xy.w}$ would take $n-3$ degrees of freedom rather than $n-2$ as used in the t test of a simple coefficient. When using the transformed correlation, z, the variance of $z_{xy.w}$ would be $\frac{1}{n-4}$, not $\frac{1}{n-3}$, as in the case of z_{xy}.

Data of this kind are, however, more profitably treated by the use of multiple regression.

43. INTRA-CLASS CORRELATION

In the example of a correlation coefficient that was considered in Section 40 the two variates, I.Q. and I.B., obtained from intelligence tests, differed quite markedly from one another. Their means were similar but their variances were very different.

It does, however, happen at times that the data requiring analysis concern the joint distribution of two like quantities. Such a case could be, for example, a set of measurements on pairs of fully grown brothers. If these were always separable into, say, elder and younger it would be possible to treat them by the correlation method already described; but if such a separation were not possible a different type of correlation coefficient, denoted as intra-class, would be necessary.

The intra-class correlation coefficient differs from the inter-class type in that during its calculation the two variates, x and y, are assumed to have the same mean and variance. No other assumption is possible if the x and y measurements, as pairs, are not separable. Even where separation is possible, the intra-class correlation is the more precise method, provided, of course, that the two measurements are of the same kind and might be expected to follow the same distribution.

In order to emphasize the similarity of the two measurements of the n pairs used in the calculation of an intra-class correlation we will refer to them as x and x', their common mean being $\bar{x} = \frac{1}{2n} S(x+x')$. Then the sum of their cross-products will be $S[(x-\bar{x})(x'-\bar{x})] = S(xx') - \frac{S^2(x+x')}{4n}$. By analogy with the inter-class coefficient this sum of cross-products will form the numerator of the fraction which provides the estimate of ρ. The denominator of the fraction in the case of an inter-class coefficient is

$$\sqrt{S(x-\bar{x})^2 S(y-\bar{y})^2} = (n-1) s_x s_y.$$

But we are now assuming that x and x', which replace x and y, have the same variance and hence the same standard deviation. Thus the equivalent denominator is $(n-1)s_x s_{x'} = (n-1)s_x^2$ or $(n-1)V_x$. Now, as $V_{x'} = V_x$, $2n-1$ degrees of freedom will be available for the estimation of V_x from the n pairs of observations. So $V_x = \frac{1}{2n-1}[S(x-\bar{x})^2 + S(x'-\bar{x})^2]$ and the denominator $(n-1)V_x$ becomes $\frac{n-1}{2n-1}[S(x-\bar{x})^2 + S(x'-\bar{x})^2]$. The equation of estimation of an intra-class correlation coefficient is thus

$$r = \frac{(2n-1)S[(x-\bar{x})(x'-\bar{x})]}{(n-1)[S(x-\bar{x})^2 + S(x'-\bar{x})^2]}$$

It is now evident why this coefficient is more precise than the inter-class type. The assumption that x and x' have the same mean and variance provides $2n-1$ degrees of freedom for the estimate of the variance, whereas in the inter-class case V_x and V_y each are estimated on the basis of $n-1$ comparisons.

Where there are two observations in each set the significance of an intra-class coefficient can be tested by transforming r into z with the help of the formula $z = \frac{1}{2}[\log_e(1+r) - \log_e(1-r)]$ and putting $V_z = \frac{1}{n - \frac{3}{2}}$.

When the number of measurements per set is three or more, e.g. where trios of fully grown brothers are measured, intra-class correlations can still be calculated. The data are cast in the form of paired observations for this purpose. A set of three observations would provide three such pairs, x and x', x and x'' and x' and x''. Each pair gives a complete sum of cross-products so that the grand total must be divided by three. The formula for the intra-class coefficient thus becomes:

$$r = \frac{(3n-1)(S[(x-\bar{x})(x'-\bar{x})] + S[(x-\bar{x})(x''-\bar{x})] + S[(x'-\bar{x})(x''-\bar{x})])}{3(n-1)[S(x-\bar{x})^2 + S(x'-\bar{x})^2 + S(x''-\bar{x})^2]}$$

The labour involved in such a calculation becomes very great as the number of observations in each set increases, but an easier approach to the analysis is possible. This is afforded by the analysis of variance, which incidentally also shows why the z transformation may be used in testing the significance of correlation coefficients.

Let us consider once more the case of n pairs of measurements, each pair including an x and an x' measurement. There are $2n$ measurements in all and hence $2n-1$ degrees of freedom between them. These may be partitioned into three groups. First, there will be 1 degree of freedom for the difference between the means of x and x'. Secondly, there will be $n-1$ degrees of freedom for differences between the pairs of observations. Finally, there will be $n-1$ degrees of freedom for the variation of the difference $(x-x')$ between the various pairs of observations. The analysis is, in fact, exactly the same as that used in the tomato example of Section 24.

If x and x' were separable, as would be the case with inter-class correlation data, the analysis could be made completely. If, however, x and x' are not separable, as in the present case, the analysis must be incomplete and the item for the difference between $\bar{x}$ and $\bar{x}'$ pooled with the third portion of the variance, viz. that concerning variation in the difference between x and x' in the different pairs of observations. In both complete and incomplete analyses the portion of the variance ascribable to differences between pairs of observations is capable of being isolated.

When x and x' are independent

$$V_{x+x'} = V_x + V_{x'}$$

but if x and x' are correlated this relation is modified by the inclusion of a covariance term which reduces the value of $V_{x+x'}$ when the correlation is negative and increases it when the correlation is positive. So the value of the mean square between pairs of observations will vary according to the type of correlation between x and x'. If it does not differ significantly from the error term, based on the variation of $(x-x')$, there is no evidence of correlation. If it is significantly higher than the error mean square the correlation is positive. If it is lower than the error mean square the correlation is negative.

The test of significance consists, of course, in the calculation of a z which is half the natural logarithm of the ratio of the two mean squares. The use of z as a transformation of the correlation coefficient for the purpose of testing significance is no longer mysterious.

The essential difference between inter- and intra-class correlation when viewed from the standpoint of the analysis of variance lies in the completeness of the partition in the analysis to which they lead. It must be added, however, that the analysis of variance may not always be applicable to inter-class correlation problems because marked differences in distribution of the two variates may be found. It is always appropriate to intra-class correlation analyses, which are based on the assumption that no such distributional differences exist.

We have already seen that the analysis of variance is a very general method and so it is clear that groups of more than two observations can be handled in this way. The following data from Mather and Lamm's account of the frequency of chiasma formation in rye chromosomes shows an application of the analysis to a case where each group consisted of seven observations.

Example 20. The majority of rye plants have seven pairs of chromosomes, i.e. bivalents, at meiosis, each of them forming from one to four chiasmata. The seven bivalents cannot be regularly distinguished from one another by inspection, and so the distribution of chiasma frequencies for any single bivalent cannot be found. It may, however, be assumed that all the bivalents have the same chiasma characteristics, whereupon the distribution of chiasma frequencies can be found by counting the chiasmata in each of the seven bivalents and treating each bivalent as a sample observation of the joint chiasma frequency distribution. Table 40 gives the results of such counts on the seven bivalents in each of 35 nuclei of a particular rye plant.

TABLE 40

The Frequency of Chiasma Formation in a Rye Plant (Mather and Lamm)

Number of chiasmata per bivalent	1	2	3	4		Total
Number of bivalents	4	150	89	2		245

Number of chiasmata per nucleus .	14	15	16	17	18	Total
Number of nuclei	1	3	12	14	5	35

In addition, the total number of chiasmata in each of the 35 nuclei was determined, it being, of course, the sum of the chiasmata in the seven constituent bivalents. These nuclear totals are also given in Table 40. The existence of a correlation between the numbers of chiasmata in the various bivalents of the same nucleus can be tested by an analysis of variance of these chiasma frequencies.

There are 245 observations in all, and so the total of degrees of freedom is 244. The corresponding total sum of squares of deviations from the general mean is found by summing the squares of the numbers of chiasmata and subtracting the correction term, which will clearly be $\frac{S^2(x)}{245}$. The calculation is thus

$$[4\times(1^2)+150\times(2^2)+89\times(3^2)+2\times(4^2)]-\frac{579^2}{245}$$
$$=1{,}437{\cdot}0000-1{,}368{\cdot}3306=68{\cdot}6694$$

This total must be partitioned into two items, one for differences between nuclei and one for differences within nuclei. The former will have 34 degrees of freedom, as there are 35 nuclei, leaving 210 for the latter item.

The sum of squares between nuclei is obtainable as

$$\tfrac{1}{7}[1\times(14^2)+3\times(15^2)+12\times(16^2)+14\times(17^2)+5\times(18^2)]-\frac{579^2}{245}$$
$$=1{,}372{\cdot}7143-1{,}368{\cdot}3306=4{\cdot}3837$$

The divisor 7 is used because each nuclear total is the sum of seven individual chiasma frequencies. The sum of squares within nuclei is then obtainable by subtraction, giving as the analysis:

TABLE 41

Item	Sum of squares	N	Mean square	Variance ratio
Between nuclei	4·3837	34	0·1289	2·3747, with a probability of about 0·001
Within nuclei	64·2857	210	0·3061	
Total	68·6694	244		

The seven bivalents of the nucleus are not separable, so that the analysis of variance is of necessity incomplete. The sum of squares within nuclei contains an item, for 6 degrees of freedom, dependent on differences between the chiasma frequencies of the seven bivalents.

The significance of the difference between the two items that are actually isolated can be tested by calculating the variance ratio $\frac{0\cdot3061}{0\cdot1289}=2\cdot3747$. The larger mean square has 210 degrees of freedom and the smaller 34, so that the variance ratio table is entered with $N_1=210$ and $N_2=34$. The probability is found to be about 0·001, so indicating a genuine discrepancy in size of the two mean squares. The same test could, of course, have been equally well performed by taking

$$z=\tfrac{1}{2}\log_e(\text{V.R.})=1\cdot1513\log_{10}(\text{V.R.})=1\cdot1513\log_{10}2\cdot3747=0\cdot4530$$

which, on entering in a table of z with $N_1=210$ and $N_2=34$, gives exactly the same probability as that found when the variance ratio itself was used.

The fact that the difference between the two mean squares is significant shows that a correlation in chiasma frequency exists between the seven bivalents of a nucleus. Furthermore, this correlation must be negative as the mean square between nuclei is lower than that within nuclei.

The intra-class correlation can be calculated from the data of Table 41, as it can be shown that the total sum of squares equals nkV_x and the sum of squares between nuclei is $nV_x[1+(k-1)r]$, where there are n sets (here 35) each of k observations (here 7), r being the correlation coefficient. Then the ratio of the sum of squares between nuclei to the total sum of squares must be $\frac{1+(k-1)r}{k}$. Arithmetically, from Table 41, this gives

$$\frac{1+(7-1)r}{7}=\frac{4\cdot3837}{68\cdot6694}=0\cdot06384=\frac{1-6r}{7}$$

and $\qquad r=\tfrac{7}{6}(0\cdot06384-0\cdot1429)=-0\cdot09219.$

This calculation also brings out one final property distinguishing intra- from inter-class coefficients. The latter may range, as we have seen, from -1 to $+1$. An intra-class correlation also has the upper limit of 1, but the lower limit is easily shown to be $-\frac{1}{k-1}$, attained when the sum of squares between nuclei, i.e. $nV_x[1+(k-1)r]$, takes its minimum value of 0. In this case $\frac{1+(k-1)r}{k}=0$ and $(k-1)r=-1$. So even when a negative intra-class coefficient is found to exist, its actual value is not of much use in determining the strength of the relation of which the correlation is a reflexion.

REFERENCES

FISHER, R. A. 1944. *Statistical Methods for Research Workers.* Oliver and Boyd. Edinburgh. 9th ed.

MATHER, K. 1940. The design and significance of synergic action tests. *J. Hyg.*, **40**, 513–31.

—— and LAMM, R. 1935. The negative correlation of chiasma frequencies. *Hereditas*, **20**, 65–70.

ROBERTS, J. A. FRASER, and GRIFFITHS, R. 1937. Studies on a child population. *Ann. Eugen.*, **8**, 15–45.

CHAPTER XI
THE ANALYSIS OF FREQUENCY DATA

44. χ^2 AND THE NORMAL DEVIATE

THE data resulting from observations or experiments are commonly of two types, which may for convenience be termed measurements and frequencies. In the former type each individual is characterized by a measurement of some kind. Most of the data so far considered have been of this type. Thus in Example 12 each observation gave the amount of Rb taken up by potato slices in a given time, and in Example 6 each tomato plant was represented by its yield in the data for analysis. In such cases the distributions of the various measurements must be reconstructed in a suitable manner from the experimental results themselves. This means that the variances used in the final tests of significance are estimated from observations. The t and z distributions are, as we have seen, appropriate to analyses of this kind. We may note that the maize data of Example 1 were of this type, though they had been recast into the form of a frequency distribution in order to lighten the arithmetic computation.

In other types of biological research the results of observation and experiment take the form of frequencies with which individuals fall into certain distinct classes. This is commonly the case with genetical experiments, such as that of Sirks discussed in Example 5, where two classes of plant, with coloured and white flowers, were recognized. With frequency data of this kind the hypothesis under test fixes the variance of the distribution expected and in consequence the test of significance will be made using a normal deviate or χ^2.

Both the normal deviate and χ^2 are found by comparing observed deviations, or squared deviations, with standard deviations, or variances, fixed by hypothesis. As has been pointed out in Chapter IV, they represent limits to t and z, in which quantities the variance or standard deviation forming the denominator is estimated from the data. The normal deviate may also be regarded as a special case of χ^2 in that its numerator consists of a single deviation while that of χ^2 may depend on any number of independent comparisons. This relation can perhaps be best seen from a further consideration of Sirks's results.

One cautionary remark must be made here. Both χ^2 and the normal deviate are derived from the continuous normal distribution, whereas frequency data are discontinuous. In consequence an error is introduced, but it will not be large unless the expected class frequencies are small. Neither χ^2 nor the normal deviate should ever be used where any class frequency has an expectation of 5 or less. Yates's correction for continuity (Section 19) helps to overcome this trouble, but the above rule is a sound safeguard against the serious overestimation of significance.

Example 21. It will be recalled from Example 5 that on self-pollinating a *Datura* plant heterozygous for the gene P,p, Sirks obtained a family containing 59 coloured (P) and 14 white (p) flowered plants. Mendelian theory leads us to expect that, on the average, $\frac{3}{4}$ of the individuals would be coloured and the remaining $\frac{1}{4}$ white; but it also tells us, and this is an important point, that the distribution of the observed frequencies of coloured individuals in such families will have the characteristic binomial variance of $p(1-p)n$, where p and $(1-p)$ are the probabilities that a given individual will be coloured or white, i.e. $\frac{3}{4}$ and $\frac{1}{4}$ respectively, and n is the number of individuals in the family, in this case 73.

So we expect to find $\frac{3}{4} \times 73$, i.e. 54·75, coloured plants and $\frac{1}{4} \times 73$, i.e. 18·25, white plants in such a family. Furthermore, the variance of the number of coloureds or whites is expected to be $\frac{3}{4} \times \frac{1}{4} \times 73$, i.e. 13·6875.

The deviation of the observed frequency of coloureds from that expected is 59−54·75 or 4·25. This may be compared with the standard deviation, found as the square root of the variance, to give a normal deviate in the form $\dfrac{4\cdot 25}{\sqrt{13\cdot 6875}} = \dfrac{4\cdot 25}{3\cdot 6997} = 1\cdot 149$.

Consultation of a table of normal deviates (Table I) shows that the probability of finding a fit as bad or worse is between 0·26 and 0·25.

The same result could be obtained equally well using χ^2. For this calculation it is necessary to compare the square of the observed deviation with the expected variance, i.e.

$$\chi^2_{[1]} = \frac{(4\cdot 25)^2}{13\cdot 6875} = \frac{18\cdot 0625}{13\cdot 6875} = 1\cdot 3196 = 1\cdot 149^2.$$

This χ^2 will have 1 degree of freedom because the numerator is based on one comparison between the data. A normal deviate is thus the square root of a χ^2 for 1 degree of freedom, a relation which is exactly the same as that holding between t and the variance ratio. The table of χ^2 (Table III) shows that the probability of finding a fit with hypothesis at least as bad as that observed lies between 0·30 and 0·20. The normal deviate permitted the probability to be stated with greater accuracy because the table of normal deviates, being one-dimensional, is more closely computed than the two-dimensional χ^2 table. This extra precision is, however, seldom of real importance in understanding the implications of experimental data.

It may be noted that Yates's correction for continuity could have been applied in the calculation of χ^2 in exactly the same way as it was used in Example 5.

45. THE VARIOUS FORMS OF χ^2

The normal deviate is confined to cases like the one above where only one observed deviation is to be tested, but χ^2 is of wider use when its general form is known.

Where only a single deviation is to be tested, χ^2, as we have seen above, can be found from the formula

$$\chi^2_{[1]} = \frac{(a_1 - m_1 n)^2}{m_1 m_2 n} = \frac{(a_2 - m_2 n)^2}{m_1 m_2 n}$$

where n is the family size, m_1 and m_2 the relative proportions expected to fall into the two classes, and a_1 and a_2 the numbers observed in the two classes. It should be noted that $m_1 + m_2 = 1$ and $a_1 + a_2 = n$. The symbols m_1 and m_2 replace p and $(1-p)$ for reasons which will become apparent when more complicated data are under discussion. In Sirks's case $a_1 = 59$, $a_2 = 14$, $n = a_1 + a_2 = 73$, $m_1 = \frac{3}{4}$, $m_2 = \frac{1}{4}$ and $m_1 + m_2 = 1$. Then

$$\chi^2_{[1]} = \frac{(a_1 - m_1 n)^2}{m_1 m_2 n} = \frac{\left(59 - \frac{3 \times 73}{4}\right)^2}{\frac{3}{4} \times \frac{1}{4} \times 73} \quad \text{as already used}$$

This formula for χ^2 is incapable of extension to more complex cases, but it can be recast into a form from which the general formula becomes obvious.

$$\chi^2_{[1]} = \frac{(a_1 - m_1 n)^2}{m_1 m_2 n} = \frac{(a_1 - m_1 a_1 - m_1 a_2)^2}{m_1 m_2 n}$$

since $n = a_1 + a_2$

$$= \frac{(m_2 a_1 - m_1 a_2)^2}{m_1 m_2 n}$$

since $m_2 = 1 - m_1$.[*]

We may pause here to note that this formula or its variant $\chi^2_{[1]} = \frac{(a_1 - la_2)^2}{ln}$ where $l = \frac{m_1}{m_2}$ is very convenient for the calculation of χ^2, testing the fit of an observed two-class segregation with

---

[*] Yates's correction for continuity results in the value, which is squared to give the numerator of this fraction, being reduced by 1 if positive or -1 if negative, i.e. if $m_2 a_1 > m_1 a_2$ it is $(m_2 a_1 - m_1 a_2 - 1)$, or if $m_2 a_1 < m_1 a_2$ it is $(m_2 a_1 + 1 - m_1 a_2)$.

the expected ratio $m_1 : m_2$, or $l : 1$ where $l = \frac{m_1}{m_2}$. It is, as will be seen later, widely used in analyses of this kind.

Resuming the general discussion, a further transformation may be made:

$$\chi^2_{[1]} = \frac{(m_2 a_1 - m_1 a_2)^2}{m_1 m_2 n}$$

$$= \frac{1}{m_1 m_2 n}(m_2^2 a_1^2 - 2m_1 m_2 a_1 a_2 + m_1^2 a_2^2)$$

Since $1 + m_1^2 + m_1 m_2 - 2m_1 = m_2$
$1 + m_1 m_2 + m_2^2 - 2m_2 = m_1$
and $m_1 + m_2 - 2 = -1$

$$\chi^2_{[1]} = \frac{1}{m_1 m_2 n}[m_2 a_1^2(1 + m_1^2 + m_1 m_2 - 2m_1) + m_1 a_2^2(1 + m_1 m_2 + m_2^2 - 2m_2)$$
$$+ 2m_1 m_2 a_1 a_2(m_1 + m_2 - 2)]$$

By expansion and rearrangement

$$\chi^2_{[1]} = \frac{1}{m_1 m_2 n}[m_2 a_1^2 - 2m_1 m_2 a_1^2 - 2m_1 m_2 a_1 a_2 + m_1^2 m_2 a_1^2 + 2m_1^2 m_2 a_1 a_2$$
$$+ m_1^2 m_2 a_2^2 + m_1 a_2^2 - 2m_1 m_2 a_2^2 - 2m_1 m_2 a_1 a_2 + m_1 m_2^2 a_1^2$$
$$+ 2m_1 m_2^2 a_1 a_2 + m_1 m_2^2 a_2^2]$$

(since $a_1 + a_2 = n$)

$$= \frac{1}{m_1 m_2 n}[m_2 a_1^2 - 2m_1 m_2 n a_1 + m_1^2 m_2 n^2 + m_1 a_2^2 - 2m_1 m_2 n a_2 + m_1 m_2^2 n^2]$$

$$= \frac{1}{m_1 m_2 n}[m_2(a_1 - m_1 n)^2 + m_1(a_2 - m_2 n)^2] = \frac{(a_1 - m_1 n)^2}{m_1 n} + \frac{(a_2 - m_2 n)^2}{m_2 n}$$

This formula has two terms each dependent on one of the two classes into which the family was divided. Applying it to Sirks's data we find:

$$\chi^2_{[1]} = \frac{\left(59 - \frac{3 \times 73}{4}\right)^2}{\frac{3 \times 73}{4}} + \frac{\left(14 - \frac{73}{4}\right)^2}{\frac{73}{4}} = 1.3196 \text{ as before}$$

It is easy to see that this formula can be extended to any number of classes in the form

$$\chi^2 = \frac{(a_1 - m_1 n)^2}{m_1 n} + \frac{(a_2 - m_2 n)^2}{m_2 n} + \ldots + \frac{(a_j - m_j n)^2}{m_j n}$$

where $a_1 + a_2 + \ldots + a_j = n$ and $m_1 + m_2 + \ldots + m_j = 1$
or more compactly $\chi^2 = S\left[\frac{(a - mn)^2}{mn}\right]$.

This formula in its turn may be re-written in a form more convenient for calculation as

$$\chi^2 = S\left[\frac{(a-mn)^2}{mn}\right] = S\left[\frac{a^2 - 2amn + m^2n^2}{mn}\right]$$
$$= S\left(\frac{a^2}{mn}\right) - 2S\left(\frac{amn}{mn}\right) + S\left(\frac{m^2n^2}{mn}\right)$$
$$= S\left(\frac{a^2}{mn}\right) - 2n + n = S\left(\frac{a^2}{mn}\right) - n$$

46. PARTITIONING χ^2

The use of these formulae allows a χ^2 to be calculated to test the fit with expectation of any number of classes in a set of data. It is, however, clear that the value of χ^2 will not be independent of the number of classes concerned. It will, in fact, have a characteristic number of degrees of freedom, as the following considerations show.

We have seen that a χ^2 testing the fit of two observed frequencies a_1 and a_2 with the expected values, $m_1 n$ and $m_2 n$, can be written in the form

$$\chi^2_{[1]} = \frac{(m_2 a_1 - m_1 a_2)^2}{m_1 m_2 n}$$

This is obviously dependent on one comparison between the observed frequencies, viz. $(m_2 a_1 - m_1 a_2)$, and so has 1 degree of freedom.

The next simplest case is that of individuals falling into three classes. Let the expected proportions be m_1, m_2 and m_3, so that $m_1 + m_2 + m_3 = 1$, and the numbers observed be correspondingly a_1, a_2 and a_3, the total being n. Applying the general formula

$$\chi^2 = \frac{a_1^2}{m_1 n} + \frac{a_2^2}{m_2 n} + \frac{a_3^2}{m_3 n} - n$$

But suppose we pool classes 1 and 2 to give a two-class segregation having the observed frequencies $(a_1 + a_2) : a_3$ and expectations $(m_1 + m_2)n : m_3 n$. A χ^2 for 1 degree of freedom testing the agreement of observations and expectation in this new two-class segregation can be calculated from the formula

$$\chi^2_{[1]} = \frac{[m_3(a_1 + a_2) - (m_1 + m_2)a_3]^2}{m_3(m_1 + m_2)n}$$

The derivation of this from the general two-class formula requires no explanation.

PARTITIONING χ^2

The formula for the total χ^2 must include this item and also another which may reasonably be supposed to be concerned with the separation of classes 1 and 2. By subtraction, this second portion is

$$\left(\frac{a_1{}^2}{m_1 n}+\frac{a_2{}^2}{m_2 n}+\frac{a_3{}^2}{m_3 n}-n\right)-\frac{[m_3(a_1+a_2)-(m_1+m_2)a_3]^2}{m_3(m_1+m_2)n}$$

(since $a_1+a_2+a_3=n$)

$$=\frac{1}{m_1 m_2 m_3 n}[a_1{}^2 m_2 m_3 + a_2{}^2 m_1 m_3 + a_3{}^2 m_1 m_2 - (a_1+a_2+a_3)^2 m_1 m_2 m_3]$$

$$-\frac{1}{m_3(m_1+m_2)n}[(a_1+a_2)^2 m_3{}^2 - 2(a_1+a_2)a_3(m_1+m_2)m_3 + a_3{}^2(m_1+m_2)^2]$$

$$=\frac{1}{m_1 m_2 m_3(m_1+m_2)n}[a_1{}^2 m_2 m_3(1-m_1)(m_1+m_2) + a_2{}^2 m_1 m_3(1-m_2)(m_1+m_2)$$
$$+ a_3{}^2 m_1 m_2(1-m_3)(m_1+m_2) - a_1{}^2 m_1 m_2 m_3{}^2$$
$$- a_2{}^2 m_1 m_2 m_3{}^2 - a_3{}^2 m_1 m_2(m_1+m_2)^2$$
$$- 2(a_1 a_2 + a_1 a_3 + a_2 a_3)m_1 m_2 m_3(m_1+m_2)$$
$$- 2a_1 a_2 m_1 m_2 m_3{}^2 + 2a_1 a_3 m_1 m_2 m_3(m_1+m_2)$$
$$+ 2a_2 a_3 m_1 m_2 m_3(m_1+m_2)]$$

$$=\frac{1}{m_1 m_2 m_3(m_1+m_2)n}[a_1{}^2 m_2 m_3(m_1 m_2 + m_2{}^2 + m_1 m_3 + m_2 m_3 - m_1 m_3)$$
$$+ a_2{}^2 m_1 m_3(m_1{}^2 + m_1 m_3 + m_1 m_2 + m_2 m_3 - m_2 m_3)$$
$$- 2a_1 a_2(m_1{}^2 m_2 m_3 + m_1 m_2{}^2 m_3 + m_1 m_2 m_3{}^2)]$$

(since $m_1+m_2+m_3=1$)

$$=\frac{1}{m_1 m_2 m_3(m_1+m_2)n}[a_1{}^2 m_2{}^2 m_3 - 2a_1 a_2 m_1 m_2 m_3 + a_2{}^2 m_1{}^2 m_3]$$

$$=\frac{(a_1 m_2 - a_2 m_1)^2}{m_1 m_2(m_1+m_2)n} = \frac{(m_2 a_1 - m_1 a_2)^2}{m_1 m_2 n'}$$

where $n'=n(m_1+m_2)$, i.e. is the total of individuals expected to fall into either class 1 or class 2.

This is clearly the formula of a χ^2 for 1 degree of freedom based solely on the comparison between classes 1 and 2. The only point requiring special note is that n', the effective total number of observations in classes 1 and 2 jointly, is the total number expected, not the total number observed.

So we see that the χ^2 calculated from a three-class segregation is divisible into two independent χ^2's each for 1 degree of freedom. The total χ^2 is thus based on two independent comparisons and has 2 degrees of freedom.

The subdivision of the total χ^2 could be made in two other ways according to whether classes 1 and 3 or classes 2 and 3 are pooled for the purpose of analysis. The three possible partitions are:

(i) $\dfrac{(m_2a_1-m_1a_2)^2}{m_1m_2n(m_1+m_2)}$ and $\dfrac{[m_3(a_1+a_2)-(m_1+m_2)a_3]^2}{(m_1+m_2)m_3n}$

(ii) $\dfrac{(m_3a_1-m_1a_3)^2}{m_1m_3n(m_1+m_3)}$ and $\dfrac{[m_2(a_1+a_3)-(m_1+m_3)a_2]^2}{(m_1+m_3)m_2n}$

(iii) $\dfrac{(m_3a_2-m_2a_3)^2}{m_2m_3n(m_2+m_3)}$ and $\dfrac{[m_1(a_2+a_3)-(m_2+m_3)a_1]^2}{(m_2+m_3)m_1n}$

There is thus scope for analysis of χ^2 into components testing those specific comparisons which the hypothesis in question suggests, exactly as was the case with sums of squares in Section 22.

The same type of analysis by subtraction can be applied to the case of a four-class segregation, and it can be shown that the total χ^2 has 3 degrees of freedom, being subdivisible into three independent components each based on a single comparison and hence each having one degree of freedom. This partition can be made in a number of ways of which two examples are

(i) $\dfrac{(m_2a_1-m_1a_2)^2}{m_1m_2n(m_1+m_2)}$, $\dfrac{[m_3(a_1+a_2)-(m_1+m_2)a_3]^2}{m_3(m_1+m_2)n(m_1+m_2+m_3)}$

and $\dfrac{[m_4(a_1+a_2+a_3)-(m_1+m_2+m_3)a_4]^2}{m_4(m_1+m_2+m_3)n}$

(ii) $\dfrac{(m_2a_1-m_1a_2)^2}{m_1m_2n(m_1+m_2)}$, $\dfrac{(m_3a_4-m_4a_3)^2}{m_3m_4n(m_3+m_4)}$

and $\dfrac{[(m_3+m_4)(a_1+a_2)-(m_1+m_2)(a_3+a_4)]^2}{(m_1+m_2)(m_3+m_4)n}$

A third type of partition of a 3 degree of freedom χ^2 which is much used in genetical analysis will be developed later.

It will be seen from the foregoing that a compound χ^2 can be partitioned into simple components each dependent on a single comparison and each taking 1 degree of freedom, in the same way that sums of squares are analysed. As with sums of squares, too, the single χ^2's are found from a comparison which is squared and divided by a characteristic divisor. With sums of squares (Section 23) the conditions which must be fulfilled for a successful partition are:

(i) In the comparison, $S(k)=0$
(ii) The divisor is $S(k^2)$
(iii) The comparisons are independent if $S(k_1k_2)=0$

Partitioning χ^2 is a somewhat more complex operation because the frequencies which are to be used in making the comparisons are not always expected to be equal, whereas in the analysis of

PARTITIONING χ^2

variance all the measurements have the same expectation. The complication introduced by this inequality of expectation is not, however, very great. The three conditions necessary for a successful partition are modified to

(i) In the comparison, $S(mk)=0$
(ii) The divisor is $nS(mk^2)$
(iii) The comparisons are independent if $S(mk_1k_2)=0$

As to the divisor, it may be noted that since χ^2 compares an observed deviation with the theoretical variance, $nS(mk^2)$ is clearly V_x, where $x=S(ak)$. This comparison, x, vanishes when a takes its expected value of mn.

Applying these three tests to the partition of a 2 degree of freedom into the two simple components

(i) $\dfrac{(m_2a_1-m_1a_2)^2}{m_1m_2n(m_1+m_2)}$ and (ii) $\dfrac{[m_3(a_1+a_2)-(m_1+m_2)a_3]^2}{(m_1+m_2)m_3n}$

we have in (i) $k_{11}=m_2 \quad k_{12}=-m_1 \quad k_3=0$
and in (ii) $k_{21}=m_3 \quad k_{22}=m_3 \quad k_{23}=-(m_1+m_2)$
and so $\quad S(mk_1)=m_1m_2-m_2m_1=0$
$\quad S(mk_2)=m_1m_3+m_2m_3-m_3(m_1+m_2)=0$
$\quad S(mk_1k_2)=m_1m_2m_3-m_2m_1m_3=0$
$\quad S(mk_1^2)=m_1m_2^2+m_2m_1^2=m_1m_2(m_1+m_2)$

giving as the divisor $\quad m_1m_2n(m_1+m_2)$
$S(mk_2^2)=m_1m_3^2+m_2m_3^2+m_3(m_1+m_2)^2$
$\quad =m_3(m_1+m_2)(m_1+m_2+m_3)=m_3(m_1+m_2)$

giving as the divisor $\quad (m_1+m_2)m_3n$

The partition satisfies all three conditions.

The application of the rules of partition to more complex cases can be illustrated by a genetical example.

Example 22. If a plant, which is heterozygous for two genes, A,a and B,b, is self-pollinated, the progeny is expected to fall into four phenotypic classes, AB, Ab, aB, ab. With no disturbance of the segregation each gene is expected to show a 3 : 1 ratio, i.e. (AB+Ab) should be three times as frequent as (aB+ab) and (AB+aB) three times as frequent as (Ab+ab). Furthermore, with unlinked genes their segregations are independent, i.e. the ratio of B : b is expected to be the same in A plants as it is in a plants. In short, with good gene segregations and no linkage the relative frequencies of the four classes are expected to be 9 AB : 3 Ab : 3 aB : 1 ab. Thus $m_1=\tfrac{9}{16}$, $m_2=m_3=\tfrac{3}{16}$ and $m_4=\tfrac{1}{16}$. Let a_1, a_2, a_3 and a_4 be the frequencies observed, with $S(a)=n$.

Using the general formula, a χ^2 for 3 degrees of freedom can be calculated to test the goodness of fit of observation with expectation in the four classes jointly. We require to analyse this into its three simple components in such a way as to tell us something about the nature of the two segregations and about the possible linkage of the two genes.

For the purpose of testing the segregation of A and a, the classes AB and Ab are pooled to give one A class, and aB and ab are pooled to give a single a class. The former is expected to be three times as large as the latter, i.e. $m_A = \tfrac{3}{4}$ and $m_a = \tfrac{1}{4}$. Then a χ^2 testing the segregation of A and a will depend on the comparison

$$(m_a a_A - m_A a_a) = \left(\frac{a_A}{4} - \frac{3a_a}{4}\right) = \tfrac{1}{4}(a_A - 3a_a)$$

The coefficients used in the calculation of this simple χ^2 must be 1 for both A classes and -3 for the two a classes. In terms of the four classes observed the comparison must then be

$$x_1 = k_{11} a_1 + k_{12} a_2 + k_{13} a_3 + k_{14} a_4$$
$$= a_1 + a_2 - 3a_3 - 3a_4$$

The first condition of partition is fulfilled as

$$k_{11} = k_{12} = 1 \quad \text{and} \quad k_{13} = k_{14} = -3$$

and $\quad m_1 k_{11} = \tfrac{9}{16}, \quad m_2 k_{12} = \tfrac{3}{16}, \quad m_3 k_{13} = -\tfrac{9}{16}, \quad m_4 k_{14} = -\tfrac{3}{16}$

so that $\quad S(mk_1) = \tfrac{1}{16}(9 + 3 - 9 - 3) = 0$

The divisor for this comparison is found from the formula $nS(mk_1^2)$ and is

$$nS(mk_1^2) = n\left[\left(\tfrac{9}{16} \times 1^2\right) + \left(\tfrac{3}{16} \times 1^2\right) + \left(\tfrac{3}{16} \times [-3]^2\right) + \left(\tfrac{1}{16} \times [-3]^2\right)\right]$$

$$= \frac{n}{16}(9 + 3 + 27 + 9) = 3n$$

So χ^2 testing the A:a segregation is $\dfrac{(a_1 + a_2 - 3a_3 - 3a_4)^2}{3n}$

It will be seen that this is simply a modification of the two-class segregation formula of Section 45, the two classes each being subdivided into two sub-classes which are then treated alike.

Similarly the χ^2 testing the B:b segregation will be

$$\frac{(a_1 - 3a_2 + a_3 - 3a_4)^2}{3n}$$

These two components are independent as

$$\left.\begin{array}{l} m_1 k_{11} k_{21} = \tfrac{9}{16} \times 1 \times 1 \\ m_2 k_{12} k_{22} = \tfrac{3}{16} \times 1 \times (-3) \\ m_3 k_{13} k_{23} = \tfrac{3}{16} \times (-3) \times 1 \\ m_4 k_{14} k_{24} = \tfrac{1}{16} \times (-3) \times (-3) \end{array}\right\} S(mk_1 k_2) = \tfrac{1}{16}(9 - 9 - 9 + 9) = 0$$

This leaves only the question of linkage χ^2 to be settled. What values should be assigned to k_{31}, k_{32}, &c.? Only one set of values can possibly be taken by these coefficients, as the deduction of the two simple χ^2's already found from the compound

χ^2 for 3 degrees of freedom can leave but one possible formula for the remaining component. It is, however, not necessary to arrive at it by the method of subtraction. Fisher's way of finding the coefficients in the comparisons on which components of sums of squares are based (Section 25) applies here also.

The two genes are each expected to show a segregation of $3:1$. Then χ^2 testing the segregation of A:a, i.e. the 'main effect' of A, can be represented by

$$(A-3a)(B+b) = AB + Ab - 3aB - 3ab$$

from which the k values are easily derived.

Similarly, the segregation of B:b is represented as

$$(A+a)(B-3b) = AB - 3Ab + aB - 3ab$$

Lastly, the linkage component or 'interaction' of A and B is

$$(A-3a)(B-3b) = AB - 3Ab - 3aB + 9ab$$

Thus $k_{31}=1$, $k_{32}=-3$, $k_{33}=-3$ and $k_{34}=9$. The divisor for this comparison is

$$nS(mk_3^2) = \frac{n}{16}[(9\times 1^2) + (3\times[-3]^2) + (3\times[-3]^2) + (1\times 9^2)]$$

$$= \frac{n}{16}(9+27+27+81) = 9n$$

and $$\chi^2 = \frac{(a_1 - 3a_2 - 3a_3 + 9a_4)^2}{9n}$$

That this is independent of the two previous comparisons is verified by

$S(mk_1k_3) = \frac{1}{16}[(9\times 1\times 1) + (3\times 1\times[-3]) + (3\times[-3]\times[-3]) + (1\times[-3]\times 9)]$
$= \frac{1}{16}[9 - 9 + 27 - 27] = 0$

and $S(mk_2k_3) = \frac{1}{16}[(9\times 1\times 1) + (3\times[-3]\times[-3]) + (3\times 1\times[-3]) + (1\times[-3]\times 9)]$
$= \frac{1}{16}[9 + 27 - 9 - 27] = 0$

The partition is now complete, the formulae for the three simple components of the χ^2 being

$$\mathbf{A:a} \quad \chi^2_{[1]} = \frac{(a_1 + a_2 - 3a_3 - 3a_4)^2}{3n}$$

$$\mathbf{B:b} \quad \chi^2_{[1]} = \frac{(a_1 - 3a_2 + a_3 - 3a_4)^2}{3n}$$

$$\text{Linkage} \quad \chi^2_{[1]} = \frac{(a_1 - 3a_2 - 3a_3 + 9a_4)^2}{9n}$$

Details of two families of the type under discussion are given in Table 42. They were recorded by Philp and Imai respectively, the plants being *Papaver* and *Pharbitis*. The gene symbols used by these authors were not A,a and B,b, but the latter are more convenient for our purpose.

TABLE 42

Philp's and Imai's Data on Two-gene Segregations

		AB	Ab	aB	ab	Total
Philp	Observed (a)	72	29	40	12	153
	Expected (mn)	86·0625	28·6875	28·6875	9·5625	153
Imai	Observed (a)	123	30	27	21	201
	Expected (mn)	113·0625	37·6875	37·6875	12·5625	201

The expectations given in the table are those based on the 9 : 3 : 3 : 1 ratio. A compound χ^2 for 3 degrees of freedom can be found from each set of data. Thus in Philp's case it is

$$\chi^2_{[3]} = S\left(\frac{a^2}{mn}\right) - n$$

$$= \frac{72^2}{86 \cdot 0625} + \frac{29^2}{28 \cdot 6875} + \frac{40^2}{28 \cdot 6875} + \frac{12^2}{9 \cdot 5625} - 153$$

= 7·3834, which has a probability of between 0·10 and 0·05. For Imai's data

$$\chi^2_{[3]} = \frac{123^2}{113 \cdot 0625} + \frac{30^2}{37 \cdot 6875} + \frac{27^2}{37 \cdot 6875} + \frac{21^2}{12 \cdot 5625} - 201$$

= 11·1393 with a probability of between 0·02 and 0·01.

The departure from expectation is clear in Imai's case and, though not quite significant in Philp's data, is at least suspiciously large and worthy of further investigation. The next step is that of partitioning $\chi^2_{[3]}$, using the formulae developed above. In Philp's case

A : a $\chi^2_{[1]} = \dfrac{[72 + 29 - (3 \times 40) - (3 \times 12)]^2}{3 \times 153}$

= 6·5904 with probability 0·02–0·01

B : b $\chi^2_{[1]} = \dfrac{[72 - (3 \times 29) + 40 - (3 \times 12)]^2}{3 \times 153}$

= 0·2636 with probability 0·70–0·50

Linkage $\chi^2_{[1]} = \dfrac{[72 - (3 \times 29) - (3 \times 40) + (9 \times 12)]^2}{9 \times 153}$

= 0·5294 with probability 0·50–0·30

The three items sum to give $\chi^2_{[3]} = 7 \cdot 3834$, so providing a check on the arithmetic.

It is now abundantly clear that the departure from expectation lies solely in the lack of agreement of the A : a segregation with its expected 3 : 1. The B : b segregation is good and there is no evidence of linkage. It may also be noted that when χ^2 is partitioned the significance of the departure of the A : a segregation is increased, because the single large χ^2 is isolated from the two smaller ones which previously masked its full effect.

The partition in Imai's data is

$$A : a \quad \chi^2_{[1]} = \frac{[123+30-(3\times27)-(3\times21)]^2}{3\times201}$$
$$= 0{\cdot}1343 \text{ with probability } 0{\cdot}80{-}0{\cdot}70$$

$$B : b \quad \chi^2_{[1]} = \frac{[123-(3\times30)+27-(3\times21)]^2}{3\times201}$$
$$= 0{\cdot}0149 \text{ with probability } 0{\cdot}95{-}0{\cdot}90$$

$$\text{Linkage} \quad \chi^2_{[1]} = \frac{[123-(3\times30)-(3\times27)+(9\times21)]^2}{9\times201}$$
$$= 10{\cdot}9900 \text{ with probability less than } 0{\cdot}001$$

Again the calculation is checked by summing the three items to give 11·1392. The difference of 1 in the last decimal place between this value and that obtained earlier is due, of course, to arithmetic approximation.

Here the situation differs from that in Philp's poppies. Both genes show good 3 : 1 segregations, but they are not independent in segregation, i.e. they must be linked.

It is now possible to see that the two families depart from expectation in quite different ways. Partitioning χ^2 has fully revealed the genetical situation in each case.

More complex χ^2's can be partitioned by exactly the same methods. Suppose there are three genes, A,a, B,b, C,c, segregating in a backcross (AaBbCc×aabbcc). Each gene is expected to show a 1 : 1 ratio and, in the absence of linkage, the three segregations are independent. Hence eight classes, ABC, ABc, AbC, aBC, Abc, aBc, abC and abc are expected in equal numbers. A compound χ^2 for 7 degrees of freedom can be calculated from the data as a whole. How should this be partitioned in order that the genetical situation can be fully appreciated?

Fisher's method may be used to find the k coefficients in the seven comparisons on which the partition is based. These must clearly consist of one for each of the three gene segregations or 'main effects', one each for the three linkage pairs or 'first-order interactions' and one for the 'second-order interaction' which here has no simple genetical interpretation. The k's are found as shown in Table 43.

TABLE 43
Coefficients for the Analysis of a Three-gene Backcross

Effect	Formula	ABC	ABc	AbC	Abc	aBC	aBc	abC	abc	$S(mk^2)$
Main Effect $\begin{cases} A:a \\ B:b \\ C:c \end{cases}$	$(A-a)(B+b)(C+c)$ $(A+a)(B-b)(C+c)$ $(A+a)(B+b)(C-c)$	1 1 1	1 1 −1	1 −1 1	1 −1 −1	−1 1 1	−1 1 −1	−1 −1 1	−1 −1 −1	1 1 1
First-order Interaction $\begin{cases} A \text{ and } B \text{ Linkage} \\ A \text{ and } C \text{ ,,} \\ B \text{ and } C \text{ ,,} \end{cases}$	$(A-a)(B-b)(C+c)$ $(A-a)(B+b)(C-c)$ $(A+a)(B-b)(C-c)$	1 1 1	1 −1 −1	−1 1 −1	−1 −1 1	−1 −1 1	−1 1 −1	1 −1 −1	1 1 1	1 1 1
Second-order Interaction $\{$No simple interpretation	$(A-a)(B-b)(C-c)$	1	−1	−1	1	−1	1	1	−1	1

THE EFFECT OF FITTING A PARAMETER

It should be noted that $(A-a)$ is used, and not $(A-3a)$ as in the previous example, since A and a are expected now to be equally frequent and not to show a 3 : 1 ratio.

In every case $S(mk^2)=1$, and so the divisor appropriate to each comparison is n. The calculation of the 21 different $S(mk_1k_2)$ quantities shows that all the comparisons are independent.

47. THE EFFECT OF FITTING A PARAMETER

Where a given number of individuals are assignable to j classes there are usually $j-1$ degrees of freedom for the calculation of a χ^2 testing the general agreement of observation and expectation over the whole of the data. Thus, in the case of the four-class segregation analysed in Example 22 a compound χ^2 was calculated for 3 degrees of freedom. This can be partitioned into three components each depending on a single comparison between the observed frequencies. It is then clear that adjustment of one or more of these comparisons will reduce the value of the total χ^2 in a characteristic way. This can perhaps be best understood from a further analysis of Philp's poppy data of Table 42.

Example 23. We have seen that the departure of Philp's observed frequencies from the 9 : 3 : 3 : 1 expectation is due to the gene A,a failing to give a 3 : 1 ratio. New expectations can be formulated using the observed A,a ratio in place of the original 3 : 1. There were 101 A plants and 52 a plants, so that the ratio is 1·9423 : 1. Since the segregation of gene B,b is still expected to be 3 : 1 and the two genes segregate independently of one another the new expectation is

$$5·8269 : 1·9423 : 3 : 1$$

which, with a total of 153 plants, gives as the expected frequencies

75·75 AB, 25·25 Ab, 39·00 aB, 13·00 ab

Using the formula $$\chi^2 = S\left(\frac{a^2}{mn}\right) - n$$

the general goodness of fit is found to be tested by $\chi^2 = 0·8450$. This is lower than the χ^2 obtained when the 9 : 3 : 3 : 1 expectation was used, but it also has 1 degree of freedom less, as will be readily appreciated when a partition is made.

The coefficients are found by Fisher's method

A:a $(A-1·9423a)(B+b) = AB+Ab-1·9423aB-1·9423ab$
B:b $(A+a)(B-3b) = AB-3Ab+aB-3ab$
Linkage $(A-1·9423a)(B-3b) = AB-3Ab-1·9423aB+5·8269ab$

It should be noticed that $(A-1·9423a)$ replaces $(A-3a)$ now that it has been agreed to discard the 3 : 1 expectation in favour of the ratio observed.

The formula $nS(mk^2)$ shows that the divisors of the three comparisons are $1 \cdot 9423n$, $3n$ and $5 \cdot 8269n$ respectively. The three portions of χ^2 are thus

A:a $\quad \chi^2 = \dfrac{1}{1 \cdot 9423n}(a_1 + a_2 - 1 \cdot 9423 a_3 - 1 \cdot 9423 a_4)^2$

B:b $\quad \chi^2 = \dfrac{1}{3n}(a_1 - 3a_2 + a_3 - 3a_4)^2$

Linkage $\quad \chi^2 = \dfrac{1}{5 \cdot 8269n}(a_1 - 3a_2 - 1 \cdot 9423 a_3 + 5 \cdot 8269 a_4)^2$

The first item, testing the A : a segregation, must clearly be 0, since the k's of the comparison are directly derived from the segregation observed. In other words, this component of χ^2 has been fixed and eliminated from the analysis by the adoption of the observed A : a segregation. Calculation of the parameter measuring the A : a segregation has removed one component of χ^2 and so reduced the total number of possible comparisons, i.e. of degrees of freedom, by 1.

On substituting the frequencies observed in the above formulae the other two components of χ^2 are found to be 0·2636 and 0·5815 respectively. These sum to 0·8451 as found for the compound χ^2, which is thus seen to be separable into only two simple components. The B:b component is exactly the same as in the previous analysis, but the linkage item has changed from 0·5294 to 0·5815. When the formulae for this component in the two analyses are compared, it will be observed that the change in the A : a expectation has altered the k's in the linkage comparison, so changing its arithmetic value a little. In general terms we might say that the previous hypothesis had been rendered unlikely and replaced by a new one. It is not to be expected that the goodness of fit will remain unchanged under these circumstances.

The principle that a degree of freedom is lost when a parameter is fitted is of general application in statistical analysis. It has earlier been seen in operation in fitting the normal distribution (Section 10), where the variance is estimated from $n-1$ degrees of freedom after the mean is calculated. If a regression coefficient is estimated another degree of freedom is lost from the material for the calculation of the residual sum of squares, and so on. The χ^2 test of goodness of fit falls into line with these others.

At the risk of anticipating the next chapter it may be stated here that the method of estimating the parameter must be a good one or the component which is supposedly lost will not actually be reduced to 0. In this way a spuriously large departure from expectation might be found as a result of faulty estimation.

The question of what constitutes a good method of estimation must be reserved for later comment.

48. HETEROGENEITY OF DATA

Frequency observations are often made in replicate, as, for example, in the case of Sirks's data on the segregation of the gene P,p in *Datura stramonium* (Example 5). In such cases it is of obvious importance to determine whether all the series of observations are in agreement with each other as well as with the expectation. A calculation designed to answer this question is generally known as a test of heterogeneity of the data.

The simplest case of this kind is that of two sets of observations in each of which the individuals may fall into either of two classes. Sirks's data referred to above are of this kind.

Example 24. As described in Example 5 two families were raised each of which was expected to show a 3 : 1 segregation for P : p plants. The details of the two families are given in Table 44.

TABLE 44
Segregation in Datura stramonium *(Sirks)*

Family	Number of plants			χ^2
	P	p	Total	
1922 . .	59	14	73	1·3196
1925 . .	103	23	126	3·0582
Total . .	162	37	199	4·3568

In effect, the data consist of a four-class table, the classes being distinguished by the simultaneous classification for type and family. The hypothesis to be tested is that the two families agree with each other in showing a 3 : 1 segregation.

Three degrees of freedom, or comparisons, are available from such a four-class table, but they are not of equal importance with respect to this hypothesis. The analysis of Section 46 shows that the three simple χ^2 can be made to test

(i) The agreement of the P : p totals with hypothesis.
(ii) The agreement of the family totals with hypothesis.
(iii) The independence of the two classifications.

The first of these is clearly found from the P : p totals as $\chi^2_{[1]} = \frac{[162-(3\times 37)]^2}{3\times 199} = 4\cdot 3568$, and tests the general agreement of the data with the 3 : 1 expected.

The second $\chi^2_{[1]}$ component cannot, however, be calculated, because the hypothesis makes no stipulation about the size of the families. The third $\chi^2_{[1]}$ can be found in exactly the same way as the linkage component in the analysis of Philp's poppy data after the expectation of 3 : 1 for the A : a segregation had been abandoned. This item is the one which will answer the question of the agreement of the two families with each other. It is an interaction term and, as such, tests whether classification into P and p is affected by the family classification.

The ratio of the family size is $\frac{126}{73} : 1$ or $1 \cdot 7260 : 1$. Hence the third or heterogeneity component of χ^2 is

$$\chi^2_{[1]} = \frac{[103 - (3 \times 23) - (1 \cdot 7260 \times 59) + (3 \times 1 \cdot 7260 \times 14)]^2}{3 \times 1 \cdot 7260 \times 199} = 0 \cdot 0210$$

with a probability of 0·90–0·80.

This heterogeneity analysis can, however, be carried out by a more general and more convenient method. We have seen in the last example how a compound χ^2 for 2 degrees of freedom can be calculated from a two-way classification when the observed ratio for one of the classifications is itself used in place of any expectation. A little consideration of this operation as carried out on Philp's data will show that the calculation of this χ^2 for 2 degrees of freedom really resolves itself into finding two simple χ^2's. Each of these tests the agreement of the data with the other expected ratio within one of the two categories separated by the classification for whose result no expectation exists. Thus with Philp's data we found, on using the general formula, that the compound χ^2 for 2 degrees of freedom was 0·8450. This could equally well have been obtained by summing the two simple χ^2's testing the agreement of the B : b segregation with the expected 3 : 1 in the A plants and in the a plants separately. These two items are

$$\frac{[72 - (3 \times 29)]^2}{3 \times 101} \quad \text{and} \quad \frac{[40 - (3 \times 12)]^2}{3 \times 52}$$

which give a sum of 0·8450.

Hence the heterogeneity analysis of Sirks's data can be carried out by calculating three χ^2, each having 1 degree of freedom, from the two single families and from their total, respectively. These three items, shown in the appropriate lines of Table 44, are found as

$$\frac{[59 - (3 \times 14)]^2}{3 \times 73}, \quad \frac{[103 - (3 \times 23)]^2}{3 \times 126}, \quad \frac{[162 - (3 \times 37)]^2}{3 \times 199}$$

giving 1·3196, 3·0582 and 4·3568. The last one is the test of agreement of the total data with expectation. The sum of the first two, viz. 4·3778, is the compound χ^2 for 2 degrees of freedom which includes the item testing total agreement, as already found, together with the heterogeneity item. The latter can then be obtained by subtraction:

$$\chi^2_{[1]} = 4\cdot3778 - 4\cdot3568 = 0\cdot0210$$

The analysis is set out in tabular form in Table 45.

TABLE 45
The Analysis of χ^2 for Sirks's Data

Item	χ^2	N	P
Deviation	4·3568	1	0·05–0·02
Heterogeneity	0·0210	1	0·90–0·80
Total	4·3778	2	

The deviation of χ^2 tests the agreement of the totals with the expected segregation. The total χ^2 is, of course, the sum of the two items from the single families.

This analysis is of some interest in consisting essentially of two steps. The first operation is that of building up a compound χ^2 from its simple items, the second step is that of breaking down this same compound into simple components on a new basis. It is a remarkable example of that power of synthesizing and re-analysing a compound along new lines which is conferred by the system of independent comparisons developed in Section 46.

When the heterogeneity analysis is carried out in this way it is easily seen that the method can be extended to data including any number of families. As an example we may take certain families of *Antirrhinum majus* which were segregating for yellow and ivory flower colour (Mather's data).

Example 25. Four plants known to be heterozygous for the gene in question were self-pollinated and the individual progenies so obtained gave the following segregations:

TABLE 46
Segregation in Antirrhinum majus (*Mather*)

Family	Numbers of plants			χ^2
	Yellow	Ivory	Total	
1	27	2	29	5·0690
2	15	12	27	5·4444
3	24	6	30	0·4000
4	25	5	30	1·1111
Total	91	25	116	0·7353

A simple χ^2 is calculated from each family separately, testing its agreement with the expected 3 : 1 ratio. Thus family 1 gives $\chi^2_{[1]} = \dfrac{[27-(3\times 2)]^2}{3\times 29} = 5\cdot 0690$. The sum of the four χ^2's obtained in this way from the separate families is itself a compound χ^2 of 12·0245 for 4 degrees of freedom. It consists of two parts, that testing the general agreement of the totals with the 3 : 1 expectation and the heterogeneity item. The former is found from the total segregation and has, of course, 1 degree of freedom. The latter is found, as in the last example, by subtraction and must clearly have 3 degrees of freedom. The analysis is set out in Table 47.

TABLE 47
Analysis of χ^2 for Mather's Data

Item	χ^2	N	P	Mean square
Deviation	0·7353	1	0·50–0·30	
Heterogeneity	11·2892	3	0·02–0·01	3·7631
Total	12·0245	4		

The result of this analysis is itself worth considering in some detail. The totals agree with the 3 : 1 expected but there is significant heterogeneity, i.e. the families disagree with one another. This last result must mean that the agreement of the totals with expectation is fortuitous, as it shows that all the component families do not themselves agree with this expectation. Heterogeneity disposes of the hypothesis as effectively as a significant deviation item.

We may note also that where heterogeneity is present the totals are subject to a variance greater than that expected on hypothesis, because the discrepancies between the families add a new item to the variation. The correct test of significance of the deviation item is thus not given by the use of χ^2 but by the comparison of the deviation χ^2 with the mean square obtained from the heterogeneity item, to give a variance ratio. In the present example the mean square is $\dfrac{11\cdot 2892}{3} = 3\cdot 7631$, which, being larger than the deviation item, shows the latter not to be significant.

When the variance is demonstrably greater than that expected from hypothesis the χ^2 test must be abandoned, as its use presupposes that an observed variance is being compared with hypothesis. In its place we must resort to the z test, or to its transformation, the variance ratio, by which two observed variances are compared.

The method of heterogeneity analysis can be adapted to more complex cases, and used in conjunction with partition by orthogonal functions, but the reader must be referred to Mather's account of such analyses for further details.

49. THE 2×2 CONTINGENCY TABLE

We have seen how one of the main comparisons in a four-class table can be removed from the analysis of χ^2 without affecting the test of agreement of either the remaining main comparison or the test of independence of the two comparisons. It is possible to take a further step and to accept the results of both classifications as their own expectations, so to speak, and yet still to be able to test the independence of the two classifications. In such analysis the two χ^2's testing the main effects or classifications are being removed from consideration, attention being confined to the third simple χ^2 testing the interaction or independence of the two methods of classification.

Example 26. Lawrence and Newell, while experimenting with the composition of soil composts, recorded the following hitherto unpublished results of a germination trial with *Primula sinensis* seeds. The seeds were divided into two groups and set to germinate in dishes containing filter papers soaked respectively in rain water and water which had been allowed to seep through loam before use. The germinations were as follows:

TABLE 48
Germination in Primula (*Lawrence and Newell*)

	Germinated	Ungerminated	Total
Loam water . . .	37	13	50
Rain water	32	18	50
Total . . .	69	31	100

Does the type of water affect germination?

The two marginal classifications are clearly uninteresting and indeed have no expectations. The number of seeds in each test can be varied at will and the percentage germination which is observed depends on many other factors such as the genetical constitution of the seeds, age, aeration, and so on. The question at issue really reduces to that of testing the independence of the two classifications. To obtain an answer it is necessary only to calculate the interaction χ^2 item.

The calculation of such a contingency χ^2 can be undertaken by an extension of the methods of Example 24. Reverting to

Philp's poppies, it was seen that, where a 3 : 1 was expected for each of the two main classifications, the interaction, or, in that case, linkage, χ^2 was found as

$$\chi^2_{[1]} = \frac{[a_1 - 3a_2 - 3a_3 + (3\times3)a_4]^2}{3n}$$

When it was decided to substitute the observed ratio, which may be denoted as $l_A : 1$, for the A : a segregation, the interaction item became

$$\chi^2_{[1]} = \frac{[a_1 - 3a_2 - l_A a_3 + (3 \times l_A)a_4]^2}{3 \times l_A \times n}$$

If the next step is taken and the observed segregation, $l_B : 1$, for B : b is used, the interaction χ^2 can be shown by Fisher's method to be

$$\chi^2_{[1]} = \frac{(a_1 - l_B a_2 - l_A a_3 - l_A l_B a_4)^2}{l_A l_B n}$$

This is the formula necessary for the analysis of Lawrence and Newell's data. The ratio of the number of seeds in the two tests, $l_T : 1$, is 1 : 1. The ratio of the two germination classes, denoted as $l_G : 1$, is $\frac{69}{31} : 1$, i.e. 2·2258 : 1. Then the contingency χ^2 is

$$\chi^2_{[1]} = \frac{(a_1 - l_T a_2 - l_G a_3 + l_T l_G a_4)^2}{l_T l_G n}$$

$$= \frac{[37 - (1\times32) - (2\cdot2258\times13) + (1\times2\cdot2258\times18)]^2}{1\times2\cdot2258\times100}$$

$$= \frac{16\cdot1290^2}{222\cdot58} = 1\cdot1688$$

which for 1 degree of freedom has a probability of 0·30–0·20, showing that there is no interaction between the classifications, i.e. that the type of water does not affect germination.

This method of finding χ^2 is not, however, the one in common use for the 2×2 contingency table. The usual formula does not require the calculation of the two marginal ratios. It is not difficult to derive from the formula used above.

The contingency table may be written out, using the values a_1–a_4 for the four observed class frequencies. It then becomes

| a_1 | a_2 | $a_1 + a_2$ |
a_3	a_4	$a_3 + a_4$
$a_1 + a_3$	$a_2 + a_4$	$a_1 + a_2 + a_3 + a_4 = n$

The margins show ratios of $\frac{a_1+a_2}{a_3+a_4}:1$ and $\frac{a_1+a_3}{a_2+a_4}:1$, which may be substituted for l_T and l_G in the formula already used for the calculation of χ^2.

$$\chi^2_{[1]} = \frac{\left[a_1 - a_2\left(\frac{a_1+a_3}{a_2+a_4}\right) - a_3\left(\frac{a_1+a_2}{a_3+a_4}\right) + a_4\frac{(a_1+a_2)(a_1+a_3)}{(a_3+a_4)(a_2+a_4)}\right]^2}{\frac{(a_1+a_2)(a_1+a_3)}{(a_3+a_4)(a_2+a_4)}n}$$

$$= \frac{[a_1(a_2+a_4)(a_3+a_4) - a_2(a_1+a_3)(a_3+a_4) - a_3(a_1+a_2)(a_2+a_4) + a_4(a_1+a_2)(a_1+a_3)]^2}{(a_1+a_2)(a_1+a_3)(a_2+a_4)(a_3+a_4)n}$$

Expanding and collecting like terms in the numerator

$$\chi^2_{[1]} = \frac{[a_1 a_4(a_1+a_2+a_3+a_4) - a_2 a_3(a_1+a_2+a_3+a_4)]^2}{(a_1+a_2)(a_1+a_3)(a_2+a_4)(a_3+a_4)n}$$

which, since $n = S(a)$, reduces to the widely used form

$$\chi^2 = \frac{(a_1 a_4 - a_2 a_3)^2 n}{(a_1+a_2)(a_1+a_3)(a_2+a_4)(a_3+a_4)}$$

Applying this to Lawrence and Newell's data, where $a_1 = 37$, $a_2 = 13$, $a_3 = 32$, and $a_4 = 18$, with $n = 100$, we find

$$\chi^2_{[1]} = \frac{[(37 \times 18) - (32 \times 13)]^2 100}{50 \times 50 \times 69 \times 31} = \frac{6{,}250{,}000}{5{,}347{,}500} = 1{\cdot}1688$$

as before.

Before leaving the subject of the 2×2 contingency table it may be noted that Yates's correction for continuity can be applied to prevent overestimation of the significance where the class frequencies are expected to be small. This is done by deducting 0·5 from each of the two classes in opposite corners giving the larger product, and adding 0·5 to each of the other two classes giving the smaller product. In the present example it would be necessary to reduce 37 and 18 to 36·5 and 17·5 respectively, and to increase 32 and 13 to 32·5 and 13·5 respectively. The effect in this case would be negligible.

For tables with very small class frequencies Fisher's exact treatment is to be recommended. This is based on the multinomial expansion and hence is an extension of the type of calculation discussed in Chapter II.

50. THE $2 \times j$ TABLE

The $2 \times j$ contingency table [*] is an extension of the type of heterogeneity analysis illustrated in Example 25 just in the same way that the 2×2 table is an extension of that of Example 24.

[*] Often referred to as the $2 \times n$ table.

It can be analysed by treating it according to the method of the heterogeneity test. In a contingency table there is, however, no expectation for the class frequencies in either margin of the table, which means, of course, that no χ^2 can be calculated to test agreement with expectation of the two totals in the bottom line of the $2\times j$ table. This simple χ^2, termed the deviation item in a heterogeneity test, is omitted and the ratio observed in this margin must be used to supply the k coefficients which are applied to the class frequencies in calculating χ^2 from the single families. The sum of the simple χ^2's found in this way from the single families will be a compound χ^2 corresponding to a number of degrees of freedom one less than the total number of families. This will be better appreciated from an example.

Example 27. G. Hartman has recorded the frequencies of men and women having certain given thresholds for tasting phenylthiocarbamide. Eleven strengths of solution of this substance were used, being labelled 0 to 10. The subjects of the test were given solutions of the various strengths to taste, the concentration immediately below that at which they commenced to taste being counted as their threshold. Twelve classes of each sex were obtained, as some subjects could taste solution 0 and were thus classed as having the threshold <0. The results of the test are given in Table 49. Do the sexes differ in the distribution of the thresholds that they show?

TABLE 49
Hartman's Data on Taste Thresholds

Threshold	Frequency in Men (a_1)	Women (a_2)	Total (n)	χ^2	$\dfrac{a_1^2}{n}$
10	15	42	57	10·7507	3·9474
9	35	52	87	2·1115	14·0805
8	46	38	84	1·5327	25·1905
7	31	30	61	0·1925	15·7541
6	23	19	42	0·7664	12·5952
5	13	17	30	0·2632	5·6333
4	9	6	15	0·8635	5·4000
3	7	5	12	0·5120	4·0833
2	10	10	20	0·0316	5·0000
1	13	19	32	0·6998	5·2813
0	25	33	58	0·5601	10·7759
<0	63	43	106	5·5391	37·4433
Total .	290	314	604	23·8231	139·2384

In the absence of detailed knowledge about the determination of the threshold there is clearly no way of formulating an expectation for the total number of people falling into each threshold class. Similarly, though approximately equal numbers of men and women are expected in the general population, there is no reason why equal numbers should be included in the experiment. The ratio obtained will depend on the circumstances under which the experiment is conducted. In this way the problem reduces to that of testing the independence of the two classifications, by sex and by taste threshold.

Now if there were an expectation of $l : 1$ for sex the heterogeneity χ^2 would be found by subtracting from the sum of the single threshold class χ^2's the χ^2 found from the total segregation, the formula $\dfrac{(a_1 - la_2)^2}{ln}$ being used to find these simple χ^2's from both single thresholds and from the total. In the absence of such an expectation it is necessary to use the observed sex totals to estimate l. In this way the χ^2 from the total is reduced to 0 and the sum of the χ^2's, found from each threshold, is itself the heterogeneity, or as we now term it, contingency, χ^2. It has 11 degrees of freedom just as the heterogeneity χ^2 would have if the calculation had been made using an expected sex segregation.

In practice it is more convenient to use the sex totals in the calculation rather than the ratio $\dfrac{290}{314} : 1$. Thus the χ^2 item from the class of threshold 10 is found from the formula

$$\chi^2 = \frac{\left[15 - \left(\dfrac{290}{314} \times 42\right)\right]^2}{\dfrac{290}{314} \times 57} = \frac{[(15 \times 314) - (42 \times 290)]^2}{314 \times 290 \times 57}$$

$$= \frac{55{,}800{,}900}{5{,}190{,}420} = 10 \cdot 7507$$

The χ^2 item from threshold 9 is

$$\chi^2 = \frac{[(35 \times 314) - (52 \times 290)]^2}{314 \times 290 \times 87} = 2 \cdot 1115$$

and so on. It will be observed that on applying this method of calculation to the totals

$$\chi^2 = \frac{[(290 \times 314) - (314 \times 290)]^2}{314 \times 290 \times 604} = 0 \text{ as expected.}$$

The sum of these χ^2 components from the 12 thresholds is 23·8231, which has, as already noted, 11 degrees of freedom. Such a value has a probability of 0·02–0·01, and so there is good evidence that the distribution of thresholds is dependent on the sex. Men appear to fall more often into class <0 and less often into class 10 than do women.

There is another method, due to Brandt and Snedecor, of finding the contingency χ^2 from a $2 \times j$ table. It is very valuable in some cases where the subdivision is more complex than in the present example. Mather has described such a complex example which brings out the full value of this method of calculation.

The $2 \times j$ table may be written in the general form of

a_{11}	a_{12}	n_1
a_{21}	a_{22}	n_2
a_{31}	a_{32}	n_3
.	.	.
.	.	.
.	.	.
a_{j1}	a_{j2}	n_j
a_{T1}	a_{T2}	n_T

Let us consider the calculation of a heterogeneity χ^2 when the total of n_T individuals is expected to consist of $m_1 n_T$ and $m_2 n_T$ of the two types respectively. Each line of the table contributes an item of the type

$$\frac{(m_2 a_{11} - m_1 a_{12})^2}{m_1 m_2 n_1}$$

to the total χ^2. The deviation χ^2, found in like manner from the totals in the bottom line of the table, is

$$\frac{(m_2 a_{T1} - m_1 a_{T2})^2}{m_1 m_2 n_T}$$

Hence the heterogeneity χ^2 obtained by subtraction is

$$S\left[\frac{(m_2 a_{11} - m_1 a_{12})^2}{m_1 m_2 n_1}\right] - \frac{(m_2 a_{T1} - m_1 a_{T2})^2}{m_1 m_2 n_T}$$

$$= \frac{1}{m_1 m_2}\left\{S\left[\frac{(m_2^2 a_{11}^2 - 2m_1 m_2 a_{11} a_{12} + m_1^2 a_{12}^2)}{n_1}\right]\right.$$
$$\left. - \frac{(m_2^2 a_{T1}^2 - 2m_1 m_2 a_{T1} a_{T2} + m_1^2 a_{T2}^2)}{n_T}\right\}$$

$$= \frac{1}{m_1 m_2}\left\{m_2^2\left[S\left(\frac{a_{11}^2}{n_1}\right) - \frac{a_{T1}^2}{n_T}\right] - 2m_1 m_2\left[S\left(\frac{a_{11} a_{12}}{n_1}\right) - \frac{a_{T1} a_{T2}}{n_T}\right]\right.$$
$$\left. + m_1^2\left[S\left(\frac{a_{12}^2}{n_1}\right) - \frac{a_{T2}^2}{n_T}\right]\right\}$$

Now $$\frac{a_{12}^2}{n_1}=\frac{(n_1-a_{11})^2}{n_1}=\frac{n_1^2-2n_1a_{11}+a_{11}^2}{n_1}=n_1-2a_{11}+\frac{a_{11}^2}{n_1}$$

and, similarly, $\frac{a_{T2}^2}{n_T}=n_T-2a_{T1}+\frac{a_{T1}^2}{n_T}$

Hence $S\left(\frac{a_{12}^2}{n_1}\right)-\frac{a_{T2}^2}{n_T}=S(n_1)-2S(a_{11})+S\left(\frac{a_{11}^2}{n_1}\right)-n_T+2a_{T1}-\frac{a_{T1}^2}{n_T}$

which, since $n_T=S(n_1)$ and $a_{T1}=S(a_{11})$, gives

$$S\left(\frac{a_{12}^2}{n_1}\right)-\frac{a_{T2}^2}{n_T}=S\left(\frac{a_{11}^2}{n_1}\right)-\frac{a_{T1}^2}{n_T}$$

It can similarly be shown that

$$S\left(\frac{a_{11}a_{12}}{n_1}\right)-\frac{a_{T1}a_{T2}}{n_T}=-\left[S\left(\frac{a_{11}^2}{n_1}\right)-\frac{a_{T1}^2}{n_T}\right]$$

The formula for the heterogeneity χ^2 then becomes

$$\chi^2=\frac{1}{m_1m_2}\left[S\left(\frac{a_{11}^2}{n_1}\right)-\frac{a_{T1}^2}{n_T}\right](m_1^2+2m_1m_2+m_2^2)$$

$$=\frac{(m_1+m_2)^2}{m_1m_2}\left[S\left(\frac{a_{11}^2}{n_1}\right)-\frac{a_{T1}^2}{n_T}\right]$$

It is also obvious that since $S\left(\frac{a_{11}^2}{n_1}\right)-\frac{a_{T1}^2}{n_T}=S\left(\frac{a_{12}^2}{n_T}\right)-\frac{a_{T2}^2}{n_T}$

$$\chi^2=\frac{(m_1+m_2)^2}{m_1m_2}\left[S\left(\frac{a_{12}^2}{n_1}\right)-\frac{a_{T2}^2}{n_T}\right]$$

The fraction $\frac{(m_1+m_2)^2}{m_1m_2}=\frac{1}{m_1m_2}$ since m_1+m_2 is chosen equal to 1

$$=\frac{n_T^2}{m_1n_T\times m_2n_T}$$

It will be seen that this formula for the heterogeneity χ^2 is divisible into two parts. One of these, $S\left(\frac{a_{11}^2}{n_1}\right)-\frac{a_{T1}^2}{n_T}$, is independent of the $m_1:m_2$ expectation, and so gives a quantity proportional to χ^2 for any expectation. It may be analysed in the same way as χ^2 itself, but without prejudice to the nature of the expectation. The results of such an analysis are then converted into χ^2's testing agreement with any expectation $m_1:m_2$ by means of the appropriate multiplier, which forms the second part of the formula. If the χ^2 in question is for a contingency test, expectations m_1 and m_2 are not available and the observed totals a_{T1} and a_{T2} are used to replace m_1n_T and m_2n_T, so giving

$$\chi^2_{[j-1]}=\frac{n_T^2}{a_{T1}a_{T2}}\left[S\left(\frac{a_{11}^2}{n_1}\right)-\frac{a_{T1}^2}{n_T}\right]$$

This formula can be applied to Hartman's data. The values of $\dfrac{a_{11}^2}{n_1}$, &c., are to be found in the right-most column of Table 49. The value in the bottom, or total, line is $\dfrac{a_{T1}^2}{n_T}$. Then

$$S\left(\dfrac{a_{11}^2}{n_1}\right) - \dfrac{a_{T1}^2}{n_T} = (3 \cdot 9474 + 14 \cdot 0805 \ldots + 37 \cdot 4433) - 139 \cdot 2384 = 5 \cdot 9464$$

The multiplier $\quad \dfrac{n_T^2}{a_{T1} a_{T2}} = \dfrac{604^2}{290 \times 314} = \dfrac{364{,}816}{91{,}060} = 4 \cdot 0063$

and $\quad \chi^2_{[11]} = 5 \cdot 9464 \times 4 \cdot 0063 = 23 \cdot 8231$

The great advantage of this method arises from the fact that the quantity proportional to χ^2 can be analysed and later, by the use of an easily determined multiplier, converted into a χ^2 depending on any given expectation. Thus, if we decided to expect equality of the sex frequencies in Hartman's data the multiplier would be $\dfrac{n_T^2}{m_1 n_T \times m_2 n_T}$, where $m_1 = m_2 = \tfrac{1}{2}$, i.e. $4 \cdot 0$ and $\chi^2 = 5 \cdot 9464 \times 4 \cdot 0000 = 23 \cdot 7856$. The major part of the work has been done before the expectation is introduced. Many additional expectations can be tested without much additional computation. With complex data this advantage may be very great.

51. THE GENERAL CONTINGENCY TABLE

The general contingency table may have any number of rows and columns. The two marginal or main classifications have no expected values and the table is used solely to test their independence. If such marginal expectations did exist the analysis would take the form

Item	N
Rows	$r-1$
Columns	$c-1$
Interaction	$(r-1)(c-1)$
Total	$rc-1$

where the table has r rows and c columns, i.e. rc entries in all.

In using the marginal totals as their own expectations, so to speak, the first two items of the analysis are removed from account. Their χ^2's are artificially made to take the value 0 and so the degrees of freedom to which they correspond are lost. Only the interaction component, with $(r-1)(c-1)$ degrees of freedom, remains.

No specially simple method of calculation has yet been

devised for such tables. The expectations for each cell of the table must be found from the marginal frequencies and the general formula $\chi^2 = S\left(\dfrac{a^2}{mn}\right) - n$ used for the calculation.

Example 28. Table 50 gives data obtained by Catcheside during his analysis of the secondary association of chromosoms in *Brassica oleracea*. The pollen mother cells were classified according to whether they had 3, 2, 1 or 0 pairs of bivalents showing secondary association at metaphase. Three preparations were studied, and it was desired to know whether the classification of the pollen mother cells could be considered as constant from slide to slide.

TABLE 50

Secondary association in Brassica (*Catcheside*)

Number of pairs	Slide 1	Slide 2	Slide 3	Total
0	14 (13·1039)	7 (9·9703)	11 (8·9258)	32
1	32 (42·1780)	36 (32·0920)	35 (28·7300)	103
2	51 (49·9585)	39 (38·0119)	32 (34·0296)	122
3	41 (32·7596)	23 (24·9258)	16 (22·3146)	80
Total	138	105	94	337

The numbers in brackets are expectations based on the marginal totals.

The first step in the analysis is to find the frequencies expected for each pairing category in each slide. Of the 337 pollen mother cells observed, 32 fall into the 0 class. If the classification is the same in all slides we should expect a fraction $\frac{138}{337}$ of these 32 to be in slide 1, a fraction $\frac{105}{337}$ in slide 2 and $\frac{94}{337}$ in slide 3. The expectations for the three cells in the top row of the table are thus $\dfrac{32 \times 138}{337}$, $\dfrac{32 \times 105}{337}$ and $\dfrac{32 \times 94}{337}$, or 13·1039, 9·9703 and 8·9258. The other expectations are found in the same way. That for the bottom right-corner cell is, for example, $\dfrac{80 \times 94}{337}$ or 22·3146.

The formula $\chi^2 = S\left(\dfrac{a^2}{mn}\right) - n$ is then applied to these figures.

There are twelve items, one from each cell, of the type $\frac{a^2}{mn}$. That from the top left-hand corner is, for example,

$$\frac{14^2}{13 \cdot 1039} = 14 \cdot 9574$$

and that from the bottom right-hand corner is $\frac{16^2}{22 \cdot 3146} = 11 \cdot 4723$. The others are found in just the same way. The sum of the twelve is found to be 346·9055 and $\chi^2 = 346 \cdot 9055 - 337 = 9 \cdot 9055$. The table has four rows and three columns, so the contingency χ^2 has (4−1)(3−1) or 6 degrees of freedom. Reference to the table of χ^2 shows that $\chi^2_{[6]} = 9 \cdot 9055$ has a probability of between 0·20 and 0·10, so that it may be concluded that the classification into secondary association types is reasonably consistent over all three preparations.

The general method of calculation could, of course, have been applied to 2×2 and 2×j tables, but it is not so convenient to use as the special methods which have been developed for these special cases.

REFERENCES

CATCHESIDE, D. G. 1937. Secondary pairing in *Brassica oleracea*. *Cytologia*. Fujii Jub. Vol., 366–78.

FISHER, R. A. 1944. *Statistical Methods for Research Workers*. Oliver and Boyd. Edinburgh. 9th ed.

HARTMAN, G. 1939. Application of individual taste differences towards phenyl-thio-carbamide in genetic investigations. *Ann. Eugen.*, **9**, 123–35.

IMAI, Y. 1931. Linkage studies in *Pharbitis Nil*. *Genetics*, **16**, 26–41.

MATHER, K. 1937. The analysis of single factor segregations. *Ann. Eugen.*, **8**, 96–105.

—— 1938. *The Measurement of Linkage in Heredity*. Methuen. London.

PHILP, J. 1933. The genetics of *Papaver Rhoeas* and related forms. *J. Genet.*, **28**, 175–204.

SIRKS, M. J. 1929. Mendelian factors in *Datura III*. *Genetica*, **11**, 257–66.

CHAPTER XII

ESTIMATION AND INFORMATION

52. PROBABILITY AND LIKELIHOOD

BROADLY speaking, statistical operations fall into two categories, viz. tests of significance and the estimation of parameters. Of these two, we have been mainly occupied up to the present with tests of significance, though some problems of estimation, concerning variances and regression coefficients, have been discussed. It is now necessary to undertake a more detailed consideration of the problems of estimation.

Tests of significance and the estimation of parameters are fundamentally operations of very different characters, though, as will be seen later, the success of a test of significance may largely depend on the proper estimation of some parameter, without which the hypothesis under consideration could not be adequately defined. When an hypothesis is adequately stated, it is possible to deduce the probabilities of all the types of observation which may be encountered in experiment. After this has been done, the probability of obtaining a fit as bad or worse than that of a given series of observations may be evaluated and used as the basis of a decision as to the competence of the hypothesis to account for the observations. This is a test of significance and, in essence, it involves the deduction of particular consequences from a general statement.

Estimation involves the reverse operation, viz. the endeavour to construct or amplify a general hypothesis from the material afforded by a particular set of observations. This induced hypothesis may later be used in a deductive test of significance.

The essential distinction in the type of argument involved may be illustrated by a consideration of genetical recombination. If two homozygous individuals who differ by two genes, i.e. have the constitutions AABB and aabb, are intercrossed, a double heterozygote AB/ab is obtained. Such an individual produces four types of gamete, AB, Ab, aB and ab. Of these four types two, viz. AB and ab, resemble the gametes which fused to give the double heterozygote itself, and may be referred to as non-recombinants. The other two types, Ab and aB, are recombinants in that they show changed combinations of the two genes. The class, recombination or non-recombination, into which any gamete falls may be discovered by the use of suitable test crosses. The relative proportions of the two types of gamete are denoted as $p : 1-p$, p being termed the recombination value.

Let us suppose that, by means of suitable crosses, n gametes have been tested and found to consist of a_1 recombinants and a_2 non-recombinants. The probability of obtaining such a result is, as shown in Section 5,

$$\frac{n!}{a_1!a_2!}(p)^{a_1}(1-p)^{a_2}$$

When p is fixed by hypothesis, as it would be, for example, if the genes were supposedly independent in inheritance, so giving $p=\frac{1}{2}$, all the possible types of family, with $a_1=0, 1, 2$, &c., and $a_2=n, n-1, n-2$, &c., could be enumerated, and their probabilities calculated for use as the basis of a test of significance.

The two genes might not, however, be independent in inheritance, in which case p could take any value between wide limits. It would then be necessary to find the value of p before the hypothesis of non-independence, or linkage, became sufficiently precise for further use. We are thus faced with the problem of estimating p from a knowledge of the value of

$$\frac{n!}{a_1!a_2!}(p)^{a_1}(1-p)^{a_2}$$

Superficially this is just the reverse calculation to the previous one, but a closer inspection shows that such a simple statement cannot be true. In each case there is a single starting-point, viz. a single hypothetical value of p or a single observed value of $\frac{n!}{a_1!a_2!}(p)^{a_1}(1-p)^{a_2}$; but whereas, when p is fixed, it is possible to enumerate all the types of family and determine the relative probability of any one observation or set of observations, it is not possible, when a single observation has been made, to enumerate all the hypothetical values of p to which it might be related. Given the hypothesis, the scope and limits of observation are determined, but given the observation the scope and limits of hypothesis are not determined.

Unless this difficulty can be resolved, estimation cannot be treated as an exercise in probability. Thomas Bayes devised an axiom which, if its truth be granted, would supply the necessary basis for such a treatment. Bayes proposed to treat the hypothetical population from which the observed sample was drawn as itself a sample of a super-population and to assign *a priori* probabilities to the constituents of this super-population. This leads to the so-called inverse probability method of approach. The difficulties of the method need not be enumerated here, but it may be noted that Bayes himself apparently doubted its value and many writers have wholly rejected it since his time.

The situation has now been completely transformed by Fisher's analysis of the question of estimation. He recognizes and accepts the differences between the calculation of probabilities from hypothesis and the estimation of parameters from observation. Mathematically the expression $\frac{n!}{a_1!a_2!}(p)^{a_1}(1-p)^{a_2}$ is a function both of the observed number a, and of the hypothetical frequency p. Regarded as a function of p, this expression is the probability with which the number a will be observed. Regarded as a function of a, it is not a probability. Fisher terms it a likelihood function. Probability and likelihood have distinct mathematical properties and the special properties of likelihood have allowed Fisher to develop a theory of estimation which is independent of the theory of probability.

The most important of these properties of likelihood is that relating to the precision of statistics to which the likelihood function leads. If from a body of data T be obtained as an estimate of the parameter θ, and if in large sample T is distributed normally with variance V_T, then the limiting value of $\frac{1}{nV_T}$, as n becomes large, cannot exceed a quantity i which is defined independently of the estimation of T. The proof of this proposition may be found in an article on the 'Statistical Theory of Estimation' by Fisher and need not be set out here. The important result for our purpose is that i can always be found from the formula

$$i = S\left[\frac{1}{m}\left(\frac{dm}{d\theta}\right)^2\right]$$

where m is the class expectation in terms of the parameter θ and S, as usual, denotes summation over all classes. This quantity i is an intrinsic property of the data and provides the necessary yardstick with which to compare the value of any estimate obtained from the observations.

Fisher has also shown that one method of estimation, viz. that of maximizing the likelihood function by adjustment of the parameter value, always provides an estimate, T, which has the property that the limiting value of $\frac{1}{nV_T}$ is i. In other words, the reciprocal of the variance of the maximum likelihood estimate supplies us with a means of assessing the value of other estimates. Unless their variances equal $\frac{1}{ni}$ they are not extracting the full amount of information available in the data, and are hence less efficient than the maximum likelihood statistic. Such comparisons of accuracy may be made in the special case of the distribution of estimates of the same parameter even when the error curves are not normal.

53. THE METHOD OF MAXIMUM LIKELIHOOD

Consider a set of n individuals separable into j classes, the observed frequencies being $a_1, a_2, a_3 \ldots a_j$, and $S(a)=n$. If the proportions expected in the various classes are $m_1, m_2, m_3 \ldots m_j$, with $S(m)=1$, m being a function of the parameter θ, then the likelihood of obtaining such a family as the one observed will be given by the appropriate term in the expansion of the multinomial

$$(m_1+m_2+m_3+ \ldots +m_j)^n$$

This term is clearly

$$\frac{n!}{a_1! a_2! a_3! \ldots a_j!}(m_1)^{a_1}(m_2)^{a_2}(m_3)^{a_3} \ldots (m_j)^{a_j}$$

Estimation of θ by the method of maximum likelihood requires that a value T be found which, on substituting for θ, makes this expression a maximum. Maximization is carried out by differentiation with respect to θ and equating the differential to 0 in order to obtain the equation of estimation. Such an expression as that given above is, however, not very easy to differentiate and resort is made to a device for this purpose. The expression and its logarithm will both show maxima at the same value of T. Hence if we find that value of T which maximizes the logarithm of the likelihood we have solved our problem.

The log likelihood is

$$L = \log\left(\frac{n!}{a_1! a_2! a_3! \ldots a_j!}\right) + a_1 \log m_1 + a_2 \log m_2 + a_3 \log m_3 + \ldots + a_j \log m_j.$$

Maximizing this logarithm gives

$$\frac{dL}{d\theta} = a_1 \frac{d \log m_1}{d\theta} + a_2 \frac{d \log m_2}{d\theta} + a_3 \frac{d \log m_3}{d\theta} + \ldots + a_j \frac{d \log m_j}{d\theta}$$

as $\log\left(\dfrac{n!}{a_1! a_2! a_3! \ldots a_j!}\right)$ is independent of θ and vanishes when differentiated.

The appropriate root of this equation supplies the necessary estimate, T, of θ.

Example 29. As an example of the application of this method consider the estimation of the parameter μ in the Poisson distribution, already mentioned in Section 12. The variate x may take the values 0, 1, 2, 3 ... j and the frequencies with which observations are expected to fall into these classes are

$$e^{-\mu}, \ e^{-\mu}\mu, \ e^{-\mu}\frac{\mu^2}{2!}, e^{-\mu}\frac{\mu^3}{3!}, \ \ldots, \ e^{-\mu}\frac{\mu^j}{j!}$$

If the observed frequencies are a_0, a_1, a_2, &c., the likelihood function is

$$\frac{n!}{a_0!a_1!a_2!a_3!\ldots}(e^{-\mu})^{a_0}(e^{-\mu}\mu)^{a_1}\left(e^{-\mu}\frac{\mu^2}{2!}\right)^{a_2}\left(e^{-\mu}\frac{\mu^3}{3!}\right)^{a_3}\ldots$$

The log likelihood then becomes

$$L = C + a_0 \log(e^{-\mu}) + a_1 \log(e^{-\mu}\mu) + a_2 \log\left(e^{-\mu}\frac{\mu^2}{2!}\right) + a_3 \left(e^{-\mu}\frac{\mu^3}{3!}\right) + \ldots$$

where C is the constant which vanishes on maximization.

This log likelihood expression may be recast in a more manageable form because

$$\log(e^{-\mu}) = -\mu \quad \text{and} \quad \log\left(e^{-\mu}\frac{\mu^2}{2!}\right) = \log(\mu^2) - \log(2!) - \mu, \text{ &c.}$$

Rewriting gives

$$L = C + a_1 \log \mu + a_2 \log(\mu^2) + a_3 \log(\mu^3) \ldots - a_2 \log(2!)$$
$$- a_3 \log(3!) \ldots \ldots - a_0\mu - a_1\mu - a_2\mu - a_3\mu \ldots$$

It may be noted that log 2!, &c., are independent of μ and will vanish on differentiating. Furthermore, as $S(a) = n$, the set of terms in μ may be replaced by a single term $-n\mu$. Maximization then gives

$$\frac{dL}{d\mu} = \frac{a_1}{\mu} + \frac{2a_2\mu}{\mu^2} + \frac{3a_3\mu^2}{\mu^3} \ldots - n = 0$$

which reduces to $\quad a_1 + 2a_2 + 3a_3 + \ldots = n\mu$

Then $$\mu = \frac{a_1 + 2a_2 + 3a_3 + \ldots}{n}$$

Now a_1 is the observed frequency of the class in which $x = 1$, a_2 that in which $x = 2$, and so on. So

$$a_1 + 2a_2 + 3a_3 + \ldots = S(x)$$

and μ is estimated by $\bar{x}$, the mean of x, as in Section 12.

Example 30. A numerical example of this type of calculation is afforded by Catcheside's data on the secondary association of chromosomes in *Brassica oleracea*. There are three pairs of bivalents, each of which may or may not show association at meiosis. In this way a meiotic nucleus may contain 0, 1, 2 or 3 pairs of associated bivalents. The frequency with which nuclei of these types were observed in certain preparations were 32, 103, 122 and 80 respectively (Table 50). If all three pairs have the same chance, p, of being associated, the expected frequencies of the four classes will be

$$(1-p)^3 \;;\quad 3p(1-p)^2 \;;\quad 3p^2(1-p) \;;\quad p^3.$$

What is the value of p which gives the best fit with the observed results?

The log likelihood is clearly
$$L = C + 32 \log [(1-p)^3] + 103 \log [3p(1-p)^2]$$
$$+ 122 \log [3p^2(1-p)] + 80 \log [p^3]$$
This expression may be rearranged as shown in Table 51.

TABLE 51

Item	log p	log $(1-p)$	log 3
32 log $[(1-p)^3]$	—	96	—
103 log $[3p(1-p)^2]$	103	206	103
122 log $[3p^2(1-p)]$	244	122	122
80 log $[p^3]$	240	—	—
Total	587	424	225

This gives
$$L = C + 587 \log p + 424 \log (1-p) + 255 \log 3$$

and
$$\frac{dL}{dp} = \frac{587}{p} - \frac{424}{1-p} = 0$$

Then
$$p = \frac{587}{424 + 587} = \frac{587}{1{,}011} = 0 \cdot 580613$$

This method of solution would always be used in practice, but if the simplification of the log likelihood expression is omitted, the data will serve to illustrate the process of solution by iteration. This latter is a very valuable method of solving complicated estimation equations when no algebraic means exists.

We have
$$L = 32 \log [(1-p)^3] + 103 \log [3p(1-p)^2] + 122 \log [3p^2(1-p)] + 80 \log [p^3]$$
and
$$\frac{dL}{dp} = -\frac{32(3 - 6p + 3p^2)}{(1-p)^3} + \frac{103(1 - 4p + 3p^2)}{p(1-p)^2} + \frac{122(2p - 3p^2)}{p^2(1-p)} + \frac{80(3p^2)}{p^3} = 0$$
which obviously simplifies to
$$-\frac{96}{1-p} + \frac{103(1-3p)}{p(1-p)} + \frac{122(2-3p)}{p(1-p)} + \frac{240}{p} = 0$$

This may be further simplified to the form used earlier, but it will be instructive to solve it by iteration as it stands. This process consists in substituting trial values of p, finding the resulting values of the maximum likelihood expression and interpolating for p on the basis of these values. The details are shown in Table 52.

TABLE 52
The Iteration Solution of the Equation
$$-\frac{96}{1-p}+\frac{103(1-3p)}{p(1-p)}+\frac{122(2-3p)}{p(1-p)}+\frac{240}{p}=0$$

p	0·5	0·6	0·58	0·581	0·5806
$-\dfrac{96}{1-p}$	−192·0000	−240·0000	−228·5714	−229·1169	−228·8984
$\dfrac{103(1-3p)}{p(1-p)}$	−206·0000	−343·0000	−312·8900	−314·3662	−313·7752
$\dfrac{122(2-3p)}{p(1-p)}$	244·0000	101·6667	130·2135	128·7961	129·3632
$\dfrac{240}{p}$	480·0000	400·0000	413·7931	413·0809	413·3655
Total	326·0000	−81·6667	2·5452	−1·6061	0·0551

$$\underbrace{\qquad\qquad\qquad}_{407\cdot6667} \quad \underbrace{\qquad\qquad\qquad}_{4\cdot1513}$$

As a first approximation we put $p=0.5$ and calculate the value of the left side of the maximum likelihood equation. The value is positive, and so the trial value for p was too low. The calculation is then repeated with $p=0.6$, which is found to be too high a value, as the remainder is negative. The next step is to make a linear interpolation putting

$$p=0\cdot5+\frac{0\cdot1\times326\cdot0000}{326\cdot0000+81\cdot6667}=0\cdot58.$$

This value for p is a close approximation as it gives a very small remainder. It is, however, slightly too low as the remainder is positive. In view of the proximity of the true value of p to 0·58 it is not worth trying $p=0.59$ and interpolating from the difference. Instead we try $p=0.581$ and find that this value is a shade too high. Interpolation then gives

$$p=0\cdot580+\frac{0\cdot001\times2\cdot5452}{2\cdot5452+1\cdot6061}=0\cdot5806,$$

which, as the last column of the table shows, is a very close approximation.

The alternate trial and interpolation can be carried on to give as accurate a value for p as may be desired. Four-figure accuracy will serve our present purpose of illustrating the method. Solution by iteration has another great advantage in the calculation of the variance of p, as will be seen below.

It has been mentioned that the reciprocal of the variance of a maximum likelihood statistic is equal to ni, where i is the amount of information extractable from a single observation of the data, irrespective of how the estimation is made. For convenience we may put $I=ni$ and refer to I as the amount of information contained in the body of data at hand.

Fisher has shown that

$$i_p = S\left[\frac{1}{m}\left(\frac{dm}{dp}\right)^2\right] = \frac{1}{nV_p}$$

This formula may be used to obtain the variance of p from Catcheside's figures. Table 53 shows how it is applied.

TABLE 53

The Calculation of an Amount of Information

Class	Expectation (m)	$\frac{dm}{dp}$	i
0	$(1-p)^3$	$-3(1-p)^2$	$9(1-p)$
1	$3p(1-p)^2$	$3(1-p)(1-3p)$	$\frac{3(1-3p)^2}{p}$
2	$3p^2(1-p)$	$3p(2-3p)$	$\frac{3(2-3p)^2}{1-p}$
3	p^3	$3p^2$	$9p$
Total	1	0	$\frac{3}{p(1-p)}$

Thus $i_p = \frac{3}{p(1-p)}$, $I_p = \frac{3n}{p(1-p)}$ and $V_p = \frac{1}{I_p} = \frac{p(1-p)}{3n}$. This result is not surprising. It will be recalled from Section 13 that the variance of p in a binomial expansion is given by $\frac{p(1-p)}{n}$. Since, however, every observation of the present data covers the behaviour of three pairs, each of which supplies an independent piece of information about p, we have in effect $3n$ observations. So V_p might be expected to take the value $\frac{p(1-p)}{3n}$.

Substituting the estimated value of p, viz. 0·5806, and the observed value of n, viz. 337, we find

$$I_p = \frac{3 \times 337}{0·5806 \times 0·4194} = 4,151·889$$

and

$$V_p = \frac{1}{I_p} = 0·00024085$$

Then $s_p = \sqrt{V_p} = 0.015519$

and we may write $p = 0.5806 \pm 0.01552$.

The formula $i_p = S\left[\dfrac{1}{m}\left(\dfrac{dm}{dp}\right)^2\right]$

has an identical form, viz.

$$i_p = -S\left[m\dfrac{d^2 \log m}{dp^2}\right]$$

For $-S\left[m\dfrac{d^2 \log m}{dp^2}\right] = -S\left[m\dfrac{d}{dp}\left(\dfrac{d \log m}{dp}\right)\right]$

$= -S\left[m\dfrac{d}{dp}\left(\dfrac{1}{m}\dfrac{dm}{dp}\right)\right]$

$= -S\left[m\left(\dfrac{1}{m}\dfrac{d^2m}{dp^2} - \dfrac{1}{m^2}\dfrac{dm}{dp}\cdot\dfrac{dm}{dp}\right)\right]$

$= -S\left[\dfrac{d^2m}{dp^2} - \dfrac{1}{m}\left(\dfrac{dm}{dp}\right)^2\right]$

$= -S\left(\dfrac{d^2m}{dp^2}\right) + S\left[\dfrac{1}{m}\left(\dfrac{dm}{dp}\right)^2\right]$

Now $S(m) = 1$ and so $S\left(\dfrac{d^2m}{dp^2}\right) = S\left(\dfrac{dm}{dp}\right) = 0$

Hence the two formulae for i are identical.

This new formula for i is of value because it is easily related to the maximum likelihood expression. The latter is

$$\dfrac{dL}{dp} = S\left[a\dfrac{d \log m}{dp}\right] = 0.$$

Hence, if we redifferentiate and substitute mn, the expected value in any class, for the corresponding observed value, we have

$$S\left[mn\dfrac{d^2 \log m}{dp^2}\right] = -ni_p = -I_p$$

This can be applied to the unsimplified form of the maximum likelihood expression from Catcheside's data, which was

$$\dfrac{dL}{dp} = -\dfrac{32\times 3}{1-p} + \dfrac{103(1-3p)}{p(1-p)} + \dfrac{122(2-3p)}{p(1-p)} + \dfrac{80\times 3}{p}$$

where $32 = a_0$, $103 = a_1$, $122 = a_2$ and $80 = a_3$. Then on redifferentiating

$$a\dfrac{d^2 \log m}{dp^2} = \dfrac{d^2 L}{dp^2} = -\left\{\dfrac{3a_0}{(1-p)^2} + \dfrac{a_1}{p^2(1-p)^2}[3p(1-p) + (1-3p)(1-2p)]\right.$$
$$\left. + \dfrac{a_2}{p^2(1-p)^2}[3p(1-p) + (2-3p)(1-2p)] + \dfrac{3a_3}{p^2}\right\}$$

Substituting mn for a, simplifying and changing the sign

$$I_p = -S\left[mn\frac{d^2\log m}{dp^2}\right] = \left[3n(1-p)+\frac{3n}{p}(1-2p+3p^2)\right.$$
$$\left.+\frac{3n}{1-p}(2-4p+3p^2)+3np\right] = \frac{3n}{p(1-p)}$$

as before.

This formula relating I_p to the maximum likelihood expression is also useful in conjunction with the solution of maximum likelihood equations by iteration. I_p is the second differential of the log likelihood expression, i.e. is the rate of change on p of the first differential, which we term the maximum likelihood expression, though always, of course, with mn in place of a. The rate of change of the actual maximum likelihood expression is $S\left(a\dfrac{d^2\log m}{dp^2}\right)$, which equals I_p provided that we are willing to accept the observed value, a, in any class as a substitute for its expectation, mn.

Now we can see from Table 52 that when $p=0.580$,

$$\frac{dL}{dp} = S\left(a\frac{d\log m}{dp}\right) = 2.5452$$

and when $p=0.581$, $S\left(a\dfrac{d\log m}{dp}\right) = -1.6061$. Thus a change of 0·001 in p changes the maximum likelihood expression by 4·1513. In other words, the rate of change of the maximum likelihood expression on p is $\dfrac{4\cdot1513}{0\cdot001} = 4{,}151\cdot3$. This is the value of I_p.

The calculation of Ip by the direct method gave its value as 4,151·889, while derivation from the iteration solution gives it as 4,151·3. The difference is due to the use, in the latter method, of a in place of mn. This can be expressed by saying that the value obtained by the direct method is the mean amount of information expected from a body of data of this type and size; but the value obtained from the iteration solution is the actual amount of information yielded by the particular body of data under examination. Either value may be used to obtain the variance and standard error of p.

54. INEFFICIENT STATISTICS

The method of maximum likelihood holds a unique position in the theory of estimation by virtue of the fact that it will always extract from the data the maximum amount of available information. Its limiting variance is equal to the reciprocal of ni, where i is the amount of information defined independently of the method of estimation. This is commonly expressed by saying that the method of maximum likelihood always leads to an efficient statistic. With an infinitely large sample all the information is extracted by an efficient statistic, but in a finite sample this is generally not the case. Special methods are then necessary for the extraction of the residuum of information not available by the ordinary estimation process. Sometimes, however, a statistic does extract all the information that the data contain, even in small samples. Such a statistic is termed sufficient, and will be found by the method of maximum likelihood where it exists.

In many types of problem other methods of estimation suggest themselves and are in some cases fully efficient, in the sense that they lead to a statistic having the same variance as that yielded by the method of maximum likelihood. Yet no other method of estimation has the property of always leading to an efficient statistic. Hence an inefficient statistic may easily result from the use of some other estimation process. As maximum likelihood is frequently not the easiest method to use it is worth examining the drawbacks of inefficient estimates. It is only by this means that the desirability of always using efficient methods, even at the expense of extra labour, will be appreciated. It is assumed that all the methods considered lead to consistent statistics. A consistent statistic is simply one which approaches more and more closely to the true value of the parameter as the size of sample increases. It will be readily appreciated that inconsistent statistics are utterly misleading and should not be used under any circumstances.

Example 31. De Winton and Haldane have recorded the results of self-pollinating and intercrossing *Primula sinensis* plants that were heterozygous for the two genes F,f and Ch,ch. These genes are linked and the 4,164 individuals observed in the progeny of coupled double heterozygotes showed the following segregation: 2,972 F Ch, 171 F ch, 190 f Ch, 831 f ch. What is the linkage value of the two genes?

Now it can be shown from simple genetical considerations that the frequencies expected in each of the four classes are $\frac{1}{4}(2+P)$ F Ch, $\frac{1}{4}(1-P)$ F ch, $\frac{1}{4}(1-P)$ f Ch, $\frac{1}{4}P$ f ch, where

$$P = (1-p_m)(1-p_f)$$

p_m being the recombination value of the male gametes and p_f that of the female gametes. It should be noted that p_m and p_f cannot be separated in data of this kind; only if they are assumed to be equal can the value of p be found from that of P. We will consider the estimation of P as the parameter characterizing the data.

The log likelihood expression is

$$L=2{,}972 \log\left(\frac{2+P}{4}\right)+171 \log\left(\frac{1-P}{4}\right)+190 \log\left(\frac{1-P}{4}\right)+831 \log\left(\frac{P}{4}\right)$$

which may be re-written as

$$L=2{,}972 \log(2+P)+361 \log(1-P)+831 \log P - 4{,}164 \log 4.$$

Then the maximum likelihood equation of estimation becomes

$$\frac{dL}{dP}=\frac{2{,}972}{2+P}-\frac{361}{1-P}+\frac{831}{P}=0$$

or $\qquad 1{,}662+1{,}419\,P-4{,}164\,P^2=0$
and $\qquad P=0\cdot 824734$

Redifferentiating and substituting expected for observed frequencies gives

$$-I_P=\frac{d^2L}{dP}=-\frac{n}{4}\left[\frac{2+P}{(2+P)^2}+\frac{2(1-P)}{(1-P)^2}+\frac{P}{P^2}\right]$$

$$=-\frac{n}{4}\left(\frac{1}{2+P}+\frac{2}{1-P}+\frac{1}{P}\right)$$

and $\qquad I_P=\dfrac{n(1+2P)}{2P(1-P)(2+P)}$

Substituting the estimated value of P

$$I_P=\frac{4{,}164 \times 2\cdot 649469}{2\times 0\cdot 824734 \times 0\cdot 175266 \times 2\cdot 824734}=13{,}509\cdot 8703$$

and $\qquad V_P=\dfrac{1}{I_P}=0\cdot 000074020$

We may note that if it is assumed that male and female recombination values are the same

$$P=(1-p)^2=0\cdot 824734$$
$$1-p=0\cdot 908149$$
$$p=0\cdot 091851$$

In order to arrive at the values of I_p and V_p we put

$$I_p=nS\left[\frac{1}{m}\left(\frac{dm}{dp^2}\right)\right]$$

but $\qquad \dfrac{dm}{dp}=\dfrac{dm}{dP}\cdot\dfrac{dP}{dp}$

and so $\qquad I_p=nS\left[\dfrac{1}{m}\left(\dfrac{dm}{dP}\cdot\dfrac{dP}{dp}\right)^2\right]$

$$=nS\left[\dfrac{1}{m}\left(\dfrac{dm}{dP}\right)^2\left(\dfrac{dP}{dp}\right)^2\right]$$

which, since $\frac{dP}{dp}$ is constant for all the classes in the data,

$$-n\left(\frac{dP}{dp}\right)^2 S\left[\frac{1}{m}\left(\frac{dm}{dP}\right)^2\right] = I_P\left(\frac{dP}{dp}\right)^2$$

Now $P=(1-p)^2$ so $\frac{dP}{dp}=-2(1-p)$

$$\left(\frac{dP}{dp}\right)^2 = 4(1-p)^2 = 4P$$

Hence $$I_p = \frac{2n(1+2P)}{(1-P)(2+P)} = 44{,}568 \cdot 2206$$

and $$V_p = \frac{1}{I_p} = 0 \cdot 0000224375$$

These estimates of P and p are fully efficient, but other estimates do not always have this property. One such estimate is related to the calculation of χ^2 testing the linkage item in this family.

In Section 46 we used the comparison

$$(a_1 - 3a_2 - 3a_3 + 9a_4)$$

to test for linkage. If this comparison can be used for the detection of linkage it seems not unreasonable to expect that it would be suitable for estimating the linkage value.

Substituting the expected for the observed values the comparison becomes

$$\frac{n}{4}(2+P_1-3(1-P_1)-3(1-P_1)+9P_1)$$
$$= n(4P_1-1)$$

The symbol P_1 is used to distinguish the present estimate from the maximum likelihood statistic which has already been obtained.

The comparisons having the observed and expected values can be equated to give the equation of estimation of P

$$n(4P_1-1) = (a_1-3a_2-3a_3-9a_4)$$
$$4nP_1 = (a_1-3a_2-3a_3+9a_4)+(a_1+a_2+a_3+a_4)$$

and $$P_1 = \frac{1}{2n}(a_1-a_2-a_3+5a_4)$$

Taking de Winton and Haldane's data

$$P_1 = \frac{1}{2 \times 4{,}164}[2{,}972 - 171 - 190 + (5 \times 831)]$$
$$= 0 \cdot 812439$$

This value is distinctly lower than that of the maximum likelihood estimate.

The variance of P_1 can be found by means of the general formula, taken from Fisher,

$$\frac{1}{n}V_{P_1}=S\left[m\left(\frac{dP_1}{da_1}\right)^2\right]-\left(\frac{dP_1}{dn}\right)^2$$

Now $\qquad P_1=\frac{1}{2n}(a_1-a_2-a_3+5a_4)$

So $\qquad \frac{dP_1}{da_1}=\frac{1}{2n}, \quad \frac{dP_1}{da_2}=\frac{dP_1}{da_3}=-\frac{1}{2n}, \quad \frac{dP_1}{da_4}=\frac{5}{2n}$

and $\qquad \frac{dP_1}{dn}=-\frac{1}{2n^2}(a_1-a_2-a_3+5a_4)=-\frac{P_1}{n}$

Then
$$\frac{1}{n}V_{P_1}=\frac{2+P_1}{4}\left(\frac{1}{2n}\right)^2+\frac{1-P_1}{4}\left(-\frac{1}{2n}\right)^2+\frac{1-P_1}{4}\left(-\frac{1}{2n}\right)^2+\frac{P_1}{4}\left(\frac{5}{2n}\right)^2-\left(\frac{P_1}{n}\right)^2$$

$$=\frac{1}{16n^2}(2+P_1+1-P_1+1-P_1+25P_1-16P_1{}^2)$$

$$=\frac{1}{4n^2}(1+6P_1-4P_1{}^2)$$

and $\qquad V_{P_1}=\frac{1}{4n}(1+6P_1-4P_1{}^2)$

Substituting the value observed for P_1 gives

$$V_{P_1}=\frac{1+(6\times 0\cdot 812439)-4(0\cdot 812439)^2}{4\times 4{,}164}=0\cdot 000194189$$

This is to be compared with the variance of the maximum likelihood statistic, $V_P=0\cdot 000074020$

V_{P_1} is much greater than V_P. In other words, the second method of estimation gives a less precise estimate of the linkage value. As Fisher has shown, we can regard $I_{P_1}=\dfrac{1}{V_{P_1}}=5{,}149\cdot 6334$ as the amount of information extracted by the second method of estimation. The available information is measured by I_P and has already been found as $13{,}509\cdot 8703$, so that the estimate P_1 uses only $\dfrac{5{,}149\cdot 6334}{13{,}509\cdot 8703}$ or 38% of the total information utilizable by an efficient estimate. This result is often stated by saying that the efficiency, E, of P_1 is

$$E=\frac{I_{P_1}}{I_P}=38\%$$

An equally precise result would have been obtained if the method of maximum likelihood had been employed with $\dfrac{38\times 4{,}164}{100}$, i.e. 1,582 plants in the family. Inefficient estimation is thus very wasteful. In the present case its use is equivalent to throwing away nearly two-thirds of the labour and materials used in raising the family.

The value of E is itself dependent on the value of P.

$$I_P = \frac{n(1+2P)}{2P(1-P)(2+P)} \quad \text{and} \quad I_{P_1} = \frac{4n}{1+6P-4P_1^2}$$

Now if $P=P_1$, as must be the case on the average, since both are consistent estimates,

$$E = \frac{I_{P_1}}{I_P} = \frac{8P(1-P)(2+P)}{(1+6P-4P^2)(1+2P)}$$

Fig. 8 shows the value of E plotted against the value of P. It will be seen that $E=1$, i.e. the second method of estimation

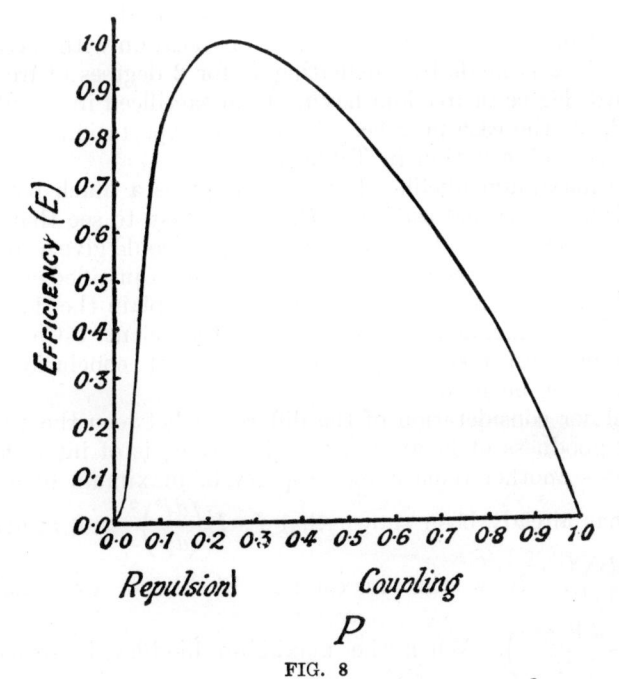

FIG. 8

The efficiency, for all linkage values, of the estimate $P_1 = \frac{1}{2n}(a_1-a_2-a_3+5a_4)$, by comparison with the maximum likelihood statistic

is fully efficient, only when $P=0.25$. At this point $p=0.5$, i.e. the genes are independent in inheritance. So the comparison $(a_1-3a_2-3a_3+9a_4)$ is fully efficient for the very purpose for which it was used in Section 46, viz. the detection of departures from independence; but it is inefficient for estimating any linkage value once linkage has been demonstrated. For close linkage in either coupling or repulsion, when P approaches 1 and 0 respectively, the method is absolutely useless as its efficiency is nearly 0.

These conclusions about the estimation of the linkage value can be reached without any reference to observed data. They rest solely on a consideration of the properties of I_P and I_{P_1}. It will thus be seen that information is a concept of great value in the planning of analyses and experiments. Another example will be given later and the subject has been further discussed by both Fisher and Mather.

Not only are inefficient statistics wasteful of data but they may also be very misleading. Once found, P and P_1 can be used to formulate new expectations for the frequencies of the four phenotypic classes into which the plants fall. In this way, it is possible to test further the hypothesis that the genes F,f and Ch,ch are linked. The comparison of observation with these new expectations is made by calculating χ^2 for 2 degrees of freedom, the third degree of freedom having been sacrificed in calculating P or P_1, as the case may be. These new expectations are compared with observation in Table 54.

The maximum likelihood statistic P gives a much better fit than does the second estimate, P_1. It is easy to see that in an extreme case the use of an inefficient statistic could give a spurious disagreement with the data, so leading to the unjustified suspicion that linkage was not in itself sufficient to explain the departure from simple mendelian expectation. Inefficient estimates of parameters can result in seriously incorrect conclusions and should never be used.

A closer consideration of the difference between the two χ^2s testing goodness of fit after fitting P and P_1 is of interest as it illustrates another remarkable property of maximum likelihood.

It has already been shown that $I_p = I_P \left(\dfrac{dP}{dp}\right)^2$ and, in general, $I_y = I_x \left(\dfrac{dx}{dy}\right)^2$. Now the maximum likelihood expression is $\dfrac{dL}{dP} = S\left(a \dfrac{d \log m}{dP}\right)$. When the maximum likelihood estimate of P is substituted this expression has the value 0. But if some other estimate, P_1, is used, $S\left(a \dfrac{d \log m}{dP}\right)$ is no longer 0. It has a value which may be called D. Then

$$\dfrac{dD}{dP} = \dfrac{d}{dP} S\left(a \dfrac{d \log m}{dP}\right) = S\left(a \dfrac{d^2 \log m}{dP^2}\right) = I_P$$

a being used in place of the corresponding expectation mn.

TABLE 54

The Agreement of Observation with Expectations found by the use of P and P_1

	Classes				Total	z^2
	F Ch	F ch	f Ch	f ch		
Observed	2,972	171	190	831	4,164	
Expected with P . .	2,940·5485	182·4515	182·4515	858·5485	4,164	2·2515
Expected with P_1 . .	2,927·7500	195·2500	195·2500	845·7500	4,164	4·0790

Now
$$\frac{dP}{dD} = \frac{1}{\frac{dD}{dP}}$$

and so
$$I_D = \frac{I_P}{\left(\frac{dD}{dP}\right)^2} = \frac{I_P}{I_P^2} = \frac{1}{I_P},$$

and $V_D = I_P$.

This variance is fixed by hypothesis, hence

$$\frac{D^2}{V_D} = \frac{D^2}{I_P} \text{ is a } \chi^2 \text{ for 1 degree of freedom.}$$

Applying this to de Winton and Haldane's data

$$D = \frac{2{,}972}{2+P_1} - \frac{361}{1-P_1} + \frac{831}{P_1} = \frac{2{,}972}{2 \cdot 81244} - \frac{361}{0 \cdot 18756} + \frac{831}{0 \cdot 81244} = 154 \cdot 86145$$

and I_P has already been found to be $13{,}509 \cdot 8703$.

Hence
$$\chi^2_{[1]} = \frac{D^2}{I_P} = \frac{(154 \cdot 86145)^2}{13{,}509 \cdot 8703} = 1 \cdot 7752$$

Thus we can expect χ^2 testing the fit given by observation to the expectation found from P_1 to be $1 \cdot 7752$ greater than that obtained when the maximum likelihood expectations are used. The corresponding difference calculated in Table 54 is $4 \cdot 0790 - 2 \cdot 2515 = 1 \cdot 8275$. This slight discrepancy is not due to faulty calculation or reasoning but to the fact that, as the values of P and P_1 are different, the $\chi^2_{[2]}$ testing the two gene ratios, without reference to the linkage item, are slightly different. The segregations of the two genes are correlated when the genes are linked. In the extreme case of complete linkage any departure from expected ratio of one gene involves a corresponding departure in the other. As the linkage becomes looser this correlated departure becomes less, and the χ^2 testing the discrepancies in gene ratios alone will become correspondingly larger. Now P_1 is less than P and so p_1 is greater than p. Hence the gene ratio χ^2 is slightly larger when the P_1 expectations are used. This coupled with the χ^2 testing the discrepancy of the inefficient and the maximum likelihood linkage values accounts for the $1 \cdot 8275$ difference of Table 54. Here the χ^2 difference due to gene ratio correlation is only $0 \cdot 0523$. The great discrepancy lies in the item of $1 \cdot 7752$ traceable to the use of an inefficient estimate of the linkage parameter. In this way we see that any departure from the maximum likelihood estimate is liable to cause a seriously large inflation of the χ^2 subsequently used to test goodness of fit. This means, in effect, that 1 degree of freedom in χ^2 is supposedly sacrificed to the estimation of P, and yet, when an inefficient estimate is used, χ^2 itself is not reduced by the full corresponding amount. Clearly, unless an efficient estimate is employed, the subsequent test of significance cannot be trustworthy.

55. SIMULTANEOUS ESTIMATION

In the examples worked above the problem involved the estimation of a single parameter. Sometimes, however, two or more parameters must be found in order to specify the hypothesis. Thus the formula of a normal distribution contains two unknowns, μ and σ. The estimation of these two parameters will serve to show how such cases are treated by the method of maximum likelihood.

Example 32. The formula of the normal distribution is

$$m = \frac{1}{\sigma\sqrt{2\pi}} e^{-\frac{(\mu-x)^2}{2\sigma^2}}$$

where m is the expected frequency of the class characterized by the value x of the diagnostic measurement. Let m_1 be the expectation of class x_1, m_2 of x_2, and so on. Further, let a_1 be the frequency observed in class x_1, a_2 of x_2, and so on.

Then the log likelihood expression is

$$L = a_1 \log\left[\frac{1}{\sigma\sqrt{2\pi}} e^{-\frac{(\mu-x_1)^2}{2\sigma^2}}\right] + a_2 \log\left[\frac{1}{\sigma\sqrt{2\pi}} e^{-\frac{(\mu-x_2)^2}{2\sigma^2}}\right] + \ldots$$

This may be re-written as

$$L = a_1 \log\left(\frac{1}{\sigma\sqrt{2\pi}}\right) - a_1\frac{(\mu-x_1)^2}{2\sigma^2} + a_2 \log\left(\frac{1}{\sigma\sqrt{2\pi}}\right) - a_2\frac{(\mu-x_2)^2}{2\sigma^2} + \ldots$$

$$= n \log\left(\frac{1}{\sigma\sqrt{2\pi}}\right) - a_1\frac{(\mu-x_1)^2}{2\sigma^2} - a_2\frac{(\mu-x_2)^2}{2\sigma^2} \ldots$$

To find the equations of estimation of μ and σ the log likelihood must be maximized by partial differentiation with respect to each of these parameters, giving

$$\frac{\partial L}{\partial \mu} = -\frac{2a_1(\mu-x_1)}{2\sigma^2} - \frac{2a_2(\mu-x_2)}{2\sigma^2} - \ldots = 0 \quad . \quad . \quad . \quad \text{(i)}$$

$$\frac{\partial L}{\partial \sigma} = -\frac{n\sigma\sqrt{2\pi}}{\sigma^2\sqrt{2\pi}} + \frac{a_1(\mu-x_1)^2}{\sigma^3} + \frac{a_2(\mu-x_2)^2}{\sigma^3} + \ldots = 0 \quad . \quad \text{(ii)}$$

Equation (i) reduces to $a_1(\mu-x_1) + a_2(\mu-x_2) + \ldots = 0$ or

$$S(a_1 x_1) - \mu S(a_1) = 0$$

and since $S(a_1) = n$, $\mu = \dfrac{S(a_1 x_1)}{n}$, i.e. $= \bar{x}$, as the numerator is the sum of all the x values in the observations.

Equation (ii) may be simplified to
$$-n\sigma^2 + a_1(\mu-x_1)^2 + a_2(\mu-x_2)^2 + \ldots = 0$$
Then substituting $\bar{x}$ for μ it becomes
$$\sigma^2 = \frac{S[a_1(x_1-\bar{x})^2]}{n}$$

The numerator of this expression is the sum of squares of deviations from the mean of x, just as in the formula used in Section 10. The denominator, however, requires a word of explanation. It is n and not $n-1$ as used before. The reasons for the use of $n-1$, the number of degrees of freedom, have been fully set out earlier. It will be remembered that if a theoretical mean is used, then n is the proper divisor, but that if μ is estimated from the data the number of degrees of freedom is reduced to $n-1$. The substitution of $\bar{x}$ for μ in the above calculation, $\bar{x}$ having already been found as the estimate of μ, requires that $n-1$ be substituted for n in the denominator, and so the formula reduces to the form used earlier, viz.
$$\sigma^2 = \frac{S[a_1(x_1-\bar{x})^2]}{n-1}$$

The necessity for the change in the denominator at the same time as the substitution in the numerator is a consequence of the use of small samples. In large samples the difference between n and $n-1$ is so small as to be negligible.

56. COMBINED ESTIMATION AND HETEROGENEITY TESTS

The method of maximum likelihood offers a solution to the problems that arise when more than one type of data each supplies information about the same parameter. Two main questions are to be answered in such cases, that of finding the best estimate of the parameter when using all the sets of data together, and that of testing the agreement of all the data with each other. A detailed discussion of these problems has been given by Mather, but the salient features of the treatment can be illustrated by a very simple example.

Example 33. Suppose we have an organism heterozygous for a single gene difference, A,a. The segregation of this gene may be investigated in either or both of two ways, viz. by self-fertilizing or intercrossing such heterozygotes to give an F$_2$ and by backcrossing the heterozygote to a recessive individual.

Let x be the proportion of a gametes, and $1-x$ correspondingly the proportion of A gametes, which are successfully represented in the next generation, x being alike for both male and female gametes. It is expected that the two phenotypic classes, A and a, will occur with the frequencies $1-x : x$ in the backcross and $1-x^2 : x^2$ in the F_2. The observed frequencies of individuals of the two phenotypes in backcross and F_2 may be denoted as:

Type of progeny	A	a	Total
Backcross	a_{B1}	a_{B2}	n_B
F_2	a_{F1}	a_{F2}	n_F

Three questions may be asked, viz.

(a) What value of x best fits the joint data?

(b) Does this agree with the simple mendelian expectation of $x=\tfrac{1}{2}$?

(c) Do the two families agree in showing the same value of x?

The likelihood of obtaining the observed backcross family is

$$\frac{n_B!}{a_{B1}!a_{B2}!}(1-x)^{a_{B1}}(x)^{a_{B2}}$$

and that of obtaining the F_2 is

$$\frac{n_F!}{a_{F1}!a_{F2}!}(1-x^2)^{a_{F1}}(x^2)^{a_{F2}}$$

Since the two families are quite independent of each other the likelihood of their simultaneous occurrence is the product of the two individual likelihoods, viz.

$$\frac{n_B!n_F!}{a_{B1}!a_{B2}!a_{F1}!a_{F2}!}(1-x)^{a_{B1}}(x)^{a_{B2}}(1-x^2)^{a_{F1}}(x^2)^{a_{F2}}$$

and the joint log likelihood becomes

$$L = C + a_{B1}\log(1-x) + a_{B2}\log(x) + a_{F1}\log(1-x^2) + a_{F2}\log(x^2)$$

The best-fitting joint estimate of x is then obtained by maximization.

$$\frac{dL}{dx} = -\frac{a_{B1}}{1-x} + \frac{a_{B2}}{x} - \frac{2x \cdot a_{F1}}{1-x^2} + \frac{2x \cdot a_{F2}}{x^2} = 0$$

As a numerical example the data of Fisher and Mather on segregation for D,d in mice may be used (Table 55).

TABLE 55

Segregation for Intense (D) and Dilute (d) in Mice (Fisher and Mather)

Family	Phenotype D	Phenotype d	Total	χ^2
Backcross . . .	648	571	1,219	4·8638
F_2	132	56	188	2·2979

Substituting these figures in the maximum likelihood equation

$$-\frac{648}{1-x}+\frac{571}{x}-\frac{2x.132}{1-x^2}+\frac{2x.56}{x^2}=0$$

which simplifies to $683-648x-1{,}595\ x^2=0$
and $\qquad x=0\cdot 482049$

The amount of information about x may be found from either of the two formulae

$$i_x = S\left[\frac{1}{m}\left(\frac{dm}{dx}\right)^2\right] = -S\left[m\frac{d^2\log m}{dx^2}\right]$$

If the second formula is used, it is clear that the second derivative of the joint log likelihood expression is the sum of the second derivatives of the two log likelihoods given by backcross and F_2 separately. Hence the total amount of information about x is the sum of the amounts yielded by the two types of data when taken separately. Once this has been established it is, however, easier to find the information value by using the first formula.

Class	Backcross			F_2		
	m	dm/dx	i	m	dm/dx	i
A	$1-x$	-1	$\dfrac{1}{1-x}$	$1-x^2$	$-2x$	$\dfrac{4x^2}{1-x^2}$
a	x	1	$\dfrac{1}{x}$	x^2	$2x$	$\dfrac{4x^2}{x^2}$
Total	1	0	$\dfrac{1}{x(1-x)}$	1	0	$\dfrac{4}{1-x^2}$

The total amount of information is thus

$$I_x = \frac{n_B}{x(1-x)} + \frac{4n_F}{1-x^2}$$

$$= \frac{1{,}219}{0\cdot 269678} + \frac{4\times 188}{0\cdot 767629} = 4{,}882\cdot 29 + 979\cdot 64$$

$$= 5{,}861\cdot 93$$

and $\qquad V_x = \dfrac{1}{I_x} = 0\cdot 000170592$ giving $s_x = \sqrt{V_x} = 0\cdot 013061$

This method of combining different groups of data to give one estimate of the parameter is worth examining a little more closely. Let $\hat{x}$ be the best joint estimate of x, as found above, and x_B and x_F be the best estimates supplied by the two bodies of data taken separately. It has already been shown (Section 53) that the rate of change of the maximum likelihood expression on the parameter is the amount of information yielded by the data. Hence $D_B = I_B(\hat{x} - x_B)$ provided that $(\hat{x} - x_B)$ is small, where D_B is the value of the backcross maximum likelihood expression when $\hat{x}$ is substituted for x_B. Similarly $D_F = I_F(\hat{x} - x_F)$. Now the joint maximum likelihood expression has the value 0 when $\hat{x}$ is used, i.e. $D_B = -D_F$. So

$$I_B(\hat{x} - x_B) = -I_F(\hat{x} - x_F)$$

and
$$\hat{x} = \frac{I_B x_B + I_F x_F}{I_B + I_F}$$

The best joint value is the mean of the separate values weighted according to their respective amounts of information. In general $I = \frac{1}{V}$, and so the reciprocal of the variance is the weight to be applied to any statistic when it is being combined with other estimates of the same parameter. The procedure used in combining different estimates of a correlation coefficient in Section 41 is of general validity.

We now turn to the problem of testing the joint agreement of the backcross and F_2 data with the simple mendelian expectation of $x = \frac{1}{2}$. If $\frac{1}{2}$ is substituted for x in the joint maximum likelihood expression the latter takes a value D_x. We can also calculate the amount of information, I_x, yielded by the joint data about x when the latter has this value of $\frac{1}{2}$. As $\frac{D_x^2}{I_x}$ is a χ^2 for 1 degree of freedom (Section 54) the appropriate test of significance is then easily made.

The joint maximum likelihood expression is

$$\frac{dL}{dx} = \frac{571}{x} - \frac{648}{1-x} + \frac{2x \cdot 56}{x^2} - \frac{2x \cdot 132}{1-x^2}$$

which, when $x = \frac{1}{2}$, becomes

$$(2 \times 571) - (2 \times 648) + (4 \times 56) - (\tfrac{4}{3} \times 132) = -106 = D_x$$

and
$$I_x = \frac{n_B}{x(1-x)} + \frac{4 n_F}{1-x^2} = (4 \times 1,219) + (\tfrac{4}{3} \times 4 \times 188) = 5,878 \cdot 6$$

Hence $\chi^2_{[1]} = \frac{(-106)^2}{5,878 \cdot 6} = 1 \cdot 9113$ and the joint data agree with mendelian expectation.

The last column of Table 55 gives the values of the two $\chi^2_{[1]}$'s testing the agreement of the separate families with this expectation of $x = \frac{1}{2}$. In the former case the segregation expected is 1 : 1 and in the latter case 3 : 1. The total χ^2 is 7·1617, which may be analysed into deviation and heterogeneity items as shown in

Table 56. The deviation item has been found above and the heterogeneity item is found by subtraction.

TABLE 56
The Analysis of Fisher and Mather's Data

Item	χ^2	N	P
Deviation	1·9113	1	0·20–0·10
Heterogeneity	5·2504	1	0·05–0·02
Total	7·1617	2	

The heterogeneity χ^2 is suspiciously large and so there is doubt whether the two sets of data agree in their x values. This heterogeneity is not sufficiently pronounced to cause any serious disturbance, but it is doubtful whether the two sets of data can properly be combined in the estimation of x.

This analysis gives the heterogeneity item appropriate to $x=\frac{1}{2}$, and, if the deviation were significant, this item would be inexact. Though the calculation of a more exact heterogeneity item is not necessary with the present data, it may be undertaken as an illustration of the method for use in other cases.

The best-fitting joint estimate of x, viz. $\hat{x}$, is substituted in the two separate maximum likelihood expressions, from backcross and F_2, which then take the values of D_B and D_F. The two separate amounts of information, I_B and I_F, are calculated and

$$\chi^2_{[1]} = \frac{D_B^2}{I_B} + \frac{D_F^2}{I_F}$$

It should be noted that this χ^2 would have 2 degrees of freedom if an expected value of x were used, but where the estimate $\hat{x}$ has been found from the data themselves 1 degree of freedom is, as usual, lost.

$$\hat{x} = 0·482049$$

$$D_B = \frac{571}{0·482049} - \frac{648}{0·517951} = -66·55$$

$$D_F = \frac{56 \times 2}{0·482049} - \frac{133 \times 2 \times 0·482049}{0·767629} = 66·56$$

$$I_B = \frac{1,219}{0·482049 \times 0·517951} = 4,882·29$$

$$I_F = \frac{4 \times 188}{0·767629} = 979·64$$

The $\chi^2_{[1]}$ is $\frac{(-66·55)^2}{4,882·29} + \frac{(66·56)^2}{979·64} = 5·4294$ with a probability of 0·02.

57. PLANNING EXPERIMENTS

The concept of the amount of information is very helpful in the understanding and planning of experiments. It is very commonly the case that some aspect of experimental technique is capable of being modified in such a way that the resulting data are to some extent altered. A comparison of the amounts of information about the parameter in question will quickly show which of the various procedures is most profitable.

As a case in point we may consider the biological assay of drugs. The dose administered may be chosen so that any proportion of the test individuals show the reaction, death, convulsion, &c., characterizing the drug's effect. Fisher has, however, shown that the most precise assay is made when 50% of the individuals react, as it is here that the quantity of information about drug strength is greatest. So, in making such assay, the drug should always be administered at approximately the strength necessary to give 50% effect.

Though perhaps of rather specialized interest, the estimation of genetical recombination values provides a very striking example of the use of information in the design of experiments. It has already been stated that an individual heterozygous for two genes, i.e. of the genotype AaBb, gives four classes of gamete, AB, Ab, aB and ab, with the characteristic frequencies

$$\tfrac{1}{2}(1-p) : \tfrac{1}{2}p : \tfrac{1}{2}p : \tfrac{1}{2}(1-p), \quad \text{or} \quad \tfrac{1}{2}p : \tfrac{1}{2}(1-p) : \tfrac{1}{2}(1-p) : \tfrac{1}{2}p,$$

p being the recombination value, according to whether the individual itself arose from the fusion of AB and ab or of Ab and aB gametes. The former type of heterozygote, symbolized as AB/ab, is usually said to show the coupling phase of linkage, the latter, Ab/aB, the repulsion phase. When the genes are unlinked $p = 1-p = \tfrac{1}{2}$ and the two phases cease to differ.

Suppose that it is desired to estimate the recombination value. It is necessary to devise some technique for determining the relative frequencies of the non-recombinant and recombinant gametic classes, i.e. AB and ab as opposed to Ab and aB in the coupling case and vice versa for repulsion. Several experimental courses are open for this purpose, but only two of them are in common use. First of all, the double heterozygote could be crossed to a double recessive aabb. Four classes of progeny, all phenotypically distinguishable, are produced, viz. AaBb, Aabb aaBb and aabb. These classes have the same expected frequencies as the four corresponding types of gamete given by the double heterozygote. Such a backcross would normally be made in animals, provided, of course, that aabb individuals were available. One type of mating is as easy as another in bisexual organisms. But in plants self-pollination may be much easier than backcrossing and so would commend itself for practical reasons. On selfing, ten genotypes are produced in the F_2. Table 57 gives the frequencies of these classes for the coupling phase, assuming that p is the same in male and female gametes.

TABLE 57

The Progeny of a Selfed Double Heterozygote

	AA	Aa	aa
BB	$(1-p)^2$	$2p(1-p)$	p^2
Bb	$2p(1-p)$	R $2p^2$ / C $2(1-p)^2$	$2p(1-p)$
bb	p^2	$2p(1-p)$	$(1-p)^2$

R=repulsion phase   C=coupling phase

The repulsion phase gives similar results but with p and $1-p$ interchanged. In the common case of dominance of both genes, only four classes are distinguishable on the basis of phenotypic differences. These classes are indicated by dotted lines in the table. Simple addition then shows that the frequencies of the four classes are

	AB	Ab	aB	ab
Coupling	$\frac{1}{4}[2+(1-p)^2]$	$\frac{1}{4}[1-(1-p)^2]$	$\frac{1}{4}[1-(1-p)^2]$	$\frac{1}{4}(1-p)^2$
Repulsion	$\frac{1}{4}(2+p^2)$	$\frac{1}{4}(1-p^2)$	$\frac{1}{4}(1-p^2)$	$\frac{1}{4}p^2$

Which of the two methods, backcrossing or self-pollinating, is to be recommended for determining the recombination value?

The first step in answering this question is that of finding the relative amounts of information about p yielded by the two types of progeny. These are easily obtained from the formula $i = S\left[\frac{1}{m}\left(\frac{dm}{dp}\right)^2\right]$, as shown in Table 58. It will be noticed that i, rather than I, is used for this purpose, so obviating any confusion due to the question of family size. The result would, however, be the same if I were employed, provided that backcross and F_2 were of the same size.

The information from both types of family varies with p, and so it is necessary to take one as a standard for comparison with the other. The backcross information is the same in both coupling and repulsion and hence is to be preferred as the standard. If the value of the backcross is taken as unity, the relative value

TABLE 58
Amounts of Information about the Recombination Value

Backcross

Class	Coupling m	$\frac{dm}{dp}$	i	Repulsion m	$\frac{dm}{dp}$	i
AB	$\frac{1}{2}(1-p)$	$-\frac{1}{2}$	$\frac{1}{2(1-p)}$	$\frac{1}{2}p$	$\frac{1}{2}$	$\frac{1}{2p}$
Ab	$\frac{1}{2}p$	$\frac{1}{2}$	$\frac{1}{2p}$	$\frac{1}{2}(1-p)$	$-\frac{1}{2}$	$\frac{1}{2(1-p)}$
aB	$\frac{1}{2}p$	$\frac{1}{2}$	$\frac{1}{2p}$	$\frac{1}{2}(1-p)$	$-\frac{1}{2}$	$\frac{1}{2(1-p)}$
ab	$\frac{1}{2}(1-p)$	$-\frac{1}{2}$	$\frac{1}{2(1-p)}$	$\frac{1}{2}p$	$\frac{1}{2}$	$\frac{1}{2p}$
Total	1	0	$\frac{1}{p(1-p)}$	1	0	$\frac{1}{p(1-p)}$

F_2

Class	Coupling m	$\frac{dm}{dp}$	i	Repulsion m	$\frac{dm}{dp}$	i
AB	$\frac{1}{4}(3-2p+p^2)$	$-\frac{1}{2}(1-p)$	$\frac{(1-p)^2}{3-2p+p^2}$	$\frac{1}{4}(2+p^2)$	$\frac{1}{2}p$	$\frac{p^2}{2+p^2}$
Ab	$\frac{1}{4}(2p-p^2)$	$\frac{1}{2}(1-p)$	$\frac{(1-p)^2}{2p-p^2}$	$\frac{1}{4}(1-p^2)$	$-\frac{1}{2}p$	$\frac{p^2}{1-p^2}$
aB	$\frac{1}{4}(2p-p^2)$	$\frac{1}{2}(1-p)$	$\frac{(1-p)^2}{2p-p_1}$	$\frac{1}{4}(1-p^2)$	$-\frac{1}{2}p$	$\frac{p^2}{1-p^2}$
ab	$\frac{1}{4}(1-2p+p^2)$	$-\frac{1}{2}(1-p)$	1	$\frac{1}{4}p^2$	$\frac{1}{2}p$	1
Total	1	0	$\frac{2(3-4p+2p^2)}{p(2-p)(3-2p+p^2)}$	1	0	$\frac{2(1+2p^2)}{(2+p^2)(1-p^2)}$

of the F_2, obtained by dividing the F_2 amount of information by the backcross amount, $\frac{1}{p(1-p)}$, is

Coupling $\frac{2(1-p)(3-4p+2p^2)}{(2-p)(3-2p+p^2)}$ Repulsion $\frac{2p(1+2p^2)}{(2+p^2)(1+p)}$

These two fractions are perhaps most easily understood when the relative value of the F_2 is plotted against p as in Fig. 9. The F_2 is as valuable, plant for plant, as the backcross in close coupling, but its value falls away to 0 in close repulsion. When $p=\frac{1}{2}$ the F_2 gives four-ninths of the precision of the backcross. So when backcrossing is as simple an operation as self-pollinating, the F_2 is only recommendable in case of close linkage in the coupling phase. In close repulsion an F_2 is relatively worthless, and even for the detection of loose linkage it has less than half the value of the backcross.

If, however, F_2 seed is more easily produced than backcross material, the advantage in precision of the latter may be offset

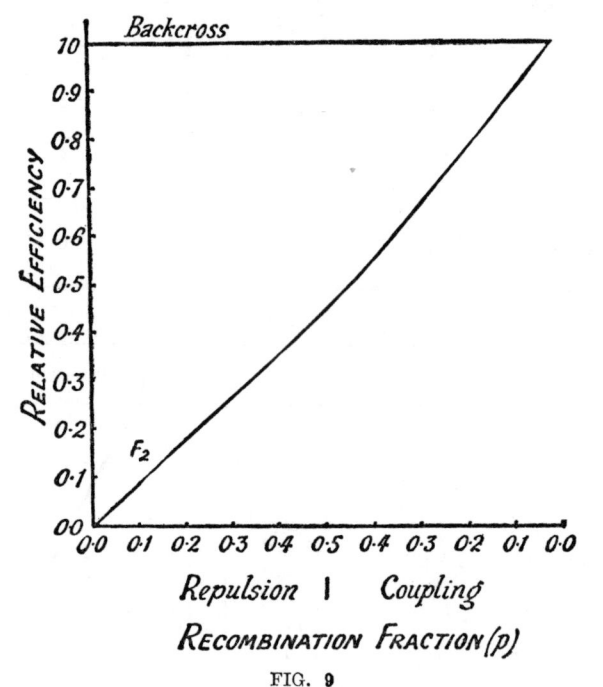

FIG. 9

The efficiency, relative to backcross data, of F_2 progenies, for the estimation of the recombination fraction

by the use of greater progenies of the former type. The experimenter, knowing his own material, can form an opinion on the point at which the ease of production of an F_2 is overborne by its poorer precision. If, for example, a given amount of labour would result in twice as big an F_2 as backcross, it would be profitable to test almost any linkage in the coupling phase by means of the F_2, always provided, of course, that no information was sought on the equality of male and female recombination values. Repulsion F_2's would still be unprofitable.

Before leaving this example a further point may be made.

An F_2 classified fully into all 10 genotypes, as given in Table 57, can, by the calculation of i, be shown to contain twice the information of a backcross. In other words, the incompletely classified F_2 never yields more than half the amount actually present in the family, and usually gives a much smaller fraction still. Incomplete separation of the classes means loss of information. So it follows that classification should always be as complete as is practicable. In the present case, however, completing the classification is very time and labour consuming and cannot be undertaken with profit except in very special circumstances.

58. FIDUCIAL PROBABILITY

A parameter is estimated for the purpose of completing some hypothesis related to the phenomenon under consideration. The hypothesis that two genes are linked is, for example, of very restricted use until the recombination value has been found. Once the parameter has been estimated, on the other hand, the hypothesis of linkage may be tested for agreement with any set of data concerning the genes in question.

We have seen that inefficient estimation leads to trouble when further tests of significance are based on the resulting statistic. But even when an efficient statistic has been found it must be used in a proper manner, or false conclusions will be drawn.

The point is well illustrated by one of the commonest operations in the realm of statistical analysis, viz. the testing of a deviation when the variance with which it is to be compared is estimated from the data. The formula

$$V_x = \frac{1}{n-1} S(x-\bar{x})^2$$

supplies not merely an efficient but a sufficient estimate of σ_x^2, the true variance of the distribution of x. To test the significance of any observed deviation of x from its expected value μ it is necessary to compute the ratio $\frac{\mu-x}{s_x}$, where s_x, found as $\sqrt{V_x}$, is the sufficient estimate of σ_x. The whole of the care devoted to the calculation of s_x is wasted if it is then forgotten that the precision of s_x is dependent on the number of degrees of freedom available for its estimation. Fisher has shown that this precision is, in fact, $\frac{n+1}{n+3}$ of σ_x, where n is the number of observations. To treat $\frac{\mu-x}{s_x}$ as a normal deviate, i.e. to treat s_x as σ_x itself, rather than as an estimate of σ_x, is to assign to the calculation of s_x a spuriously high precision. There is then a real danger of overestimating the significance of the deviation under test. But to treat the fraction as a t for the appropriate number of degrees of freedom is to give it its proper weight. Its true significance will then be apparent. This quantity t is derived solely from the data at hand and it carries no unproved, and unprovable, implications about the hypothetical nature of the population from which the sample is supposedly drawn. It is known exactly and its distribution is also known exactly. It permits the experimenter to draw rigorous conclusions.

The two recent great developments in statistics are (i) the calculation of the distributions of the various exact tests of significance, as described in Chapter IV, and (ii) the demonstration that data contain a definite amount of information about any parameter upon which they depend, and that this information can always be extracted by suitable methods of estimation. Statistical methods developed from these two findings lead to conclusions which are based solely on the data and which are as precise as the data will allow. In this way proper statistical analysis leads to rigorous inferences. These are of necessity stated in terms of uncertainty, but the degree of uncertainty is known and can be given.

The ratio t, for example, usually takes the form

$$t = \frac{\mu - x}{s_x}$$

Of the four quantities involved, three, t, s_x and x, are known exactly. So the equation may be used for a purpose other than that of testing the deviation of x from some hypothetical value μ. It may equally well be written as

$$\mu = x \pm t s_x$$

When given probability levels are assigned to t, this form of the equation allows us to state rigorously, on the basis of the available observations and with no resort to hypothesis, that μ lies between the levels $x + t_p s_x$ and $x - t_p s_x$ with a probability of p, where t_p is the value of t at that level of probability.

This approach is of general validity. In the example of Section 32, concerning the uptake of Rb ions by potatoes, $b = 0.172985$, $s_b = 0.007186$ and t for 3 degrees of freedom has the value 3·182 at the 0·05 level of probability. Then β, the parameter of which b is an estimate, lies between the values 0·1730+(3·182×0·007186), i.e. 0·1959 and 0·1730−(3·182×0·007186), i.e. 0·1501 with a 5% probability of error. Such a statement is one of Fiducial Probability. It is a property of those data which are its origin and it is rigorous because sound statistical methods have been used in the analysis of the data. Only by the use of such analytical methods can the experimenter avoid the twin dangers of over-assessment and under-assessment of the meaning of his results.

REFERENCES

CATCHESIDE, D. G. 1937. Secondary pairing in *Brassica oleracea*. *Cytologia*, Fujii Jub. Vol., 366–78.

FISHER, R. A. 1937. *The Design of Experiments*. Oliver and Boyd. Edinburgh. 2nd ed.

—— 1938. *Statistical Theory of Estimation*. Calcutta University Readership Lectures.

—— and MATHER, K. 1936. A linkage test with mice. *Ann. Eugen.*, **7**, 265–80.

MATHER, K. 1935. The combination of data. *Ann. Eugen.*, **6**, 399–410.

—— 1938. *The Measurement of Linkage in Heredity*. Methuen. London.

WINTON, D. DE, and HALDANE, J. B. S. 1935. The genetics of *Primula sinensis*—III. *J. Genet.*, **31**, 67–100.

CHAPTER XIII

SOME TRANSFORMATIONS

59. THE ANGULAR TRANSFORMATION

WHEN an object may fall into either of two classes, the probability of it falling into one being p and into the other q $(=1-p)$, and n such objects are observed, the probabilities of finding all n to be of the first type, $n-1$ of the first and 1 of the second types, and so on, are given, as we have seen in Section 5, by the expansion of the binomial expression $(p+q)^n$. If a series of such groups of n objects are observed the mean proportion of objects in the first class is expected to be p and the variance of the proportion to be $\frac{pq}{n}$ (Section 13). Thus the precision with which we determine p is a function of p, as well as of n, so that even if n is held constant, the variance will not be constant when p itself varies.

This means that we cannot combine proportions by simple averaging, since each proportion will be determined with a different precision and hence should be weighted by the inverse of its variance in any combining operation. Similarly we are debarred from the use of such a simple and powerful technique as the analysis of variance in dealing with data consisting of proportions as this involves the assumption that each datum, in this case each proportion, is subject to the same variance. Over small ranges of p, especially near $p=0.5$, this assumption may be sufficiently nearly true for the errors arising therefrom to be negligible; but over wider ranges of p the available analytical methods must be seriously limited by the dependence of V_p on p.

The angular transformation, which consists of replacing p (or q) by an angle ϕ such that $p = \sin^2 \phi$, is of great value in overcoming this handicap. For

$$I_\phi = I_p \left(\frac{dp}{d\phi}\right)^2 = \frac{n}{pq}\left(\frac{dp}{d\phi}\right)^2$$

Now $$\frac{dp}{d\phi} = \frac{d}{d\phi}\sin^2\phi = 2\sin\phi \frac{d\sin\phi}{d\phi} = 2\sin\phi\cos\phi$$

when ϕ is measured in radians. Furthermore

$$q = 1-p = 1-\sin^2\phi = \cos^2\phi$$

Therefore $$I_\phi = \frac{n}{\sin^2\phi\cos^2\phi}(2\sin\phi\cos\phi)^2 = 4n$$

and V_ϕ is independent of the value of ϕ.

When, as is usually more convenient, ϕ is measured in degrees

$$\frac{d}{d\phi}\sin\phi = \frac{\pi}{180}\cos\phi$$

and $$I_p = \frac{4n\pi^2}{180^2} = \frac{n}{820\cdot 7}$$

V_ϕ then becomes $\frac{820\cdot 7}{n}$.

Hence the angular transformation replaces proportions by angular values which can be treated by simple averaging, the analysis of variance, and similar methods.

Example 34. The value of the angular transformation may be illustrated by the analysis of an experiment, which formed part of an investigation into the precautions necessary to ensure effective isolation of varieties in the production of seed of crop plants. It was desired to know the amount of inter-varietal cross-pollination occurring between two varieties of the radish when no spatial isolation was attempted. Fifty plants of each of the two varieties, one white rooted and the other red rooted, were grown in a square of ten plants side, the representatives of the two varieties being randomly sited within the square. Radishes set no seed with their own pollen and so all seed comes from crossing with other plants. The chance of the pollen grain, effective in giving any one seed, coming from a plant of the opposite variety to the mother, is rather greater than 0·5, since there are 50 potential fathers of the opposite kind to 49 of the mother's own variety, and even the pollen of some of these 49 may be ruled out by the same mechanism as prevents effective self-pollination. To avoid complications, however, in our illustration we will assume expectations of 0·5 probability of the effective pollen coming from the mother plant's own variety, and 0·5 of it being from the other variety. Progenies of 30 seedlings were grown from the seed of each of 20 white- and 20 red-rooted mothers taken at random from the square. Inter-varietal crosses were recognizable by the resulting seedling having purple pigment. Table 59 shows the numbers of seedlings resulting from inter-varietal crosses in each of the 40 progenies. Do these data accord with the expectation of 50% inter-varietal crossings, and if not, do the two varieties agree in the percentages they show?

TABLE 59

Frequency of Contamination by Foreign Pollen in Radishes

No. of hybrids (in 30 seedlings)	p	ϕ in °	Frequency observed in White series	Red series
1	0·033	10·5	0	1
3	0·100	18·4	0	1
4	0·133	21·4	0	1
5	0·167	24·1	1	1
6	0·200	26·6	0	2
7	0·233	28·9	1	1
8	0·267	31·1	1	0
9	0·300	33·2	1	0
10	0·333	35·3	1	2
11	0·367	37·3	2	0
12	0·400	39·2	3	0
13	0·433	41·2	1	3
14	0·467	43·1	0	2
15	0·500	45·0	1	2
16	0·533	46·9	2	0
17	0·567	48·8	0	1
18	0·600	50·8	1	1
19	0·633	52·7	2	0
20	0·667	54·7	1	0
21	0·700	56·8	1	0
22	0·733	58·9	1	0
23	0·767	61·1	0	1
26	0·867	68·6	0	1
			20	20

The value of ϕ may be found from the proportions of hybrid seedlings either by the use of the relation $p = \sin^2 \phi$ or, more easily, from Fisher and Yates's table of this transformation. Here, where the observations are on 30 individuals in each case, Fisher and Yates's Table XIII relating ϕ to the actual numbers of observations in the two classes may be used, so obviating the calculations of the proportions. The sum of ϕ in the white series is 851·4, giving a mean of 42·57, the sum in the red series is 756·2, giving a mean of 37·81, and the overall sum is 1,607·6, giving a general mean of 40·19. Thus in both series the mean is below 45, which is the value of ϕ corresponding to the expectation of $p = 0·5$.

The values of ϕ may be subjected to an analysis of variance. Taking the expected $\phi = 45$ as the mean from which deviations are calculated, each value of ϕ will contribute 1 degree of freedom, giving 40 in all. Of these, 1 will clearly be concerned with the deviation of the general mean of the observations from $\phi = 45$, 1 will be concerned with the difference between the means of the white and red series, while 38 will be concerned with the variation of ϕ within the two series, each of which will contribute 19 degrees of freedom.

In obtaining the sum of squares of ϕ it is easier to use the working mean of 0, and perform the analysis as though it comprised only 39 degrees of freedom, the one concerned with the general deviation from the expectation of 45 being omitted. In this way we find

$$S(\phi^2)=70{,}510{\cdot}460 \text{ and } \frac{1}{n}S^2(\phi)=\frac{1}{40}(1{,}607{\cdot}6)^2=64{,}609{\cdot}444$$

leaving $5{,}901{\cdot}016$ as $S(\phi-\bar{\phi})^2$ for 39 degrees of freedom. Of this total $\frac{1}{20}(851{\cdot}4^2+756{\cdot}2^2)-64{,}609{\cdot}444$ or $226{\cdot}576$ is ascribable to the degree of freedom concerned with the difference between the white and red series means, leaving $5{,}901{\cdot}016-226{\cdot}576$ or $5{,}674{\cdot}440$ for the 38 degrees of freedom concerned with the pooled variation within the two series. On finding the sum of squares for each series separately, round its own mean, it appears that this pool contains $1{,}777{\cdot}482$ from the white series and $3{,}896{\cdot}958$ from the red.

The sum of squares for the deviation of the general mean from 45 is found as $\frac{1}{40}(1{,}800-1{,}607{\cdot}6)^2$, 1,800 being the expected total of ϕ and $1{,}607{\cdot}6$ that observed. This reduces to $925{\cdot}444$. The full analysis of variance may then be set out as in Table 60.

TABLE 60
Analysis of Variance of Radish Data

Item	Sum of Squares	N	χ^2	Mean Square	t	Probability
General Deviation	925·444	1	33·825	925·444	2·491	0·02–0·01
Difference of W and R Means	226·576	1	8·281	226·576	1·232	0·3–0·2
Variation within series	5,674·440	38	207·399	149·327		
Total	6,826·460	40				
White ⎰ Deviation	118·098	1	4·316	118·098	1·123	0·3–0·2
series ⎱ Heterogeneity	1,777·482	19	64·967	93·552		
Red ⎰ Deviation	1,033·922	1	37·790	1,033·922	2·245	0·05–0·02
series ⎱ Heterogeneity	3,896·958	19	142·433	205·103		

Now ϕ is, as we have seen, subject to a theoretical variance of $\dfrac{820{\cdot}7}{n}$, or, in this case, with progenies of 30 seedlings, $27{\cdot}36$. Therefore, if each sum of squares in the analysis is divided by $27{\cdot}36$, a χ^2 will be obtained testing the significance of that item. When this is done every item is found to have a significantly low probability; and, in particular, that for the variation within series has a very small probability of occurrence by chance. We must, therefore, abandon the use of the theoretical variance and use the mean square for the variation within series as an estimated error. The mean squares may be obtained by dividing either the sums of squares or the χ^2 values by the numbers of degrees of freedom. A constant factor difference of 27·36 is involved between the two methods, and this vanishes in calculating t for the test of significance. In Table 60 the mean squares have been found from the sum of squares.

The general deviation from the mean and the difference between the white and red series means are then tested by finding t as the square root of the ratio of the appropriate mean square to the error mean square. The general deviation gives a $t_{[38]}=2\cdot491$, which may be entered in the table of c since $N>30$. It has a probability of 0·02–0·01 and so affords good grounds for deciding that the general mean is below the expected value of 45. In the case of the difference between the white and red series means $t_{[38]}=1\cdot232$ and this is not significant. The series do not, therefore, differ in so far as the present evidence goes. We may, therefore, take a combined mean ϕ for both series. This has already been found as 40·19 or, reconverting to proportions, $p=0\cdot418$.

The lower part of Table 60 shows the test of deviation from the expected value of 45 as applied to each series separately. It will be seen that the mean square error for the white series is only 93·5517, while that of the red series is 205·1031. These give a variance ratio of 2·192 for $N_1=N_2=19$, and the table of variance ratios shows the probability of obtaining such a difference due to chance to be only about 0·05. There is, therefore, some suspicion that the internal variations of the series differ; but since there is no obvious reason for expecting such a result and since the significance is only at the suggestive level, it might reasonably be assumed that the apparent departure was fortuitous, until further investigations, which are clearly desirable, provide unambiguous evidence of a difference in variation.

If, however, the deviations of the white and red series means from the expectation of 45 are tested against their respective intra-series mean squares, the deviation of the white series mean is insignificant, and even that for the red series is barely significant. The advantage of the joint test described above is clear. The series means are shown by it not to differ from one another, and so are capable of being tested for their joint deviation from expectation. This is more significant than either single deviation when tested alone.

It may be noted that the sum of squares for general deviation and that for difference of white and red means in the upper analysis of Table 60 together equal the pooled sums of squares for the separate deviations of the series means in the lower analyses. The advantage of the joint test arises, therefore, from the more informative partition of the sum of squares in the upper analysis as compared with the lower. This freedom to adopt the more valuable partition depends on the use of the analysis of variance technique, which, as we have seen, is made possible by the angular transformation. Without this transformation the available analytical methods would have been less informative as well as more cumbersome.

One further value of the angular transformation may be noted in passing. Since the values of V_ϕ and I_ϕ are independent of ϕ itself, any required level of precision may be secured merely by adjustment of the number of observations or individuals. In planning an experiment we can thus decide at once the number of observations necessary for the attainment of any given level of precision in the results, or for the detection of deviations of a given magnitude at a given level of probability. This is impossible, of course, if the results are to be expressed and tested in terms of the untransformed proportion p, where the variance is dependent on the value of p itself.

The benefits accruing from the angular transformation of proportions may be secured also with data which take the form of Poisson series. As we have seen in Section 12, the Poisson series is completely described by its mean to which its variance is equal. The variance of the mean, $\bar{x}$, is therefore $\frac{\bar{x}}{n}$, where n observations are used. Then if we put $y=\sqrt{\bar{x}}$, $\frac{d\bar{x}}{dy}=2\sqrt{\bar{x}}$, and $I_y=\frac{n}{\bar{x}}(2\sqrt{\bar{x}})^2=4n$. The square root of the mean of a Poisson series has, therefore, a variance independent of its own value.

60. THE PROBIT TRANSFORMATION

The transformation of a variate may also be of value in giving a simpler relation with a second variate than does the untransformed form. Thus, as we have seen in Section 31, the compound interest law, relating growth to time, leads to a logarithmic transformation, since if growth follows this law the relation between log size (or weight) and time is linear and therefore easier to manage statistically than that between untransformed size and time. The probit transformation is widely used for this purpose in toxicology, biological assay and similar work where response is quantal, i.e. all or none.

In order to see what this transformation is, let us consider the type of data which such experiments yield. A number, n, of animals are exposed to a poison and s of them survive, the rest dying. First of all this implies variation in the individual's capacity to resist the poison. The variation may be genetic or it may depend on fortuitous circumstances in the administration of the poison, or it may arise from both causes; but in any case, all those whose individual lethal dose is below that which they receive will die, and the rest will survive. If the frequencies of individuals requiring the various possible lethal doses are normal in the population from which the test animals are taken, an ordinate at the point on the abscissa representing the dose in question divides the curve into two parts, whose areas are determined by the distance of that point from the mean when expressed in terms of the standard deviation, i.e. expressed as a normal deviate. Furthermore, the area to the left of the ordinate gives the proportion of animals of lethal dose below the dose given, i.e. those who will die, and the area to the right of the ordinate the proportion of animals of lethal dose above that administered, i.e. those who will survive (Fig. 10).

Now, if we plot the proportion of animals dying, i.e. the area of the curve on the left of the ordinate, against the dose we shall clearly obtain a sigmoid curve (or ogive as Galton called it) relating mortality to dose. But if we plot the normal deviate which corresponds to the proportion dying, in the sense that the ordinate at this normal deviate cuts off an area of the correct proportion under the normal curve, we must obtain a straight-line relation to dose; for we are in fact replacing the proportion of deaths by a kind of hypothetical dose whose relation to the dose of poison known to have been administered we can now investigate.

In practical toxicology and biological assay the frequency distribution of individual lethal doses is generally not normal when the actual dose of poison or drug is used as the abscissa. It is, however, normal, or very nearly so, when the logarithm of the dose of poison or drug is used. A double transformation is therefore used to obtain the desired linear relation, viz. that of the dose into log dose to give a normal distribution and that of proportion of deaths into normal deviates to remove the sigmoid shape of the integrated normal curve. This log transformation of dose is not, however, an essential part of the treatment. It is an addition, empirically known to be desirable in most cases, though not in all. With any new poison or drug, or any new method of preparation or measurement, the use of the log transformation requires rejustification. If it should prove unsuitable, and the actual scale used in measuring the dose administered is also unsuitable, other more effective transformations should be sought.

The normal deviates corresponding to the various proportions of deaths can be read from any table of normal integrals, such

FIG. 10

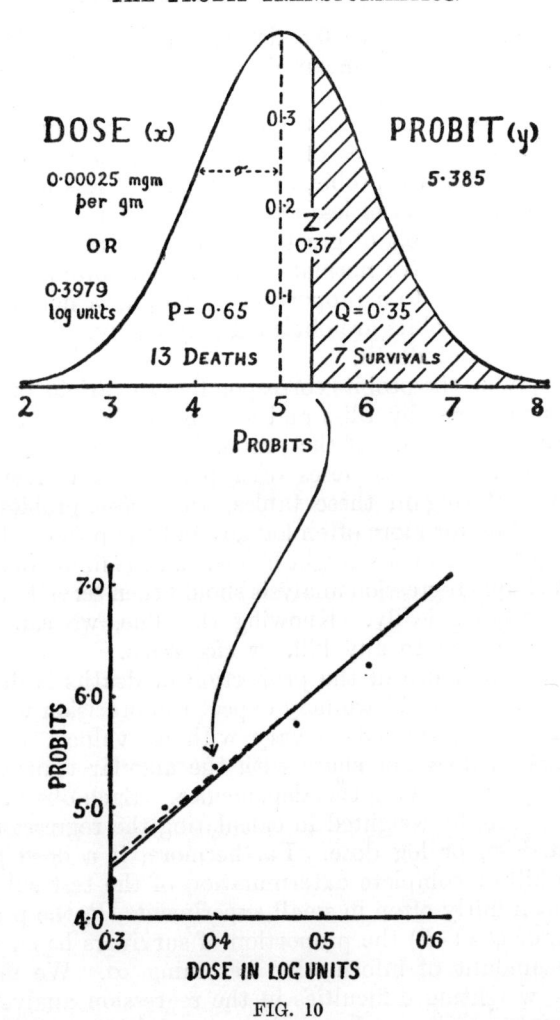

Above. Diagram to show the relation of the probit value (y) to the corresponding proportion of deaths (P) and survivals (Q). Probits are normal deviates to which 5 has been added, and the ordinate (Z) at y is used in calculating working probits and weighting coefficients

Below. The visually fitted provisional line (broken) and the regression line calculated from it (solid) for Smith's data on ouabain with frogs. The arrow marks the point to which the upper part of the figure refers

as the table of c used in finding the probabilities corresponding to deviations of a quantity from its expected value (see Section 14 and Fig. 1), for the area of the curve cut off by any ordinate is the integral of the curve up to that ordinate. It is, however, then necessary to use – and + signs to denote proportions below and above 0·5 deaths. (This proportion corresponds to the centre, i.e. mean of the normal distribution, which for the purpose of tabulation is taken at 0.) Bliss has pointed out that the inconvenience of the − sign can generally be removed by adding 5 to the values of the normal deviates. The value so obtained is called a probit, and a probit of less than 5 corresponds to a proportion of less than 0·5, i.e. to a negative normal deviate, while a probit of greater than 5 indicates a proportion over 0·5, i.e. a positive normal deviate. The probit value 5, of course, corresponds to a proportion of 0·5 and a normal deviate of 0. Negative probits are obtained only rarely, with extremely low proportions of death.

Tables giving the probits corresponding to various proportions have been prepared by Bliss and are also to be found in Fisher and Yates's collection. If the proportions of deaths among the test animals at various doses of a poison are converted into probits by entering in these tables, and these probits plotted against the dose (or more often log dose) of the poison, the points are expected to fall on a straight line within the limits of sampling error. A simple regression analysis should then serve to elucidate the relation statistically. Knowing this line, we can find the dose corresponding to any kill, or *vice versa*.

Since the variance of the proportion of deaths is dependent on the proportion itself, we may expect the precision with which any probit is determined to vary with its value. The probit transformation does not share with the angular transformation the property of removing this dependence. Each observed point must, therefore, be weighted in calculating the regression line of probit on dose, or log dose. Furthermore, if a dose produces either no kill or complete extermination of the test subjects, as must happen fairly often in small experiments, P, the proportion of deaths, or $Q(=1-P)$ the proportion of survivors has a variance of 0, the amount of information becoming ∞. We may then anticipate weighting difficulties in the regression analysis. The proper weights to be used and the way of dealing with cases of zero or total survival can be derived by use of the method of maximum likelihood, as Fisher has shown in an appendix to one of Bliss's papers.

At any given dose of poison let there be s survivors out of n test subjects. Then P, the probability of death is estimated as $1-\frac{s}{n}$ and $Q=1-P=\frac{s}{n}$. Further, let these proportions of death and survival correspond to a probit of y. With a probability P of death and Q of survival, we expect s survivors out of n in $\frac{n!}{s!(n-s)!}P^{n-s}Q^s$ of cases. Each experiment with its characteristic dose will give a likelihood expression of this kind, and fitting the regression line of y on dose or log dose by the method of maximum likelihood involves equating to zero the sum of the differentials with respect to y of the logarithms of these likelihood expressions (Section 53). The log of each likelihood expression is of the form $C+(n-s)\log P + s\log Q$, C being the constant which vanishes on differentiating, leaving us with a differential coefficient with respect to P of $\dfrac{n-s}{P}-\dfrac{s}{Q}$ or $\dfrac{Qn-s}{PQ}$. But we need the differential coefficient with respect to y, the probit value, and this is found by multiplying by $\dfrac{dP}{dy}$. Now P, the probability of death, is the integral of the normal curve from probit value $-\infty$ to y. The value of $\dfrac{dP}{dy}$ must therefore be the value of the ordinate to the normal curve at y, which we may, following Fisher, call Z (see Fig. 10). (This Z is, of course, not to be confused with the z used in tests of significance.) The contribution to the maximum likelihood expression is then $\dfrac{Qn-s}{PQ}\dfrac{dP}{dy}=(Qn-s)\dfrac{Z}{PQ}$.

The first part of this expression is the difference between the expected survival, Qn, and that observed, s. If n and s are large enough for the distribution of s, which will be given by the binomial expansion, to be treated as normal, this factor $Qn-s$ must be proportional to the difference between the probit expected and that corresponding to the observed kill. But the rate of change of the probit difference on y will again be $\dfrac{dQ}{dy}$ times that of the difference expressed in terms of proportions. In other words, we may replace $(Qn-s)$ by $n(Y-y)\dfrac{dQ}{dy}$ or $n(y-Y)Z$, where Y is the probit expected. The differential coefficient thus becomes $(y-Y)\dfrac{nZ^2}{PQ}$. The solution to the maximum likelihood (which consists of a series of such differential coefficients, one from each test of the different doses) thus consists of finding, by minimizing the sum of squares of $(y-Y)$, the values of Y which have a linear relation to the dose of poison, x, as expressed in appropriate units. This is, of course, the method of least squares already used in regression calculations (Section 31), but with each point given its individual weight of $\dfrac{nZ^2}{PQ}$ in the calculation.

The values of P and Q used in calculating the weight must, of course, be based on the kill expected from the regression line, not that actually observed.

If, however, either n or s is too small for the distribution of s to be treated as normal $Qn-s$ will not generally be proportional to $Y-y$. This discrepancy is most strikingly shown by the case of no survivors, for then $s=0$ and y becomes infinite, even though $Qn-s$ must still be finite. In such cases, however, where s is not normally distributed, in place of y, the probit corresponding to the observed kill, we may substitute a working probit y_w such that the equation $Qn-s=nZ(y_w-Y)$ is satisfied. The maximum likelihood equation may then be solved as before.

The value of y_w cannot be found from the single test in question because it demands a knowledge of Y, the probit expected. It is found, together with the values of P and Q, to be used in calculating the weighting coefficient $\dfrac{nZ^2}{PQ}$, by drawing a provisional regression line on a graph of the observations and using the appropriate points on this line to give the expectations. A more accurate line can then be calculated by means of these provisional expectations, and itself used to provide expectations for the calculation of a still more exact line, and so on, if desired. Even this second calculation is often unnecessary if the provisional first line has been drawn with reasonable accuracy.

To return to the working probit, y_w, it is found from the equation established above $Qn-s=nZ(y_w-Y)$ when recast in the form

$$y_w = Y + \frac{1}{Z}\left(Q - \frac{s}{n}\right)$$

Where there are no survivors $s=0$ and

$$y_w = Y + \frac{Q}{Z}$$

Tables to facilitate the calculation of y_w have been given by Bliss and also by Fisher and Yates. These give the value of $Y+\dfrac{Q}{Z}$ for each value of Y. They also give $\dfrac{1}{Z}$ for each value of Y, so that y_w can be found when $s \neq 0$, by subtracting from the tabulated value of $Y+\dfrac{Q}{Z}$, corresponding to the probit Y expected from the provisional regression line, $\dfrac{1}{Z}$ multiplied by the observed fraction $\dfrac{s}{n}$ which survive, and which we may denote by q.

When less than half the test animals are expected to die,

i.e. $Y < 5$, it may be more convenient to use the complementary expression

$$y_w = Y - \frac{1}{Z}\left(P - \frac{n-s}{n}\right)$$

and Bliss's table gives the material for this too. Both Bliss and Fisher and Yates give for the various values of Y the corresponding weighting coefficients $\frac{Z^2}{PQ}$, which must, of course, be multiplied by n the number of individuals in the test. It will be seen that the weight is at a maximum when $Y=5$ (see p. 227) and falls off symmetrically on each side of this value. Thus the weight when $Y=5+a$ is the same as that when $Y=5-a$. This symmetry is seen too in another connection, for the probit for a kill of s out of n animals is the complement of the probit for a survival of s out of n animals in that they depart equally from the value 5 but in opposite directions. The one can be found by subtracting the other from 10. This property is used in finding y_w when $Y < 5$ from Fisher and Yates's tables which cover the range $Y=5.0$ to $Y=8.9$.

The use of the transformation tables in arriving at the probits and of the weights in calculating the regression lines will be better seen from an arithmetic example.

Example 35. Table 61 gives the numbers of frogs (*Rana pipiens*) tested with various doses of anhydrous ouabain and the numbers dying in the various test classes as observed by Smith. The dose was adjusted to the weight of each individual frog and so is expressed as milligrams of ouabain per gram live weight of frog. Gaddum has shown that the log transformation is required if these data are to give a linear relation of probit to dose, and so the dose is expressed in log milligrams per gram. Since in every case the logarithm lies between −3 and −4, 4 has been added to each log dose to ease calculation by removing the minus signs. These doses may therefore be regarded as log milligram per 10 Kg. of frog.

The proportions killed (p) were used to find the empirical probits (y) from Fisher and Yates's Table IX. No probit can, of course, be given for the highest dose when all frogs died. These empirical probits are plotted against the dose, in log units, in Fig. 10, and the provisional regression line (shown broken in the figure) drawn in by eye. If this line is drawn so as to give a reasonably good fit, it may be unnecessary to use the first calculated regression line as the provisional for a second calculation. It is therefore profitable to devote some consideration to drawing this first visual provisional line. In Fig. 10 it passes through the points representing probit 4·5 at $x=0.3$ and probit 6·9

TABLE 61

Assay of Ouabain on Rana pipiens *(M. I. Smith)*

DOSE mgm. per gm.	log units (x)	FROGS Tested (n)	Survived (s)	p	q	y	Y (visual)	y_w	w	Y (calculated)
0·000200	0·3010	20	15	0·25	0·75	4·326	4·51	4·3346	11·659	4·4632
0·000225	0·3522	20	10	0·50	0·50	5·000	4·92	5·0002	12·695	4·8869
0·000250	0·3979	20	7	0·65	0·35	5·385	5·28	5·3834	12·367	5·2650
0·000300	0·4771	18	4	0·77	0·22	5·765	5·92	5·7528	8·368	5·9203
0·000350	0·5441	10	1	0·90	0·10	6·282	6·45	6·2576	2·855	6·4747
0·000400	0·6021	10	0	1·00	0·00	—	6·92	7·3544	1·497	6·9546

at $x=0.6$. Its slope is therefore 8.0 probits for a change of 1 in x. Then starting from the point $Y=4.5$, $x=0.3$ (these are now expected probits, Y, as they are obtained from the provisional line), we find $Y=4.5+(0.0010\times 8.0)=4.51$, for our lowest dose at $x=0.3010$, and so on, as shown in Table 61.

The next step is to find y_w, the working probits, from Y, the expected probit, and $q\left(=\dfrac{s}{n}\right)$, the proportion of survivors observed in each experiment. The easiest case is that of the test at the highest dose where no frogs survived. Here $Y=6.92$ and $q=0$. Then $y_w=Y+\dfrac{Q}{Z}$, the so-called maximum working probit. From Fisher and Yates's Table XI we find $y_w=7.3376$ when $Y=6.9$, and $y_w=7.4214$ when $Y=7.0$. Linear interpolation then gives $y_w=7.3544$ for $Y=6.92$. At the next dose, $x=0.5441$ we have $Y=6.45$ and $q=0.10$. Then $y_w=Y+\dfrac{Q}{Z}-0.10\dfrac{1}{Z}$. For $Y=6.4$ the table gives $Y+\dfrac{Q}{Z}=6.9394$ and $\dfrac{1}{Z}=6.6788$, so that $y_w=6.9394-0.6679=6.2715$. Similarly at $Y=6.5$, $y_w=6.2437$ and by interpolation, $y_w=6.2576$ when $Y=6.45$.

The remaining working probits are obtained in the same way, the only comment being required by the cases where $Y<5$, as, for example, at the lowest dose where $Y=4.51$. The working probit in such a case can be found directly from Bliss's table using the formula $y_w=Y-\dfrac{P}{Z}+\dfrac{p}{Z}$, where p is the observed proportion of survivors. Fisher and Yates's table does not include values of Y lower than 5.0, so that the direct calculation is not possible. We have, however, already seen that the case where, say, s survive out of n is the complement of that where s die out of n in that the two probits deviate equally, but in opposite directions, from 5. To put it another way, the sum of the two probits is 10. If, therefore, when $Y<5$, we take the complementary probit Y' such that $Y'=10-Y$, and interchange the proportions of those surviving and dying, we can calculate y_w' from the table and then, by reversing the process, find $y_w=10-y_w'$. Thus when $x=0.3010$, Smith's data give $Y=4.51$ and $q=0.75$. Then we find $Y'=10-4.51=5.49$ and take 0.25, the proportion of deaths, in place of q. From the table an expected probit of 5.4 with 0.25 survivors gives $y_w'=5.6569$ and an expected probit of 5.5 similarly gives 5.6663. Interpolation then gives $y_w'=5.6654$ for $Y'=5.49$. The complementary working probit corresponding to $Y=4.51$ is then found as $y_w=10-y_w'=10-5.6654=4.3346$. The working probit for dose 0.3522 is similarly calculated as 5.0002.

The weighting coefficients, $w = \dfrac{nZ^2}{PQ}$, are also found from Fisher and Yates's Table XI, using the expected probits Y. Thus when $Y=6\cdot 9$, the table gives $\dfrac{Z^2}{PQ}=0\cdot 15436$ and when $Y=7\cdot 0$, $\dfrac{Z^2}{PQ}=0\cdot 13112$, so that by interpolation when $Y=6\cdot 92$, $\dfrac{Z^2}{PQ}=0\cdot 1497$. Since at this highest dose $n=10$, $w=1\cdot 497$. When $Y<5$ use is made of the fact that the weight for the expected probit equals that for the complementary probit Y'. Thus for $Y=4\cdot 51$ we use the weight given by $Y'=10-4\cdot 51=5\cdot 49$.

The rest of the analysis follows the lines of simple regression calculations as discussed in Sections 31 and 32, with the slight complication that each point (y_w, x) is given its individual weight. We have already seen, in Section 41, how weights are used in calculating weighted means, and the formulae for calculating weighted regression lines can easily be derived in the same way from those used in unweighted regression analysis.

Giving a weight w to a point may be regarded as equivalent to saying that that point has been observed w times, each hypothetical observation having weight 1. Then the total number of such hypothetical observations is given by $S(w)$, and the sum of y_w for the hypothetical assay is similarly $S(wy_w)$. Hence $\hat{y}_w = \dfrac{S(wy_w)}{S(w)}$. Similarly $\hat{x} = \dfrac{S(wx)}{S(w)}$.

Turning to the sum of squares and cross-products, the sum of squares of deviations of x from zero is clearly $S(wx^2)$ and the correction term must be $\dfrac{S^2(wx)}{S(w)}$. The sum of squares of deviations of x from $\hat{x}$ is thus

$$S[w(x-\hat{x})^2] = S(wx^2) - \frac{S^2(wx)}{S(w)}.$$

Similarly
$$S[w(y_w - \hat{y}_w)^2] = S(wy_w^2) - \frac{S^2(wy_w)}{S(w)}$$

and
$$S[wy_w(x-\hat{x})] = S(wxy_w) - \frac{S(wy_w)S(wx)}{S(w)}$$

Applying these formulae to the data of Table 61

$S(w)=49\cdot 441$ $\qquad S(wx)=19\cdot 3485$ $\qquad S(wy_w)=257\cdot 6056$
$S(wx^2)=7\cdot 881733$ $\qquad S(wy_w^2)=1,364\cdot 566361$ $\qquad S(wxy_w)=103\cdot 376004$
and so $\qquad \hat{x}=0\cdot 3913$ $\qquad \hat{y}_w=5\cdot 2104$

$$S[w(x-\hat{x})^2] = 7\cdot 881733 - \frac{19\cdot 3485^2}{49\cdot 441} = 0\cdot 309797$$

$S[w(y_w-\hat{y}_w)^2]=22\cdot 347836 \qquad S[wy_w(x-\hat{x})]=2\cdot 563345$

Then $a = \hat{y} = 5 \cdot 2104$ and $b = \dfrac{S[wy_w(x-\hat{x})]}{S[w(x-\hat{x})^2]} = 8 \cdot 2743$.

The calculated regression line is thus
$$Y = 5 \cdot 2104 + 8 \cdot 2743(x - 0 \cdot 3913),$$
Y now being the probit expected from this new line and so replacing the expectations from the visual provisional line.

We must next enquire into the adequacy of this line as a representation of the data, and also find the standard errors of the regression constants. The amount by which the sum of squares of y_w is reduced in fitting the regression line will, by analogy with unweighted regression, be $\dfrac{S^2[wy_w(x-\hat{x})]}{S[w(x-\hat{x})^2]}$, which in the present case becomes $\dfrac{2 \cdot 563345^2}{0 \cdot 309797}$ or $21 \cdot 209817$. This must correspond to 1 degree of freedom, leaving 4, out of the 5 between 6 observations, for the remainder, or error, sum of squares.

Before the full significance of this analysis of the sum of squares of y_w can be appreciated, it must be observed that the weighting coefficients are themselves the theoretically fixed amounts of information concerning the probits to which they are attached. Now the variance of p in the binomial expansion of $(p+q)^2$ was seen in Section 13 to be $\dfrac{pq}{n}$, where $p+q=1$. The amount of information about P, the proportion of deaths, is therefore $\dfrac{n}{PQ}$, and the amount of information about the corresponding probit Y will, as seen on p. 218, be $\dfrac{n}{PQ}\left(\dfrac{dY}{dP}\right)^2$. But $\dfrac{dY}{dP} = Z$ and so $I_Y = \dfrac{nZ^2}{PQ} = w$.

Weights of this kind are therefore equivalent to dividing each observation in the calculation of the mean, and each squared and cross-multiplied deviation in the calculation of sums of squares and cross-products, by the corresponding theoretically fixed variance. The sums of squares for regression and remainder are thus $\chi^2 s$, because each of their constituent parts is the ratio of an observed squared deviation to a variance fixed by hypothesis. Our analysis of the sum of squares of y_w thus becomes

Item	χ^2	N	Probability
Regression	21·209817	1	very small
Remainder (Error) .	1·138019	4	0·9–0·8
Total	22·347836	5	

The regression line clearly accounts for all but an insignificant portion of the variation in probit value, and so affords an adequate description of the probit dose relation.

Since the error χ^2 is insignificant, we take the residual variance of y_w round the regression line as 1, the average contribution each degree of freedom is expected to make to a χ^2. (With a significant error χ^2 it would have been necessary, of course, to treat χ^2 as a sum of squares, divide it by N and take the resulting mean square as Vy, (as on p. 192). Then, once again by analogy with unweighted regression,

$$V_a = V\hat{y} = \frac{Vy}{S(w)} = \frac{1}{49 \cdot 441} = 0 \cdot 020226 \text{ and } s_a = \sqrt{V_a} = 0 \cdot 1422$$

$$V_b = \frac{Vy}{S[w(x-\hat{x})^2]} = \frac{1}{0 \cdot 309797} = 3 \cdot 227920 \text{ and } s_b = \sqrt{V_b} = 1 \cdot 7967.$$

The regression coefficient b represents the rate of change of mortality, as measured in probits, on the dose expressed in this case in log units. It is, however, helpful to look at it in another way. The reciprocal of b, in this case $\frac{1}{8 \cdot 2743}$ or $0 \cdot 1209$, is the increase in dose, here expressed in logarithmic units, required to increase the probit value by 1, i.e. is the standard deviation of the frequency distribution of individual lethal doses of the test animals (Fig. 10). The less the variation in individual lethal dose of the test animals, the greater the slope of the regression line, and the more precisely will the dose, necessary to give a particular percentage kill, be estimated.

The dose giving 50% death is widely used in connection with dosage mortality relations. It is generally denoted by $LD50$ and, since it is the dose corresponding to $Y=5 \cdot 0$, is found as

$$LD50 = \hat{x} + \frac{5 \cdot 0 - a}{b}$$

This is a special case of the general relation considered on p. 118.

$$Y_1 = a + b(x_1 - \hat{x})$$

where, instead of fixing x_1 and so finding Y_1, we set $Y_1 = 5 \cdot 0$ and so find $x_1 = LD50$. Now as we have seen, $V_{Y_1} = V_a + (x_1 - \hat{x})^2 V_b$, which in weighted regression, when V_y is taken to be 1, becomes

$$V_Y = \frac{1}{S(w)} + \frac{(x-\hat{x})^2}{S[w(x-\hat{x})^2]}$$

But since
$$I_x = I_Y \left(\frac{dY}{dx}\right)^2$$

$$V_x = V_Y \bigg/ \left(\frac{dY}{dx}\right)^2$$

$\dfrac{dY}{dx}$ is the ratio of change of Y on x, i.e. is here the slope of the regression line b.

Hence
$$V_x = \frac{1}{b^2} V_Y = \frac{1}{b^2}\left[\frac{1}{S(w)} + \frac{(x-\hat{x})^2}{S[w(x-\hat{x})^2]}\right]$$

and, in particular, the variance of $LD50$ is
$$\frac{1}{b^2}\left[\frac{1}{S(w)} + \frac{(LD50-\hat{x})^2}{S[w(x-\hat{x})^2]}\right]$$

In the present case $a = \hat{y}_w = 5\cdot2104$, $\hat{x} = 0\cdot3913$, $b = 8\cdot2743$, $S(w) = 49\cdot441$ and $S[w(x-\hat{x})^2] = 0\cdot309797$. Hence
$$LD50 = 0\cdot3913 + \frac{5\cdot0 - 5\cdot2104}{8\cdot2743} = 0\cdot3659 \text{ in log units}$$

(or 0·0002322 mgm. ouabain per gm. frog weight) and
$$V_{LD50} = \frac{1}{8\cdot2743^2}\left[\frac{1}{49\cdot441} + \frac{0\cdot0254^2}{0\cdot3098}\right] = 0\cdot0003259$$

Then $s_{LD50} = \sqrt{V_{LD50}} = 0\cdot01805$ log units (or 0·00001145 mgm. per gm.).

This first calculated regression line may itself be used as the provisional line in the calculation of a second, and presumably still better fitting, regression. Indeed, if the visual provisional line was a poor fit, the first calculated regression line cannot be expected to give a fully satisfactory representation of the data, and it must be used on the provisional line for a second calculation. In the present case, however, the use of our calculated relation

$$Y = 5\cdot2104 + 8\cdot2743(x - 0\cdot3913)$$

as the provisional line gives, after the second fitting

$$Y = 5\cdot2087 + 8\cdot2824(x - 0\cdot3912).$$

The remainder or error χ^2 is now 1·1701, a value slightly higher than that obtained after the first fitting. The second calculation shows no improvement on the first and none of the statistics obtained from the second fitting differed by so much as their standard errors from those given by the first calculation. In particular, the second estimate of $LD50$ is 0·3660±0·01810 as compared with the first estimate of 0·3659±0·01805.

The first regression must therefore be judged to have been adequate. The visual provisional line used as the basis of the first fitting was satisfactory. By removing the need for a second fitting it well repaid the care expended in drawing it.

Once a regression line has been found to represent the relation between dose and effect, it may be compared with other such lines, differing from it in slope or position or both, for such purposes as comparing the potencies of two samples of a drug, or standardizing a sample of unknown potency against one whose potency is known. A dosage-effect regression line may also be used to estimate the dose of poison required to achieve a specified percentage kill in insecticidal work, in a way similar to that used for finding the $LD50$. These uses of the line have been fully described by Gaddum, Bliss, and Irwin, to whose works reference should be made for the methods to be employed in the various circumstances.

REFERENCES

BLISS, C. I. 1935a. The calculation of the dosage-mortality curve. *Ann. Appl. Biol.*, **22**, 134–67.
—— 1935b. The comparison of dosage-mortality data. *Ann. Appl. Biol.*, **22**, 307–33.
—— 1938. The determination of the dosage-mortality curve from small numbers. *Quart. J. Pharm.*, **11**, 192–216.
GADDUM, J. H. 1933. Reports on biological standards. III. Methods of biological assay depending on quantal response. *Med. Res. Council Spec. Rep. No.* 183, H.M. Stat. Office.
FISHER, R. A. 1935. The case of zero survivors. Appendix to Bliss (1935a) above.
—— and YATES, F. 1943. *Statistical Tables for Biological, Agricultural and Medical Research.* Oliver and Boyd. Edinburgh. 2nd ed.
IRWIN, J. O. 1937. Statistical method applied to biological assays. *Suppl. J. Roy. Statistical Soc.*, **4**, 1–60.
SMITH, M. I., quoted by GADDUM, J. H. 1932. The biological assay of Strophanthus (Kombé) in comparison with Ouabain. *Quart J. Pharm.*, **5**, 274–300.

GLOSSARY OF TERMS

Bias. A consistent and false departure of an observed quantity from its proper value. The average error of an estimate.
Binomial series. The series obtained by expanding to any power the sum of two quantities.

c. The normal deviate. The ratio of an observed deviation to the appropriate standard deviation fixed by hypothesis.
Confounding. The deliberate sacrifice of a potentially interesting comparison by identifying it with one which it is intended to eliminate in order to reduce the error variation. Such a comparison is said to be *confounded.*
  Partial ———. The confounding of a comparison in part of a design, or in such a way that, after the elimination of ill-controlled comparisons, it is estimated with accuracy less than if such comparisons had been reliable.
Contingency table. A table of frequencies distinguishing two classifications simultaneously.
Correlation. The interdependence of two variates. The opposite of independence. Applied also to the analysis of such interdependence by methods involving the two variates symmetrically.
  ——— *coefficient.* The ratio of the covariance of two variates to the geometrical mean of their variances.
  Inter-class ———. The correlation of variates which are distinguished from each other in the data.
  Intra-class ———. The correlation of variates which are not distinguished from each other in the data.
  Partial ———. The correlation of variates when due allowance is made for the effects of other uncontrolled variates.
Covariance. The mean product of the deviations of two variates from their means. Estimated as the ratio of a sum of cross-products to the corresponding number of degrees of freedom.
  Analysis of ———. The simultaneous analysis of the sums of squares and cross-products of two or more variates.
Cross-products. Sum of ———. Sum of the products of corresponding deviations of two variates from their individual means.
χ^2. The ratio of an observed sum of squares to the corresponding variance fixed by hypothesis.
  Simple ———. One in which the observed sum of squares is based on a single comparison. The square of a normal deviate.
  Compound ———. One in which the observed sum of squares is based on several independent comparisons, and which can hence be resolved into two or more simple χ^2's.

Degree of freedom. A comparison between the data, independent of the other comparisons used in the analysis.
  Number of ———. The number of independent comparisons that can be made in the data.
Deviate. Normal ———. See *c.*
Deviation. Departure of any observation or quantity from its expected value.
  Standard ———. The distance, measured along the abscissa, of the

point of inflection, or maximum slope, from the mean in a normal curve. Generalized as the square root of the variance. Called the *Standard Error* when the deviation can properly be regarded as an error, as in the case of estimates of parameters.

Discriminant function. Linear compound of a series of variates with coefficients chosen to maximize the difference between the classes of object, of which the variates are measurements, relative to the variation within classes.

Distribution. Frequency ———. The distribution obtained when the frequencies with which observations fall into certain classes are plotted against those classes.

Normal ——— (or *Normal Curve of Errors*). The limit to the binomial and multinomial series when the power is large and none of the summed quantities very small. The frequency distribution expected from a series of observations on a variate whose magnitude is influenced by a large number of agents having small independent effects.

Effect. Main ———. The direct effect of any treatment or agent, without reference to the effects of other treatments or agents.

Interaction ———. The mutual effects of two or more treatments on one another's action.

Efficiency of a method of estimation. The amount of information extracted from the data by the method, as a fraction of that extracted by maximizing the likelihood.

Error. Control of ———. The reduction of error variation by the use of restraints in experimental design.

Sampling ———. The variation in value of a statistic arising from the use of finite samples.

Standard ———. See *Standard Deviation*.

——— *variance*. The variance arising from agents uncontrolled in the experiment, with which the apparent effect of any controlled agent must be compared.

Estimate. Consistent ———. A statistic which tends to approach the parameter in value as the sample size increases.

Efficient ———. A statistic which tends, as the sample size increases, to use all of the information available in the data.

Sufficient ———. A statistic which uses all the relevant information in the data, even in small samples. Sufficient statistics are not always available.

Estimation. Combined ———. The calculation of a statistic or statistics from several sets of unlike data taken together.

Simultaneous ———. The calculation of two or more statistics from data simultaneously.

Factorial experiment. One in which all the treatments or agents under investigation are varied simultaneously and combined in such a way that any desired main or interaction effect may be isolated and evaluated.

Fiducial probability. The probability that a parameter lies within certain limits, the *Fiducial limits*, as exactly determined from the information afforded by direct observation, without resort to any hypothetical information.

Grouping. The process of arranging measurements in such a way that the observations falling within a given range are replaced, for the

GLOSSARY OF TERMS

purposes of calculation, by an equal number of hypothetical measurements at the centre of that range (see also *Sheppard*).

Heterogeneity. Test of ——. A test of agreement of different bodies of data in showing the same value of a parameter common to them all.

Independence. The relation between two variates each of which takes values uninfluenced by those of the other. The opposite of dependence and correlation.

Independent comparisons. Comparisons, between observations, whose values are uninfluenced by changes in each other. Such comparisons are also said to be *Orthogonal*, and the functions from which they are calculated are *Orthogonal functions*.

Information. Amount of ——. The quantity which characterizes a body of data with respect to a parameter, independently of the method of estimating that parameter. Generalized as the reciprocal of the variance of an efficient statistic.

Invariance. The reciprocal of the variance.

Iteration. The method of solving equations by a series of similar calculations each leading to the next.

Kurtosis. The departure of a symmetrical frequency distribution, from the normal, by excessiveness or deficiency in the shoulders as opposed to the tails and top.

Likelihood. —— *function.* The function relating an unknown parameter to observations from which it can be estimated. The inverse of a probability function.

Method of Maximum ——. The method of estimation depending on the maximization of the log likelihood and hence of the likelihood function.

Mean. The arithmetic average of a series of observations or quantities. Used as an abbreviation for *Arithmetic Mean*.

Weighted ——. A mean obtained when each observation or quantity is given a characteristic weight in the calculations.

Working ——. A value, more or less approximating to the true mean, used for the purpose of lightening the calculation of the true mean, the sum of squares and other quantities.

Median. That value of the variate on each side of which lie equal numbers of observations.

Mode. That value of the variate shown by the most frequent observational class.

Multinomial series. The series obtained by expanding, to any power, the sum of three or more quantities.

Null hypothesis. The hypothesis which is the basis of a test of significance, and from which the expectations are formulated.

Orthogonal. See *Independent*.

Parameter. A quantity whose value is necessary for the specification of a hypothetical population.

Partition. The breaking down of a sum of squares or a compound χ^2 into simple components, for the purpose of analysis.

Polynomial. A simple power series, of any order, of a variate.

    Orthogonal ——*s*. Polynomials which take out independent sums of squares of the dependent variate in regression analyses.

Population. The hypothetical infinitely large series of observations or individuals of which those observations or individuals actually obtained form a sample.

Precision. The exactness with which a quantity or statistic is ascertained.

Probability. —— *function*. The function relating observations to the parameter from whose value their frequencies may be predicted. The inverse of a likelihood function.

    Simple ——. Probability relating to the occurrence of single event.

    Compound ——. Probability relating to the occurrence of more than one event.

Random. Arrived at by chance without the exercise of any choice.

    ——*ization*. The process of arriving at a random arrangement.

    ——*ized block*. An experimental design involving one restraint.

Regression. The dependence of one variate, termed dependent, on another, termed the independent variate.

    —— *coefficient*. The coefficient representing the rate of change of the dependent variate on the independent variate.

    Cubic ——. A regression involving the independent variate to the third power.

    —— *line*. The line or curve showing the regression in a geometrical representation.

    Linear ——. A regression involving the independent variate to the first power.

    Multiple ——. Regression, usually linear, on two or more independent variates which may themselves be correlated. (Also called *Partial Regression*.)

    Polynomial ——. A regression in which the dependent variate is related to a polynomial function of the independent variates.

    Quadratic ——. A regression involving the independent variate to the second power.

    Simple ——. Linear regression on one independent variate.

Replication. The equal incorporation of all treatments or other agents two or more times in an experimental design, which is then called a *Replicated design*.

Restraint. A limitation of the random arrangement of treatments in an experimental design, so that the error variation, though still capable of unbiased estimation, is reduced or potentially reduced.

Sample. A finite series of observations or individuals taken from the hypothetical infinitely large population of possible observations or individuals.

Selection. The exercise of discrimination in sampling or in arrangement. Opposed to randomness.

Sheppard's correction for grouping. A correction applied in the calculation of variances to allow for the inflationary effect of grouping.

Significance. The measure of reality of an apparent discrepancy between observation and expectation. A departure is said to be *Significant*, i.e. to be judged real, if the probability of obtaining one as large or larger is lower than some chosen level, which is then referred to as the *Level of significance*.

    Test of ——. A test designed to assess significance, and so to

GLOSSARY OF TERMS

distinguish deviations due to sampling error from those indicating real discrepancies between observation and hypothesis.

Skewness. Asymmetry in a frequency distribution.

Square. Graeco-Latin ———. An experimental design involving three restraints.

    Latin ———. An experimental design involving two restraints.

    Mean ———. Average of the squared deviations of observations from their mean. The ratio of the sum of squares to the number of degrees of freedom. Synonymous with estimated variance.

    Method of Least ———*s.* A method of estimation, depending on the minimization of sums of squares, widely used in regression analyses.

    Sum of ———*s.* The sum of the squared deviations of observations from their mean.

Statistic. The estimate of a parameter arrived at from observed samples. It bears the same relation to the sample as the parameter does to the population.

t. The ratio of an observed deviation to its estimated standard deviation.

Variance. Mean square deviation of a variate from its mean. Estimated as the *Mean square* (q.v.). The square of the standard deviation.

    Analysis of ———. A technique for the isolation of particular components of variation for assessment by comparison with error variation.

    ——— *ratio.* The ratio of two estimated variances. Twice the natural antilog of z.

Variate. A variable quantity whose measurements or frequencies form all or part of the data for analysis.

Weight. The relative value assigned to an estimate when it is being combined with other estimates of the same quantity. Usually the weight is the invariance or amount of information.

Yates's correction for continuity. A correction applied in the calculation of normal deviates or χ^2's to allow for the discrepancy arising from the fact that the observations are discontinuous while the tables of c and χ^2 are calculated on the supposition of continuity of the variate.

z. The natural logarithm of the ratio of two estimated standard deviations. (See also *Variance ratio.*)

TABLES

TABLE I
Table of c (the Normal Deviate)

Probability	0·95	0·90	0·80	0·70	0·60	0·50	0·40
c	0·063	0·13	0·25	0·39	0·52	0·67	0·84
Probability	0·30	0·20	0·10	0·05	0·02	0·01	0·001
c	1·04	1·28	1·64	1·96	2·33	2·58	3·29

[Abridged from *Statistical Tables for Biological, Agricultural and Medical Research* by R. A. FISHER and F. YATES, with the kind permission of the authors and publishers, MESSRS. OLIVER AND BOYD.]

TABLE II
Table of t

N	\	\	\	\	Probability	\	\	\	\	\	\
	0·90	0·80	0·70	0·50	0·30	0·20	0·10	0·05	0·02	0·01	0·001
1	0·16	0·33	0·51	1·00	1·96	3·08	6·31	12·71	31·82	63·66	636·62
2	0·14	0·29	0·45	0·82	1·39	1·89	2·92	4·30	6·97	9·93	31·60
3	0·14	0·28	0·42	0·77	1·25	1·64	2·35	3·18	4·54	5·84	12·94
4	0·13	0·27	0·41	0·74	1·19	1·53	2·13	2·78	3·75	4·60	8·61
5	0·13	0·27	0·41	0·73	1·16	1·48	2·02	2·57	3·37	4·03	6·86
6	0·13	0·27	0·40	0·72	1·13	1·44	1·94	2·45	3·14	3·71	5·96
7	0·13	0·26	0·40	0·71	1·12	1·42	1·90	2·37	3·00	3·50	5·41
8	0·13	0·26	0·40	0·71	1·11	1·40	1·86	2·31	2·90	3·36	5·04
9	0·13	0·26	0·40	0·70	1·10	1·38	1·83	2·26	2·82	3·25	4·78
10	0·13	0·26	0·40	0·70	1·09	1·37	1·81	2·23	2·76	3·17	4·59
11	0·13	0·26	0·40	0·70	1·09	1·36	1·80	2·20	2·72	3·11	4·44
12	0·13	0·26	0·40	0·70	1·08	1·36	1·78	2·18	2·68	3·06	4·32
13	0·13	0·26	0·39	0·69	1·08	1·35	1·77	2·16	2·65	3·01	4·22
14	0·13	0·26	0·39	0·69	1·08	1·35	1·76	2·15	2·62	2·98	4·14
15	0·13	0·26	0·39	0·69	1·07	1·34	1·75	2·13	2·60	2·95	4·07
16	0·13	0·26	0·39	0·69	1·07	1·34	1·75	2·12	2·58	2·92	4·02
17	0·13	0·26	0·39	0·69	1·07	1·33	1·74	2·11	2·57	2·90	3·97
18	0·13	0·26	0·39	0·69	1·07	1·33	1·73	2·10	2·55	2·88	3·92
19	0·13	0·26	0·39	0·69	1·07	1·33	1·73	2·09	2·54	2·86	3·88
20	0·13	0·26	0·39	0·69	1·06	1·33	1·73	2·09	2·53	2·85	3·85
22	0·13	0·26	0·39	0·69	1·06	1·32	1·72	2·07	2·51	2·82	3·79
24	0·13	0·26	0·39	0·69	1·06	1·32	1·71	2·06	2·49	2·80	3·75
26	0·13	0·26	0·39	0·68	1·06	1·32	1·71	2·06	2·48	2·78	3·71
28	0·13	0·26	0·39	0·68	1·06	1·31	1·70	2·05	2·47	2·76	3·67
30	0·13	0·26	0·39	0·68	1·06	1·31	1·70	2·04	2·46	2·75	3·65

When N is greater than 30, t may be treated as a normal deviate without serious inaccuracy resulting.

[Abridged from *Statistical Tables for Biological, Agricultural and Medical Research* by R. A. FISHER and F. YATES, with the kind permission of the authors and publishers, MESSRS. OLIVER AND BOYD.]

TABLE III
Table of χ^2

N	0·90	0·80	0·70	0·50	Probability 0·30	0·20	0·10	0·05	0·02	0·01	0·001
1	0·016	0·064	0·15	0·46	1·07	1·64	2·71	3·84	5·41	6·64	10·83
2	0·21	0·45	0·71	1·39	2·41	3·22	4·61	5·99	7·82	9·21	13·82
3	0·58	1·01	1·42	2·37	3·67	4·64	6·25	7·82	9·84	11·34	16·27
4	1·06	1·65	2·20	3·36	4·88	5·99	7·78	9·49	11·67	13·28	18·47
5	1·61	2·34	3·00	4·35	6·06	7·29	9·24	11·07	13·39	15·09	20·52
6	2·20	3·07	3·83	5·35	7·23	8·56	10·65	12·59	15·03	16·81	22·46
7	2·83	3·82	4·67	6·35	8·38	9·80	12·02	14·07	16·62	18·48	24·32
8	3·49	4·59	5·53	7·34	9·52	11·03	13·36	15·51	18·17	20·09	26·13
9	4·17	5·38	6·39	8·34	10·66	12·24	14·68	16·92	19·68	21·67	27·88
10	4·87	6·18	7·27	9·34	11·78	13·44	15·99	18·31	21·16	23·21	29·59
11	5·58	6·99	8·15	10·34	12·90	14·63	17·28	19·68	22·62	24·73	31·26
12	6·30	7·81	9·03	11·34	14·01	15·81	18·55	21·03	24·05	26·22	32·91
13	7·04	8·63	9·93	12·34	15·12	16·99	19·81	22·36	25·47	27·69	34·53
14	7·79	9·47	10·82	13·34	16·22	18·15	21·06	23·69	26·87	29·14	36·12
15	8·55	10·31	11·72	14·34	17·32	19·31	22·31	25·00	28·26	30·58	37·70
16	9·31	11·15	12·62	15·34	18·42	20·47	23·54	26·30	29·63	32·00	39·25
17	10·09	12·00	13·53	16·34	19·51	21·62	24·77	27·59	31·00	33·41	40·79
18	10·87	12·86	14·44	17·34	20·60	22·76	25·99	28·87	32·35	34·81	42·31
19	11·65	13·72	15·35	18·34	21·69	23·90	27·20	30·14	33·69	36·19	43·82
20	12·44	14·58	16·27	19·34	22·78	25·04	28·41	31·41	35·02	37·57	45·32
22	14·04	16·31	18·10	21·34	24·94	27·30	30·81	33·92	37·66	40·29	48·27
24	15·66	18·06	19·94	23·34	27·10	29·55	33·20	36·42	40·27	42·98	51·18
26	17·29	19·82	21·79	25·34	29·25	31·80	35·56	38·89	42·86	45·64	54·05
28	18·94	21·59	23·65	27·34	31·39	34·03	37·92	41·34	45·42	48·28	56·89
30	20·60	23·36	25·51	29·34	33·53	36·25	40·26	43·77	47·96	50·89	59·70

When N is greater than 30, use $\sqrt{2\chi^2} - \sqrt{2n-1}$ as a normal deviate.

[Abridged from *Statistical Tables for Biological, Agricultural and Medical Research* by R. A. FISHER and F. YATES, with the kind permission of the authors and publishers, MESSRS. OLIVER AND BOYD.]

TABLE IV
Table of Variance Ratio
(i) 0·20 Probability Point

N_2 \ N_1	1	2	3	4	5	6	12	24	∞
1	9·5	12·0	13·1	13·7	14·0	14·3	14·9	15·2	15·6
2	3·6	4·0	4·2	4·2	4·3	4·3	4·4	4·4	4·5
3	2·7	2·9	2·9	3·0	3·0	3·0	3·0	3·0	3·0
4	2·4	2·5	2·5	2·5	2·5	2·5	2·5	2·4	2·4
5	2·2	2·3	2·3	2·2	2·2	2·2	2·2	2·2	2·1
6	2·1	2·1	2·1	2·1	2·1	2·1	2·0	2·0	2·0
7	2·0	2·0	2·0	2·0	2·0	2·0	1·9	1·9	1·8
8	2·0	2·0	2·0	1·9	1·9	1·9	1·8	1·8	1·7
9	1·9	1·9	1·9	1·9	1·9	1·8	1·8	1·7	1·7
10	1·9	1·9	1·9	1·8	1·8	1·8	1·7	1·7	1·6
11	1·9	1·9	1·8	1·8	1·8	1·8	1·7	1·6	1·6
12	1·8	1·8	1·8	1·8	1·7	1·7	1·7	1·6	1·5
13	1·8	1·8	1·8	1·8	1·7	1·7	1·6	1·6	1·5
14	1·8	1·8	1·8	1·7	1·7	1·7	1·6	1·6	1·5
15	1·8	1·8	1·8	1·7	1·7	1·7	1·6	1·5	1·5
16	1·8	1·8	1·7	1·7	1·7	1·6	1·6	1·5	1·4
17	1·8	1·8	1·7	1·7	1·7	1·6	1·6	1·5	1·4
18	1·8	1·8	1·7	1·7	1·6	1·6	1·5	1·5	1·4
19	1·8	1·8	1·7	1·7	1·6	1·6	1·5	1·5	1·4
20	1·8	1·8	1·7	1·7	1·6	1·6	1·5	1·5	1·4
22	1·8	1·7	1·7	1·6	1·6	1·6	1·5	1·4	1·4
24	1·7	1·7	1·7	1·6	1·6	1·6	1·5	1·4	1·3
26	1·7	1·7	1·7	1·6	1·6	1·6	1·5	1·4	1·3
28	1·7	1·7	1·7	1·6	1·6	1·6	1·5	1·4	1·3
30	1·7	1·7	1·6	1·6	1·6	1·5	1·5	1·4	1·3
60	1·7	1·7	1·6	1·6	1·5	1·5	1·4	1·3	1·2
120	1·7	1·6	1·6	1·5	1·5	1·5	1·4	1·3	1·1
∞	1·6	1·6	1·6	1·5	1·5	1·4	1·3	1·2	1·0

(ii) 0·05 Probability Point

N_2 \ N_1	1	2	3	4	5	6	12	24	∞
1	161·4	199·5	215·7	224·6	230·2	234·0	243·9	249·0	254·3
2	18·5	19·0	19·2	19·3	19·3	19·3	19·4	19·5	19·5
3	10·1	9·6	9·3	9·1	9·0	8·9	8·7	8·6	8·5
4	7·7	6·9	6·6	6·4	6·3	6·2	5·9	5·8	5·6
5	6·6	5·8	5·4	5·2	5·1	5·0	4·7	4·5	4·4
6	6·0	5·1	4·8	4·5	4·4	4·3	4·0	3·8	3·7
7	5·6	4·7	4·4	4·1	4·0	3·9	3·6	3·4	3·2
8	5·3	4·5	4·1	3·8	3·7	3·6	3·3	3·1	2·9
9	5·1	4·3	3·9	3·6	3·5	3·4	3·1	2·9	2·7
10	5·0	4·1	3·7	3·5	3·3	3·2	2·9	2·7	2·5
11	4·8	4·0	3·6	3·4	3·2	3·1	2·8	2·6	2·4
12	4·8	3·9	3·5	3·3	3·1	3·0	2·7	2·5	2·3
13	4·7	3·8	3·4	3·2	3·0	2·9	2·6	2·4	2·2
14	4·6	3·7	3·3	3·1	3·0	2·9	2·5	2·3	2·1
15	4·5	3·7	3·3	3·1	2·9	2·8	2·5	2·3	2·1
16	4·5	3·6	3·2	3·0	2·9	2·7	2·4	2·2	2·0
17	4·5	3·6	3·2	3·0	2·8	2·7	2·4	2·2	2·0
18	4·4	3·6	3·2	2·9	2·8	2·7	2·3	2·1	1·9
19	4·4	3·5	3·1	2·9	2·7	2·6	2·3	2·1	1·9
20	4·4	3·5	3·1	2·9	2·7	2·6	2·3	2·1	1·8
22	4·3	3·4	3·1	2·8	2·7	2·6	2·2	2·0	1·8
24	4·3	3·4	3·0	2·8	2·6	2·5	2·2	2·0	1·7
26	4·2	3·4	3·0	2·7	2·6	2·5	2·2	2·0	1·7
28	4·2	3·3	3·0	2·7	2·6	2·4	2·1	1·9	1·7
30	4·2	3·3	2·9	2·7	2·5	2·4	2·1	1·9	1·6
60	4·0	3·2	2·8	2·5	2·4	2·3	1·9	1·7	1·4
120	3·9	3·1	2·7	2·5	2·3	2·2	1·8	1·6	1·3
∞	3·8	3·0	2·6	2·4	2·2	2·1	1·8	1·5	1·0

(iii) 0·01 Probability Point

N_2 \ N_1	1	2	3	4	5	6	12	24	∞
1	4,052	4,999	5,403	5,625	5,764	5,859	6,106	6,234	6,366
2	98·5	99·0	99·2	99·3	99·3	99·3	99·4	99·5	99·5
3	34·1	30·8	29·5	28·7	28·2	27·9	27·1	26·6	26·1
4	21·2	18·0	16·7	16·0	15·5	15·2	14·4	13·9	13·5
5	16·3	13·3	12·1	11·4	11·0	10·7	9·9	9·5	9·0
6	13·7	10·9	9·8	9·2	8·8	8·5	7·7	7·3	6·9
7	12·3	9·6	8·5	7·9	7·5	7·2	6·5	6·1	5·7
8	11·3	8·7	7·6	7·0	6·6	6·4	5·7	5·3	4·9
9	10·6	8·0	7·0	6·4	6·1	5·8	5·1	4·7	4·3
10	10·0	7·6	6·6	6·0	5·6	5·4	4·7	4·3	3·9
11	9·7	7·2	6·2	5·7	5·3	5·1	4·4	4·0	3·6
12	9·3	6·9	6·0	5·4	5·1	4·8	4·2	3·8	3·4
13	9·1	6·7	5·7	5·2	4·9	4·6	4·0	3·6	3·2
14	8·9	6·5	5·6	5·0	4·7	4·5	3·8	3·4	3·0
15	8·7	6·4	5·4	4·9	4·6	4·3	3·7	3·3	2·9
16	8·5	6·2	5·3	4·8	4·4	4·2	3·6	3·2	2·8
17	8·4	6·1	5·2	4·7	4·3	4·1	3·5	3·1	2·7
18	8·3	6·0	5·1	4·6	4·3	4·0	3·4	3·0	2·6
19	8·2	5·9	5·0	4·5	4·2	3·9	3·3	2·9	2·5
20	8·1	5·9	4·9	4·4	4·1	3·9	3·2	2·9	2·4
22	7·9	5·7	4·8	4·3	4·0	3·8	3·1	2·8	2·3
24	7·8	5·6	4·7	4·2	3·9	3·7	3·0	2·7	2·2
26	7·7	5·5	4·6	4·1	3·8	3·6	3·0	2·6	2·1
28	7·6	5·5	4·6	4·1	3·8	3·5	2·9	2·5	2·1
30	7·6	5·4	4·5	4·0	3·7	3·5	2·8	2·5	2·0
60	7·1	5·0	4·1	3·7	3·3	3·1	2·5	2·1	1·6
120	6·9	4·8	4·0	3·5	3·2	3·0	2·3	2·0	1·4
∞	6·6	4·6	3·8	3·3	3·0	2·8	2·2	1·8	1·0

(iv) 0·001 Probability Point

N_2 \ N_1	1	2	3	4	5	6	12	24	∞
1	405,284	500,000	540,379	562,500	576,405	585,937	610,667	623,497	636,619
2	998·5	999·0	999·2	999·2	999·3	999·3	999·4	999·5	999·5
3	167·5	148·5	141·1	137·1	134·6	132·8	128·3	125·9	123·5
4	74·1	61·3	56·2	53·4	51·7	50·5	47·4	45·8	44·1
5	47·0	36·6	33·2	31·1	29·8	28·8	26·4	25·1	23·8
6	35·5	27·0	23·7	21·9	20·8	20·0	18·0	16·9	15·8
7	29·2	21·7	18·8	17·2	16·2	15·5	13·7	12·7	11·7
8	25·4	18·5	15·8	14·4	13·5	12·9	11·2	10·3	9·3
9	22·9	16·4	13·9	12·6	11·7	11·1	9·6	8·7	7·8
10	21·0	14·9	12·6	11·3	10·5	9·9	8·5	7·6	6·8
11	19·7	13·8	11·6	10·4	9·6	9·1	7·6	6·9	6·0
12	18·6	13·0	10·8	9·6	8·9	8·4	7·0	6·3	5·4
13	17·8	12·3	10·2	9·1	8·4	7·9	6·5	5·8	5·0
14	17·1	11·8	9·7	8·6	7·9	7·4	6·1	5·4	4·6
15	16·6	11·3	9·3	8·3	7·6	7·1	5·8	5·1	4·3
16	16·1	11·0	9·0	7·9	7·3	6·8	5·6	4·9	4·1
17	15·7	10·7	8·7	7·7	7·0	6·6	5·3	4·6	3·9
18	15·4	10·4	8·5	7·5	6·8	6·4	5·1	4·5	3·7
19	15·1	10·2	8·3	7·3	6·6	6·2	5·0	4·3	3·5
20	14·8	10·0	8·1	7·1	6·5	6·0	4·8	4·2	3·4
22	14·4	9·6	7·8	6·8	6·2	5·8	4·6	3·9	3·2
24	14·0	9·3	7·6	6·6	6·0	5·6	4·4	3·7	3·0
26	13·7	9·1	7·4	6·4	5·8	5·4	4·2	3·6	2·8
28	13·5	8·9	7·2	6·3	5·7	5·2	4·1	3·5	2·7
30	13·3	8·8	7·1	6·1	5·5	5·1	4·0	3·4	2·6
60	12·0	7·8	6·2	5·3	4·8	4·4	3·3	2·7	1·9
120	11·4	7·3	5·8	5·0	4·4	4·0	3·0	2·4	1·6
∞	10·8	6·9	5·4	4·6	4·1	3·7	2·7	2·1	1·0

[Abridged from *Statistical Tables for Biological, Agricultural and Medical Research* by R. A. FISHER and F. YATES, with the kind permission of the authors and publishers, MESSRS. OLIVER AND BOYD.]

INDEX

analysis of χ^2, 191, 192
analysis of covariance, 124, 128
analysis of variance, 69, 86, 115, 119, 134, 170, 171, 234
   incomplete ——, 79, 129, 170
Antirrhinum, 191
apple, 89
Ashby, 129
asparagus, 104
assay, 227

backcross, 15, 19, 21, 185, 223, 227
barley, 72
Bath, 161
Bayes, 204
bias, 30
binomial, 17, 25, 26, 35, 38 *et seq.*, 52, 210, 234
Blackman, 36
Bliss, 242, 244, 245, 247, 252
Bortkewitch, 36
Brandt, 198
Brassica oleracea, 201, 207
Buck, 149

c, 42, 43, 46 *et seq.*, 50, 51, 85, 192
Catcheside, 201, 207
children, 161
combination, 166
combinations, 17
comparisons, 63, 65, 71, 178, 180, 181, 191
compound interest, 109
concomitant observations, 123, 128
confounding, 104, 108
   partial ——, 107
contingency table, 193 *et seq.*, 196 *et seq.*, 200 *et seq.*
continuity, 51, 174
   Yates' correction for ——, 51, 175, 176, 195
correction term, 55, 58, 68
correlation, 109, 160 *et seq.*
   —— coefficient, 160, 162, 168, 169, 173
   inter-class ——, 161, 173
   intra-class ——, 168, 173
   partial ——, 167
   transformed ——, 164, 165, 168, 169
covariance, 35, 54, 147, 148

Crane, 55
cubic curve, 133
χ^2, 46 *et seq.*, 174 *et seq.*, 192, 220, 226, 237, 249

Datura stramonium, 50, 175, 189
decomposition, 107
deductive reasoning, 9
degrees of freedom, 33, 40, 43, 45, 46, 47, 57, 60, 61 *et seq.*, 69, 72, 114, 133, 148, 155, 164, 170, 178, 189, 231
   loss of ——, 33, 115, 188, 200, 220, 226
deviation, 42, 44, 231
   —— χ^2, 191, 192, 196, 225
diagrams, 12
difference, variance of, 54
discriminant function, 152 *et seq.*
Dobzhansky, 79, 156
Drosophila melanogaster, 21
Drosophila pseudo-obscura, 79, 156
drugs, 227

East, 28
Eden, 35
efficiency, 216, 230
   —— index, 109
Emerson, 28
error, 66, 68, 69, 70, 78, 85, 87, 93, 94, 110 (*see also* sampling error)
   control of ——, 89, 93 *et seq.*
Eryngium maritimum, 36
estimate, 11, 28
estimation, 203 *et seq.*
   combined, ——, 222
   simultaneous, ——, 221

F_2, 16, 223, 228
factorial experiment, 87, 91, 93, 102
   —— notation, 16
fireflies, 149
Fisher, 12, 28, 36, 38, 43, 44, 71, 86, 97, 102, 108, 138, 148, 152, 159, 164, 183, 185, 187, 194, 195, 204, 210, 216, 218, 223, 227, 231, 234, 242, 243, 244, 245, 247
frequencies, 48, 174
frequency distribution, 29, 161
   —— surface, 160

Gaddum, 245, 252
gene, 14, 19, 21, 38, 50, 175, 181, 191, 213, 222, 227
genetical experiments, 50
goodness of fit, 46
Graeco-Latin square, 101
graph, 12
Griffiths, 161
grouping, 30
  Sheppard's correction for ——, 32
growth, 109

haemacytometer counts, 36
Haldane, 213
Harrison, 116
Hartman, 196
Hayes, 72
heterogeneity, test of, 189, 192, 225 et seq.
histogram, 34
hypothesis, 10, 165, 188, 204
  null ——, 65

Imai, 183
Immer, 72
incomplete classification, 231
independent comparisons, 64, 91, 103
  —— observations, 53
  —— regressions, 142, 147
inductive reasoning, 9
information, amount of, 166, 205, 210, 212, 218, 224, 227, 232, 249
integral coefficients, 136, 143
interaction, 70 et seq., 79, 183
invariance, 166
Iris, 159
Irwin, 252
iteration, 208, 212

kurtosis, 35

Lamm, 171
Latin square, 95 et seq.
Lawrence, 193
*LD*50, 250 et seq.
least squares, 113, 146, 243
likelihood, 205, 223, 243
  log ——, 206, 223
line, straight, 109, 132
linearity, 129
linkage, 181 et seq., 213, 215, 217, 218, 220

main effect, 70, 183
maize, 25, 28
Mather, 38, 55, 79, 156, 165, **171**, 191, 193, 198, 218, 222, 223
maximum likelihood, 113, 205 *et seq.*, 221, 222, 243
mean, 26, 28, 30 et seq., 36, 38, 40, 54, 55, 166
  weighted ——, 167
mean deviation, 27
mean square, 32, 68, 69, 192
measurements, 48, 174
median, 26
mice, 38, 223
misclassification, 153, 158, 159
mode, 26
moments, 35
multinomial, 18, 26, 195, 206

Newell, 193
normal curve, 25 et seq., 221, 240
  —— deviate, 42, 43, 50, 51, 174, 231, 240

observations, 10, 204
orthogonal functions, 64, 65, 72
  —— polynomials, 133 et seq.
  —— treatments, 95
ouabain, 245

Papaver, 183, 187
parameter, 10, 28, 33, 115, 148, 188, 204
partition, 61 et seq., 139, 180 et seq., 193, 239
Pearson, 12, 46
permutations, 16
Pharbitis, 183
phenylthiocarbamide, 196
Philp, 183, 187, 190, 194
plating, 36
Poisson series, 35 et seq., 206, 239
population, 10, 11, 204
  super ——, 11, 204
potatoes, 97, 116
Powers, 72
precision, 107, 166, 205, 216, 230
Primula sinensis, 14, 18, 25, 193, 213
probability, 14, 19 et seq., 29, 41, 205
  compound ——, 15 et seq.
  fiducial ——, 232
  inverse ——, 204
probit, 242 et seq.

INDEX

quadrat, 36
quadratic curve, 132

radish, 235
Rana pipiens, 245
random numbers, 23
—— sampling, 23, 28, 94
randomized block, 95, 102
recombination, 203, 227
regression, 109 *et seq.*, 160, 242
—— coefficient, 113, 119
   multiple ——, 146 *et seq.*, 152, 167
   partial ——, 167
   polynomial ——, 129, 133 *et seq.*, 152
   weighted ——, 245 *et seq.*
restraints, 95, 99, 101
rigour, 11, 49, 232
Roberts, 161
rye, 171

sample, 10
sampling error, 10, 11, 28, 41, 46, 67, 76, 87, 113
segregation, 181 *et seq.*, 222
selection, 23, 110
self-pollination, 181, 227
Shippy, 89
significance, 21 *et seq.*, 51
   test of ——, 10, 19, 21, 23, 24, 41 *et seq.*, 69, 87, 165, 203, 221, 231, 232
Sirks, 50, 51, 175, 189
skewness, 35
Smith, 245
Snedecor, 44, 198
standard deviation, 27, 28, 30 *et seq.*, 40, 43, 50, 52, 166
—— error, 50, 78

statistic, 10, 35
   consistent ——, 213
   efficient ——, 213, 231
   inefficient ——, 213 *et seq.*
   sufficient ——, 213, 231
Steward, 116
Student, 12, 43
sum, variance of, 54
sum of cross products, 54, 64
   —— squares, 31, 36, 39, 46, 61 *et seq.*, 66, 69

t, 43, 44, 46 *et seq.*, 69, 78, 85, 174, 232
taxonomic data, 152, 159
Tedin, 44
tomato, 55, 65, 79, 129
toxicology, 239 *et seq.*
transformation, 109, 234 *et seq.*
trout, 123

uncertainty, 11, 232

variance, 32, 35, 36, 38, 40, 50, 52 *et seq.*, 166, 231
   —— formula, 216
   —— ratio, 44 *et seq.*, 78, 85, 192
variate, dependent, 110, 160
   ——, independent, 110, 160

Washbourn, 123
weight, 166, 225, 243, 248, 249
Winton, de, 213
Wishart, 104
working mean, 31 *et seq.*

Yates, 35, 43, 44, 97, 108, 138, 175, 234, 242, 244, 245, 247

z, 44 *et seq.*, 78, 85, 164, 167, 168, 170, 174, 192